THE MEDIEVAL ENGLISH BOROUGH

STUDIES ON ITS ORIGINS AND CONSTITUTIONAL HISTORY

BY

JAMES TAIT, D.Litt., Litt.D., F.B.A.

Honorary Professor of the University

MANCHESTER UNIVERSITY PRESS
BARNES & NOBLE INC., NEW YORK

© 1936 MANCHESTER UNIVERSITY PRESS
Published by the University of Manchester at
THE UNIVERSITY PRESS
316–324 Oxford Road, Manchester 13

U.S.A.
BARNES & NOBLE, INC.
105 Fifth Avenue, New York, N.Y. 10003

First published 1936
Reprinted 1968

G.B. SBN 7190 0339 3

Printed in Great Britain by Lowe & Brydone (Printers) Ltd.,
London

PREFACE

As its sub-title indicates, this book makes no claim to be the long overdue history of the English borough in the Middle Ages. Just over a hundred years ago Mr. Serjeant Mere- wether and Mr. Stephens had *The History of the Boroughs and Municipal Corporations of the United Kingdom*, in three volumes, ready to celebrate the sweeping away of the medieval system by the Municipal Corporation Act of 1835. It was hardly to be expected, however, that this feat of bookmaking, good as it was for its time, would prove definitive. It may seem more surprising that the centenary of that great change finds the gap still unfilled. For half a century Merewether and Stephens' work, sharing, as it did, the current exaggera- tion of early "democracy" in England, stood in the way. Such revision as was attempted followed a false trail and it was not until, in the last decade or so of the century, the researches of Gross, Maitland, Mary Bateson and others threw a flood of new light upon early urban development in this country, that a fair prospect of a more adequate history of the English borough came in sight. Unfortunately, these hopes were indefinitely deferred by the early death of nearly all the leaders in these investigations. Quite recently an American scholar, Dr. Carl Stephenson, has boldly attempted the most difficult part of the task, but his conclusions, in important respects, are highly controversial.

When in 1921 an invitation to complete Ballard's un- finished *British Borough Charters* induced me to lay aside other plans of work and confine myself to municipal history, I had no intention of entering into thorny questions of origins. A remark of Gross in the introduction to his *Bibliography of British Municipal History* (1897) that "certain cardinal features of the medieval borough, such as the *firma burgi*, the judiciary and the governing body, still need illumination" suggested the studies, printed, chiefly in the *English Historical Review*, between 1925 and 1930, which, with some revision, form chapters VII-XI of the present volume. Another, on the borough courts and assemblies, had been planned when my attention was diverted to the pre-Conquest period by the appearance in the *English Historical Review* in July, 1930, of a revolutionary article by Dr. Stephenson in which he sought to prove that, with inconsiderable exceptions, the Anglo-Saxon boroughs were still no more than administrative and military centres in 1066. A thorough re-study of all the evidence for that very difficult period took so long that, save for a chapter on its origins, the subject of borough jurisdiction has had regretfully to be left to younger investigators. Another and more deliberate omission is the history of formal incorporation on which, I am glad to say, my friend Dr. Martin Weinbaum has a book in the press.

The chapters dealing with the Anglo-Saxon borough were nearly complete when Dr. Stephenson's enlarged treatment of the subject in his book *Borough and Town* appeared, in 1933. His modifications of his views as originally stated are, however, practically confined to a large extension of his list of exceptions, his conception of the " ordinary " borough remaining unaltered, so that it was not necessary to recast completely what I had written. When required, references are given to a summary (chapter VI) of the exceptions Dr. Stephenson now allows.

In his article of 1930, the late Professor Pirenne's conception of town life in the Netherlands as the result of mercantile settlement under the shelter of fortified administrative centres was applied to England with such rigour as virtually to make the Norman Conquest the starting-point of its urban development. And though in his book Dr. Stephenson admits earlier mercantile settlements in the populous boroughs of the Danelaw and makes some wider but vaguer concessions, he still retains in his title and general exposition the sharp antithesis between borough and town. For this he claims, as forerunners, Maitland and Miss Bateson, but, apart from his " garrison theory," Maitland was much more cautious and Miss Bateson's estimate of French influence upon the post-Conquest borough is pressed too far. She did not, for instance, regard it as inconsistent with the view that the Anglo-Saxon borough had a distinctively urban court, a view which Dr. Stephenson strongly combats.

Even in the country of its first statement the antithesis tends to be less sharply drawn. M. Paul Rolland's study of

" the origins of the town of Tournai " (1931) shows that in suitable spots a trading population could develop gradually from an agricultural one.[1] At Tournai there was no large mercantile settlement from without (See *English Historical Review*, 1933, p. 688).

At first sight Dr. Stephenson's concession that even if there had been no Norman Conquest " London's charter might well have contained the same major articles, if it had been granted by a son of Harold, rather than by a son of William " might seem to yield more ground than has been indicated. But it is qualified by a statement that by 1066 Anglo-Saxon England was only just coming under the influence of the commercial revival on the Continent. It is difficult to reconcile this with the fact that London's foreign trade *c.* 1000 was as wide, if not as great, as it was under Henry I.

This limited recognition of an urban continuity across the Conquest does not extend to the agricultural aspect of the borough. A stronger contrast could hardly be imagined than that between the manorial system which Dr. Stephenson conceives to have prevailed in the cultivation of the fields of the Anglo-Saxon borough and that which is found in working after the Conquest, and no explanation of this unrecorded transformation is offered.

Dr. Stephenson deserves every credit for his pioneer effort of reconstruction, he has done good service in diverting attention from vain attempts to find precise definitions in a non-defining age to the safe ground of social and commercial development, while his treatment of the problem of early borough jurisdiction, though not wholly acceptable, rightly emphasizes the very general origin of burghal courts as units in the hundred system of the country at large. But his book contains too much that is disputable to constitute the first part of a definitive history of the English borough.

Dr. Stephenson's own criticisms of some of the views advanced in my reprinted articles, *e.g.* as to the influence of the Continental commune upon the communal movement in England at the end of the twelfth century, are discussed in appendices to the respective articles. This has involved some repetition, but the articles were already sufficiently controversial and the opportunity has been gained of adding a little fresh matter. The document of 1205 preserved by

---

[1] With its bishop's see Tournai may have been more favourable to such growth than the ordinary feudal *burg*.

Gervase of Canterbury (below, p. 253) has apparently never been considered in its bearing on the communal movement nor has its early reference to the new office of mayor been previously noted. The appendix on the barons of London and of the Cinque Ports will, it is hoped, do something to remove that uncertainty as to the precise origin and meaning of the title which is found in the older books.

With some hesitation, I have appended my British Academy lecture of 1921 on the study of early municipal history in England. It much needed revision and may serve as a general introduction to the post-Conquest studies and a supplement to their casual treatment of the seignorial borough.

I have to thank the editor and publishers of the *English Historical Review*, the Council of the British Academy, and the Tout Memorial Committee for kind permissions to reprint articles. My indebtedness to younger scholars who have kept me in touch with recent research in borough archives, closed to me by impaired eyesight and advancing years, will be found frequently acknowledged in footnotes.

JAMES TAIT.

THE UNIVERSITY,
MANCHESTER, *March 7th, 1936.*

CONTENTS

ADDENDA AND CORRIGENDA

Page 83, *l.* 20   "Opus in curia" might, however, include lifting and stacking hay (Vinogradoff, *Villainage*, p. 444).

,,   89, *l.* 16   Eight virgates. Cf. *ibid.* p. 381.

,,   97, *l.* 8   *For* fripeni *read* fripene.

,,   98   For the charter, probably of Abbot Robert de Sutton (1262-73), to the men of Peterborough "which offers release from seignorial exploitation (including merchet), but in the most restricted terms" see *V.C.H., Northants*, ii. 425. A similar charter was granted to Oundle.

,,   118   For the importance of the English textiles industry in the tenth century and their export to France see *E.H.R.* xlii. (1927), 141.

,,   131, *l.* 13   *For* weigh *read* way.

,,   145, *l.* 17   Earl William's houses were perhaps private, not comital.

,,   149, *n.* 2   Although *D.B.* in the passage quoted says quite clearly that William gave to Robert de Stafford half of his own share of the revenues of the borough, Robert is reported under his own fief (f. 248*b*, 2) to be claiming 70*s.*, which was half of the combined shares of king and earl, then both in William's hands.

,,   184   Though Dover rendered £54 in 1086, its true value was estimated to be £40.

,,   230, *l.* 6   The burgesses of Gloucester having had a bare grant of fee farm in 1194 (*B.B.C.* i. 224), it seems clear that the importance of such a full grant of liberties as John's is underestimated here and on p. 250. In his reign these grants perhaps carried with them, unexpressed, allowance of sworn association (see pp. 251-2).

Page 235 (*cf.* 226)   According to two charters in the cartulary of St. Frideswide's (i. 26, 33) the dispute between the canons and the citizens went back to the reign of Stephen, who confirmed a grant by the latter to the canons of their rent of 6*s.* 8*d.* from Medley " ad restaurandum luminare predicte ecclesie quod amiserant pro stallis que per eos perdiderant."

„ 292, *n.* 1   I owe this fact to Miss Catherine Jamison.

„ 304, *l.* 10   The Winchester court was called *burghmote* not *burwaremote.*

„ 353   The " inferior limit of burgality " can hardly have been lower than at Peterborough (see the *addendum* to p. 98 above) before the thirteenth-century charter, itself grudging enough.

„ 364   *S.v.* Gilds. *For* trade and craft *read* craft.

„ „   *S.v.* Gloucester. Add reference to p. 102.

BIBLIOGRAPHY

The following abbreviations have been used in the footnotes to the text and in the bibliography :—

A.S.C.	= Anglo-Saxon Chronicle.
A.S.I.	= Chadwick, Anglo-Saxon Institutions.
B.B.C.	= British Borough Charters.
B.C.	= Bateson, Borough Customs.
B.M.	= British Museum.
C.C.R.	= Calendar of Close Rolls.
C.Ch.R.	= Calendar of Charter Rolls.
C.P.R.	= Calendar of Patent Rolls.
C.S.	= Birch, Cartularium Saxonicum.
D.B.	= Domesday Book.
D.B. and B.	= Maitland, Domesday Book and Beyond.
E.E.T.S.	= Early English Text Society.
E.H.R.	= English Historical Review.
P.R.	= Pipe Rolls.
P.R.O.	= Public Record Office.
R.L.C.	= Rotuli Litterarum Clausarum.
R.S.	= Rolls Series.
V.C.H.	= Victoria History of Counties.

Anglo-Norman Custumal. See Exeter.
Anglo-Saxon Chronicle (*A.S.C.*). Ed. C. Plummer. 2 vols., 1892-99.
Antiquity. Ed. O. G. S. Crawford and R. Austin. Vol. viii., 1934.
Archaeologia Aeliana. Fourth ser., vol. i. Newcastle-upon-Tyne, 1925.
Asser, bp. Life of King Alfred. Ed. W. H. Stevenson, 1904.

Ballard, A. The Domesday Boroughs, 1904.
    The Burgesses of Domesday. *E.H.R.*, 1906.
    The Walls of Malmesbury. *E.H.R.*, 1906.
    Castle-guard and Barons' houses. *E.H.R.*, 1910.
    The English Borough in the Twelfth Century, 1914.
    British Borough Charters. Vol. i. 1042–1216 ; vol. ii. (with J. Tait) 1216–1307, 1913–23.
    An Eleventh Century Inquisition of St. Augustine's, Canterbury. Brit. Acad., 1920.
    The Theory of the Scottish Borough. *Scott. Hist. Rev.*, 1916.

Bateson, M. Records of Leicester. 3 vols., 1899–1905.
    Borough Customs (*B.C.*). Selden Soc. 2 vols., 1904–6.
    Review of Ballard's Domesday Boroughs. *E.H.R.*, 1905.
    The Burgesses of Domesday and the Malmesbury Walls. *E.H.R.*, 1906.
Bede. Historia Ecclesiastica. Ed. C. Plummer. 2 vols., 1896.
Benham, W. G. See Colchester.
Bilson, J. Wyke-upon-Hull in 1293, 1928.
Birch, W. de G. See Cartularium Saxonicum (*C.S.*). Catalogue of Seals in the department of MSS. in the British Museum. 6 vols., 1887–1900.
Bird, R. Civic Factions in London and their relation to political parties. [Unprinted London University thesis.]
Black Book of the Admiralty. Monumenta Juridica, vol. ii. Ed. Travers Twiss. *R.S.*, 1873.
Black Book of St. Augustine's. See St. Augustine's.
Black Book of Warwick. Ed. T. Kemp, 1898.
Black Book of Winchester. Ed. W. H. B. Bird, 1925.
Blakeley, G. S. The City of Gloucester, 1924.
Book of Fees, The, commonly called Testa de Nevill, reformed from the earliest MSS. P.R.O. 3 vols., 1920–31.
Bridges, J. and Whalley, P. History and Antiquities of Northamptonshire, 1791.
Bristol. See Red Book.
British Borough Charters (*B.B.C.*). See Ballard.
Brownbill, J., and Nuttall, J. R. Calendar of Charters and Records belonging to the Corporation of Lancaster, 1929.
Bugge, A. Die nordeuropäischen Verkehrswege im frühen Mittelalter. Vierteljahrschrift fur Social- und Wirtschaftsgeschichte. Vol. iv., 1906.

Cam, H. Francia and England, 1912.
    Manerium cum Hundredo. *E.H.R.*, 1932.
    The Origin of the Borough of Cambridge. Proc. Camb. Antiq. Soc. Vol. xxxv., 1935.
Calendar of
    Charter Rolls. (*C.Ch.R.*). P.R.O.
    Close Rolls. (*C.C.R.*). P.R.O.
    Rolls of the County Court of Chester, etc. Ed. R. Stewart-Brown. Chetham Soc., 1925.
    Letter-Books of the City of London (A-L). Ed. R. R. Sharpe, 1899–1912.
    Miscellaneous Inquisitions. 2 vols. P.R.O.
    Patent Rolls (*C.P.R.*). P.R.O.
    Plea and Memoranda Rolls of the City of London. Ed. A. H. Thomas. Vol. i., 1323–64 ; vol. ii., 1364–81, 1926–29.
    See also Brownbill, J.
Cambridge Historical Journal. Vol. iv., 1933.
Canterbury, Gervase of. Works. Ed. W. Stubbs. *R.S.* 2 vols., 1879–80.
    See also Ballard, Cotton, Domesday Monachorum and St. Augustine's.

Cartularium Saxonicum (*C.S.*). Ed. W. de G. Birch. 3 vols., 1885–93.
Cartulary of
    The Abbey of St. Werburgh, Chester. Ed. J. Tait. Chetham Soc. 2 vols., 1920–23.
    Eynsham Abbey. Ed. H. E. Salter. Oxf. Hist. Soc. 2 vols., 1907–8.
    The Priory of St. Frideswide, Oxford. Ed. S. R. Wigram. 2 vols., 1895–96.
    Oseney Abbey, Oxford. Ed. H. E. Salter. Oxf. Hist. Soc. 4 vols., 1928–34.
    The Priory of Worcester. Ed. R. R. Darlington. [In preparation.]
Chadwick, H. M. Studies on Anglo-Saxon Institutions, 1905.
Chester Archæological Society, Journal of, 1857, etc.
Chronicon
    Monasterii de Bello. Anglia Christiana Soc., 1846.
    Abbatiae Rameseiensis. Ed. W. D. Macray. *R.S.*, 1886.
Clemesha, H. W. History of Preston in Amounderness, 1912.
Close Rolls (*C.R.*). For reign of Hen. III. from 1227. P.R.O.
Colby, C. W. The Growth of Oligardy in English Towns. *E.H.R.*, 1890.
Colchester, Court Rolls of. Ed. W. G. Benham and I. H. Jeayes. Vol. i. (1310–53), 1921.
    Oath Book of. Ed. W. G. Benham, 1907.
    Red Paper Book of. Ed. W. G. Benham, 1902.
Cooper, C. H. Annals of Cambridge. Vols. i.-ii., 1842–43.
Coopland, G. W. The Abbey of St. Bertin, 900–1350. Oxf. Stud., ed. Vinogradoff, iv., 1914.
Corbett, W. J. In Cambridge Medieval History. Vol. iii.
Cotton, C. The Saxon Cathedral of Canterbury, 1929.
Court Rolls. See Colchester.
Coventry, Leet Book of. Ed. M. Dormer Harris. 4 vols., 1907–13.
Curia Regis Rolls. P.R.O., 1923, etc.
Custumals of Battle Abbey. Ed. S. R. Scargill-Bird. Camden Soc., 1887.

Davis, H. W. C. England under the Normans and Angevins, 1905.
    Regesta Regum Anglo-Normannorum (1066–1100), 1913.
Dilks, T. B. The Burgesses of Bridgwater in the 13th cent. Proc. Somerset Arch. Soc. Vol. lxiii., 1917.
    Bridgwater Borough Archives (1200–1377). Somerset Record Soc. Vol. 48, 1933.
Domesday Book (*D.B.*). With Additamenta. 4 vols., 1783–1816.
Domesday Book and Beyond (*D.B. and B.*). See Maitland.
Domesday Monachorum. Somner, W. Antiquities of Canterbury. Pt. 1, app. 40, 1703. See Ballard, Inquisition.
Douglas, D. C. Feudal Documents from the Abbey of St. Edmunds. Brit. Acad., 1932.
Dover Charters. Ed. S. P. H. Statham, 1902.
Drake, F. Eboracum, 1736.
DuCange. Glossarium Mediae et Infimae Latinitatis. Niort, 1883–87.

Durham, Simeon of. Opera Omnia. Ed. T. Arnold. *R.S.* 2 vols., 1882–85.

East, R. Extracts from the Municipal Records of Portsmouth, 1891.
Ellis, H. General Introduction to Domesday Book. Record Com. 2 vols., 1833.
English Gilds. Ed. T. Smith. *E.E.T.S.*, 1870.
English Historical Review (*E.H.R.*), 1886, etc.
English Register of Osney Abbey. Ed. A. Clark. *E.E.T.S.*, 2 pts., 1907–13.
Exeter, Anglo-Norman Custumal of. Ed. Schopp, J. W. and Easterling, R. C., 1925. See also Wilkinson.
Eyton, R. W. Key to Domesday—Dorset Survey, 1878.
Somerset Survey, 1880.
Court, Household and Itinerary of Henry II., 1878.

Farrer, W. Early Yorkshire Charters. 3 vols., 1914–16.
Itinerary of Henry I. *E.H.R.* and reprint, 1919.
Feudal Aids. P.R.O., 1899, etc.
Foedera (O). Ed. T. Rymer and R. Sanderson. Orig. ed., 1704–35. (Rec.). Ed. A. Clarke, etc. Record Com. 4 vols., 1816–69.

Freeman, E. A. History of the Norman Conquest of England. 2nd ed., 1870–76.
Furley, J. S. City Government of Winchester, 1923.
Ancient Usages of the City of Winchester, 1927.

Gesta Regis Henrici secundi et Ricardi [Benedictus Abbas]. Ed. W. Stubbs. *R.S.* 2 vols., 1867.
Gesta Stephani. In Chronicles of the reigns of Stephen, etc. Ed. R. Howlett. *R.S.* Vol. iii., 1886.
Gilbert, J. T. Historic and Municipal Documents of Ireland. *R.S.*, 1870.
Giraldus Cambrensis. Opera. *R.S.* 8 vols., 1861–91.
Giry, A. Histoire de la ville de Saint-Omer, 1877.
Les Établissements de Rouen. 2 vols., 1883–85.
Glanvill, de Legibus et Consuetudinibus Anglie. Ed. G. E. Woodbine, 1932.
Gneist, R. Geschichte der Communalverfassung, 1863.
Green, Mrs. J. R. Town Life in the Fifteenth Century. 2 vols., 1894.
Gretton, R. H. The Burford Records, 1920.
Gribble, J. B. Memorials of Barnstaple, 1830.
Griffiths, R. G. History of Clifton-on-Teme, 1932.
Gross, C. Gild Merchant. 2 vols., 1890.

Harland, J. Mamecestre. Chetham Soc. 3 vols., 1861–62.
Hegel, K. Städte und Gilden der Germanischen Völker im Mittelalter. 2 vols., 1891.
Historical Manuscripts Commission, Reports of. Parl. papers, 1870, etc.

Hudson, W. and Tingey, J. C. Records of Norwich. 2 vols., 1906–10.
Hunt, W. Bristol. Historic Towns, 1887.
Hutchins, J. History and Antiquities of Dorset. 3rd ed., 4 vols., 1861–70.

Inquisition of St. Augustine's, Canterbury. See Ballard.
Ipswich, Custumal of. See Black Book of the Admiralty.

Jacob, G. Law Dictionary, 1782.
Jacob, E. F. Baronial Reform and Rebellion, 1258–67. Oxford Studies, ed. Vinogradoff., 1925.
Jolliffe, J. E. A. The Hidation of Kent. *E.H.R.*, 1929. The Domesday of Sussex and the Rapes. *E.H.R.*, 1930.
Jones, W. H. Domesday for Wiltshire, 1865.

Keutgen, F. Ursprung der deutsche Stadtverfassung, 1895.

Lapsley, G. L. Buzones. *E.H.R.*, 1932.
Law Merchant, The. Ed. C. Gross and H. Hall. 3 vols., 1908–32.
Lees, B. A. Records of the Templars in England. Brit. Acad., 1935.
Legras, H. Le Bourgage de Caen, 1911.
Lewis, E. A. Mediæval Boroughs of Snowdonia, 1912.
Liber Albus. See Munimenta Gildhallae.
Liber de Antiquis Legibus Londoniarum. Chronicon maiorum et vicecomitum. Ed. T. Stapleton. Camden Soc., 1846.
Liber Custumarum. See Munimenta Gildhallae.
Liber Eliensis. [Ed. D. J. Stewart] Anglia Christiana Soc., 1848.
Liber Winton. See Domesday Book. Vol. iv.
Liebermann, F. Die Gesetze der Angelsachsen. 3 vols., 1903–16.
Lincoln Cathedral, Registrum Antiquissimum of. Ed. C. W. Foster. Linc. Rec. Soc. Vols. i.-iii., 1931–35.
Lincolnshire Assize Rolls (1202–9). Ed. D. M. Stenton. Linc. Rec. Soc., 1926.
Domesday. Ed. C. W. Foster and T. Longley. Linc. Rec. Soc., 1924.
Lobel, M. D. The Borough of Bury St. Edmunds, 1935.
Luchaire, A. Manuel des institutions Françaises, 1892.
Lynn Regis. See Red Register.

Madox, T. Firma Burgi, 1726.
History of the Exchequer. 2 vols., 1769.
Maitland, F. W. The Origin of the Borough. *E.H.R.*, 1896.
Domesday Book and Beyond, 1897.
Township and Borough, 1898.
See also Pollock and Maitland.
Malmesbury, W. of. De Gestis Regum Anglorum. Ed. W. Stubbs. *R.S.* 2 vols., 1887–89.
Markham, C. A. and Cox, J. C. Records of the Borough of Northampton. 2 vols., 1898.
Mayo, C. H. Municipal Records of Dorchester, 1908.

Memorials of St. Edmund's Abbey. Ed. T. Arnold. *R.S.* 2 vols., 1890–96.
Merewether, H. A. and Stephens, A. J. History of the Boroughs and Corporations of the United Kingdom. 3 vols., 1835.
Monasticon Anglicanum. Ed. W. Dugdale, etc., 1846.
Morris, R. H. Chester in Plantagenet and Tudor Times, 1893.
Morris, W. A. The Mediæval English Sheriff to 1300, 1927.
Muir, Ramsay. History of Liverpool, 1907.
    and Platt, E. M. History of Municipal Government in Liverpool to 1835, 1906.
Munimenta Gildhallae Londoniensis. Vol. i., Liber Albus ; vol. ii., Liber Custumarum ; Vol. iii., Liber Horn, etc. *R.S.*, 1859–62.
Murray, K. M. E. Constitutional History of the Cinque Ports. 1935.

Napier, A. S. and Stevenson, W. H. Crawford Charters, 1895.
Neilson, N. Customary Rents. Oxford Studies, ed. Vinogradoff. Vol. ii., 1910.
Norgate, K. John Lackland, 1902.
Norton, G. Commentaries on the History, Constitution and chartered Franchises of London. 3rd ed., 1869.

Oak Book of Southampton. Ed. P. Studer. Southampton Record Soc. 3 vols., 1910–11.
Oath Book of Colchester. See Colchester.
Oman, C. England before the Norman Conquest. [1910.]
Ordericus Vïtalis. Historia Ecclesiastica. Ed. A. le Prévost. 5 vols., 1838–55.
Ormerod, G. History of Cheshire. 2nd ed. Ed. T. Helsby, 3 vols., 1882.

Page, W. London : its Origin and Early Development. 1923.
Palgrave, F. Normandy and England. 2nd ed. 4 vols., 1919–21.
    Rotuli Curiae Regis. Rec. Com. 2 vols., 1835.
Palmer, W. M. Cambridge Borough Documents, 1931.
Pape, T. Mediæval Newcastle-under-Lyme, 1928.
Parker, J. Early History of Oxford. Oxford Hist. Soc., 1885.
Parliamentary Writs. Ed. F. Palgrave. Record Com. 2 vols. in 4, 1827–34.
Patent Rolls for reign of Henry III (*Pat. R.*). P.R.O.
Petit-Dutaillis, C. and G. Lefebvre. Studies supplementary to Stubbs' Constitutional History of England. 3 vols., 1908–29.
Pipe Rolls (*P.R.*) 31 Hen. I. and 2 Hen. II. to 2 John. P.R.O. and Pipe Roll Soc., 1833 [repr. 1929]–1934.
Pirenne, H. Histoire de Belgique. 3 vols., 1902–7.
Place-Names of England. Ed. A. Mawer and F. M. Stenton. English Place-Name Society, 1924, etc.
Pollock, F. and Maitland, F. W. History of English Law. 2nd ed. 2 vols., 1898.
Powell, F. York. Review of Grueber and Keary's Catalogue of English Coins in B.M. (Vol. ii.). *E.H.R.*, 1896.

Powicke, F. M.   The Loss of Normandy (1189–1204), 1913.

Ramsay, J.   The Angevin Empire, 1903.
Ramsey Abbey.   See Chronicon.
Red Book of the Exchequer.   Ed. H. Hall.   *R.S.*   3 vols., 1896.
Red Books of Bristol,
 Great.   Ed. E. W. W. Veale.   Bristol Rec. Soc., 1931–
 Little.   Ed. F. B. Bickley.   2 vols., 1900.
Red Paper Book of Colchester.   See Colchester.
Red Register of Lynn.   Ed. H. Ingleby.   2 vols.   *c.* 1920–22.
Registrum Antiquissimum.   See Lincoln.
Reid, R. R.   The Office of Warden of the Marches.   *E.H.R.*, 1917.
Riley, H. T.   Memorials of London and London Life, 1868.
Rotuli Litterarum Clausarum (1204–27).   Record Com.   2 vols.,
 1833–44.
Rotuli Chartarum.   Record Com., 1837.
Rotuli Hundredorum.   Record Com.   2 vols., 1812–18.
Rotuli Litterarum Patentium (1201–16).   Record Com., 1835.
 See also Patent Rolls.
Rotuli Parliamentorum.   6 vols., *c.* 1783.
Round, J. H.   Ancient Charters.   Pipe Roll Soc., O.S., x., 1888.
 Geoffrey de Mandeville, 1892.
 Feudal England, 1895.
 Commune of London, 1899.
 Calendar of Documents preserved in France, illustrative of the
  History of Great Britain and Ireland, 1899.
 " Burhbot " and " Brigbot," in Family Origins, ed. W. Page,
  1930.

St. Augustine's Abbey, Canterbury, Black Book of.   Ed. G. J.
 Turner, and H. E. Salter.   Brit. Acad.   2 vols., 1915–24.
 See also Ballard.
Salter, H. E.   Early Oxford Charters, 1929.
 Munimenta Civitatis Oxonie.   Oxf. Hist. Soc., 1917.
Schopp, J. W.   See Exeter.
Scott, J.   Berwick-upon-Tweed.   The History of the Town and
 Guild, 1888.
Smith, T.   See English Gilds.
Southampton.   See Oak Book.
Speculum.   Mediæval Academy of America.   Vol. vii., 1934.
Statutes of the Realm.   Ed. A. Luders, etc., 1810–28.
Stenton, D. M.   See Lincolnshire.
Stenton, F. M.   Danelaw Charters.   Brit. Acad., 1920.
 The Danes in England.   Proc. Brit. Acad.   Vol. xiii., 1927.
 The First Century of English Feudalism, 1932.
Stephenson, C.   The Aids of the English Boroughs.   *E.H.R.*, 1919.
 The Origin of the English Town.   Americ. Hist. Rev., 1926.
 The Anglo-Saxon Borough.   *E.H.R.*, 1930.
 Borough and Town.   Med. Acad. of America, 1933.
Stevenson, W. H.   Trinoda Necessitas.   *E.H.R.*, 1914.
 See also Asser and Crawford Charters.
Stow, J.   Survey of London.   Ed. C. L. Kingsford.   2 vols., 1908.

Stubbs, W.   Constitutional History of England.   2nd and 3rd ed.,
      1878–80.
   Select Charters.   9th ed.   Ed. H. W. C. Davis, 1913.
Sussex Archæological Collections, 1848, etc.

Tait, J.   Mediæval Manchester, 1904.
   See Ballard and Cartulary.
Thorpe, B.   Diplomatarium aevi Saxonici, 1865.
Tout, T. F.   Historical Essays presented to, 1925.
Trenholme, N. M.   English Monastic Boroughs.   University ,of
      Missouri Studies, ii. 3, 1927.
Turner, G. J.   The Sheriff's Farm.   Trans. Roy. Hist. Soc., N.S.
      Vol. xii., 1898.
   See also St. Augustine's.
Turner, W. H.   Selections from the Records of Oxford, 1509–83,
      1880.

Unwin, G.   The Gilds and Companies of London, 1908.

Victoria History of the Counties of England (*V.C.H.*).

Walsingham, T.   Gesta Abbatum Monasterii S. Albani.   Ed. H. T.
      Riley.   *R.S.*   3 vols., 1867–69.
Warwick.   See Black Book.
Wilkinson, B.   The Mediæval Council of Exeter.   With introduction
      by R. C. Easterling, 1931.
Willard, J. F.   Taxation Boroughs and Parliamentary Boroughs, in
      Historical Essays in honour of James Tait, 1933.
Winchester.   See Black Book, Furley and Liber Winton.
Wodderspoon, J.   Memorials of Ipswich, 1850.

York Memorandum Book.   Ed. M. Sellers.   Pt. i.   Surtees Soc.,
      1912.

THE ANGLO-SAXON PERIOD

I

THE ORIGINS OF THE BOROUGH

1. INTRODUCTORY

THE revival of urban life in England when the Teutonic invaders had settled down and accepted Christianity was not an isolated development. Everywhere in Western Europe successive waves of barbarian invasion had washed out Roman municipal organization, a nascent recovery was temporarily checked by the ravages of the Northmen in the ninth century, but with their repulse or settlement proceeded steadily, though at varying rates as local conditions favoured or impeded it. The rise of towns in England cannot therefore be safely studied without some knowledge of the parallel movement on the Continent.

The strong similarities which are observable in urban organization on both sides of the Channel and North Sea may be due, at first at all events, rather to the working of like causes than to direct influence. In nomenclature, for example, the fact that towns were necessarily almost always fortified seems sufficiently to account for the general application to them of the Germanic *burh, burg, bourg*,[1] without supposing borrowing. Certain features of their organization as it gradually developed, within or beyond the period with which we are immediately concerned, were in the nature of the case alike in all countries. Markets, fairs, a body of *probi homines* acting as administrators and, in the more advanced communities, as judges were urban requisites everywhere. In the case of these more highly organized communities there

---

[1] In the Gothic Gospels of the fourth century *baurgs* is used to translate the Greek πόλις, "city," as contrasted with κώμη, "village," which is translated *haims*—O.E. *ham* (Mark, i. 33, vi. 56; Luke, x. 10). The early application of the cognate *burg, burh* to the walled town in England is seen in Canterbury (*Cantwaraburh*).

are always two main problems to be solved. When and in what circumstances did the town become a separate judicial area ? At what date and by what means did it secure the right of self-government ? The materials for answers to these questions, especially the first, are unfortunately imperfect in all countries and a massive literature has gathered round them, especially in Germany. The view that municipal life had survived from Roman times has long been discredited, but the hot controversy whether the town was in the beginning essentially a mere natural extension of a rural community or a fortress (or an appendage of one) or the locality of a market, has not yet been settled to everybody's satisfaction, though the last suggestion has now few, if any, continental supporters.

If the early growth of the English borough has much in common with that of the continental town, it has also some marked peculiarities, due to the insular position of the country and the course of its history. The chief of these is the limited hold which feudalism obtained here as compared with Germany and still more with France. Even in Germany the Ottonian dynasty (10th century) delegated public justice in the great episcopal cities to their bishops, not without risk of confusion between the unfree inhabitants of episcopal domain and the citizens outside its bounds.[1] In thoroughly feudalized France cities had to wrest liberties from episcopal lords. In England, on the other hand, the crown retained its direct authority over all but a few small boroughs in the south-east down to the Norman Conquest and though some larger towns were mediatized by the new rulers of the land, the process never went to dangerous lengths. This direct relation to the king was doubtless in part accountable for the slower development of towns in England than abroad and for the complete absence during the Anglo-Saxon period of such urban charters as were being granted, sparingly enough, by feudal lords in France in the eleventh century and even occasionally in the tenth. Athelstan's alleged charter to Malmesbury [2] is of course the most obvious of post-Conquest forgeries and there is not even a medieval copy of that to Barnstaple.[3]

---

[1] F. Keutgen, *Ursprung der deutschen Stadtverfassung* (1895), pp. 14 ff.
[2] *C.S.*, no. 720, vol. ii., p. 428.
[3] In an inquisition taken shortly before 1344 it was found that " there was nothing certain about the charter of king Athelstan whereby the burgesses pretend that certain liberties were granted to them " (*C.P.R.*

The absence of military and political feudalism in Anglo-Saxon England explains a further marked difference between the early English borough and a large class of continental towns. In the Low Countries the *burg* was the feudal castle round which or a fortified ecclesiastical settlement the towns (*poorte*) mostly grew up, while in France similar settlements below the feudalized walled *cités* of Roman origin came to be distinguished from them as *bourgs* when in their turn they were surrounded with walls. This distinction between old and new was unknown in pre-Conquest England [1] where urban life began within the walls [2] of old Roman towns and the new *burhs* founded by Alfred and his family, when not mere forts, were normally existing settlements, now for the first time surrounded by a wall or stockaded rampart.

The scientific investigation of the origins of the English borough began much later than corresponding studies abroad and was strongly influenced by them. It was not until 1896 that Maitland, much impressed by Keutgen's theory of the vital part played by the defensive *burg* in the rise of towns in Germany, gave a forecast in the *English Historical Review* [3] of the "garrison theory" of the origin of English towns which he expounded at length in the next year in *Domesday Book and Beyond*. Briefly, his theory was that the burgesses and houses recorded in Domesday Book as paying rent to manors outside the borough in the eleventh century were relics of a duty of the shire thegns of the ninth and tenth to keep men in the boroughs for their defence, who became the nucleus of the borough community.

Though slightly guarded by his admission that "no one theory will tell the story of any and every particular town" [4] and that "we must not exclude the hypothesis that some

---

1343-45, p. 290). Yet in 1930 the corporation publicly celebrated the millenary of the granting of the charter to " the oldest borough in the kingdom." Malmesbury wisely made no protest.

[1] Except perhaps in a minor degree at Worcester. See below, p. 20.

[2] At Canterbury these had been extended northwards before the coming of St. Augustine (Bede, bk. i. c. 33 ; C. Cotton, *The Saxon Cathedral at Canterbury* (1929), p. 4) ; but the Burgate, the " Borough Gate," was in the old Roman wall. Dr. Mortimer Wheeler has recently advanced the theory that Saxon London originated in the western half of the area within the Roman wall because that, always thinly populated, had probably been found deserted, while the nucleus of *Londinium*, east of the Walbrook was still occupied through the fifth and sixth centuries by a Romano-British population, " if only as a sub-Roman slum " (*Antiquity*, viii. (1934), pp. 290 ff., *cf. ib.*, 437 ff.). This suggestion is still under discussion and in any case the first Saxon settlement would not have been one of traders.

[3] xi. (1896), pp. 13 ff.   [4] *D.B. and B.*, p. 173.

places were fortified and converted into *burgs* because they were already the focuses of such commerce as there was,"[1] Maitland's theory found practically no supporter but the late Adolphus Ballard, whose exaggerated development of it and illogical attempts to link it up with the Norman castle-guard did not tend to secure its acceptance. With the death of most of the protagonists the controversy subsided without producing an alternative theory, fully worked out.

It was not until 1930 that the problem was attacked again, by an American scholar, Dr. Carl Stephenson, in an important article,[2] in which the whole evidence is reviewed and a conclusion reached which has features both of agreement and disagreement with Maitland's view. Dr. Stephenson rejects the "garrison theory," but goes much further in emphasizing the military character of the early boroughs. For him the normal borough remained primarily a fortress and administrative centre until the Norman Conquest. He claims to have established from the old English laws and from Domesday that, except for a few sea-ports of the south-east,[3] the Anglo-Saxon borough had no really urban character. Its market, like its mint, was official, its court only a unit of the general system of hundred courts. Its population was a microcosm of the countryside, containing all its social ranks from thegn down to slave. There was no land tenure peculiar to boroughs, no burgage tenure as we know it after the Conquest. *Burgenses* (*burgware, burhwaru*) meant no more than inhabitants of a walled centre. There was little trade and that local. For their subsistence the burgesses mainly depended on the borough fields, which the majority of them cultivated for the benefit of a wealthy land-owning minority. Free communal life did not yet exist. It was first called forth by the settlement of French traders in the old boroughs and in new ones created by Norman barons. Uniform burgage tenure was introduced and a rapid succession of other privileges was embodied in charters from the reign of Henry I. The origin of our municipal towns is thus found not in legal criteria, such as the possession of a separate court, but in the

---

[1] *D.B. and B.*, p. 192 ; *cf.* p. 195.

[2] *E.H.R.* xlv. 177 ff. Since my article was written, Professor Stephenson has restated his thesis more fully and with some notable modifications in his book : *Borough and Town : a Study of Urban Origins in England* (Medieval Academy of America, 1933).

[3] In his later work the large populations of York, Lincoln, and Norwich are recognized as evidence of Scandinavian trade. See below, p. 131.

development of a mercantile community, whose chief instrument was the merchant gild. It was essentially a social, not a legal, change.

This change, Dr. Stephenson goes on, falls into its place in the general growth of town life in Western Europe created by the revival of trade in the eleventh century. In England, as on the Continent, the *burgus* was a small lifeless unit until the age of mercantile settlement. This is of course the view for which, as regards the origin of continental towns, Professor Pirenne has secured wide acceptance. The great cities of the Netherlands are traced by him to the settlements of traders in *poorts* under the shelter of *burgs* fortified, like the English *burhs*, for defence against the Northmen. While reserving judgement on Dr. Stephenson's conception of the Anglo-Saxon borough until we have reconsidered the evidence, it may be well to note here that the parallel which he suggests is by no means exact. The boroughs founded by Alfred and his family—not to speak of the old Roman towns early re-occupied, were themselves called *ports*[1] from the first in virtue of their markets. The king's reeve in the borough was *port*reeve not *borough*reeve. While the few dozen *ministeriales*, with the household serfs, of the *burg* in the Low Countries were consumers only, it was, we shall see, the definite policy of Edward and Athelstan to restrict trading as far as possible to the borough-ports. The Northmen here, but not in the Netherlands, settled down as active traders. It is only as royal and revenue-yielding creations that these early markets can be called " official," [2] and the crown continued to retain control of the creation of markets after the Norman Conquest. Again, English boroughs were usually much larger than the *burgs* of the Netherlands.[3]

2. BEFORE THE DANISH INVASIONS

It seems clear that urban life in its most general sense, the aggregation of exceptional numbers at certain points, began in this country with the re-occupation of the old Roman walled towns which for a while had stood wholly or practically

---

[1] Professor Pirenne himself notes this early parallel. Below, p. 21, *n.* 3.
[2] There is no evidence, Professor Pirenne says, of official markets in the *burgs* of the Low Countries. Stephenson, *Borough and Town*, p. 213 *n.*
[3] With the 25 acres of the *vieux-bourg* of Ghent, *cf.* the 80 acres of Oxford, Wallingford, and Wareham, boroughs of middle size.

deserted.[1] The more important became capitals of kingdoms and, in some cases, bishops' sees. In none, however, did the bishop acquire the feudal authority which passed into the hands of the French bishops in the old Roman episcopal cities of Gaul or enjoy even the delegated public authority of the German bishops in the Roman towns along the Rhine and Danube. Such administrative and ecclesiastical centres would naturally attract settlers to supply their wants, many of whom would be attached to the royal domain and the episcopal and monastic estates. There would be a market.[2] These centres were already, in one sense, " boroughs " for *burh* [3] the general name for a fortification, was specially applied to walled towns, but we shall not expect to detect in them all the features of the later Anglo-Saxon borough. There is evidence, for instance, that a court was held in them, but it seems to have been the king's court for a wider district than the *civitas*. With rare exceptions, such communal organization as they yet possessed would be mainly of an agricultual type. Most, if not all, of them had arable fields and their appurtenant meadow, pasture and wood, which suggests that the original settlers had formed agricultural communities which differed from others only by living within walls. The germ of a more thoroughly urban communalism lay in their market, though royal policy afterwards, though reluctantly, decided that markets and fairs were not to be exclusive marks of a borough.

That London at least was the centre of much more than local trade as early as the seventh century we know from Bede's description of the metropolis of the East Saxons as " multorum emporium populorum terra marique uenientium." [4] A law of Hlothere and Eadric reveals Kentishmen as frequent purchasers in London.[5] Signs of increasing trade elsewhere in the eighth and ninth centuries will come before us later. It is significant that when at the latter date the place of minting is given on the coins, eight out of the ten mints on

---

[1] As regards London, this is disputed by Dr. Wheeler (see above, p. 3, *n.* 2). Haverfield pointed out that the correct Roman names of Canterbury and Rochester, Doruuernis and Dorubreuis, were known to Bede, apparently by tradition only. He ascribed this to the first English settlement in Kent having been by agreement (*E.H.R.* x. (1895), 710-11), but it may also perhaps indicate an early re-occupation of these *civitates*.

[2] The *venalis locus* at Canterbury is mentioned in a charter of 786 (*C.S.* no. 248, i. 344).

[3] Latin, *urbs* in Bede, etc., *arx* usually in charters.

[4] *Hist. Eccl.*, ed. Plummer, i. 85.

[5] Liebermann, *Ges.* i. 11 (c. 16), a. 685-6.

record were in old Roman *civitates*.[1] This is far from ex-
hausting the Roman sites which developed into boroughs.
Of the seventy-one unmediatized boroughs which appear in
Domesday, some eighteen are of this type and Carlisle and
Newcastle raise the number to twenty.

Apart from Bede's testimony to the trade of London, we
are not altogether left to conjecture and inference from later
evidence in estimating the stage reached by the future boroughs
in this early period. Royal grants of land in Canterbury and
Rochester, to Christ Church and St. Augustine's Abbey in
the one and the see in the other, and similar gifts to thegns,
have fortunately been preserved and throw a little welcome
light upon the two Kentish cities. The charters attributed
to Ethelbert are forgeries and the earliest genuine grant is
that of Egbert, king of Kent, to Bishop Eardulf of Rochester
in 765.[2] This is a gift of land within the walled area (*cas-
tellum*)[3] described as " unum viculum cum duobus jugeri-
bus adjacentem plateae quae est terminus a meridie hujus
terrae." This and some later grants of *jugera* with houses in
Rochester and Canterbury have been claimed as revealing the
existence within their walls of large estates ranging up to six
ploughlands and so " indicating the survival in the *civitas* of
only a scanty population living by agriculture."[4] The argument is, however, vitiated by two errors into which Professor
Stephenson has fallen. He identifies *jugerum*, " acre " with
jugum, the fourth part of a ploughland,[5] and fails to notice
that the acres were in most cases wholly or largely outside the
walls. The only certain evidence of acres within them is
confined to the two acres of the Rochester grant quoted above
and ten in Canterbury.[6] Even these of course are large
tenements for a town, but in the ancient borough, we must not
expect the small and uniform lots of those of later creation.[7]
That there was some agricultural land even within the walls

---

[1] *E.H.R.* xi. (1896), 759. It has even been questioned whether the
evidence for Alfred's mint at Oxford is trustworthy (J. Parker, *Early History
of Oxford*, pp. 366 ff.). The most recent opinion, that of Sir Charles Oman,
rejects this scepticism.

[2] *C.S.* 196, i. 278.

[3] *Cf.* W. H. Stevenson, *Asser*, p. 331.

[4] *E.H.R.* xlv. (1930), 204-5.

[5] The 30 *jugera* on the north side of Canterbury granted (a. 823) in
C.S. 373, i. 511 are " ŏritiges *aecra* " in the contemporary English endorsement.

[6] *Ibid.* 426, i. 597.

[7] An acre for the burgage seems to have been a maximum allowance
in the new boroughs of the thirteenth century (*B.B.C.* ii. 47, 51, 62).

we need not deny. There were closes within the walls of Lincoln as late as 1086.[1]

The Latin terms applied to city messuages in these Kentish charters do not indeed on their face suggest a tenement specifically urban and on the contrary have a rural sound. *Villa* and *vicus*, if not *villulum* and *viculum*, were common Latin versions of the Anglo-Saxon *tun* and *wic* in the sense of " dwelling-place," " homestead " and by extension " village " or, more widely, any populated place, as our word " town " witnesses. While in the country at large, however, the wider meaning tended to become predominant, the original narrower sense persisted in the Kentish cities. Charters of 786[2] and 824[3] preserve the English names of two messuages in Canterbury, Curringtun and Eastur Waldingtun. The contemporary English endorsement of the sale of a plot of land there in 868 describes it as " ðisne tuun."[4] But a more specialized term was coming in. As early as 811 we find a Mercian king transferring to Archbishop Wulfred " duas possessiunculas et tertiam dimidiam, id est in nostra lingua ðridda half haga "—*i.e.*, 2½ haws—in Canterbury with their appurtenant meadows on the east bank of the Stour,[5] and twelve years later another king of Mercia added a small adjoining plot measuring 60 feet by 30, together with 30 acres on the north side of the city, 25 in the arable (*in arido campo*) and 5 of meadow.[6] A Rochester charter of 855 granted " unam villam quod nos Saxonice *an haga* dicimus in meridie castelli Hrobi " with the appurtenances of land, etc., which of old belonged to it.[7] *Haga*, afterwards softened to *haw*, was, like *tun*, a general term for an enclosed area, a dwelling-place, but it never obtained such a wide extension of application and came to be almost exclusively applied to urban tenements. Even when the word dropped out of ordinary use, it long survived in the " hawgable " rents of some old boroughs.[8]

The descriptions of the appurtenances of the Canterbury and Rochester haws, one or two of which have been quoted, show clearly that these *civitates* were in the eighth and ninth

---

[1] *D.B.* i. 336a, 2. They were called crofts.
[2] *C.S.* 248, i. 344.   [3] *Ibid.* 382, i. 526.
[4] *Ibid.* 519, ii. 134. It measured 6 rods by 3, a moderate area. Such plots could also be called " wics." See *ibid.* 373, i. 512. Hence the Latin *vicus* and *viculum.*
[5] *Ibid.* 335, i. 467.   [6] *Ibid.* 373, i. 511.   [7] *Ibid.* 486, ii. 86.
[8] *E.g.* Cambridge. See Maitland, *Township and Borough*, p. 48 and *passim ;* W. M. Palmer, *Cambridge Borough Documents*, i (1931), lviii f., 57 ff.

centuries no mere aggregations of small agricultural estates within their Roman walls, but exhibit all those agricultural features of the English borough with the later aspect of which Maitland has made us familiar, the messuage within the walls, or suburb, and the appendant arable, meadow, pasture, wood and marsh further out. Especially noteworthy is the mention of the *urbanorum prata*[1] and *burhwarawald*,[2] " the boroughmen's wood," of Canterbury.

The eighth-century charter which supplies the latter name has a further interest in the combination of the grant of a large agricultural estate at Ickham with that of " the *vicus* called Curringtun," on the north side of the market-place in Canterbury. This looks very like an early instance of those town houses attached to rural manors, so numerous in Domesday Book, which Maitland wished to trace to military arrangements of tenth century date.[3]

In regulating the use of unenclosed fields and pastures and woods and marshes enjoyed in common, the *burgware* had constant necessity to act as a community, but the charters give hints of wider common action. Land in Canterbury was sold between 839 and 855 with the witness of the *portweorona*[4] who were present, and a few years later a sale was witnessed among others by *innan burgware*, headed by an Athelstan who was probably the reeve of the city.[5] The existence of other *burgware*, living without the walls is implied.[6]

The application of the term *port* to Canterbury in the first of these documents is of vital importance as showing that the city in the ninth century did not subsist on agriculture alone, but was a place of trade. That this was already the well-established meaning of *port* is clear from a contemporary London charter (857) by which Ælhun, bishop of Worcester,

---

[1] *C.S.* 449, ii. 30 (a. 845). Perhaps the *burgwara meda* of *C.S.* 497, ii. 102 (a. 859) in which a half *tun* participated. It is not clear to what *burh* the *burware felda* in the bounds of Challock (*C.S.* 378, i. 519) belonged.

[2] *C.S.* 248, i. 344 (a. 786). A Canterbury grant of 839 included two cartloads of wood in summer, by ancient custom, " in commune silfa quod nos Saxonice *in gemennisse* dicimus" (*ibid.* 426, i. 597). For the Middle English *menesse* in this transferred sense see *Place Names of Sussex*, ed. Mawer and Stenton, ii. 560.

[3] Possibly another case is that of the half *tun* mentioned in note 1 above, which is said to have formerly belonged to a " Wilburgewell." For the tenement in Canterbury granted to the nuns of Lyminge in 811 " ad refugium necessitatis " see below, p. 15.

[4] *I.e.* " Portmen," *C.S.* i. 599.   [5] *C.S.* 515, ii. 128.

[6] They appear together in 958 as witnesses of *C.S.* 1010, iii. 213 : " iii geferscipas innan et utan burhwara."

acquired the haw of Ceolmund the reeve (*praefectus*) at a
yearly rent of 12*d*. in addition to the purchase price. With
the haw, it is stated, went the liberty of having " modium
et pondus et mensura, *sicut in porto mos est*." [1] The privilege
was one of exemption from royal dues, as is more clearly
brought out in the grant more than thirty years later to
Ælhun's successor of the *curtis* called by the Londoners " At
Hwaetmundes Stane," to which was attached " urnam et
trutinam ad mensurandum in emendo sive vendendo ad usum
suum ad necessitatem propriam," free from all toll to the
king. This, however, became payable if any of the bishop's
men traded outside the house, either in the public street or on
the quay (*in ripa emptorali*).[2]

There is much earlier evidence of royal tolls at London
and elsewhere. Exemptions were granted by Ethelbald of
Mercia *c.* 732–745 for ships belonging to the abbess of Minster
in Thanet and to the bishops of Rochester and Worcester,
both in the port (*in portu*, " harbour ") or hythe of London
and at Fordwich and Sarre on the Stour below Canterbury.[3]
Already in the eighth century there was some foreign trade.
In 789 Charles the Great in a quarrel with King Offa closed
all the Frankish ports to English merchants and, when the
embargo was removed on both sides, stipulated that merchants
and smugglers should not enter in the guise of pilgrims.
Merchants of both nations were to have royal protection as
before and direct appeal to emperor or king as the case might
be. Charles wrote to Offa that his subjects complained of
the length (*prolixitas*) of the cloaks (*sagi*) sent from England,
and asked him to see that they were made as of old.[4] There
is no hint that any of these *negotiatores* were slave-traders.

---

[1] *C.S.* 492, ii. 95. *Portus* in this sense seems always declined as a
noun of the first declension.

[2] *Ibid.* 561, ii. 200. In later London the tron (*trutina*) or great beam
was for weighing coarse goods by the hundredweight (Riley, *Memorials of
London*, p. 26 *n*.).

[3] *Ibid.* 149, i. 216 ; 152, i. 220 ; 171, i. 246 ; 188, i. 267 ; 189, i. 268.
For salt toll at Droitwich (*emptorium salis*) *c.* 716 see *ibid.* 138, i. 203,
and in the ninth century *ibid.* 552. ii. 174 and 579, ii. 222.

[4] This and other evidence is collected by Miss H. Cam in *Francia and
England* (1912), pp. 15 f. " Cloak " is her translation of *sagus*, but these
sagi may possibly be the " drappes ad camisias ultramarinas quae vulgo
berniscrist (see Du Cange, *s.v.*) vocitantur " purchased by the monks of St.
Bertin (Giry, *Hist. de Saint.-Omer*, p. 276). About 975 Irish traders
brought *saga* with other merchandise to Cambridge (*Lib. Eliensis*, p. 148).
Ethelwerd's story that the Danes who first landed on the south coast
were taken for traders, from whom the king's official to collect toll,
may be true.

An important result of this commercial intercourse with Francia was the substitution of the silver penny for the sceatt in England and the adoption there of the gold coin known as the *mancus*. It is first mentioned in an undoubtedly genuine charter of 799.[1]

The evidence which is available for a view of the condition of urban centres in England before the age of fortification against the Danes is not, to say the least, abundant and it is almost confined to the south-east, but, so far as it goes, it does not reveal a purely agricultural economy. It is a striking illustration of the little light that can be expected from the early land charters that those of Rochester and Canterbury only once mention a trader as such. A royal grant of land in Canterbury to a thegn in 839, already referred to, conveyed also, in close conjunction with two weirs on the Stour, " unum merkatorem quem lingua nostra *mangere* nominamus." [2] It would certainly be rash to infer that this " monger " was personally unfree [3] and in any case unreasonable to draw from one instance any general conclusions as to the status of the class to which he belonged. At the best, they were clearly very humble folk, compared with the churchmen and royal servants to whom the kings were " booking " considerable portions of their domain within and without the old walls. It is possible that some of them held small tenements by folkright derived from the original agricultural settlers, but it seems likely that for the most part they were tenants or grantees of the great churches [4] and thegns, and in the latter case it is very improbable that the tenements were conveyed by charter.[5] There is evidence that in some quarters at any rate houses in Canterbury closely adjoined one another on the street frontages. An endorsement on a charter of 868 recording the sale for 120*d.* of a small *tuun*, measuring six rods by three and bounded on all four sides by the land of different owners, mentions that by customary law (*folcaes*

---

[1] *C.S.* 293, i. 409.   [2] *C.S.* 426, i. 598.

[3] In the twelfth and thirteenth centuries burgesses and other undoubted freemen were sometimes transferred with the land they rented. See, for example, *Reg. Antiquissimum Cath. Linc.*, ii. no. 324.

[4] In the exemption from toll of a London house of the bishop of Worcester (*C.S.* 561 ; see above, p. 10) the case of the bishop's men trading outside the privileged tenement is provided for. If they do, they must pay the king's toll.

[5] But the *burhware*, who in the tenth century had " book acres " in the fields, may have included merchants (*C.S.*, no. 637, ii. 314).

folcryht) two feet had to be left between houses to allow eavesdrip.[1]

That any members of the thegnly class engaged in trade at this early period seems unlikely. Its junior members, the *cnihts*, had indeed a gild in Canterbury in the middle of the ninth century [2] and it is tempting to see in them fore-runners of the *cnihts* of the chapmengild there which made an exchange of houses with Christ Church about the beginning of the twelfth century.[3] But it is a serious obstacle to this identification that the earlier gild witnessed a charter which reveals its existence separately from the inner *burgware*.[4] This may possibly be a case of illogical classification, but it is safer not to take refuge in anomalies.

It will have been observed in the foregoing analysis of the Rochester and Canterbury charters that the " tenurial heterogeneity " of towns which Maitland imaginatively deduced from a supposed obligation imposed on the shire thegns of the tenth century to garrison the *burhs* and repair their walls, was already a feature in the eighth and ninth centuries in those towns for which we have detailed evidence. Tenements in *burhs* or *ports* were being granted to churches and thegns with or without definite association with estates outside, as a matter of privilege, conferring honour and profit and in no case with any military obligation beyond that which lay on land everywhere to construct and repair *burhs* (*burhbot*) and bridges and do military service.[5]

The *burhbot* did not apply to all *burhs*. This word, as we have seen, was a general term for fortified enclosure. It covered the deserted hill " camps " of earlier races as well as the re-occupied Roman *civitates* and the fortified dwellings of the English higher classes as well as those of their kings, but it was only for the old walled town and the royal house [6] that the *burhbot* was available.

In view of the municipal future of *burh*, it may seem sur-prising that our local nomenclature preserves it much oftener—

---

[1] *C.S.* 519, ii. 134.   This must have been in the main an urban law.

[2] *C.S.* 515, ii. 128.

[3] C. Gross, *Gild Merchant*, ii. 37.   See below, p. 120.

[4] Above, p. 9.

[5] Commonly, but inaccurately known as the *Trinoda Necessitas*. *Cf.* W. H. Stevenson's article in *E.H.R.* xxix (1914), 689 ff., especially p. 698.

[6] In a Mercian charter of 836 it appears in another association than that of the *Trinoda Necessitas*.   Hanbury monastery is freed " a pastu regis et principum et ab omni constructione regalis ville et a difficultate illa quam nos Saxonice *fæstingmenn* dicimus (*C.S.* 416, i. 581).

in the suffix -bury or borough—in village names than in those of towns, either of Roman or later origin. In the former *ceaster*, borrowed from Latin *castra*, was usually preferred to the native *burh* in either form as suffix, the only exceptions being Canterbury and Salisbury,[1] while the latter often grew out of villages with names of a different type.

For the same reason as that last mentioned, *port*, though it came to be a synonym for town, in its trading aspect, and, unlike *burh*, was exclusively urban, has left few traces in local names. Much better represented in them, because it was in older and less exclusive use, is *wic*, *wich*. A loan-word from Latin *vicus*, its original sense was "dwelling-place," "abode," from which, like *tun*, it developed the meaning "village." By a further, but early, development it was used in a sense similar to that of *port*. London was known as Lundenwic already in the last quarter of the seventh century;[2] its chief officer was the *wic-gerefa*. The salt workings in Cheshire and Worcestershire were *wiches*.

In this early period then the urban community had three aspects: it formed an agricultural group, its house area was usually fortified and it was to some extent engaged in trade. Of these aspects the most primitive was the agricultural, though in *burhs* of Roman origin the walls were older than the first English settlements. It is not unreasonable to suppose that such settlements, though afterwards overlaid by administrative and ecclesiastical elements, contributed a germ of communalism which later expanded under the influence of commerce. Without subscribing to von Below's theory of the origin of the town (*Stadt*) in the self-governing village (*Landgemeinde*), we may note that Maitland, though maintaining that in the absence of some further ingredient the courtless village could never have developed into the borough, admits even in *Domesday Book and Beyond*, and more fully in *Township and Borough*, that the medieval borough belonged to the genus *tun*, as indeed the name "town" and the equivalent use even in official language of *villa* and *burgus* (or *civitas*) sufficiently attest. The equivalence, it is true, was really very imperfect, ignoring a vital distinction, and its significance chiefly retrospective. In the very early period with which we have been dealing, however, the distinction

---

[1] Lundenburh proved a transient form. See below, p. 23.
[2] *Laws of Hlothaere and Eadric* (685–686), c. 16, in Liebermann, *Ges.* i. 11. Cf. *C.S.* 335, i. 466; *A.S.C.* s.a. 604, ed. Plummer, i. 23.

between urban and rural units was as yet material, not legal. There was nothing paradoxical in the description of Canterbury as " regalis villa Dorovernie civitatis." [1] Nothing in the organization of the urban vill distinguished it from the *villa regalis* which still remained purely rural. Each was governed by a royal reeve (*gerefa*), though the *wic-gerefa* of London or the *port-gerefa* of other considerable places was doubtless a more important personage than the *tun-gerefa* of the ordinary royal vill. He may have found it necessary from time to time to consult with the more important *burgware* on questions of markets and tolls, if not of administration, and in these consultations we may, if we like, see faint foreshadowings of still far distant municipal self-government. A regular assembly with a share in the town government only became possible when urban courts were created, and for these the time had not yet arrived. It may be taken as certain, indeed, that a court of justice met in these urban centres, but it was not purely urban. There is strong reason to believe that the country in this period was divided for judicial purposes into districts each of which had a *villa regalis* as its centre [2] and if this was so, the court meeting in London or Canterbury would not have differed essentially from that of any other such district. The name Borowara Lathe [3] suggests that this was the district judicially dependent on Canterbury and the London folkmote of the twelfth century was perhaps a relic of a court which had once exercised jurisdiction over Middlesex at least.

The practical differences between the urban and the rural *villa regalis*, especially the intensive trade of the former, would doubtless of themselves in the long run have compelled division of the urban centre from its district as a distinct judicial area, but the process was much hastened by the Danish invasions and settlement which gave an urgent importance to fortified centres and played no small part in bringing about a readjustment of the areas for local justice and administration. [4]

[1] *C.S.* 852 (416 B), ii. app. xv, a charter of Egbert of Wessex, dated 836.
[2] See below, p. 36.
[3] The Borwart Lest of Domesday. *Cf. E.H.R.* xliv (1929), 613
[4] See below, pp. 28-9.

3. THE NEW *BURHS* FORTIFIED IN THE DANISH WARS

In the foregoing pages the first period in the urban life of England has been taken to extend roughly to the accession of Alfred. The Danish raids, it is true, had been in progress for three-quarters of a century, the " heathen " were now firmly established in the North and Midlands and the fate of Wessex hung in the balance. Until Alfred's reign, however, there is no sign of any general scheme of defensive fortifications or of reorganization. The value of existing fortified centres was indeed recognized. As early as 804 the abbess and convent of Lyminge received a grant of land in Canterbury " ad necessitatis refugium." [1] In several charters the military services of the old " trinoda necessitas " are noted to be directed " in paganos," and in one of these the duty of destroying their fortifications is added to that of building defensive *burhs*.[2] Yet even Roman walls did not always give a secure refuge in this necessity. Canterbury and, according to the oldest MS. of the Chronicle, London were stormed in 851.[3] The defences of the lesser *villae regales* would in most cases oppose a much weaker resistance to the fierce assaults of the Danes. It is at first sight surprising to find Alfred's contemporary biographer merely referring to these as buildings of stone which he sometimes removed to positions more becoming the royal power [4] and distinguishing them from the cities and *burhs* (*civitates et urbes*) which he has previously mentioned as repaired by him or constructed in places where there had been none before. But Asser is reviewing the work of Alfred's reign, and a leading feature of the period which opens with it was an increasing restriction of the term *burh* to the more strongly fortified centres.

It is unlucky that the bishop did not think it necessary to specify more than one of Alfred's fortifications, the two *arces* which protected the bridge into Athelney,[5] for had he done so, there might have been no dispute as to the date of the difficult but very important document, which in the absence of any heading is now known as The Burghal Hidage.[6] Maitland

[1] *C.S.* 317, i. 444.

[2] *Ibid.* 332, i. 462 (a. 811); 335, i. 467 (a. 811); 370, i. 509 (a. 822). The last has " arcis munitione vel destructione in eodem gente."

[3] *A.S.C.*, ed. Plummer, *s.a.*

[4] Asser, ed. W. H. Stevenson, c. 91, p. 77.

[5] Asser, c. 92, p. 80. However, he mentions casually the east gate of Shaftesbury (*ibid.* c. 98, p. 85).

[6] Maitland, *D.B. and B.*, pp. 502 ff.

was inclined to think that it was drawn up under Edward the Elder, and Professor Chadwick argues from internal evidence for a date between 911 and 919.[1] Sir Charles Oman, however, in 1910,[2] and more recently the late W. J. Corbett,[3] have claimed it as in the main an Alfredian document. Imperfect at the beginning and perhaps at the end, it contains (1) a list of thirty-one *burhs*, the hidages assigned to which are added up, and (2) an appendix, apparently later, comprising only Essex, Worcester and Warwick. The chief argument for the later date is the inclusion in the former of the Mercian Oxford and Buckingham, though it is otherwise a purely southern list. Professor Chadwick suggests that this limited inclusion was only possible shortly after the death of the Mercian ealdorman Ethelred, Alfred's son-in-law, about 911, when Edward took into his own hands London and Oxford with their districts and the intervening Buckingham was probably, he thinks, included. On the other hand, Sir Charles Oman argues that when Ethelred, according to the Chronicle, had received London in 886 from Alfred it was as his personal representative and not as ealdorman of Mercia,[4] so that he probably obtained Oxford and Buckingham at the same time and on the same terms and their grouping with Wessex is not therefore inconsistent with an Alfredian date. But Sir Charles has already, in another connexion,[5] accepted without demur, except at its date, a pretty obvious slip of 880 for 887, a charter which, if genuine, shows Ethelred disposing of land in the Oxford district as " dux et patricius gentis Merciorum." [6] The question of his status would be further cleared up if Birch's identification of Hrisbyri, the scene of a Mercian witenagemot in which Ethelred made a grant three years earlier,[7] with Prince's Risborough in Buckinghamshire could be sustained. But the name, it is said, " cannot be reconciled with the other certain forms for Risborough." [8] A further objection, that English rule in

---

[1] *Anglo-Saxon Institutions*, p. 207.

[2] *England before the Norman Conquest*, pp. 468 ff.

[3] *Cambridge Medieval History*, iii. 357.

[4] This is inferred from its resumption (with Oxford) after Ethelred's death, though Ethelfled retained the ealdormanry for some years longer.

[5] *Op. cit.*, p. 464 *n.*   [6] *C.S.* 547, ii. 166.   [7] *Ibid.* 552, ii. 174.

[8] Mawer and Stenton, *Place-Names of Buckinghamshire*, p. 171 *n.* Risbury (*D.B.* Riseberie) might be suggested as an alternative, but *Hrisbyri* is not a possible ninth-century form even for that and as *C.S.* 552 is only known from Smith's edition of Bede, the name may be a late copyist's corruption of a correct form of Risborough. *Cf.* the *Riseberie* of a charter *c.* 1155 quoted *op. cit.*, p. 170.

central Buckinghamshire in 884 is very unlikely, would lose force if Liebermann was right in his argument,[1] on independent grounds, that the peace between Alfred and Guthrum which fixes the frontier so as to leave London and all west of the Lea English did not, as now generally held, follow a recapture of London in 886, but may have been concluded as early as 880, the siege and recovery of London at the later date, if there was such an event, being the result of a temporary success of the East Anglian Danes who in 884 " broke the peace." [2]

So far Professor Chadwick has certainly the best of the argument, and he might have strengthened his case by pointing out that Edward and not Alfred is recorded in the Chronicle [3] to have made two *burhs* at Buckingham. Professor Stenton has further called my attention to charter evidence that Porchester, which is included in the main list, belonged to the see of Winchester in Alfred's time and was not exchanged with the crown for (Bishop's) Waltham until 904.[4] On the other hand, with the exception of Oxford and Buckingham, the main part of the Burghal Hidage seems to have constituted a complete scheme of defence for Wessex and its dependencies and for them only.

Moreover, Oxford at least, in the hands of Alfred's son-in-law, might be considered as a bridgehead of Wessex.[5] Save Buckingham, the list contains none of the *burhs* founded by Ethelred and his wife or her brother in their offensive against the Danes. Even their *burh* at Worcester, built in Alfred's life-time, appears only in the obviously later appendix. That *burhs*, old and new, played an important part in Alfred's last campaigns against the Danes we know from Asser and the Chronicle. Unfortunately, the annalist only mentions four by name and those all with Roman walls,[6] but by good

[1] *Ges.* iii. 84.   [2] *A.S.C.*, ed. Plummer, i. 80.
[3] *Ibid.* p. 100. Sir Charles Oman unconvincingly ·assumes that Buckingham here is an error for Bedford (*op. cit.*, p. 500 *n.*). His appeal to the Burghal Hidage of course begs the question.
[4] *C.S.* 613, ii. 274.
[5] The assignment in the list of a joint hidage to Oxford and Wallingford, an undoubted West-Saxon borough, may be significant in the light of the curious fact that in each the royal demesne was an area of eight virgates (*D.B.* i. 56a, 2, 154a, 1 ; see below, p. 89) and of the interrelations of the two boroughs and their counties revealed in Domesday Book. For Alfred's Oxford mint, see p. **7** *n.*
[6] Exeter, London, Chester and Chichester. Of these only Exeter and Chichester are in the Burghal Hidage, though Sir Charles Oman implies (*op. cit.*, p. 469) that there were a good many more and includes Twyneham first mentioned in the Chronicle under Edward and Wimborne, which is not in the list and is described as a *ham* not a *burh* in 901.

chance Asser not only describes his early fortifications at Athelney, but quite casually reveals the fact that Shaftesbury, to which in the Hidage 700 hides are assigned, was surrounded by a wall with gates.[1] It is significant, too, that the fortresses of the Hidage stand thickest in central Somerset, the starting-point of Alfred's recovery of his kingdom, round his bridge-head " work " at Lyng, the " arx munitissima " of Asser,[2] which completed the isolation of Athelney.

The scheme as a whole is skilfully devised to stay Danish attacks at all vulnerable points inland or on the coast.[3] It is surely too elaborate to have been devised during the early difficulties of Edward's reign before he took the offensive against the Danes. Any measures of defence that he resorted to must have been mainly based upon the work of his father as we see it revealed by his biographer and chronicler. It is conceivable that the original of the corrupt MS. of the Burghal Hidage, which is all we have, was copied in the reign of Edward from an earlier document, and any anachronisms, if there be such,[4] may have come in then.

About a third of the thirty-one [5] *burhs* in the main list were small military centres of temporary importance and never developed into towns. Only twenty-two were accounted boroughs in the later sense, and not all these became corporate towns.[6] Some twelve are mentioned as *ports* before the Norman Conquest, and nineteen are known to have had mints, twenty are described in Domesday Book either as *burgi* or as having *burgenses*.

The nine or ten *burhs* which never became *ports*, mint-places or boroughs may have owed their fate to the greater suitability of neighbouring places for trade and administration,[7] but this only shows that walls alone did not make a

---

[1] Ed. Stevenson, c. 98, p. 85.   [2] *Ibid.* c. 92, p. 80.

[3] Its purely military object seems attested by the absence of the Dorset Dorchester. The *burhs* were on the northern frontier and the sea coast of the shire.

[4] Buckingham, in its strong natural position and with perhaps early slighter fortification, may have been reckoned a *burh* before Edward's time. Porchester, though belonging to the see of Winchester, may, like episcopal Worcester, have been fortified in the public interest under Alfred.

[5] Of the two hitherto unidentified, Sceaftesege has been located by Professor Stenton as an island in the Thames, near Marlow.

[6] Watchet, Cricklade and Lydford never attained this status.

[7] Burpham was apparently outshadowed by Arundel, Eashing by Godalming (of which it became a tithing), Porchester by Portsmouth, Tisbury by Hindon, Bredy by Bridport, Halwell by Totnes, and Pilton by Barnstaple.

borough in the municipal sense, though, where conveniently situated, they normally provided the natural shell for the growth of town life in stormy times.

The conditions under Alfred were not favourable to urban growth. It is hardly likely that even the comparatively quiet period after the settlement of Guthrum-Athelstan in East Anglia (880) saw much revival of trade. When the Danes were not raiding England they were ravaging Francia, and commerce with that natural market was cut off. The organization of the *burhs* for national defence must have depressed the trading element where it existed and proportionately increased the predominance of the thegnly class who no doubt bore the brunt of the defence.[1] On the other hand, too much has perhaps been made of the absence of any reference to trade in Alfred's Laws except in c. 34 which required chapmen to give security in folkmoot for the good conduct of those whom they proposed to take up country with them.[2] Traders who moved about with a train of attendants cannot fairly be dismissed as mere " wandering pedlars." We have seen Charles the Great insisting on similar security from English merchants in his country.[3] Nor must it be forgotten that Alfred of set purpose added as little as was possible to the enactments of his predecessors, not knowing, he says, what additions of his would be approved by his successors.

Although a study of the map shows that the sites of the *burhs* of the Burghal Hidage were chosen for military reasons and most of their names are not recorded before the ninth century, some of these unrecorded names imply earlier settlements and there is strong probability that important fords like Oxford, Wallingford and Cricklade or the rarer bridge, as at Axbridge, had already attracted population. Such passages and the confluences of streams were the natural *nuclei* of early trade as well as obvious points to defend. That a market was the central point of the *burhs* constructed by Alfred and his Mercian son-in-law we know from the only record of such a fortification, either now or later, that affords a glimpse within

---

[1] But the *burgware* of London and Chichester who sallied forth against the Danes in 894-5 are clearly distinguishable from the king's thegns " at home in the forts " who gathered from all the *burhs* of the west to meet the Danes on the middle Severn. The " men who were to keep the *burhs* " have previously been mentioned as an exception from Alfred's division of the *fyrd* into two halves, one at home, and the other in the field. The thegns were for the present permanently " at home " in the *burhs*, but their residence would presumably end with the return of peace.

[2] Liebermann, *Ges.* i. 68-9.   [3] Above, p. 10.

the ramparts.[1] At some date between 885 and 900 Ethelred and Ethelfled, at the instance of Werfrith, bishop of
Worcester, ordered the construction of a *burh* there for the
protection of " all the folk." [2] On the completion of the fortifications, Ethelred and his wife, with the approval of Alfred
and of the Mercian *witan*, for the support of the church and
in return for religious services on their behalf in life and after
death, bestowed upon St. Peter and the bishop one-half of the
revenue accruing to them as lords from the market or from
the streets within and without the *burh*. This public revenue
is more fully defined later in the charter as comprising *landfeoh*,
perhaps the rent from demesne land later known as *landgafol*
(*landgabulum*), and a tax for the repair of the wall (*burhwealles
sceating*) together with the issues of justice from theft, fight-
ing, market offences (*wohceapung*) and all others for which
compensation (*bot*) was possible, so far as these breaches of
law occurred in market or street. Outside these limits the
bishop was to enjoy all the land and dues which the grantors'
predecessors had given to the see. It would appear from this
and later evidence that the bishop was the chief landowner
in the area enclosed by the wall and had " sake and soke,"
that is the right to take the profits of justice arising out of
offences upon his land.

The other half of the revenues which were divided was
reserved to the grantors. The market profits did not include
the most valuable tolls, for it is expressly stated that the
shilling on the waggonload and the penny on the horseload
were to go to the king, as they had always done at Saltwich,
i.e., Droitwich. This evidence of a revenue derived by the
West Saxon kings from tolls on trade in English Mercia is
noteworthy.

It seems fairly clear from the arrangements described
in this unique charter that the old unfortified Worcester had
been a mere appendage of the cathedral church, whose rights
flowed from grants by Mercian or Hwiccian kings and that
the market-place and the streets which led to it with the
jurisdiction over them, the profits of which were to be shared
with the church, were new, like the tolls reserved to the king,
and constituted the return exacted by the present " lords of
Mercia " for the costly work of fortification. A few years
later, in 904, the church added a life-lease of a great tenement

---

[1] *C.S.* 579, ii. 221 f.   [2] " Eallum thæm folc(e) to gebeorge."

(*haga*) in the north-western corner of the *burh*, along with land at Barbourne outside it on the north.[1]

The Worcester *burh* was exceptional in not being founded on land that was wholly or in large part royal domain. The bargain effected with Bishop Werfrith and his chapter can have been rare indeed, if not unique. It is important also to observe that the duty of repairing the walls was acquitted by a money payment not by personal service. The grouping of this payment with revenues otherwise entirely derived from the *burh* suggests that it fell upon the inhabitants only. It is perhaps possible that the reference is only to the urban portion of a wider tax levied upon the 1200 hides which are assigned to Worcester in the appendix to the Burghal Hidage. This seems less likely, however, and if the tax was purely internal, we must suppose that the military connexion between the hides and the *burh* was confined to personal service when required.

A parallel to the English *burhs* was found by Keutgen and Maitland [2] in the purely artificial *burgs* which Henry the Fowler a little later was raising in newly conquered lands on the north-eastern frontier of Germany and peopling from without, but the likeness is somewhat superficial. England was a long settled land. The very small *burh*, designed or adapted for military defence only and without urban possibilities may have approximated to the German type, but usually the place selected for walling had already a certain population and such elaborate arrangements as Henry was driven to make for the manning and support of the *burg* from the country round were not needed. The Worcester case might suggest a more plausible parallel with the *castra* of the Low Countries, fortified feudal and ecclesiastical centres at the foot of which trading settlements (*poorts*) grew up and were ultimately walled.[3] But the absence of feudalism in England at this date makes the parallel misleading. The cathedral precincts were probably but slightly fortified and the charter of Ethelred and Ethelfled hardly suggests that the dependent population outside before the walling was chiefly occupied in trade.

---

[1] *C.S.* 608, ii. 266. The northern side of the haw was 28 rods long, the southern 19 and the eastern 24 ; no figure is given for the western, parallel with the river.

[2] *E.H.R.* xi. (1896) 13 ff. ; *D.B. and B.*, p. 189.

[3] Pirenne, *Histoire de Belgique*, i. 2, § 1. He remarks on the equivalence of *poort* with the English *port*.

What light does this invaluable charter throw upon the vexed question of the origin of the medieval borough ? Here it was the wall which made possible the trading centre, the *port*, not the trading centre which was given a protecting wall. All or nearly all of the features on which the discussion has turned appear here in full or in germ, walls, market, separate profits of justice if not a separate court, divisions of revenue between king and earl, probably an earlier agricultural community. It is not the deliberate foundation and fortification of a trading town that the charter reveals. The walls were built as a refuge for the population of a wide region, liable to sudden Danish attacks, a market was an indispensable provision for the needs of temporary and permanent inhabitants alike. Had it not been for the military necessities of the time, episcopal Worcester might have had to wait long for urban growth, for the making of markets as of walls was a prerogative of the state. Yet the market, though at the outset an incidental result of the fortification, was a vital germ of the future borough, the fortification merely the occasion which called it into existence. Circumstances decided that most towns should grow up behind walls, but exceptions can be found. Droitwich, the " Wicum emptorium salis " of an early eighth-century character,[1] never appears as a *burh*, but it was accounted a borough in 1086 and its burgesses received a charter from King John.

The jurisdiction over market and streets at Worcester involved a local court, but it seems unlikely that this would be a purely Worcester court at this date. Elsewhere the court may usually have been that of a district centring in a royal residence, *burh* in one of its older senses, for the new *burhs* were, it would seem, nearly always fortified royal *tuns*. Worcester was not, but it would be rash to claim for it the distinction of having the first purely burghal court.

It does not seem possible to accept the opinion of the editors of the *Place-names of Worcestershire* [2] that the area walled at Worcester was the comparatively small district of Sudbury at the south-eastern corner of the city. A refuge for the population of a wide area must have enclosed a much greater space and not only is this confirmed by the size of the holding in one corner of it which the bishop leased to Ethelred and his wife in 904,[3] but the mention of the north

---

[1] *C.S.* 138, i. 203 (a. 716-7).   [2] P. 22.   [3] Above, p. 20.

wall and the Severn in its bounds shows that their *burh* lay in the same position north of the cathedral church as the later borough and may have been co-extensive with it.

Fortification did not usually, if ever, lead to a change in the earlier name of the place. New *burhs* with names ending in -bury or -borough generally owed them to some more primitive defences. London is a partial exception. Until now it had, as we have seen, been very commonly called Lundenwic, but this seems to have been quite superseded in the last centuries of the Anglo-Saxon period by Lundenburh. This, however, proved no more permanent. The uncompounded form Lundene, London, derived from the Roman *Londinium*, continued in use alongside it and ultimately prevailed. It is more than likely that Lundene in virtue of its walls had sometimes been called Lundenburh in the preceding age. Bede's " urbs Lundoniae " points to that. The increased use of the compound name may perhaps be explained by the fact that *burh* was now in everybody's mouth rather than by any repairs of the walls that Alfred may have carried out when, in 880 or shortly after,[1] he recovered the town from the Danes and entrusted its custody to his son-in-law. Some years later, in 889, Alfred and Ethelred made that gift of a tenement at Hwaetmundes Stane in the city to Bishop Werfrith of Worcester which has been mentioned above [2] on account of the privilege conferred with it of buying and selling within the messuage for its necessities and taking the resultant tolls, which in the streets and quay would go to the king. This is interesting as showing that the London tolls were not granted to Ethelred with the custody of the city, but, as at Worcester, were retained by the crown. It was to Alfred too, if we may trust a somewhat dubious document, as part of the restoration of London after the Danish occupation, that the sees of Worcester and Canterbury owed their adjoining sokes of an acre each by Ethelredshithe, the later Queenhithe, with quays (*navium staciones*) of equal width outside the wall.[3] It seems likely that the much larger soke of Queenhithe, east of the Worcester soke, represents an earlier grant to Ethelred.[4]

London, like Worcester, must of course have been the seat of a court, but in this case we are pretty safe in identifying it with an actual later court, the *folksmote* and conjecturing

---

[1] See above, pp. 16-17.   [2] P. 10.   [3] *C.S.* 577, ii. 220.
[4] W. Page, *London ; its Origin and Early Development* (1923), p. 130.

that its jurisdiction was not then confined to the city, but extended over a district which at least comprised Middlesex.

If the scheme of the Burghal Hidage was the work of Alfred, the fortification of Worcester seems to occupy a somewhat isolated position between the purely defensive *burhs* of that system and those erected by Edward the Elder and his sister Ethelfled in the course of their long offensive against the Danes. Like the former it was undertaken for defence only, but it was not, so far as we know, part of any general scheme. The later series of fortifications were steps in a converging advance from London and south-west Mercia upon the fortresses of the central Danelaw, but the new *burhs* were not all on the direct lines of advance for on the east Essex had to be occupied to prevent outflanking from East Anglia and on the west a combination of the Welsh and the Dublin Northmen with the Danes must at all costs be averted.

In all twenty-five *burhs* were constructed by Edward and his sister, if we include Chester and Manchester where old Roman walls were repaired. There were, however, two each at Buckingham and Hertford, and those at Bedford and Nottingham were merely bridgeheads for the attack on these Danish *burhs*. Of the twenty-one which remain after the necessary deduction only eight [1] are found as municipal boroughs later in the Middle Ages, though Manchester and Bakewell attained a quasi-burghal status under mesne lords. This small proportion, which more than reverses that of the Burghal Hidage is easily understood, since a majority of these forts were on the borders of Wales, a region much less favourable than Wessex to urban growth. Four of them are shown by their names to have been adaptations of more primitive fortifications. Four or five were so obscure that they still remain unidentified. Some were probably only temporary.

These facts emphasize the conclusion we drew from the Burghal Hidage that the mere fortification of a spot, whether already settled or not, did not secure its future as a town. For that its site must present special advantages for trade or administration or both, and this Edward himself recognized in his law restricting trade to *ports*.[2] Of the eight *burhs* which were to show that they possessed these advantages, all but

[1] Chester, Bridgenorth, Tamworth, Stafford, Hertford, Warwick, Buckingham, and Maldon.
[2] Liebermann, *Ges.* i. 138.

Bridgenorth were selected as mint-places before the Norman Conquest, indeed, with the exception of Buckingham, by Edward's son, Athelstan. Of the *burhs* which did not win special jurisdiction or corporate privileges, Witham in Essex had a mint, but this was only in the reign of Harthacnut when mints were more indiscriminately distributed.[1]

None of the eight more important new *burhs* is called *port* in the Chronicle. This need not be significant, however, for *port* and *burh* were practically equivalent in the tenth century in the sense of " town," and in a region not yet free from the danger of Danish invasion the term which implied fortification might easily obtain predominance before it did elsewhere. Yet Northampton, one of the captured Danish *burhs*, is called *port* by the chronicler in 1010, and Worcester as late as 1087.[2]

Speaking generally, the chief Edwardian foundations had a less important future than the well-chosen centres which the Danes had fortified and made district capitals.

A study of the maps in the *Reports of the Commissioners on Municipal Boundaries and Wards* (1837), drawn before the modern growth of towns, usually detects a marked difference in lay out between the towns which first appear as Anglo-Saxon *burhs* and those which grew up later without the constriction of ramparts. Putting aside the old Roman sites, the greater compactness of such towns as Oxford, Worcester or Derby as compared with, say, Andover, Coventry or Chesterfield at once strikes the eye. It is generally held that many of the new *burhs*, both English and Danish, were modelled upon the Roman *civitates* or *castra*, and this may have been so to some extent, though the English settlers within Roman walls, Haverfield pointed out, do not seem to have taken over the old street plans and a quadrangular rampart or wall with a gate on each side is the simplest form of fortification to enclose a considerable inhabited area and therefore likely to suggest itself without imitation. Early settlements were often made at cross-roads and if walled would, as at Oxford, reproduce the Roman plan without deliberately copying it.

4. After Fortification

Nearly all the chief English towns of the Middle Ages are found either among the Roman *civitates* or *burhs* re-occupied and their walls repaired, sometimes very early, or the new

---

[1] *E.H.R.* xi. (1896), 761 ff.   [2] *A.S.C.*, ed. Plummer, pp. 141. 223.

burhs of the ninth and tenth centuries. " Borough " became a technical term which covered walled and unwalled towns alike. Must we therefore conclude with Maitland that fortification was the vital moment in the origin of the borough ? We may certainly agree that it gave an urgent and widespread impulse to urban aggregation, which would otherwise have been a slower process, even if peace and quiet had obtained, and that it provided shelter for the trader and artisan. In an age of constant warfare walls were everywhere a necessary condition of urban growth. But Maitland's conjectural picture of the typical tenth-century *burh* as first and foremost a fortress garrisoned by the landowners of its district, who kept houses and warrior " boroughmen " (*burgware*) in it for its defence and wall-repair, has failed to secure general assent.[1] It leaves out of account the early settled *civitas* like Canterbury and the general predominance of royal domain in the borough which is so evident in Domesday. It is essentially based upon a supposed foreign parallel of more than doubtful pertinence and the bold assumption that the burgesses who were paying rent to rural lords in 1066 represented armed retainers of the predecessors of these lords less than a century and a half before. It is not supported by the solitary contemporary piece of evidence on the incidence of wall-repair which has come down to us,[2] and two important charters show that within less than twenty years after Edward's death a haw in a neighbouring borough was regarded as a profitable appurtenance of a rural estate, not as an acquittal of a military obligation.[3]

[1] A short list of the chief contributions to the controversy over this garrison theory may be of use. I. In support : F. W. Maitland, *E.H.R.* xi. (1896), 16-17 ; *D.B. and B.* (1897), pp. 186 ff. ; *Township and Borough*, pp. 44 f., 210 f. ; A. Ballard, *The Domesday Boroughs* (1904), pp. 11-40 ; " The Walls of Malmesbury," *E.H.R.* xxi. (1906), 98 ff. ; " The Burgesses of Domesday," *ibid.*, pp. 699 ff. ; " Castle-Guard and Barons' Houses," *ibid.* xxv. (1910), 712 ff. ; H. M. Chadwick, *Studies on Anglo-Saxon Institutions* (1905), pp. 220 ff. ; R. R. Reid, *E.H.R.* xxxii. (1917), 489 *n*. II. Against : J. Tait, *E.H.R.* xii. (1897), 772 ff. ; M. Bateson, *ibid.* xx. (1905), 143 ff., 416 ; " The Burgesses of Domesday and the Malmesbury Wall," *ibid.* xxi. (1906), 709 ff. ; C. Petit-Dutaillis, *Studies Supplementary to Stubbs' Constitutional History* (1908), pp. 78 ff. ; J. H. Round, " ' Burhbot ' and ' Brigbot ' " in *Family Origins*, ed. W. Page (1930), pp. 252 ff. ; C. Stephenson, " The Anglo-Saxon Borough " in *E.H.R.* xlv. (1930), 183, 203 ; *Borough and Town*, pp. 17 f.
[2] See above, p. 20.
[3] In *C.S.* 757, ii. 483 (a. 940) a grant of ten hides in Wily, Wilts, to the thegn Ordwald, there is a note that a certain meadow, the haw in Wilton that belongs to Wily, the town-hedge *bot* at Grovely and every third tree in Monnespol wood were all appurtenant to Wily, to Ordwald's *tun*. *C.S.*

Maitland's over-emphasis of the military aspect of the borough—we may now conveniently use the later form of *burh*—involved an underestimate of its trading importance and a one-sided theory of the origin of the borough court. The enumeration of offences punishable at Worcester lends no support to his suggestion that the court was called into existence to repress the turbulence of a military population. It is likely indeed, as we shall see, that the purely urban court did not come until the military aspect had waned after the conquest of the Danelaw and that up to then the only courts meeting in boroughs had jurisdiction over wider areas.

Dr. Stephenson rejects the " garrison " theory, but his conception of the late Anglo-Saxon borough is equally one-sided in another direction. The normal borough, he holds, differed only from the country round in being a place of defence and therefore a natural centre of royal administration. Its trade was negligible, its social and economic system just as aristocratic and agricultural as elsewhere. Mint and market were there merely for the shelter of its walls. It is difficult, however, to reconcile this view with the legislation of Edward and Athelstan. When Edward in his first law, passed certainly before his conquests were complete and perhaps before they were begun, forbade all buying and selling outside fixed centres,[1] he did not call them *burhs* but *ports*, a term with none but trading implications and, as we have seen, already familiar in the pre-Danish period.[2] The chief town officer, who is normally to witness all such transactions, is not *burhgerefa*, but *portgerefa*, " portreeve," a title which was to have a long burghal history. Athelstan, again, ordered that (in Kent and Wessex) no man should mint money except in a *port*. Twelve of these ports are named in a further clause, with the number of moneyers authorized for each ; " for the other *burhs*, the list concludes, ' one each.' [3] The use of *burh* here as equivalent to *port* seems to imply that the former was losing its military significance and coming to mean little more than ' town,' although an ordinance just above requires that every *burh* should be repaired by a fortnight after the Rogation days."

From the list just mentioned and the British Museum

786, ii. 529, a. 943 (*cf.* 765, ii. 495), after granting seven hides at Tisted, Hants, to a thegn, adds the haws within the borough of Winchester which belong to these seven hides, with the same immunities as the land.

[1] Liebermann, *Ges.* i. 138, iii. 93.
[2] See above, p. 9.   [3] Liebermann, i. 158.

Catalogue of Coins [1] we learn that there were fourteen mints working in Kent and Wessex in Athelstan's reign, eight of which were new. The Catalogue supplies the names of thirteen in the Midlands, all of which were new, and the old Northern mint at York was now working for the English king. The total of twenty-eight mint-places bespeaks a considerable demand for coin, but most significant of active trade is the number of moneyers allowed to the chief *ports* by Athelstan's law, eight to London, six to Winchester, four to Canterbury (besides one each to the archbishop and the abbot of St. Augustine's), and even the two each allotted to Lewes, Southampton, and Wareham reveal a growing importance. It is clear that, thanks to the victories of Alfred and his successors, things were settling down and that, in the South more especially, trade was reviving. The crown had strong inducements to foster this revival of trade and to restrict it to the walled towns for it derived an increasing revenue from tolls, profits of justice and moneyers' fees, while the restriction simplified collection and by the greater publicity of transactions made it easier to prevent fraud.

The attempt to confine all buying and selling to boroughs was not, however, successful. Athelstan found himself obliged first to except purchases under 20*d*.[2] and later to withdraw the whole requirement.[3] And so in Edgar's law fixing the number of witnesses of sales,[4] the same number was assigned to rural hundreds, to undertake this supervision, as to small boroughs. Nevertheless, the advantages of the boroughs for trading were too great to leave any considerable volume of it to other centres.

Fortified towns, rare before the Danish invasions, were now numerous and widely dispersed. Even if their walls were often only of earth, like those still to be seen at Wareham, they clearly marked off these boroughs or ports from the rural " tuns " of the country side.[5] Centres of administration,

---

[1] Conveniently summarized for this late Anglo-Saxon period by York Powell in *E.H.R.* xi. (1896), 759 ff.

[2] II Athelst. 12, Liebermann, *Ges.* i. 156. The witness of the reeves in the folkmoot was accepted as an alternative to that of the portreeve or other unlying man of Edward's law. The folkmoot was no doubt the district court, soon to be reorganized as the hundred court (see below, p. 36), which, there is reason to believe, usually met in a *burh* (see below, *ibid*).

[3] IV Athelst. 2, Liebermann, *Ges.* i. 171 ; VI. 10, *ibid.*, p. 182. It was now lawful to buy and sell out of port, provided it was done with full and credible witness.   [4] IV Edg. 5, Liebermann, *Ges.* i. 210.

[5] I Edw. I, 1, Liebermann, *Ges.* i. 138 ; IV Edg. 6, *Ges.* i. 210 ; II Cnut, 24, *Ges.* i. 326.

many of them had long been, but fresh centres were needed in the re-united and re-organized kingdom and as market towns and mint places, exclusively at first and predominantly always, they concentrated the new growth of trade after the storms of the invasions. Obscurely, but steadily, we may believe, a class of burgess traders was growing up within and about their walls. Materially most of the medieval English boroughs had come into existence and the difference of these urban units from ordinary agricultural communities was clearly recognized in nomenclature. Dorchester, in Dorset, for instance, which is merely a " king's tun " in the Chronicle's account of the first Danish landing in the South,[1] is a port and borough in Athelstan's mint law. How far did this comparatively new type of local community receive special treatment in form of government and legal status? We must put out of our minds at once of course any idea of a self-governing community electing its own head, the portreeve. That position was only gained, and not by all the tenth-century boroughs, after a long process of development which was not completed until the thirteenth century and only faintly shadowed forth by the end of the Anglo-Saxon period. The government of the borough remained essentially the same as that of any royal estate under a reeve (*gerefa*) of the king's appointment, with such check as was involved in customary consultation with the elders of the community. The chief difference was that in the freer air of the borough this check was more serious and in the long run became control. A really municipal constitution was still remote in 1066, nor did the Norman Conquest bring any immediate change. Indirectly, however, the way was already paved for it when in the second half of the tenth-century judicial reorganization created a primitive form of the medieval borough court, not of course as a concession to the burgesses, though it was destined to be of great use to them in their long struggle for autonomy, but merely in recognition of the needs of a populous area and of royal interests. Unfortunately, the origin of this court, the germ of the *burewaremot* and the *portmanimot* of the twelfth century, has become subject of controversy, owing chiefly to the ambiguity of the Laws in their references to courts held in boroughs. The question is complicated and demands a new chapter.

[1] *A.S.C.* s.a. 787. The identification with Dorchester is Ethelwerd's.

D

II

BOROUGH AND COURT

1. The Pre–Domesday Evidence

The main features of the tenth century vill, or portion of one, that was also a borough, which distinguished it from the ordinary agricultural vill, can be but brokenly discerned in the glimpses afforded by the Laws, the charters and the Chronicle. For fuller information we have to wait until Domesday Book affords material for retrospect. Meanwhile, it is possible to make some definite statements from contemporary evidence.

The borough was a place of defence against the Danish enemy, or *vice versa*, fortified or refortified by the public authority and often a natural centre for local administration whether of the shire or of some small area. It was also a place of trade, a " port," yielding a growing revenue in tolls which would have been even more important had the son and grandson of Alfred succeeded in their effort to confine all trading to the " ports." They did restrict the royal minters to these urban centres, though later kings seem to have authorized exceptions to this rule. If the public status of these centres were not sufficiently obvious, it might be safely inferred from the sharing of their revenue between king and earl which is recorded at Worcester at the first foundation of its borough, though not elsewhere until Domesday comes to our aid. The earl had no such pecuniary interest in the ancient demesne of the kingdom held by the king, being probably already provided for by the special comital estates of which we only hear later, albeit the arrangement sounds more primitive than the earl's burghal share.

The borough-port further differed from the royal vill " upland " [1] in the division of tenure which it commonly

---

[1] *Cf.* sy hit binnan byrig, sy hit up on lande (II Cnut, 24). Two and a half centuries later the same distinction is implied in the " viles de uppelaunde " of the Statute of Winchester (Stubbs, *Select Charters*, ed. Davis, p. 466).

exhibited. The king kept much of its soil in demesne, but a more or less considerable part was granted to religious houses and local magnates. That both the king and the private landholders settled " burgesses " on their holdings is a natural presumption, though the positive evidence for it first appears in Domesday Book. No one now, with Maitland and Ballard, traces this " tenurial heterogeneity " to a territorialization of the duty of the shire or other district to garrison and repair the walls of the borough. Other reasons, such as the need of a *hospicium* or lodging for visits of business to the local centre or of a refuge in time of war, as well as the financial attraction of urban house property, sufficiently account for this tenurial connexion between town and country. Surviving charters to churches and thegns show the growth of this connexion in Kentish boroughs long before the Danish invasions.

With rare exceptions, mostly old Roman towns, the fortified area, in the nature of the case, was of small extent ; houses and population were much more closely crowded together than in the countryside, and this of necessity involved some differentiation from the rural vill. Of the inner life and growth of the boroughs we know little until the eve of the Norman Conquest. In the later struggle with the Danes, the burgesses of London at least proved themselves still an effective military force. By that time they had an active trade with the Continent. Municipal growth or even aspirations we should scarcely expect to find among the slow-moving Anglo-Saxons, especially as the impulse given to it abroad by feudal tyranny was entirely absent in England. The boroughs were still primarily domanial, governed by reeves of the king's appointment, though already even in the smaller boroughs of Devon we hear of a body of *witan* [1] with whom no doubt the reeve consulted. It is safe to say that the burgesses did not yet dream even of securing direct communal responsibility to the crown for the collection of its revenue, still less of license to elect their own officers, not that there is any doubt that at least the more important Anglo-Saxon boroughs from the tenth century onwards possessed the organ in which the first strivings towards municipal autonomy were before long to make themselves felt and which moulded the body (*communitas*) that was, nominally at any rate, sovereign in the self-governing medieval town. It does not follow that this early borough court exhibited such marked differences from

[1] *Crawford Charters,* ed. Napier and Stevenson (1895), p. 9.

other local courts as did the boroughmoots or portmoots or
hustings of a later age.   It is not easy, indeed, so scanty and
perplexed is the evidence, to get a clear idea of this court.
On the strength of Edgar's ordinance that the *burhgemot*
should be held three times a year [1] it was thought until comparatively recently that such a court was a feature of all
boroughs, which was more than could be said of the late
medieval towns.   On the other hand, the very infrequency of
these meetings led Ballard to assert that the normal borough
court was not independent, did not exclude the jurisdiction
of the neighbouring hundred court with its monthly sessions.[2]
A vigorous criticism from Miss Bateson [3] induced him to
withdraw this hasty pronouncement.[4]   From an ambiguous
premise he had drawn a conclusion impossibly wide, though,
as will presently be seen, not without an element of truth.[5]
Unfortunately, Liebermann had accepted it,[6] and never saw
the retraction or realized that Ballard's view was inconsistent
with his own general theory of the borough court.   Almost
simultaneously, Professor Chadwick put forth a very different
theory, namely that the later borough courts were the dwindled
relics of courts which from the reign of Edward to that of
Edgar served for more or less wide districts centred in the
new *burhs*.[7]   The hypothesis is more applicable to the Midlands
than to the South for which it was constructed, but discussion
of it must be deferred for the moment.

Professor Chadwick's theory is an aberration from the
general line of inquiry, which has aimed at fixing the place
of the borough and its court in that new hundred organization
which was carried out in the South in the first half of the tenth
century and in the Midlands and East, somewhat later in
the century.   Maitland's cautious statement that the borough
court was probably, " at least as a general rule," co-ordinate
with a hundred court,[8] has met with almost universal agreement.   This leaves open the question whether a new type of
court was created for the borough or whether it merely received separate hundredal jurisdiction.   Maitland himself
appears to have had no doubt that the second alternative was

[1] III Edg. 5, 1 ; Liebermann, *Ges*. i. 202.
[2] *The Domesday Borough* (1904), pp. 53 f., 102 f., 120 ff. and Preface.
[3] *E.H.R.* xx. (1905), 146 ff.
[4] *The English Borough in the Twelfth Century* (1914), p. 34.
[5] See below, p. 54.   [6] *Ges*. ii. 451, 12 g.
[7] *Anglo-Saxon Institutions*, pp. 219 ff., especially pp. 222-3.
[8] *D.B. and B.*, p. 209.

the right one. " At starting," he says, " the borough seems
to be regarded as a vill which is also a hundred." He notes
that the later borough court was sometimes called a "hundred,"
and suggests that, at least in the earliest time, it had jurisdiction over an area considerably larger than the walled space.
" In this case the urban would hardly differ from the rural
hundred. A somewhat new kind of ' hundred ' might be
formed without the introduction of any new idea." [1] Boroughs
with such territory, even comprising several rural vills, are,
of course, not uncommon, but they belong chiefly to the
region north of the Thames. Maitland's generalization will
hardly cover the case of such southern boroughs as Bath and
Dorchester which were originally *capita* of ordinary hundreds,
but appear later in possession of hundred courts of their own
and of little or no extra-mural territory.

Miss Bateson, overlooking or silently rejecting this suggestion of Maitland, took the " vill that was a hundred " quite
strictly and saw a " legal thought " behind it.[2] She was com-
bating Ballard's argument that if a vill by exception was
also a hundred, that was a mere accident and the court was
an ordinary hundred court. The legal thought was the
deliberate co-ordination of the typical borough and its court
with the hundred and its court. In her view, too, the borough
court was already differentiated from that of the rural hundred
for she identified the three annual meetings of Edgar's *burhgemot*
with the " great courts " of the fully-fledged borough.[3] Dr.
Stephenson, however, sees no evidence of such differentiation
before the Norman Conquest.[4] He brushes aside the *burhgemot* in question as the court of a district meeting in a borough,
and agrees with Ballard that the court of the borough which
was a hundred in itself was just an ordinary hundred court.
He differs from him only in holding that such burghal hundreds,
though not universal, were common and not merely isolated
cases, and in finding confirmation of his view in what he
believes himself to have shown to be the purely agricultural
and non-urban economy of the Anglo-Saxon borough. There
is no " legal thought " behind the vill-hundred, for non-
burghal hundreds were often quite small and even the single
vill hundred was not unknown.

A review of the whole of the evidence, upon which these

[1] *D.B. and B.*, p. 209, *n.* 6. [2] *E.H.R.* xx. (1905), 147.
[3] *Ibid. ; Borough Customs*, i. (1904), pp. xii f. ; ii. (1906), cxlv ff.
[4] *E.H.R.* xlv. (1930), 196 ff.

divergent conclusions have been based, seems to be needed.
Unluckily, the study of the problem has been somewhat let
and hindered by the variety of meanings which words took
on in the course of the rapid development of an early society.
Perhaps the most striking illustration of this feature is afforded
by the A.-S. *tun*, our " town." Originally, as we have seen,
applied to a single homestead, it came, without wholly losing
this meaning, to be used for an aggregation of homesteads, a
village, to use a post-Conquest word, especially as a local
unit of administration, for which Maitland devised the convenient term " vill " from its Latin equivalent *villa*, and it
ended in being restricted, save in remote corners of the land,
to the most highly specialised of such aggregations.

The interpretation of the word *burh* in the Laws of the
Anglo-Saxon kings, which, next to Domesday Book, are our
main source of information on the pre-Conquest borough,
is hampered by the fact that, since its original meaning was
simply " fortification," it could be applied to the fortified
houses of the king, as indeed of all above the rank of common
freeman, as well as to fortified towns. Counsel is still further
darkened when a *burh* appears as seemingly the seat of a court,
the area of whose jurisdiction is left vague, but cannot with
any probability be identified with that of a borough. It
is hardly surprising that a Norman translator of the Laws
into Latin, within half a century of the Conquest, came to
the conclusion that *burh* in these difficult passages must have
the derived sense of " court " and turned it by *curia*.[1] Modern
students of the Laws have found themselves equally em-
barrassed. Liebermann, who published his great work,
Die Gesetze der Angelsachsen, in sections between 1898 and
1916, changed his view more than once. At first he felt no
difficulty in translating *burh* in such contexts by " town "
(*Stadt, Gerichtsstadt*), but in his glossary (1912) substituted
" king's fortified house " (in one instance) or " court " (*Gericht*),
and in his final commentary (1916) suggested as a general
equivalent " meeting place of a court " (*Gerichtsstätte*).[2]

---

[1] *Quadripartitus* in Liebermann, *Ges.* i. 161, translates "the to thære
byrig hiron " "qui ad eam curiam obediunt," and again, *op. cit.* i. 389.
Also in a passage of later date, *ibid.* i. 324. See below, pp. 37, 41 *n*.

[2] Curiously he retained *Gericht* in one passage, but, apparently feeling
it inappropriate in its ordinary sense, explained it as *Amtsprengel*, " district " (*Ges.* i. 146, iii. 97). In this passage (I Athelst. 1), where the king's
reeves in every *burh* are ordered to render tithes from his goods, it seems
more natural to take *burh* as a fortified house which was a centre of
royal domain. It is used even later for the king's house as a sanctuary
(II Edm. 2), where Liebermann translates it " festes haus " (*Ges.* iii. 127).

This does not seem to be an improvement upon his second thoughts in the most important of these troublesome passages.

When King Athelstan ordains that the seniors (*yldestan men*) belonging to a *burh* shall go out (*ridan*) and put under surety the man who has neglected repeated summons to the *gemot* or confiscate the property of the persistent thief,[1] and when the same seniors, acting as doomsmen, decide whether one found guilty of arson or of secretly compassing murder shall live or die,[2] the court is clearly not purely urban. Maitland suggested that it was a shire court meeting in a borough,[3] but there is no evidence of shire courts before the reign of Edgar and as *ridan* had then the general sense of " to go," the fact that " there was riding to be done " does not presume a very wide area.[4] Professor Chadwick agrees with Maitland in taking the meeting-place of the court to be a borough in the ordinary sense, but sees in the passage confirmation of his theory that the Burghal Hidage represents a re-division of the southern shires into administrative and judicial districts round the new *burhs* fortified against the Danes.[5] But the Burghal Hidage, whether it is to be assigned to the reign of Alfred or that of his son is, as we have seen, a plan of defence not a settlement of local areas.[6] The wide variations in the hidages and the position of the boroughs, in Dorset, for instance, on northern border and sea coast only, make it hard to believe that the scheme could have served as the basis of local government. The mention in the Chronicle [7] under 918 (915) of the seniors of Bedford and Northampton may seem to support Professor Chadwick's view, but they do not appear in any judicial capacity and the large districts appendant to such boroughs in the still unshired Midlands stand in strong contrast to the majority of those included in the Burghal Hidage.

However this may be, it can be shown, I think, that the *gemot* of Athelstan's law, though a district court, was no innovation of Edward's reign, as Professor Chadwick supposes, but belonged to a much older scheme of jurisdictional areas. In Edgar's revision of his grandfather's law [8] the *gemot* is

---

[1] II Athelst. 20, 1.

[2] Liebermann, *Ges*. i. 388. The law is anonymous but the editor agrees that Thorpe was probably justified in attributing it to Athelstan (*ibid*. iii. 228).

[3] *D.B. and B.*, p. 185.

[4] Liebermann, *Ges*. iii. 105.

[5] *A.S.I.*, pp. 219 ff.

[6] See above, p. 18.

[7] Ed. Plummer, i. 100.

[8] III Edg. 7 ; Liebermann, i. 204.

the hundred court, which he had recently organized or re-organized, the " riding " is now done by men chosen from the hundred instead of the seniors of the *burh*, and the hundred shares with the offender's landlord (*l.-hlaford*) the confiscated goods which at the earlier date had been divided between the king and the seniors themselves. Now there is strong reason for believing that the hundred court was a remodelling of the ancient folkmoot which seems to have been the only regular local court in the ninth century,[1] and can be safely identified with the court mentioned in the second law of Edward.[2] Both this court and the hundred court met every four weeks, the same class of cases came before them and the name folkmoot still clung to its successor. The natural conclusion is that the *gemot* of Athelstan's law, which also met frequently and did business which was later done by the hundred court, was, essentially at any rate, the old monthly folkmoot. If so, we learn from this law that the meeting-place of the folkmoot was a *burh*, and as the nature of its busi-ness limited the area of its jurisdiction, and there must have been far more folkmoots than boroughs, *burh* here must have its old wider sense of " king's fortified house," which might or might not have become by this date the nucleus of a village or of a fortified town. This was the interpretation of the facts before us which approved itself to Liebermann in 1912,[3] and though four years later he chose, strangely enough,[4] to translate *burh* by the colourless *Gerichtsstätte*, he still held fast to the identification of the *gemot* in question with the ancient folkmoot.

The supposed temporary re-division of the shires of the South, in the first half of the tenth century, into burghal districts, each with its court in one of the new boroughs, re-mains an unproven hypothesis, which has gained more colour of probability than it deserves from the actual existence of such districts in the unshired Danelaw. The borough " thing " in each of the Five Boroughs at the end of the century, breach of whose peace involved a penalty six times as high as that of the wapentake peace, was clearly no mere urban court.[5]

---

[1] Liebermann, *Ges.* ii. 451, § 13 *et seq.*   [2] *c.* 8 ; *ibid.* i. 144.
[3] *Ibid.* ii. 450, § 4 g.
[4] Since *burh* could only have got this general sense because the folk-moots met at such centres and he had no evidence that they had ceased to do so.
[5] III Ethelr. 1, 2 ; Liebermann, *Ges.* i. 228. *Cf. ibid.* ii. 451, § 12 e, where Liebermann does not seem to realize that the court was a district tribunal.

Professor Chadwick's theory and that which I have preferred to it above have alike to face the re-appearance of the
ambiguous *burh* in a judicial context as late as the laws of
Cnut, when the burgal district court, according to its advocate,
had long ceased to exist and the old folkmoot, remodelled
as a hundred, had its meeting-place quite exceptionally in any
sort of *burh*. The passage in Cnut's laws [1] regulates the oath
which an accused man must take with compurgators to clear
himself from the charge. If of hitherto unblemished reputation, he was allowed to choose his own compurgators in
minimum number (simple oath) within his own hundred.
A man with a bad record had to clear himself by a simple
oath with compurgators chosen for him from three hundreds
or, if strongly accused, by a three-fold oath similarly chosen
" as widely as belongs to the *burh*." Liebermann's ultimate
explanation of *burh* here is that it is used in the general sense
of " meeting-place of a court," and the court is the hundred
already mentioned.[2] This is not only awkward in itself,
but it breaks the widening range of choice for compurgators in
merciful proportion to the badness of the offender's local reputation. If the concession were made in one case, why not in
the other ? The passage is obscure, but it seems possible that
the reference is after all to a borough and that the explanation
lies in some such centralization of the more elaborate part of
judicial procedure as we find in certain quarters after the
Conquest. Failure in making the oath involved resort to the
ordeal, and this required a church, a priest, if not a bishop,
apparatus for the hot iron and hot water tests and a deep
pit (*fossa*) for that of cold water.[3] The hundred centres were
often uninhabited spots convenient as meeting-places, but
not for such procedure as this. There is perhaps actual record
of this centralization in Ethelred's ordinance that all vouching
to warranty and every ordeal in the district of the Five
Boroughs should take place in " the king's borough " (*byrig*),[4]
and in Cnut's general law that there should be the same system
of purgation in all boroughs,[5] though Liebermann preferred

---

[1] II Cnut, 22 ; Liebermann, *Ges.* i. 324.   [2] *Ibid.* iii. 205.
[3] A thirteenth-century custumal of the manor of Wye in Kent, the
caput of the possessions of Battle Abbey in that county, records that
seven hundreds had no *fosse* of their own and their men had to go to Wye
for the ordeal (*Custumals of Battle Abbey* (Camden Soc., 1887), p. 126).
The abbey took two-thirds of the *perquisita* accruing, the remaining third
going to the king.
[4] III Ethelr. 6, 1 ; Liebermann, *Ges.* i. 230.
[5] II Cnut, 34 ; *op. cit.* i. 336.

a different interpretation of these texts. There is no ambiguity, at any rate, in the testimony of Domesday Book, that all who dwelt in a wide district round Taunton had to go to that borough to take oaths or undergo the ordeal.[1] It may be objected that Taunton was a mediatized borough and that its episcopal lord, the bishop of Winchester, was responsible for the centralization, but it is recorded in close association with the regal privileges which had been conferred with this great estate.

So far, rejecting Liebermann's counsel of despair, we have caught fleeting glimpses of courts in "boroughs," new and old, but a borough court in the urban sense has not come in sight. Until a comparatively recent date, no one doubted that the *burhgemot* which Edgar ordered to be held three times a year was such a court.[2] Its three annual meetings were linked up with the three "great courts" of the London folkmoot and of a number of other town courts after the Conquest, and parallels were found in the three *echte dinge* of some early urban courts on the Continent.[3] But this, too, is now claimed by Professor Chadwick and his followers, including Dr. Stephenson, as a district court with a borough as its centre, though they are not in accord as to its precise nature. Professor Chadwick, adopting Maitland's "garrison" theory, suggested that "it was a meeting of the landowners who possessed *hagan* in the borough and had to provide for its defence."[4] Dr. Stephenson[5] discards that unlucky hypothesis, but follows Professor Chadwick in inferring from the close association of the *burhgemot* with the *scirgemot* in Edgar's ordinance that the boroughmoot was simply the equivalent of the southern shiremoot in the (as they suppose) still unshired Midlands. This is an ingenious suggestion and may be thought to gain support from the closely connected clause that follows,[6] which may be read as prescribing the presence in the one as in the other of the shire bishop (*ðaere scire biscop*) and the ealdorman, to declare respectively ecclesiastical and secular law. On the internal evidence alone, however, several objections may be taken to so construing these clauses. The abrupt introduction of two sets of courts which differ only

---

[1] *D.B.* i. 87b, 1.   [2] III Edg. 5, 1 ; Liebermann, *Ges.* i. 202.
[3] See *e.g.* Miss Bateson in *E.H.R.* xv. 503 ; xx. 146. "The whole question," she says, "is of great importance in tracing out the origin of the borough court."
[4] *A.S.I.* p. 220.   [5] *E.H.R.* xlv (1930), 200-1.   [6] III Edg. 5, 2.

in name, locality and frequency of meeting, is unusually awkward even for the Anglo-Saxon Laws. The division of the clauses, again, is not original and read continuously, as they were intended to be, the second may quite well refer only to the last mentioned court, the shiremoot. Indeed, the description of the bishop as " the shire bishop " would not be applicable to a region which still remained unshired. Lastly, if *burhgemot* and *scirgemot* were the same court under different names, why should the one have met oftener than the other ? The external evidence against the suggestion under consideration is still stronger, for Cnut re-enacted Edgar's ordinance [1] long after the Midlands had been divided into shires,[2] and this cannot be explained away as the inclusion of an obsolete law in a general code, since Cnut himself introduced an amendment which allowed the two courts to be held oftener if necessary. That the *burhgemot* in Cnut's time was no equivalent of a shire court appears clearly in the clause [3] which provides for appeal for defect of justice in the hundred court to the shiremoot, but not to the boroughmoot.

The theory that Edgar's *burhgemot* was a Midland district-court may therefore be put aside, but the new court (if new it was) still presents a difficult problem. Cnut's amendment itself adds a fresh complication, for if the court was urban and the three meetings "great courts," *echte dinge*, which imply intermediate petty or ordinary meetings, why was special authorization needed for these ? Unfortunately, too, there is no further record of a *burhgemot* in the Laws or other Anglo-Saxon sources, and indeed the name is not found again until the twelfth century. Continuity cannot be assumed without strong corroborative evidence, and this is, to say the least, not abundant. The complete absence of the unambiguous *portmanimot* in Anglo-Saxon records and literature deprives us of what would have been an invaluable link. Add to all this the undoubted fact that the courts of many of our medieval boroughs, including several of the more important, developed

---

[1] II Cnut, 18 (1028-34) ; Liebermann, *Ges*. i. 320.

[2] With one exception indeed the Midland shires are not mentioned in the Chronicle before 1011, but they owed that mention to renewed Danish attacks and there is nothing to show that they were of quite recent origin. Cheshire appears as early as 980. The region of the Five Boroughs was still unshired about 997 (Liebermann, *Ges*. iii. 156), but Lincolnshire and Nottinghamshire appear in the Chronicle under 1016. In any case these Danish boroughs were not taken into account in Edgar's ordinance which was enacted for his English subjects only (*op. cit*. iii. 134, § 11, 139, § 11).   [3] II Cnut, 19 ; *op. cit*. i. 321-2.

from hundred courts and not from any originally purely urban tribunal and the difficulties which beset the attempt to estab-lish the urban character of the tenth century *burhgemot* and to connect it up with the post-conquest borough courts may be properly appreciated.

It is easier to find evidence of the existence of borough law and of borough courts in the first half of the eleventh century than to identify these courts with Edgar's *burhgemot*. The contemporary author of a tract on the duties of bishops,[1] writing apparently at Worcester, may have exaggerated their powers partly from ecclesiastical bias and partly from local usage, for the bishop of Worcester, as we have seen,[2] had lord-ship in his see town, but he cannot have invented the dis-tinction (c. 6) between borough law (*burhriht*) and rural or, shall we say, common law (*landriht*),[3] both of which, he says, should be administered by the bishop's advice (*raede*) and witness, not necessarily, we may presume, in the same court. There is no need to suppose that the further duty ascribed to the bishop of seeing that every borough measure (*burhgemet*) and every weight was correctly made could be exercised in-dependently of a court, for it so happens that the first mention of an Anglo-Saxon court which was beyond dispute purely urban introduces it not in its judicial capacity but as the authority for a borough weight.

Towards the close of the tenth century, between 968 and 985, Ramsey Abbey received a gift of two silver cups of twelve marks *ad pondus hustingiae Londoniensis*.[4] A court of some standing is implied, but its name, which shows strong Scan-dinavian influence, forbids the assumption of any long previous existence. Can it be identified with the *burhgemot* of Edgar's law, which was enacted between 959 and *c.* 962, according to Liebermann? Unluckily our next information about the husting is of post-Conquest date, but if we can venture, with

---

[1] *Episcopus ;* Liebermann, *Ges.* i. 477, iii. 270-1. The editor dates it *c.* 1000–1050. [2] Above, p. 20.

[3] This distinction was apparently long preserved at Cambridge in the name of Landgrytheslane (now Pembroke Street) which ran just outside the town ditch. Maitland inferred that it marked the boundary between the ordinary land-peace and the stricter *burhgrið* within the ditch (*Township and Borough*, p. 101 ; *cf.* p. 74). That the king's *grith* or special peace was enforced in boroughs as in his court or on highways by the heavy fine of £5 we know from IV Ethelred, 4, 1 (Liebermann *Ges.* i. 234), though *burhbrece* is probably a misreading for *borhbrece* (*ibid.* iii. 165).

[4] *Chron. Abb. Rameseiensis* (Rolls Series), p. 58. For a later reference—in 1032—to the *hustinges gewiht* see Napier and Stevenson, *Crawford Charters*, p. 78.

all reserves, to argue back from that to the tenth century, such identification is difficult. The later husting was a weekly court without trace of three or any smaller number of " great courts." Three special courts yearly were, however, a feature of the larger open-air folkmoot of post-Conquest London and, so far as that goes, there is a stronger case for seeing in it an instance of Edgar's *burhgemot*. But if it were, it might have been re-organized by him, but could hardly have been a new creation, since the evidence of its pre-existence implied in the very title of the husting, and confirmed by the primitive constitution of the folkmoot, indicates a court that went back beyond the reign of Edgar. It has been suggested above [1] that the folkmoot may have been a curtailed relic of the district court with its centre in London which seems to be implied in the so-called *Judicia civitatis Lundonie* of Athelstan's time,[2] but this is to venture still further into the wide and dangerous field of conjecture.

More difficult to interpret than the London evidence is that contained in the invaluable record of the land suits and purchases of Ely Abbey under Ethelred II preserved in the twelfth century, *Liber Eliensis*. The abbey had been deprived of an estate at " Staneie," apparently in the isle of Ely, by relatives of the donor, " without judgment and without the law of citizens and hundredmen " (*civium et hundretanorum*). Alderman Æthelwine frequently summoned the offenders to sessions (*placita*) of the said citizens and hundredmen, but they always refused to appear. Nevertheless the abbot continued to bring up his case at " pleas " both within the borough (*urbem*) and without, and to complain to the people (*populo*) of the injury to his house. At last Æthelwine held a *grande placitum* at Cambridge of the citizens and hundredmen before twenty-four judges who gave judgment in favour of the abbot.[3] These " pleas " were clearly not sessions of a borough court in the later sense, they look more like meetings of a county court,[4] though the clumsy title does not favour this supposition, but the prominence given to the *cives* deserves attention.

[1] P. 14.
[2] VI Athelst. ; Liebermann, *Ges.* i. 173. It is not necessary, however, with Liebermann, following *Quadripartitus*, to translate the *byrig* in the Lundenbyrig of the Prologue by " judicial-political centre " (*ibid.* iii. 116). For Lundenburh as a regular name for the city in this age, see above, p. 23.
[3] *Liber Eliensis*, i. (Anglia Christiana Soc.), p. 137.
[4] Or district court with the borough of Cambridge as centre. But the references elsewhere to the *comitatus* of Cambridge and to the *comitatus* and *vicecomitatus* of Huntingdon (p. 139) may not be wholly anachronisms.

We hear also of the purchase money of estates being paid at Cambridge before the whole city (*coram tota civitate, coram coetu civium*), and on one of these occasions when the abbot asked for sureties (*vades*) from the seller, all cried out that Cambridge and Ipswich and Norwich and Thetford enjoyed such freedom (*libertas*) and dignity that anyone buying land there needed no sureties.[1] Was this *coetus civium* a mere casual assemblage or a regular meeting of their body, largely perhaps for administrative purposes, but conceivably also for the administration of justice among themselves? If Cambridge was a hundred in itself, as it was sixty years later, we may have here an urbanized hundred court.[2]

If the burgesses of Cambridge witnessed sales of land which lay remote from their walls, the *witan* of the four Devon boroughs, Exeter, Totnes, Lydford, and Barnstaple were officially informed (1018) by Bishop Eadnoth, of a life-grant of a piece of land near Crediton which he had made in return for a loan.[3] The likeness between these *burhwitan* and the *optimates* who bore rule in the twelfth century borough court is unmistakable. *Witan* was certainly used sometimes in the sense of " judges."[4] Liebermann was inclined to think that the duty imposed on *buruhwaru* in the truce with Olaf, thirty years earlier, implies a local court in each borough.[5]

What answer does our survey of the pre-Domesday evidence enable us to give to the question with which we started, whether the distinctive features which marked off the typical borough from the ordinary vill already included, as after the Norman Conquest, a separate court of justice? If we put aside the *burhgemot* of Edgar's law on the ground that its nature is still in dispute, the only direct mention of such a court is that of the London husting,[6] but the distinction between borough law and country law attested by the tract *Episcopus*[7] and supported by a post-Conquest survival suggests a distinction of courts, and some more indirect evidence seems to point in the same direction. To this last there ought perhaps to be added Edgar's ordinance for the creation of panels of witnesses (of sales) in all boroughs as well as in

[1] *Liber Eliensis*, i., p. 140.
[2] Doubts have occasionally been suggested as to the trustworthiness of the *Liber Eliensis* for this period, but there can be no real question that it is based on genuine contemporary materials.
[3] Napier and Stevenson, *Crawford Charters*, pp. 9, 77.
[4] Liebermann, *Ges.* ii. 245, *s.v.* Wita, 5 ; 565, 6a.
[5] II Ethelr. 6 ; *op. cit.* i. 222-4, ii. 451, § 12 f.
[6] See above, p. 40. [7] Above, p. 40.

every hundred.[1] It seems likely that in the one case as in the other the panel would be an emanation of a local court. A distinctive *burhriht*, again, must in the nature of things have dealt largely with cases arising between traders, often of a technical kind which could only be fairly tried by an urban body.

2. THE DOMESDAY EVIDENCE

The evidence derivable from Domesday Book is still scanty, which is not surprising in a financial record, and in part not altogether clear. Most of it comes from the North and the North Midlands. The *lagemen*, "lawmen," of Lincoln, Stamford, and York, who were or had been twelve in number in the first two towns and in all probability the same at York, where their name is Latinized *judices*, had by 1086 lost or were losing their collegiate function of judgment-finders, if that was their function,[2] at any rate in the Lincolnshire boroughs, for *lagemen* are there defined as " holders of sake and soke." They were thus comparable, as Professor Stenton has pointed out,[3] with the owners of " sokes " within the city of London. The office was normally hereditary and there were still twelve lawmen at Stamford, as late as 1275.[4] For a longer or shorter time the lawmen, being leading citizens, may still have played an important part in their respective borough courts, but as individuals not as an official body.

Of the lawmen of Cambridge we only learn that their heriot was that of the thegn class,[5] but the fact is important because it raises a doubt whether Liebermann was right in concluding from the Domesday details as to the soke of the Stamford lawmen that their wergeld was only that of the ordinary freeman.[6]

[1] IV Edg. 3, 1-6. The larger boroughs were to appoint thirty-six, small boroughs and hundreds normally twelve. If a court is rightly inferred, this may seem to imply a minor borough court not sensibly different from that of the hundred, but it equally suggests a wider difference in the court of the major borough.

[2] Vinogradoff suggested that they may have been official exponents of the law, as the lawmen of Scandinavia were (*Engl. Society in the Eleventh Century*, pp. 5-6) and is followed by Mr. Lapsley (*E.H.R.* xlvii. 557). But *cf.* Liebermann, *Ges.* ii. 565.

[3] *Lincolnshire Domesday* (Lincs. Rec. Soc. 19), p. xxix.

[4] *Rot. Hund.* i. 354. Alexander Bugge mistakenly concluded that the lawmen became the governing bodies of their towns (*Vierteljahrschrift für Social- und Wirtschaftsgeschichte*, iv. 2 (1906), 257).

[5] *D.B.* i. 189.

[6] *Ibid.* i. 336b, 2 ; Liebermann, *loc. cit.* and ii. 732, § 6a. See below, p. 80.

The twelve *judices* of the city of Chester may very well,
like those of York, have been known in the vernacular as
lawmen, for Chester and Cheshire, though in English Mercia,
came very strongly under Scandinavian influence and the
number of these judges is therefore possibly significant.
Domesday Book gives less space to them than to the lawmen
of Lincoln and Stamford, but that little is fortunately more
to our purpose. In the time of King Edward they were
drawn from the men of the king, the bishop and the earl, and
if any of them absented himself from the Hundred court
(*hundret*) on the day of its session, without sufficient excuse, he
paid as penalty 10s. to the king and the earl.[1] From this it
would seem clear that, even if these Chester judges bore the
same name, they had not the same status as the lawmen of
the Danelaw boroughs. The mention that the city court was
called the Hundred will be seen to be of vital importance
when we come to discuss the nature and origin of the Anglo-
Saxon borough court.

The brief glimpse of the Chester court in 1066, given by
Domesday Book, owes its special value to the great rarity of
such information for the pre-Conquest period, but otherwise
the chief interest of the Domesday description of the city lies
in its exceptionally long list of offences and their penalties.
The question arises whether all these pleas, including the
highest, the profits of which the king seldom granted to a
subject, such as breach of his peace, came before the Hundred
and its twelve doomsmen.[2] The palatine earls of Chester
are afterwards found holding a special court of crown pleas for
Chester presided over by their justiciar, minor offences coming
before a court called the pentice, where the city sheriffs
presided, while the portmote held by the bailiffs dealt with
civil business only.[3] It is obvious, however, that, in the form

[1] *D.B.* i. 262b, 2.

[2] The list of " the laws which were there " draws no line between the
reserved pleas and other offences. At Shrewsbury they are separated by
intervening matter, though the pleas are said to be the king's " there "
(*ibi*), at Hereford the pleas are mentioned as in the royal demesne and so
outside the customs farmed by the city reeve and shared between the king
and the earl, while the description of Worcester mentions them as being
the king's in the whole county. This might seem to suggest that there
and elsewhere they came before the shire court, held in the borough, but
before the Conquest there were no grades of jurisdiction in local courts.
The hundred court could apply the severest method of proof, the ordeal,
and inflict the extreme penalty of death (Liebermann, *Ges.* ii. 454, § 25b).

[3] See the *Calendar of Rolls of Chester County Court*, etc., 1259–97
(Cheth. Soc. N.S. 84), Introduction.

it comes before us at any rate, this distinction of courts was of post-Conquest creation. On the whole, it seems likely that the Anglo-Saxon borough court, if Chester was at all typical in this respect, could entertain cases which from the twelfth century at least would be tried by royal justices or those of great immunists like the earl of Chester. If this were so, the withdrawal of " high justice " from the borough court must have given it a more domestic character and so proportionably have facilitated its use as an organ of the municipal aspirations of the burgesses.

With one doubtful exception, to which we shall come presently, the Chester court is the only borough court which is directly mentioned in Domesday Book. It is there called the Hundred. How far was this a general name for this class of courts and if it was, what inferences are to be drawn as to their origin ?

The Chester Hundred was the court of a hundred (or more accurately half-hundred) district which besides the city comprised four adjacent vills contributing about one-fourteenth to the danegeld due from the hundred. Thirteen other boroughs are definitely described in the great survey as forming hundreds or half-hundreds in themselves, with or without a rural belt outside.[1] To these we ought perhaps to add Malmesbury.[2] Bath, which while held by Queen Edith (d. 1075) had paid geld with the rural hundred of its name,[3] was in the thirteenth century accounted a hundred and its court was called the hundred, as at Chester, the rural hundred being distinguished as the forinsec or out hundred.

Later evidence further suggests that other boroughs than Malmesbury which are not described as hundreds in Domesday Book were actually reckoned as such in the eleventh century. The Worcester city court was known as the hundred so late as 1241 [4] and Gloucester was reported by the sheriff in 1316 to

---

[1] Shrewsbury, Winchcombe, Bedford, Cambridge, Norwich, Thetford, Ipswich, Colchester, Maldon, Canterbury, Rochester, Fordwich, and Sandwich. Pevensey hundred in the Anglo-Saxon period was probably an ordinary agricultural hundred with its *caput* in the borough and its union with the borough as the " lowey " of Pevensey a Norman innovation. For its constitution in 1256, see *Sussex Arch. Coll.* iv. 210.

[2] See below, p. 53.

[3] *D.B.* iv. 106. When it reverted to the crown after the queen's death, it was evidently claimed as an ingeldable royal manor of the south-western type (see below, p. 51), the collectors of the geld of 1084 reporting that it had not paid on the twenty hides at which it had been assessed (*D.B.* iv. 68).

[4] *V.C.H. Worc.* iv. 382.

E

form a hundred in itself.[1]   Both of these boroughs belong to that important type which is given separate treatment at the head of each county in Great Domesday, and has therefore been presumed fairly enough to have possessed a court in-dependent of any rural hundred and co-ordinate with its court, but, as hundred rubrics are not attached to them, as they are in Little Domesday, the probability that the borough court was still very generally a hundred court itself has not always been duly appreciated.

It may very well be that the great condensation of the original returns imposed upon the clerks who compiled Great Domesday, caused them to omit hundred rubrics in these cases as unnecessary, while those who put together Little Domesday, having a much freer hand, inserted them together with much other detail which was suppressed in Great Domesday.   It is true that the latter often gives the assess-ment of the borough to danegeld, and where this is exactly a hundred hides, as at Cambridge and Shrewsbury, there can be no doubt that it had a complete hundred organization.   But the assessment of many boroughs, especially in the south-west,[2] was so low that it tells us nothing.   Even Worcester was rated at no more than fifteen hides and that in a non-adjacent rural hundred.   The obvious unlikel.hood that the citizens of Worcester did suit to the distant court of Fishborough hundred may help to resolve the m re difficult problem presented by Northampton and Huntingdon.   According to the Northamptonshire Geld-Roll (1066-75, the county town was rated as twenty-five hides *byrigland* in the hundred of Spelho,[3] perhaps a fourth of its original assessment.   Domesday Book itself records that until King William's time Huntingdon paid geld on fifty hides as a fourth part of Hurstingstone

---

[1] *Feudal Aids*, ii. 263-4.   Hereford, however, was returned as in Grims-worth hundred (*ibid.*, p. 385).   It lay close to the southern border of the hundred.   Hertford occupied a similar border position in the hundred to which it gave its name.   In 1066 it paid geld as ten hides.   It does not necessarily follow that either town was subject to the hundred court. A court of the vill of Hertford is mentioned in 1359 (*V.C.H. Herts.* iii. 459-6).   On the other hand, the hundred court of Bristol, which is evidenced as early as 1188 may very well be of post-Conquest origin.   In *Domesday Book* the borough is surveyed with the adjacent royal manor of Barton in Edredestane hundred (*D.B.* i. 163a, 2).

[2] Where, indeed, it was not an assessment to the danegeld.   See below, p. 51.

[3] Ellis, *Introduction to Domesday Book*, i. 186 ; Round, *Feudal England*, p. 153.   The hundred adjoined the town.

hundred, a double hundred.[1] Each borough stands centrally in its county, after the Midland fashion, and, as at Leicester, three rural hundreds converge upon it. We may be practically as certain in the one case as in the other that these hundreds stopped short at the borough boundary and that the borough itself, as a separate administrative and judicial area, was an integral part of the division of the county into hundreds. As in the case of Worcester, their danegeld payments were allocated to a neighbouring rural hundred to make up its full hundred or two hundred hides. This was merely a matter of convenience and it does not imply any judicial dependence upon rural hundred courts, the meeting-places of which were some miles away. Low assessments, such as Worcester enjoyed, were evidently due to reduction by royal favour, beneficial hidation as it has been called, but there were many boroughs, even county boroughs, whose resources could not bear the taxation of even half a rural hundred, and their assessments sometimes came in useful to make a round number of hides in one of these.

Ballard suggested in 1914[2] that the convergence of rural hundreds upon the bounds of old Roman towns like Leicester is a very early feature, going back to their resettlement by the English, whose first bishoprics and mints were fixed in them, and indicating that they were treated as urban hundreds with independent courts. The new boroughs fortified long afterwards during the struggle with the Danes were given the same type of organization. This theory, it will be seen, assumes the early origin of the hundred and its court, a theory which was never applicable to the regions north of the Thames and is now pretty generally abandoned in the case of those south of the river. Nothing is known of the area over which the folkmoot, the predecessor of the southern hundred court, exercised jurisdiction, but there is a possibility, not altogether unsupported by evidence, that its centre was a royal *burh*[3] and the court of an old Roman town may have been a district court, such as there is some reason to conjecture was the case at London,[4] and not the purely urban tribunal of Ballard's theory. However this may be, the convergence of rural

---

[1] *D.B.* i. 203a, 2. William I had substituted for it a " geldum monete." The Northampton assessment was also obsolete. The " boroughland " is recorded with waste land, etc., as not having paid danegeld (Round, *op. cit.*, p. 156), but we are not told what had taken its place.

[2] *The English Borough in the Twelfth Century*, p. 37.

[3] See above, p. 36. [4] Above, p. 41.

hundreds upon them was not, as he himself admits, a universal feature of boroughs which had been Roman towns, nor was it confined to them [1] It was inevitable in the Midlands where towards the end of the tenth century many shires were drawn each round a borough as centre and divided into hundreds or wapentakes. A majority of these centres had never been Roman. Where the shires were ancient and often contained several boroughs, such neat planning was impossible, but a fairly central position, if only for a wide section of the shire area, would produce the same effect, as it did at Canterbury and at Winchester. On the other hand, Colchester, formerly so important a Roman *colonia*, occupied such a cramped position in the north-eastern corner of Essex that it was almost completely surrounded by the rural hundred of Lexden, even after it had become a full hundred by the annexation from Lexden, probably not long before the Conquest, of four adjacent vills, including the hundred *caput* itself. [2]

The distinction between a borough which was a full hundred, as Colchester was, and one which, like Ipswich, ranked only as a half-hundred, was financial not administrative or judicial. Outside the borough proper Ipswich had a rural " liberty " not much more than a fourth less than that which surrounded Colchester. [3] The " half-hundred of Ipswich," which in 1086 gave evidence as to the land belonging in 1066 to St. Peter's church in the borough, [4] was clearly parallel with the hundred court elsewhere and just as clearly the court of the borough. Its clumsy title soon went out of use, but the Colchester court continued to be known as the Hundred right through the Middle Ages. [5]

Maldon, like Ipswich, was reckoned as a half-hundred.

[1] Three hundreds, for example, met at Northampton which had no Roman past.

[2] It is a curious coincidence, if no more, that the liberty of Ipswich, which with the borough constituted a half-hundred, was later also reckoned to contain four vills or hamlets, four men and the reeve from each of which were associated with a jury of twelve from the borough in coroners' inquests (*Hist. MSS. Comm.* 9 Rep., pt. 1, app., p. 226 ; *cf.* pp. 233, 236). The vills which with Chester composed the hundred of the city (*D.B.* i. 262b) may similarly have been reckoned as four in number. In Shrewsbury hundred there were three rural vills, one of which (Meole) was divided into two manors.

[3] Area in 1836 (including the borough) 8450 acres (*Rep. of Municipal Boundaries Commission*, 1837), while that of Colchester was 11,700.

[4] *D.B.* ii. 393.

[5] *Colchester Court Rolls.* ed. W. Gurney Benham, vol. i. (1310–52), *passim*.

It is a most interesting case, for here we get a glimpse of the process of forming a borough. The borough in this instance was clearly cut out of the hundred of Witbrichtesherna (later Dengie), by which it is entirely surrounded except on the side of the Blackwater estuary, since Little Maldon, though it remained in the parish of St. Mary in the borough, was left in its old hundred.[1] Maldon is described among the manors on the *terra regis* and so does not comply with the canon that boroughs of any importance are separately described in Domesday Book.[2] The explanation probably is that the burgesses were all on the royal demesne and, so far as we know, the earl did not share the revenue of the borough with the king. Yet Maldon had nearly two hundred houses, as a half-hundred it had its own court, it provided a horse for land warfare and a ship for sea service, there was a mint, it received charters from Henry II and Edward I, and was incorporated by Philip and Mary in 1554. It seems possible that heterogeneous tenure and the earl's third penny were not essential to the status of a borough.

The hundred-borough was also general in Kent. Canterbury, Rochester, Fordwich, and Sandwich appear as hundreds in Domesday Book, the two cities each having a good deal of agricultural land outside their walls. There was a hundred of Hythe later, and each of the Cinque Ports, including Hastings [3] in Sussex, had its hundred (court). That of Dover is mentioned as early as *c*. 1202–04.[4]

---

[1] *D.B.* ii. 29, 73, 75. *Cf.* 5b, 48.

[2] Ballard (*op. cit.*, p. 36) tried to draw a real distinction among these between the boroughs which are placed under a hundredal rubric in Domesday Book as the East-Anglian towns are, and those which have no such rubric. The former, with or without other vills, were hundreds in themselves, the latter were outside the ordinary hundred organization but had a court, co-ordinate with that of the hundred, which originated in Edgar's legislation (above, p. 38). This will not do, for neither Chester nor Shrewsbury has a hundred rubric, yet they are incidentally shown to be hundreds by Domesday itself. A practical distinction may perhaps be detected between the borough which, like Gloucester, does not appear as a hundred until later and then without other vills and the hundredal borough of Domesday with associate vills. Instances of the former type are found, however, in 1086. Maldon is one. So, too, apparently are the smaller borough-hundreds of Kent, Fordwich, and Sandwich.

[3] The " Cinque Port Liberty " of Hastings has every appearance of having been cut out of the hundred of Baldslow, and Baldslow itself is just within the northern boundary of the liberty, as Lexden is within the hundred of Colchester (above, p. 48). See *Place-Names of Sussex*, ed. Mawer and Stenton, vii. 534 and map.

[4] S. P. H. Statham, *Dover Charters* (1902), p. 456. For the " little borough " of Seasalter, see below, p. 67.

The south of England, outside Kent, where large boroughs were rare, but small boroughs were many, shows the borough community in quite a different relation to the division into hundreds. The borough which is an area entirely distinct from the rural hundreds around it occurs,[1] but is never actually called a hundred in Domesday Book.[2] More often, the southern borough is physically imbedded within some rural hundred to which it not infrequently gives a name and a place of meeting.[3] Even Exeter lay within the great hundred of Wonford, the meeting-place of which at Heavitree was only a mile from the city. This broad contrast between the Midland and the southern borough is not surprising in view of the later date of the hundred divisions north of the Thames and the comparative fewness of boroughs there. What is unexpected is the conformity of the Kentish borough to the Midland type.

In central and, to a less extent, eastern and south-eastern England the boroughs could be treated as distinct hundredal areas when the hundreds were first plotted out. In the south and south-west, where the hundred first appears *ipso nomine* in the second quarter of the tenth century, that would have been usually impracticable. With few exceptions, the boroughs were too small and too awkwardly situated. It seems possible, even likely, however, that the problem had not normally to be faced and that the boroughs were founded within local administrative and judicial areas, with their centres in royal *burhs* or *tuns*, which were often substantially the same as the later hundreds. The hundred court was apparently here, we have seen,[4] a re-organization of an earlier local court, the folkmoot of the ninth century. A complete system of local judicial areas would appear to be implied in the existence of this early court, and these may not have been very greatly altered in the re-organization of the next century. This was substantially Liebermann's view,[5] it affords a reasonable explanation of the *burh* courts of Athelstan's reign without resorting to Professor Chadwick's theory of special creation, and recent research tends to confirm it.[6] Professor Chadwick

---

[1] Three rural hundreds, for example, adjoined Chichester.

[2] For a suggestion that Malmesbury may have had a hundred organization, see below, pp. 51, 53. Ilchester was perhaps another instance.

[3] *E.g.* Bath, Bruton, Frome, Cricklade, Dorchester, Pevensey.

[4] Above, p. 36.   [5] *Ges.* ii. 450, § 4g ; 452, §§ 13d-k ; 518, § 10.

[6] J. E. A. Jolliffe, " The Hidation of Kent," *E.H.R.* xliv (1929), 612 ff. ; " The Domesday Hidation of Sussex and the Rapes," *ibid.* xlv. (1930), 427 ff. ; H. Cam, " Manerium cum Hundredo," *ibid.* xlvii (1932), 353 ff.

himself was the first to call attention to this continuity,[1] but unfortunately gave an entirely different interpretation to what seems to be the most cogent piece of evidence for it.

In the south-west, the classical land of the West Saxon small borough, we get our clearest glimpse of its relation to the hundred in 1066. The borough here is actually or originally on the demesne that pertained from of old to the crown and, like all estates of that demesne, it was free from danegeld. It usually stood within a hundred and was quite commonly its *caput*, but for this particular tax it was an exempt area. An exemption shared with every rural manor of the crown did not of course constitute a burghal distinction or imply a separate borough court. A real burghal distinction, on the other hand, was possessed in 1066 by the Devon and Dorset boroughs and one in Wiltshire,[2] which owed certain military or naval services, some of which were commuted, and this may have been one reason why, with the exception of the three smaller Devon boroughs, they were surveyed separately at the head of their counties, though the exception is a warning not to press the suggestion too strongly. These not very onerous services, perhaps of recent origin, did not, however, relieve the boroughs of Dorset at any rate, except Shaftesbury,[3] from the ancient and much heavier burden of the *firma unius noctis* which accounts for the general exemption from danegeld of the ancient demesne of the crown and the boroughs which arose upon it. The evidence of Domesday is not complete, but it shows that all the boroughs of Somerset save Bath and three out of four in Dorset were included in one or other of the groups of ancient demesne estates among which this now commuted food-rent was apportioned, while four out of the six great Wiltshire manors which are recorded as rendering each a full *firma noctis* had already burgesses at their centres. Involved in hundreds and often in *firma noctis* groups, limited to local trade, the lesser boroughs of the south-west had for the most part little future, even where they did not sink into mere market towns or villages as at Bruton and Frome. More prosperous places such as Ilchester and Milborne Port in Somerset and Calne and Cricklade in Wiltshire, though they afterwards ranked as boroughs by prescription and were represented in Parliament, never attained the status of towns of separate jurisdiction. It is not surprising that their

---

[1] *A.S.I.* pp. 233 ff., 249 ff. [2] Malmesbury.
[3] Two-thirds of which had been alienated to the abbey (*D.B.* i. 75a, 1).

possession of separate courts in an earlier age has been seriously questioned.

In the absence of any direct information upon this point, a solution of the problem may be sought by an examination of a feature of local jurisdiction, almost confined to the south and particularly to the region with which we are now concerned, that distinction between the *in* hundred and the *out* or *forinsec* hundred which Miss Cam has recently investigated with such thoroughness.[1] The recognition of the manor which was the administrative centre of a hundred and gave its name to it, as a separate inner hundred was far from being confined to manors which were early boroughs, or which developed burghal features later. Yet the fact that a number of boroughs, Andover,[2] Basingstoke,[3] Bath,[4] Leominster,[5] Reading,[6] and Wells [7] were associated or contrasted with forinsec hundreds of their name, and that at Bath the distinction is possibly as old as Domesday, suggests that this reveals at least one way in which separate borough courts came into being. These in-hundred courts developed urban features while those in manors which remained mere market towns, or not even that, became purely manorial.

As Bath alone among the six boroughs mentioned above is a known Anglo-Saxon borough and the Domesday date of its in-hundred is not certain, while the evidence for the others is not earlier than the twelfth century, we are not in a position to state definitely that this particular source of borough courts goes back beyond the Norman Conquest. The distinction of in- and out-hundred is certainly not found in every case of a pre-Conquest borough in this quarter which (or a wider manor of its name) was the *caput* of a hundred. The Dorset Dorchester, for instance, at the time of the Domesday survey was locally in, and gave its name, to a hundred of more than seventy hides. Like other royal domains and their boroughs, however, in this and the neighbouring counties, it was financially independent of the hundred, contributing nothing to its geld,[8] and by the thirteenth century

---

[1] In the article quoted above, p. 50, *n*. 6.
[2] *B.B.C.* i. 229.　　　　　　　　　[3] *Ibid.* ii. 307.
[4] Eyton, *Somerset Domesday*, i. 105.
[5] Cotton MS. Domit. A. iii. f. 116 (duo hundreda de Leom').
[6] *E.H.R.* xlvii. (1932), 360. *Cf.* B.M. Harl. MS. 1708, f. xix b.
[7] *E.H.R.* xlvii. (1932), 362.
[8] In the Geld Roll for Dorset (1084) the distinction is in one case expressed by a statement that Whitchurch hundred contained 84¾ hides *praeter firmam regis* (Eyton, *Key to Domesday; Dorset Survey*, p. 141 *n*.).

the hundred, with some additions, appears as a distinct hundred of St. George,[1] taking its name apparently from the saint to whom the parish church of Fordington, another ingeldable royal manor, running up to the walls of Dorchester, was dedicated. It is, however, possible that before this re-organization the geldable hundred was known as the forinsec hundred of Dorchester, though there is no trace of this in the Pipe Rolls or, so far as we know, in other records. In the case of the Wiltshire borough of Malmesbury, on the other hand, the question does not arise, for Domesday tells us that in its pre-Conquest farm there was included the king's share of the pleas of the two (adjacent) hundreds of Cicementone and Sutelesberg.[2] As it is very unlikely that the borough owed suit to two hundreds, the presumption is that it had always been reckoned as a hundred, and this seems confirmed by an early thirteenth-century record that the abbot of Malmesbury had by the king's grant three hundreds, Malmesbury, Sterkeley, and Cheggeslawe,[3] the two latter being those mentioned in Domesday under more archaic names.

If this reasoning be sound, we may with some probability trace urban jurisdiction in the two boroughs to inclusion in the original division into hundreds or some later revision of it in the case of Malmesbury and to the fission of a primitive hundred, before the Conquest, in the case of Dorchester.

Of the eight towns [4] in Somerset, the status of which as boroughs in 1066 is proved by the payment of the " third penny " of the total revenue from each of them to the local earl, though in two instances no burgesses are mentioned, five gave their names to hundreds, but it is only at Bath, the chief town of the county, that we have clear evidence then or later of fission and the establishment of an in-hundred of the borough.[5] Bath and Milverton were in the hands of Queen Edith, the rest were included with royal manors in one or other of the *firma unius noctis* groups. Of the three which were not *capita* of hundreds, Axbridge and Langport were grouped with the neighbouring *capita* of the hundreds in

---

[1] *Book of Fees*, i. 88 (Inquest of 1212). [2] *D.B.* i. 64b, 1.
[3] *Book of Fees*, i. 379. A modern statement (quoted by W. H. Jones, *Domesday for Wiltshire* (1865), p. 223) that the boundary of the two latter hundreds ran through the centre of the borough, is apparently merely a false inference from the passage in Domesday, for Cheggeslawe (Chedglow) is called Cicementone, a name which is not found after 1086.
[4] Bath, Ilchester, Milborne, Axbridge, Langport, Bruton, Frome and Milverton. [5] Above, p. 45.

which they lay, but Ilchester, the second town of the shire in population and wealth, was associated with Milborne (Port), a royal manor and borough ten miles away. Here, at any rate, there can have been no jurisdictional tie, and the burgesses must either have attended the court of one of the adjoining hundreds, perhaps that of Stone which their successors are found farming from Henry II,[1] or they had a hundred court of their own. One fact seems *prima facie* to favour the first alternative. The items of the borough revenue which was shared between king and earl are given in Domesday Book, and they do not include the perquisites of a court. This is not, however, conclusive, for the perquisites of a borough hundred court may have been comprised with those of the rural hundred courts in the profits of the pleas of the shire which king and earl shared in the same proportion as they did the render of the borough.

But whether or not Ilchester, with its 108 burgesses and found worthy of the liberties of Winchester by Henry II, had already a separate court, there seems less likelihood that the minor Somerset boroughs, only one of which had more than forty burgesses and two had none,[2] enjoyed that privilege, especially those in which a hundred court for a wide area regularly met.[3] So far, then, as this type of village borough, the future market town, is concerned, Ballard might perhaps have had a good defence for the heterodox view which he developed in his *Domesday Boroughs* but afterwards retracted in deference to the stern reprehension of Miss Bateson.[4] The mistake he made was in extending his theory of the subjection of burgesses to the jurisdiction of rural hundred courts to boroughs in general and in combining it with an unquestioning acceptance of that interpretation of Edgar's *burhgemot*, which sees in it a purely burghal court established in most, if not all, boroughs.[5]

---

[1] *Book of Fees*, i. 79.

[2] Frome and Milverton are not credited with burgesses either in 1066 or 1086. There was a market in both. Milverton, but not Frome, was afterwards accounted a " Borough town " and had a portreeve down to 1835.

[3] The hundred which with the market at Bruton was granted to the priory before 1205 (*Mon. Angl.* vi. 336 ; *cf. Book of Fees*, i. 80) was clearly not a burghal hundred and the pleas (*placita*) which the men of Milborne (Port) were farming in 1212 with the market for £5 (*ibid.* p. 79) were doubtless those of the whole hundred of Milborne.   [4] See above, p. 32.

[5] One of his main arguments for the burghal suit to external hundreds was the insufficiency of the three meetings a year of the *burhgemot* (above, p. 38) for the needs of a trading community.

As the smallest boroughs of the south-west almost certainly did not possess separate courts, hundredal or other, while the place given to a small minority of its boroughs at the head of the survey of their counties suggests that they at least had such courts, the questions arise where was the line drawn and by what tests. The number of the burgess population would no doubt be a chief factor in the decision, and with one exception the six boroughs which occupy this exceptional position [1] had more burgesses on the royal demesne in 1066 than those which were allotted a humbler place, save Bath and Ilchester. These had almost exactly the same number of burgesses as Bridport, which is described " above the line," and the only reason apparently why they were not thus isolated was that the Domesday commissioners in Somerset adopted a different arrangement, surveying all the king's boroughs under their respective *firma noctis* groups and Queen Edith's under her separately described estate. We have seen that independently of this population test, there is some probability that they already had separate courts. Where the test seems to break down is at Malmesbury, but Domesday only gives the 1086 figure (51) and the borough may have been more populous before the Conquest. It is some slight confirmation of this line of argument that the six boroughs, with Bath, are the only mint towns, save episcopal Taunton, recorded in Domesday Book for this region. All six, with Bath and, for a time, Ilchester, are afterwards found in possession of courts of their own, while of the other seventeen royal boroughs in the four counties which are mentioned in Domesday, only seven appear later as towns of separate jurisdiction. In this land of petty boroughs, burghal status was precarious. Cricklade, Calne, Bedwin, and Milborne, though they attained to no chartered privileges, were recognized as boroughs by prescription and sent members to Parliament, but Tilshead, Warminster, Bruton, Frome, Milverton, and Lydford dropped out of the list altogether. Frome and Milverton, as we have seen, had practically ceased to be boroughs by the date of Domesday, though Milverton retained some burghal features.

An intensive study of the ecclesiastical relations between the boroughs and their vicinities may some day throw light upon the problem we have been discussing. There seems to

[1] Malmesbury, Dorchester, Bridport, Wareham, Shaftesbury, Exeter. Yet it is difficult to deny separate courts to the lesser Devon boroughs. They had *burhwitan* like Exeter (above, p. 42).

be no instance in the south-west in which the principal church of a borough was only a chapel of a rural church, as was common enough in the new boroughs founded after the Norman Conquest, but at Dorchester the parish of Frome Whitfield to the north of the town, and (in the 13th century) in the hundred of St. George, extended within the walls at one point and exemption from the borough jurisdiction was claimed for this *enclave* as late as 1670.[1] In 1086, on the other hand, the glebe of the town church was outside the borough, in the hundred of Dorchester.[2] At Wareham, also, the parishes of several of the town churches stretched beyond the ramparts into rural hundreds of which they formed part. It is possible that these in- and out-parishes, as they were called, represented the single parish of one original church of Wareham, a parish which was too extensive to be included as a whole within the fortifications or even within the " liberties " of the borough.[3] The case may be somewhat parallel to that of Maldon.[4]

The borough which was the *caput* of a rural hundred is found elsewhere than in the south-west. Sussex, as we have seen, contained two, Pevensey and Steyning. Unfortunately they were both mediatized boroughs at the date of Domesday Book and so throw no light upon the problem of the urban court. Pevensey receives special treatment and had a mint, while the rural part of the hundred, the lowey of Pevensey, as it was afterwards called, is surveyed as a whole elsewhere, but no judicial profits are included in the unusually full enumeration of revenues derived from the burgesses. The Pevensey court was doubtless then as later a feudal court, which had absorbed the original hundred court.[5]

The court held by the abbot of Fécamp at Steyning would also be feudal, but he was not lord of the whole hundred, as the count of Mortain was of Pevensey hundred, and the hundred court of Steyning seems to have belonged to the lord of the rape.[6]

---

[1] C. H. Mayo, *Records of Dorchester* (1908), pp. 470 ff. For aggression on the borough by Fordington, east of the town, see pp. 469 f.

[2] Eyton, *Dorset Domesday*, pp. 73, 124.

[3] *Ibid.* p. 73.   [4] Above, p. 49.

[5] In the fourteenth century it was a three-weeks court presided over by the lord's steward and entertained pleas of the crown as well as of lands and tenements (*Sussex Archæological Collections*, iv. 212). The vill supplied only three of the twelve jurats of the vill and lowey as a member of the Cinque Ports confederation (*ibid.* p. 211).

[6] In 1168 it is called the hundred of Bramber, which was the *caput* of his honour (*Pipe R. 14 Hen. II*, p. 196).

There still remain to be discussed those boroughs which lay within rural hundreds but were not the meeting-places of their courts, which were sometimes five or more miles away. In this class fall the three smaller boroughs of Devon. They have a very independent appearance in a casual mention of them [1] some seventy years before the Domesday survey in which, however, one, Totnes appears as a mediatized town and the others are entered on the *Terra Regis*. The subsequent mediatization of Barnstaple and the decay of Lydford obscure their earlier relation, if any, to the hundred courts.

In Wiltshire all the pre-Conquest boroughs were extra-hundredal, for geld at any rate, except Salisbury which was an ancient possession of the bishops and as a mesne manor paid geld in the hundred of Underditch.[2] But we may be sure that there was an episcopal court there, though perhaps not for the town alone. Indeed no burgesses are actually recorded in the town, either in 1066 or twenty years later, though the earl's " third penny " attests its burghal status.[3]

In Berkshire, Wallingford was locally in Hesletesford hundred, but is described at great length at the head of the county survey and the distinction which is there carefully drawn between the jurisdiction of certain immunists in their houses and that of the king, represented by his reeve,[4] leaves no doubt that the borough had a royal court. In Hampshire there can be almost as little doubt that Southampton, which is also independently described, had its own court, though the town was surrounded by the hundred of Mansbridge. The borough of Twyneham (now Christchurch), mentioned in 1086 as having then thirty-one masures, if of pre-Conquest date,[5] was still doubtless judicially dependent upon the hundred of Egheiete under which the manor and borough are surveyed.

Three of the Sussex boroughs, Hastings, Arundel, and Lewes, were locally situate in hundreds with other names, but Arundel and Lewes are each described, without hundred rubric, at the head of their rapes, and their possession of urban courts, even before their mediatization by the Conqueror, is hardly doubtful. It seems to be implied at Lewes in the fines for various offences quoted as customary in the time of King Edward.[6] Hastings unfortunately is not surveyed at all.

[1] See above, p. 42.
[2] W. H. Jones, *Domesday for Wiltshire*, pp. 23, 188.
[3] This is also true of Marlborough.   [4] *D.B.* i. 56b, 1.
[5] It is included in the Burghal Hidage (above, p. 15).
[6] *D.B.* i. 26a, 1. Hastings was locally in the hundred of Baldslow (above, p. 49).

A borough might be attracted into another hundred than that in which it was locally situated, for financial reasons, for payment of geld or of farm. Worcester, though probably already a hundred of itself, was placed, as we have seen, in another hundred for geld, and a further case will meet us presently in the east of England. An illustration of the second type is found in Surrey, where Southwark, though it lay actually in Brixton hundred, is surveyed in Domesday Book under the hundred of Kingston, for no other reason apparently than that the royal revenue from the borough was included in the farm of the king's important manor of that name. It is not necessary to suppose that the men of Southwark had to go to Kingston for justice, and indeed the Domesday account contains a passage which points almost as directly to the existence of a court within the borough as the similar but more explicit record at Wallingford.[1]

The same kind of association may explain the survey of the other Surrey borough Guildford under Woking hundred, for though it actually lay within that hundred the king's reeve there is recorded as taking amends for forfeitures within the vill.[2]

It has been claimed [3] that the nature of the relation of boroughs to hundred courts is settled by a passage, unique in Domesday, which relates to a borough at the opposite side of the Thames, but here again mediatization makes certainty unattainable. Dunwich, which lay in Blythburgh hundred, Suffolk, four miles from its *caput*, belonged to Edric of Laxfield before the Conquest, and to Robert Malet, his Norman successor, afterwards. Domesday reports that the king had this right (*consuetudo*) in Dunwich that two or three should go to the hundred (court) if properly summoned and if they failed to appear were amerced, and that if a thief was taken there he should be judged in Dunwich, but his execution should take place at Blythburgh. His goods, however, were to fall to the lord of Dunwich.[4] There is a court therefore at Dunwich which can try even a capital case, though it cannot carry out the sentence, but it is a feudal court and we cannot be sure that it has ever been anything else. Or the other hand, the small and special attendance at the hundred court reserved by the king does not seem absolutely clear evidence of an earlier and fuller hundred suit from the town. If the arrange-

---

[1] *D.B.* i. 32a, 1.   [2] *Ibid.* f. 30a, 1.
[3] Ballard, *Domesday Boroughs*, p. 53.   [4] *D.B.* ii. 312.

ment was Norman, and it is not said to be older, it may only be an early instance of the common stipulation which bound feudal tenants to afforce higher courts in certain cases. Whether such a custom could have arisen before the Conquest in the case of a mesne borough, it would be idle, in the present state of our knowledge, to speculate.[1]

Two other East Anglian boroughs are surveyed in Domesday Book under rural hundreds which did not bear their name. Yarmouth is given separate treatment among the other Norfolk boroughs at the end of the *Terra Regis*. Sudbury appears on the Suffolk *Terra Regis* as an escheated possession of Ælfgifu, mother of Earl Morcar. Sudbury, therefore, as well as Yarmouth, was in the king's hand in 1086. Both were considerably less populous than Dunwich in 1066 and very much less twenty years later. They have lived to see that already doomed town almost vanish into the sea. Yarmouth, which was subject to the earl's " third penny," may have been the meeting-place of the hundred of East Flegg to the danegeld of which it contributed no more than one-twelfth. Its borough court first appears, but not as a novelty in John's charter of 1208 with the name husting which is certain evidence of London influence.

Sudbury was locally situated on the south-western border of Babergh hundred in Suffolk, but at some unknown date it had been transferred to Thingoe hundred, though ten miles from its nearest point. Round has shown [2] that this was done to replace the exactly equal assessment to danegeld of Bury St. Edmunds in Thingoe, the tax having been granted to the abbey. Babergh, being a double hundred, could afford the loss. It is surely most unlikely that this book-keeping change involved suit to the Thingoe courts for the Sudbury burgesses, any more than a somewhat similar allocation of the Worcester assessment did.[3] Perhaps the remark: *soca in eadem villa*, with which the Domesday description ends, means that Morcar's mother had left a court there. The usual phrase when hundred soke was claimed by the crown was : " the king and the earl have soke." Sudbury, unlike Yarmouth, was a rural manor with an urban centre, but the latter had undoubtedly two of the supposed criteria of a national borough, " hetero-geneous " tenure and a mint.

---

[1] On Malet's forfeiture under Henry I, Dunwich reverted to the crown. It was in the queen's hands in 1156 (*Pipe R.* 1156, p. 9), but this did not last long (*ibid.* 1169, p. 99).

[2] *Feudal England*, pp. 100, 101 *n*.　　　　[3] See above, p. 46.

The results of the foregoing analysis may be briefly sum-marized. They lend no support to Ballard's first hasty theory that besides the infrequently meeting *burhgemot* of Edgar's law, the burgesses of every borough had to attend a hundred court without their walls ; [1] a theory so soon retracted that it need not have been mentioned, had not Liebermann incautiously committed himself to it just before the retraction was published. On the other hand, the facts are hardly to be reconciled with the older view, most clearly voiced by Miss Bateson, that every pre-Conquest borough had a court co-ordinate with that of the rural hundred. The small boroughs of Somerset and Wiltshire which were farmed with vills of ancient demesne, were themselves often heads of hundreds, and in many cases, even after the Norman Conquest, remained boroughs by prescription without separate jurisdiction or sank into mere market towns, are difficult to fit into this view. The supposed universality of borough courts in the Anglo-Saxon period rests, indeed, almost entirely on the apparent generality of Edgar's institution of a *burhgemot*. If his law applied only to the unshired Midlands, as has been not very convincingly argued, or only to the greater boroughs in which, by another law of his, three times as many witnesses of sales were to be provided as in small boroughs or hundreds, burghal history before the Conquest would be much simplified. [2]

Whatever may be the correct interpretation of this puzzling law, the evidence of Domesday Book, confirmed by the later title of certain borough courts, leads to the conclusion that the burghal court of the Middle Ages was very generally in origin a hundred court, a unit in the complete system which was gradually worked out for the whole country except the far north, in the tenth century, though confirmation of this extension is hardly derivable from Cnut's ordinance that every freeman should be in a hundred and a tithing, [3] the tithing

---

[1] The burgesses of some small boroughs may, we have seen (p. 54), have done suit to the court of the hundred in which their borough lay, meeting either within or without the town, but the case does not really fall under Ballard's theory, since they certainly had not a four-monthly *burhgemot* as well.   [2] See above, p. 42.

[3] II Cnut, 20 ; Liebermann, *Ges.* i. 322. It would be rash to assert that the division of boroughs into wards, which under that or other names is already found in Domesday Book at Cambridge, Huntingdon, Stamford, and York, originated in Cnut's legislation, but it was certainly utilized in the working of the frankpledge system. At Canterbury, indeed, after the Conquest the corresponding division was the *borgh*, the usual local name for the tithing. Before the thirteenth century these *borghs* were reorganized as aldermanries with hundred courts, in pretty obvious imitation of the London wards and wardmoots (*Black Book of St. Augustine's* i. 394, 397; *Hist. MSS. Com.* 9 Rep. pt. 1, App. *passim; B.B.C.* i. 130).

being apparently the territorial tithing of the South. The larger boroughs could be treated as hundreds or half-hundreds in themselves, or in the case of London as a group of hundreds, but the smaller boroughs would have to be fitted into rural hundreds.

To Dr. Stephenson this character of the normal Anglo-Saxon borough court before 1066 as " merely a part of an ancient territorial organization " forbids us to regard it as in any sort a communal institution. " It was no more significant of urban life," he says, " than the wall that enclosed it ; for both had been the work of the king, not of the community." [1] The absurdity of attributing to the Anglo-Saxon boroughs municipal liberties, which even after the Conquest were only very slowly obtained from the crown, needs no demonstration, but to make an absolute break in the history of the English borough community at the Conquest is to go too far in the opposite direction, further, indeed, than Professor Stephenson had been prepared to go in an earlier section of his article, where he admits that there are some traces of communal liberty before the Conquest, primarily in the great seaports.[2] Apart from such traces, however, his conception of the hundred court of the borough seems open to criticism as too static. At the date of the Conquest it had been in existence for a century at least, time enough to develop a character of its own. If at first only a unit in the general system of courts in the land at large, it shared that origin with the courts of the continental communes and free towns,[3] and by the early part of the eleventh century, as we have seen,[4] it had already evolved a *burhriht*,[5] a body of law, which, as contrasted with *landriht*, must have dealt chiefly with the special problems of

---

[1] *E.H.R.* xlv. (1930), 202. [2] *Ibid.* p. 195.
[3] The ministers of royal justice in the Carolingian empire were the schöffen (*scabini*) and the civic court originated in the assignment of a separate body of these to the urban area. [4] Above, p. 40.
[5] The *burgherist* or *burgeristh* which occurs twice in the Somerset Domesday is a Norman mis-spelling of the same word, but it is apparently used in a different sense. Earl Harold had received in his manor of Cleeve the third penny of *burgherist* from four hundreds (*D.B.* i. 86b, 2—correcting " de " for " et " from the Exon. *D.B.*), and the list of the bishops of Winchester's customs at Taunton is headed by *burgeristh* (*ibid.* p. 87a, 1). Interpretation is difficult for *D.B.* records no borough in the four hundreds, but as one of them contained Watchet which is in the Burghal Hidage and had a mint under Ethelred II, it seems most likely that the earl's borough " third penny " is in question. Philip de Colombières, baron of Nether Stowey, had by royal grant from 1156 to 1181 ten shillings yearly *de uno burgricht* (*Pipe R.*) and the " third penny " of Langport, of Axbridge, and perhaps of Bruton, in 1086 was ten shillings. (*Cf. D.B.* i. 87a, 2 with iv. 100.)

F

a compact group of freemen traders and is mentioned in close
association with weights and measures.[1] Even the highest
class of burgesses who did not usually buy to sell, but only to
supply the needs of their own households, would not be
free from these problems. Apart from burgess rents, the
chief sources of the king's and the earl's revenue from the
borough were tolls and the profits of the court.

It was mainly in these hundredal courts adapted to the
needs of burgesses that their aspirations to greater liberty
and self-government first woke to life and found in them an
instrument which, powerfully aided by merchant gilds, ultimately secured the realization of those aspirations and became the sovereign body, the *communitas*, of the fully developed
municipality. Who can safely say that the foundations of
this revolution were not being silently laid in the two centuries
preceding the Conquest? It seems unsafe to argue that,
because a rate-book like Domesday tells us little or nothing
of these courts and is too often ambiguous in its references to
the features of the borough which might be communal, there
was no sense of community among its burgesses nor had they
any experience in translating it into action.

The hundred court was in one respect well fitted to foster
the growth of communalism in the borough. Although a
royal court and presided over by a king's reeve, it had a strong
popular aspect in its doomsmen and in its second officer, the
hundreds-ealdor, who was certainly not a royal officer and
who very probably, before as after the Conquest, was elected
by his hundred. What became of him in the towns is not very
clear, but perhaps he sank to be the sergeant of the borough
as the alderman of the rural hundred ultimately dropped to
the position of its *bedellus* or beadle.[2]

Though the borough court of the later Middle Ages would
seem to have its fountain-head in that of the hundred, it was
much influenced by a tribunal of different origin, the London
husting,[3] the most important of the three unique courts,
folkmoot, husting, wardmoot which the quite exceptional city
possessed. Unfortunately, our knowledge of the composition and working of these bodies is of entirely post-Conquest
date, but for the husting it goes back to the first half of the

---

[1] In the larger boroughs the hundred organization had to be modified.
See Edg. iv. 4, Liebermann, *Ges.* i. 210. For the king's peace in boroughs
cf. ibid. ii. 551 ff., 555 and 661, § 11 f. See also below, p. 119, *n.* 3.
[2] *Rot. Hund.*, ii. 214.   [3] See above, p. 40.

twelfth century, by the end of which the older open-air folk-moot had become a mere survival as a court of justice. Its decline had doubtless begun when the " house court " was set up in the tenth century with the object, one may surmise, of providing more suitable conditions than were possible in a large popular assembly.[1] Thus the jurisdiction which the open-air hundred court exercised in other boroughs [2] was in London, for the first time, used under a roof. That side of the hundred's work which was concerned with the keeping of the peace is here found in the hands of the wardmoots after the Conquest and the presumption is strong that it was done by them in Anglo-Saxon times, though the wards are not mentioned in any extant source of that date. It can hardly be without significance that the aldermen, who presided in the wardmoots, were also the judges of the Anglo-Norman husting.[3]

The most obvious formal differences between the fully-developed medieval borough court and the rural hundred court are its weekly or fortnightly, instead of monthly, session, and its meeting in Gild Hall, Moot Hall, or Tolbooth,[4] instead of in the open air. In both these features, especially the former, the influence of the London husting can be seen. The restriction of the husting meetings to not more than one a week in Henry I's and Henry II's charters to London was copied in a whole series of town charters before the end of the twelfth century,[5] and sometimes fixed the name husting upon their local court.

The conclusions to which the foregoing inquiry has led seem definitely to discourage the hope of finding a universal criterion of the early borough in the possession of a court of

---

[1] For this court, see W. Page, *London : its Origin and Early Development* (1923), pp. 213 ff. ; *E.H.R.* xvii. 502.

[2] At Leicester in the twelfth century in the common churchyard (M. Bateson, *Records of Leicester*, i. 4), at Oxford in the churchyard of St. Martin (J. Parker, *Early History of Oxford*, p. 122), at Norwich in Tombland (vacant land) near St. Michael de Motstowe or ad placita (W. Hudson and J. C. Tingey, *Records of Norwich*, i. Introd. V), and at Ipswich in the Thingstead (*H.M.C.* 9 Rep. pt. 1, p. 233).

[3] *E.H.R.* xvii. 487, 493.

[4] If a court for the old English borough at Norwich continued to be held separately from that of the Norman new borough for some time after the Conquest, it was merged with the latter before the thirteenth century, the single court meeting in the new borough or Mancroft, as it was now called, no longer in the open, but in the king's Tolboth.

[5] *B.B.C.* i. 442. The rule was applied to the hundred court of Bristol (*ibid.* p. 143).

its own. Taking the country over, such a court is a normal
burghal feature, but the smaller boroughs of the south-west
are exceptions both before and after the Norman Conquest.
The " borough by prescription," without special jurisdiction,
remains always a bar to easy generalization.

The separate court is only one of the features which have
been investigated as possible criteria of the borough. In
a useful table [1] Ballard has enumerated from Domesday and
coin lists, seventy-three Anglo-Saxon boroughs possessing
one or more of the following four features : (1) a court co-
ordinate with the rural hundred court, " the *burhgemot* of
Edgar's law " ; (2) heterogeneous tenure, " where different
tenants paid their rents to different lords " ; (3) payment of
one-third of the royal revenue from the borough (the " third
penny ") to the local earl or (occasionally) sheriff ; (4) a mint.
He finds 46 hundredal boroughs, 64 with heterogeneous
tenure, 39 subject to the third penny, and 56 with pre-Conquest
mints. All four features are found in 22 boroughs, three in
a further 22. But for omissions in Domesday, known or suspected, these figures would be higher. London and Winchester,
for instance, being only casually mentioned in the survey,
are credited merely with mixed tenure and early mints.

Were any of these features fundamental ? A court, as
we have just seen, was apparently not. Nor, it would seem,
was heterogeneous tenure. It was rather a natural and very
general, but not universal, result of burghal growth than
the essential pre-requisite implied in the " garrison " theory
of Maitland and Ballard. Mints, again, were not an invariable
feature of Anglo-Saxon boroughs, and in the eleventh century
at any rate are recorded in places which were never recognized
as boroughs.

More likely than any of these internal features to have
been characteristic of all new boroughs, and of no other kind
of vill, might seem the third penny. The Domesday figure is
low, but there was often no occasion to mention this feature.[2]
Luckily it tells us that the simplest of south-western boroughs,
without separate court, heterogeneous tenure, mint or apparently even burgesses, were subject to this payment. Of
course, they must have once had burgesses, if indeed their
seeming absence is not merely one of Domesday's omissions,

---

[1] *The English Borough in the Twelfth Century,* pp. 43-5. *Cf.* p. 37.
[2] This is perhaps the reason why nothing is said of it at Cambridge
and Bedford, where it is known to have been paid. But *cf.* p. 49.

and their places might yet be filled. It is plain in any case that we have not yet reached the minimum feature or features which distinguished the borough from any other royal vill and gave to it or maintained the public character implied in the earl's right to share its revenue with the king. Originally no doubt, leaving the older walled towns aside, this character would be imparted by the fortification of an open vill or group of vills for the defence of the surrounding population, and the earl's share would be the reward of his co-operation in the work. After the re-conquest of the Danelaw, however, the defensive aspect became secondary and the borough primarily a centre of local trade and administration. It is even possible that a few new centres of this kind were set up and called boroughs, though they were not fortified. At all events, there is no evidence that the minutest of the Somerset boroughs in 1066, Bruton, Frome, and Milverton, had ever been fortresses.[1]

Except at Bath, which had a mint, the revenues of the Somerset boroughs which were subject to the earl's third were apparently confined to the rents of the burgesses and the profits of markets. Unfortunately no markets are recorded at Axbridge, Bruton, and Langport and, as we have seen, no burgesses at Frome and Milverton, while no rent is assigned to the five burgesses at Bruton. However this may be accounted for, whether by Domesday omissions or by the lumping of borough revenues with those of the manors in which they were imbedded, it seems very unlikely that Axbridge and Langport, which were afterwards full-fledged municipalities, or even Bruton which was less fortunate, can have been without a market at this date, while Frome [2] and Milverton, with apparently no burgesses, possessed one.

Despite these difficulties, the Somerset evidence on the whole suggests that tenements held by rent alone and a market were enough to constitute a borough in the middle of the eleventh century. A market by itself was not sufficient, for Domesday records some thirty in places which were not, then at any rate, reckoned as boroughs, and though some certainly and perhaps most of these were Norman creations,

[1] This seems very likely too (above p. 54) in the case of a much more important borough, Droitwich, which is known to have been a market for salt as early as the eighth century.

[2] As the revenue from Frome market in 1086 was £2 6s. 8d. and the earl's third only 5s. (Eyton, *Somerset Domesday*, pp. 2, 4), it would seem likely that its profits had increased since 1066.

a few are definitely stated to have existed before the Conquest.[1] Whether these went very far back may be doubted. Edward and Athelstan's attempt to restrict marketing to boroughs had failed, but it was in favour of permitted buying and selling with hundred court witnesses not of private markets. The vital importance of the market in the borough is well seen in the record of the building of the *burh* at Worcester towards the end of the ninth century.[2] Only the universality of this feature will explain the equivalence of borough and port. It was the chief source from which king and earl could recoup the cost of fortification and secure a permanent income.

Before the Norman Conquest then, as indeed after it, the species borough of the genus vill comprised communities of the widest diversity in size and importance. Once planned out, they had prospered or decayed, as local and national conditions favoured or restricted their growth, without much regulation from above. Trade of some sort they all had and the free tenure without which trade cannot be carried on, but beyond these uniformity must not be expected. These, however, are fundamental and form in favourable circumstances the necessary basis of all future municipal growth. A new institution has grown up capable of great expansion and full of unforeseen possibilities.

A very different conception of the Anglo-Saxon borough has recently been put forth by Dr. Stephenson. Save in the case of a few seaports it was, in his view, not really urban at all, but merely a special kind of agricultural group. The Norman Conquest is not to be regarded as supplying a new and vigorous impulse to a somewhat lethargic earlier development, but as effecting a complete transformation in the character of the borough community. The history of the English borough as an urban institution might, in fact, without much loss, be begun at 1066.[3] In considering the case presented for this novel and interesting view, it will be convenient to deal first with the evidence offered in proof of the essentially agricultural character of the normal borough in the Anglo-Saxon period.

[1] Those at Launceston and " Matele " in Cornwall (*D.B.* i. 120b, 1), and at Hoxne and Clare in Suffolk (*ibid.* ii. ff. 379, 389b). Launceston was afterwards reckoned as a borough.

[2] Above, p. 20.

[3] In his book *Borough and Town*, Dr. Stephenson has made his conclusion somewhat less sweeping. See below, p. 131.

Note on the "Little Borough" of Seasalter in Kent

The "parvum burgum" of Seasalter by Whitstable, which Domesday Book (i. 5a, 1) says belonged to the archbishop of Canterbury's kitchen, but the "Domesday Monachorum" of Christ Church (*Mon. Angl.*, i. 101a) calls "burgus monachorum," has been a stumbling-block to those seeking a criterion of the borough in the eleventh century. It was largely agricultural and the only population mentioned is forty-eight bordars. Being only a little over five miles from Canterbury, it never seems to have had a market nor is there any record of burgesses or burgages, of court or third penny.[1] Ballard concluded that it was impossible from the evidence of Domesday to define the difference between a borough on an agricultural estate and a village. The only distinction that appears in this case is that Seasalter had valuable (oyster) fisheries which yielded in 1086 a rent of 25s., increased to £5 by the date of the "Domesday Monachorum." This local industry probably accounts for its being charged at the higher rate of 1/10th, with boroughs and manors of ancient demesne, in the parliamentary taxation of the fourteenth century and so sometimes described as a borough in the chief taxers' accounts (Willard in *Essays in honour of James Tait*, p. 422). The use of the term in the eleventh century must either be explained similarly or as a case of that south-eastern survival of *burh* as a manor-house which is found in the well-known London names Aldermanbury and Bucklersbury and in the more obscure *burh* of Werrington in Essex, given by Edward the Confessor to Westminster Abbey (*Mon. Angl.*, i. 299, no. xxi.). A further possibility might seem to be raised by the mention in 1463 of the " Borg of Seasalter " (9 *Rep. H.M.C.*, app., pt. 1, p. 103b), for *borg(h)*, " tithing," and *burg*, *burh*, " borough," were inevitably confused in Kent. But the evidence is too late for any safe inference.

---

[1] It was a liberty and so not in any hundred. Fordwich is also described as a small borough in Domesday Book (i. 12a, 2), but it had ninety-six masures, *i.e.* burgess tenements, in 1066.

III

THE BOROUGH FIELDS AND PASTURES

In the article [1] to which reference has already so often been made, Dr. Stephenson finds no difference between the hundred court of the borough and those outside it, and sees in this a confirmation of his main thesis that the Anglo-Saxon borough, with a few exceptions in the south-east, was merely a walled microcosm of the rural world without. Domesday Book, he claims, shows that it had the same social and economic structure as the countryside.[2] Trade played little part and the burgesses were still essentially an agricultural group. It was only the growth of commerce stimulated by the Norman Conquest which transformed such groups into urban communities, towns in the modern sense of the word.

That the student of burghal history, no less after than before the Conquest, " has fields and pastures on his hands " we learnt long ago, but it is new doctrine, unknown to Maitland, that in the middle of the eleventh century they were being cultivated by peasant burgesses for their richer fellows. The evidence offered for this view consists substantially of the mention in Domesday Book of "burgesses outside the borough" at the small Devon boroughs of Barnstaple, Lydford, and Totnes,[3] and of bordars at Buckingham, Huntingdon, and Norwich. Of the former, it is only those at Totnes, a mesne borough since the Conquest, who are reported to be *terram laborantes*, and even they may have been cultivating it for themselves or for the whole of the burgesses. Buckingham

---

[1] *E.H.R.* xlv. (1930), 177 ff.; *Borough and Town*, pp. 111 ff.

[2] For his similar deduction from the *tuns* of the early grants of land in Canterbury and Rochester, see above, p. 7. It is more plausible at that date, but the amount of agricultural land there could have been within the walls is greatly exaggerated.

[3] The in-burgesses were respectively 40, 28 and 95, the out-burgesses 9, 41 (not 48 as Professor Stephenson says (p. 179)), and 15 (*D.B.* i. 100a, 2 ; 108b, 1). The further suggestion that the *burgenses Exonie urbis* who had outside the city 12 carucates of land (*ibid.* 100a, 1) were individual rich burgesses, employing such out-burgesses, is surely rash. See below, p. 114.

was a small borough on a royal manor,[1] like those of the south-west, the bordars belonged to the manor and are carefully distinguished from the burgesses. So are the 100 bordars at Huntingdon who indeed are expressly said to be subordinate to the burgesses (*sub eis*), though helping them in the payment of the king's geld.[2] The 480 bordars of Norwich who first appear in 1086, contrasted with the burgesses as paying no custom owing to poverty, were clearly former burgesses impoverished by the rebellion, fire, taxation and official extortion which had almost halved the burgess body in twenty years.[3] They had lost all burgess qualification and become mere cottagers,[4] getting their living, we must suppose, in the minor employments of town life. A similarly impoverished class of " poor burgesses " at Ipswich and Colchester is claimed by Dr. Stephenson as evidence that the Domesday compilers used " burgensis " and " bordarius " indifferently, but is really proof of a careful distinction, for, unlike the Norwich bordars, these poor burgesses, though they had ceased to pay the full custom, were still able to pay a poll tax.[5] In any case, this class could have found little agricultural work at Norwich or Ipswich, for both had a singularly small amount of borough arable.

It is true that this arable at Derby and Nottingham was divided (*partita*) between a fraction of the burgesses, about a sixth in the first case and a fifth in the other, but these were not rich landowners for their " works " (*opera*) and, according to one possible interpretation of a difficult passage, their rent, were part of the royal revenue nor were they bordars for, at least at Nottingham in 1086, they had bordars under them.[6] They ought perhaps rather to be compared with the lessees of borough land of whom we hear at Huntingdon, where the officers of the king and the earl seem to have allotted the leases among the burgesses.[7] The tenure of the twenty-one burgesses (out of 720) of Thetford who held more than six

---

[1] " Buchingeham cum Bortone " (*D.B.* i. 143a, 1). Bourton may mark the site of the southern of the two forts built there by Edward the Elder (*Place-Names of Bucks.*, p. 60).

[2] *D.B.* i. 203a, 1. These bordars, whose existence is only mentioned for 1086, are not definitely said to have worked in the fields, which the burgesses cultivated (*ibid.* 2).   [3] *Ibid.* ii. 116b, 117b.

[4] Borde, " hut," " cottage " had no inherent rural meaning.

[5] *D.B.* ii. 290, 106b. At Dunwich in 1086 there were 236 burgesses and 178 *pauperes homines*. The population had largely increased since 1066 when there were only 120 burgesses (*ibid.* ii. 311b).

[6] *Ibid.* i. 280a, 1. These twenty bordars are mentioned in connexion with the agriculture of the burgesses.   [7] *Ibid.* f. 203a, 2.

ploughlands of the king there is not clear, but this was in 1086 and they are not said to have had bordars.[1] In short, the attempt to show from Domesday Book that the Anglo-Saxon borough contained a considerable element of peasants in subjection to richer townsmen and that it was a matter of indifference whether these peasants were called bordars or burgesses cannot be sustained. The contention that " burgess " at this date meant no more than an inhabitant or contributory of a borough or walled vill must be made good, if at all, by other arguments.

The importance of " fields and pastures " even to the eleventh century borough can easily be exaggerated. At the Conquest much borough territory was in the hands of magnates, lay and ecclesiastical. This was perhaps inevitable where the territory was wide and included an outer belt of pure country. Queen Edith and Earl Gurth had had granges of four and two ploughlands respectively,[2] and the abbey of Ely the manor of Stoke, comprising three,[3] in the half-hundred of Ipswich. In the outer ring of Colchester hundred Godric " of Colchester," perhaps a wealthy citizen, had held Greenstead and, according to the burgesses in 1086, five hides in Lexden which had been rated with the city in 1066 but no longer paid its share of the farm.[4] The wide and rather barren tracts of arable and pasture which the king and earl are recorded as holding at Thetford[5] were doubtless rated with the borough, but there is no indication that the burgesses had any agricultural interest in them. The six ploughlands held of the king by twenty-one of the burgesses in 1086[6] were probably nearer the town. The remoter land of Thetford was still national in 1086 save that the Conqueror had enfeoffed Roger Bigot with the earl's former share of the portion which lay in Norfolk, but the wide region west of York, afterwards known as the wapentake of the Ainsty, though it paid geld and shared in the *trinoda necessitas* with the citizens, was held before the Conquest almost entirely by Earl Morcar, the archbishop and other landowners.

Even the nearer fields and pastures which were all that many boroughs had inherited from a purely rural past did not always escape the encroachments of the manorial lord. There is evidence, more or less direct, of this process in Domesday Book, though the survey does not always take

---

[1] *D.B.* ii. 119. [2] *Ibid.* ff. 290, 294. [3] *Ibid.* f. 382b.
[4] *Ibid.* f. 104. [5] *Ibid.* ii. 118b. [6] Above, p. 69.

note of the borough land, an incidental mention of sheriffs' requisition of burgess ploughs being, for instance, its only reference to the double fields of Cambridge.[1] It is a curious coincidence, if no more, that in a number of the larger boroughs, widely dispersed over the country, the amount of arable land, apart from royal demesne, was exactly or approximately twelve ploughlands.[2] Cambridge—on later evidence[3]—had about twenty, Nottingham and Thetford (?) six, and small boroughs like Torksey and Lydford only two. Yet Huntingdon with nearly four times as many burgesses as Lydford had hardly more.[4] Some boroughs, especially among those which were founded late on royal estates, Bridport for instance, had little or none. Maldon had apparently only 81 acres which was held by no more than 15 of about 180 burgesses who possessed houses.[5] Even Dorchester, an old Roman town, seems, as we have seen,[6] to have had no open fields of its own. But much more populous and important boroughs were little better provided with land. Norwich with its 1320 burgesses had no more than Maldon within its boundaries,[7] though it had another 80 acres in the neighbouring hundred of Humbleyard.[8] Ipswich, with 538 burgesses and 40 acres among them,[9] stands still lower in the scale. Nothing but abundance of urban employment will explain these figures.

In large boroughs like these the growth of suburbs may have reduced the arable area, but a more general cause was the extension of manorialism into town fields. At Ipswich the granges of Queen Edith and Earl Gurth perhaps intruded upon them.

This eating away of burghal arable probably began earliest round the old Roman cities. The oldest Canterbury charters

---

[1] *D.B.* f. 189a, 1. Later evidence shows that this does not mean that no custom was due from them. The survey records, however, that the lawmen and burgesses of Stamford had 272 acres free of all custom (*ibid.* i. 336b, 2) while the burgesses' land of Exeter paid it only to the city (*ibid.* i. 100a, 1).

[2] Exeter and Derby each 12, Lincoln, 12½ (excluding the bishop's ploughland), Colchester about 11½ (computed from details including 80 acres " in commune burgensium ").

[3] Maitland, *Township and Borough*, p. 54.

[4] *D.B.* i. 203a, 2. [5] *Ibid.* ii. 5b. [6] Above, p. 56.

[7] *D.B.* ii. 116. Not including 181 acres of arable and a little meadow belonging in alms to churches held by burgesses, 112 acres and meadow belonging to Stigand's church of St. Michael and 180 acres held by the king and the earl. [8] *Ibid.* f. 118.

[9] *Ibid.* f. 290. A further 85 acres belonged to the churches of the borough.

show that tenements in the city had appendant land outside
the walls, but Domesday Book records little such arable.
Much of the land on the northern and south-eastern sides of
the city now formed the large manors of Northwood and
Langport, belonging to the archbishop and the abbey of St.
Augustine's respectively.[1] Between them, they had no fewer
than 167 burgesses in the city, whose gable or ground rent
went to them, not to the king. The only land outside York
which its burgesses are said to have cultivated[2] belonged to
the archbishop. Ten ploughlands at Leicester, including
the greater part of the eastern field of the borough, were in
the fief of the bishops of Lincoln,[3] and had perhaps been so
when their see was in the town (680–869). The Countess
Judith's possession of six ploughlands outside it, belonging
to the borough, is only recorded for 1086,[4] but they may have
been held by her husband Waltheof before the Conquest.
At Lincoln, apart from the bishops *maneriolum* of Willingthorpe
or Westgate with its one ploughland,[5] which may or may not
have dated from before the Conquest, there were, it has been
seen, twelve and a half ploughlands in which the burgesses
had an interest, but four and a half of these had been granted
by 1066 to lawmen and churches.[6] In the latter they would
possibly pay an economic rent, but in the eight which were
demesne of king and earl the *landgable* of their town houses
might cover the agricultural appurtenances. Gloucester
seems to have had less than 300 acres outside its walls.[7]
Possibly the royal manor of the Barton of Gloucester, outside
its east gate, represented its older, wider territory.[8]

Of towns not of Roman origin or episcopal, few can have
had so little arable land as Oxford. Its northern suburb grew
up on land which from before the Conquest formed a rural
hundred, later known as Northgate Hundred and not incorporated with the borough until the sixteenth century. In
1066 the manors of Walton and Holywell in this hundred
came up to the north wall of the town. Maitland was inclined

[1] *D.B.* i. 5a, 1, 12a, 1.   [2] In part (*per loca*) : *D.B.* i. 298a, 2.
[3] *Ibid*. f. 230b, 2.   [4] *Ibid*. f. 230a, 1.
[5] *Ibid*. f. 336a, 2 ; *Registrum Antiquissimum*, ed Foster, i. 189, 268.
[6] *D.B. loc. cit.*   Queen Edith's tenure of the two carucates at Torksey
was temporary. They reverted to the royal demesne at her death.
[7] Blakeway, *The City of Gloucester* (1924), p. 99.   There were at least
300 burgesses in 1066 (H. Ellis, *Introd. to Domesday*, ii. 446).
[8] *Cf*. Barton by Bristol in the farm of which the issues of the borough
were included in 1086.

to fancy that they were formed out of the fields of an older, more agricultural Oxford.[1]

Where the borough arable had always been limited in amount, as at Huntingdon, manorialism was less likely to creep in.[2]

Too much stress must not be laid, therefore, upon the agricultural aspect of the Anglo-Saxon borough. Clearly there were some boroughs which were practically as urban as a modern town, while those which retained most arable land were often much less agricultural than they may seem since its cultivation was left to a small number of the burgesses. There is one conspicuous instance, however, in which the land is known to have been very generally distributed among them. This was at Colchester, where it was so important a feature that a complete census of these royal burgesses and the houses and land held by them was taken and included in Domesday Book.[3] The number of burgesses was 276 and the number of acres divided among them 1297 or not far short of eleven plough-lands. Round, anticipating Professor Stephenson, remarks : " The whole effect produced is that of a land-owning community, with scarcely any traces of a landless, trading element." [4] Closer examination modifies this impression, despite the complete absence of trade descriptions. In the first place nearly one-half of these burgesses, 124, had houses only and must in most cases have got their living otherwise than off the land. Secondly, the burgesses had often more houses than one, in two cases as many as ten and a half and thirteen. There were seventy-seven more houses than burgesses and their tenants must be added in part to the landless class, though perhaps they included the twenty-two burgesses who had land but no houses. Again, the land shares were usually small, only 8 acres per head on the average and less than half that for two-thirds of the landholding burgesses as the following table will make clear :—

[1] *Township and Borough*, p. 45. *Cf.* p. 7. He included Wolvercote, but this was in a different hundred.
[2] Only king and earl drew custom from the fields which " belonged " to the borough (*D.B.* i. 203a, 2).
[3] *Ibid.* ii. 104-6. The figures resulting are those of 1086. There may have been changes since 1066 which are not recorded.
[4] *V.C.H. Essex*, i. 417.

Landholding Burgesses.	Number of acres apiece.	Total acreage.
1	42	
22	20 to 30	907½
31	10 to 19	
98	½ to 9	389½
152		1297

We have only to compare these holdings with the villein's yardland of 30 acres to see that, as there was no question of impoverishment here, all paying the full royal customs, the land can only have been a subsidiary element of their livelihood, especially as those who had about as much as a villein were obviously the leading people in the town. The list is primarily rather one of tenements than of burgesses since, besides seven priests and some women, it includes the abbot of St. Edmunds and three lay Norman lords.

Round's further remark that many of these small holdings must have been distant from the walls suggests that he did not realize that they all lay, as it is pretty clear they must have done, in open fields belonging to the borough.[1] The outer rural zone of its territory, an addition of no great age,[2] was at this time largely, if not wholly, manorial.

The Colchester terrier enables us to get an idea of what the Cambridge fields must have been like before gifts and sales to monasteries and colleges, with other changes, had obscured their original features in the manner described so vividly by Maitland in *Township and Borough*.

It is very unlikely that there was a borough in England which still fitted into what has been called its arable " shell " more closely than Colchester did. Nevertheless the foregoing analysis tends to confirm the conclusions we have drawn from the evidence of Domesday as to burghal agriculture in general. It gives absolutely no support to Professor Stephenson's theory that, in boroughs where agriculture still prevailed, a class of dependent peasants, occasionally called burgesses in the general sense of inhabitants of a borough, cultivated the land of the richer men, who, he holds, are always so called in the survey. The theory, as we have seen, still more markedly breaks down where, as at Norwich, the agricultural shell has almost disappeared—though it is just here that

---

[1] A " Portmannesfeld " is mentioned in an early charter of the local abbey of St. John (Round, *op. cit.* p. 423).

[2] Above, p. 48.

Professor Stephenson finds nearly five hundred burgess peasants—and where, as at Maldon, it has never been more than a small appendage to a borough which had been cut out of a larger estate. The features in certain boroughs on which the theory is based are capable of other explanation.[1]

At Lincoln two of the lawmen held a ploughland apiece and a third was joint holder of another, but it is doubtful whether they ranked as burgesses.[2] Here, if anywhere, were the theory sound, one would expect mention of peasant burgesses or " bordars," but there is none. Nor do we hear elsewhere of these peasant burgesses, dependent on fellow burgesses, who, had they existed, must have become as unfree as rural bordars.[3] Manorialism in borough fields came from without not from within, and even this extraneous manorialism contained no threat to the personal or economic freedom of the burgess. On the contrary, for there is much truth in the remark of Maitland that " we may even regard an arable ' shell ' as an impediment to the growth of municipality." [4]

If the Anglo-Saxon boroughs, which had agricultural pasts, could lose more or less of their fields and yet be able to support such large populations, for those times, as many of them contained, it is clear that economically they were substantially urban and not agricultural units. Domesday supplies plenty of figures for estimates of these burghal populations, but they do not lend themselves to such precise calculations as we could wish. The numbers given are often those of messuages (*mansiones, masurae*) or more rarely houses, and it may be sometimes doubtful whether each messuage harboured one house or burgess only.[5] Moreover, the figures

---

[1] Above, p. 68. [2] See below, p. 87.

[3] If the poorer burgesses had had to cultivate richer burgesses' land, it might be thought that *a fortiori* they would have been called upon for the same service on the little demesne estates of arable, meadow and pasture, which the king or the king and earl reserved at Colchester (92 acres of arable, 10 meadow and 240 pasture and meadow : *D.B.* ii. 107), Lincoln (231 acres in land and 100 acres meadow : *ibid.* i. 336a, 2) and Nottingham (3 ploughlands and 12 acres meadow : *ibid.* 280a, 1). But where mentioned the cultivators are villeins and bordars of the ordinary rural type. *Cf.* Derby (*ibid.* 280a, 2—Litchurch).

[4] *Township and Borough*, p. 45.

[5] At Northampton it is stated that there were as many messuages as burgesses, and at Derby and Ipswich the equivalence of burgess and messuage is involved in the comparison of the state of things in 1066 and 1086. On the other hand, the " 140 burgesses less half a house " (*domus*) at Huntingdon who had only 80 haws or messuages (not 20 as Professor Stephenson reads) among them (*D.B.* i. 203a), and the three haws at Guildford where dwelt six men (*ibid.* f. 30a, 1) suggest that the half burgage

for baronial burgesses are not usually stated for both 1066 and 1086, as are usually those of the burgesses on royal demesne, but for the latter date merely. Nevertheless, by assuming the equation of burgess = tenement, choosing the clearer cases and occasionally using a 1086 figure with all reserves, some rough estimates may be reached which will be below rather than above the truth. The usual multiplication by five for the household has been adopted. The figures of course would be increased if the number of non-burgesses, who did not hold tenements rendering royal customs, could be estimated, but no evidence is available. As London and Winchester do not appear in the survey, York comes out easily first. Our estimate of the population on the royal demesne and in the archbishop's exempt " shire " is over 8000, and if the barons' burgesses were as numerous as twenty years afterwards, 700 or so would have to be added. Next in the list is Norwich, the most satisfactory figure, for it includes all *burgesses* in 1066, in number 1320, and gives a total population of 6600. Lincoln comes third with a royal burgess population alone of 5750, and as there were about 120 baronial burgesses in 1086, the city may have been only slightly less populous than Norwich. Thetford ranks fourth with a total population approaching 4750. There is a considerable drop to Ipswich which had, however, over 3000 burgess inhabitants, if we carry back the seventy-one baronial burgesses of 1086. It is abundantly evident that such populations must have been predominantly urban in occupations and means of subsistence.

The validity of Dr. Stephenson's theory can be tested in yet another way. If the Anglo-Saxon borough had been, as he supposes, essentially a group of agricultural units, each similar to the villein and bordar unit of the rural manor, we should expect in the one case as in the other to find the unit treated as a whole for purposes of taxation and charged with its due proportion of the danegeld laid upon the borough. But this was not the case. It is true that the borough was assessed for the tax in hides or carucates, like the open country, but, as Domesday clearly shows, there was never any question of the hide (carucate) or its fractions in the repartition of the geld among the burgesses. It was charged upon the house

of later times was already not unknown. At Colchester there were more houses than burgesses, but this was in 1086 (above p. 73). They were not " waste " houses, however, such as were many in the boroughs at that date.

within the walls,[1] or the messuage on which it was built,[2] any agricultural land outside being for this purpose, as it was perhaps usually for rent, regarded as merely an appendage of the urban tenement. The amount of money due upon the hidage of the borough was divided equally between these tenements.

The theory under discussion is, indeed, impossible to re-concile with the plain facts of Domesday Book. What we find there is a twofold division of the burgesses into king's tenants and tenants of external magnates. The theory involves a cross division into burgess landlords and their agricultural dependents, who might or might not be called burgesses, for which there is absolutely no direct evidence and indeed every presumption to the contrary. It is based upon a mistaken interpretation of certain passages in Domesday and a misunderstanding of some features—in part, temporary —of the urban life there described. Maitland's conclusion in the case of Cambridge still stands fast, *mutatis mutandis*, for early boroughs of the type which had a good deal of agricultural land :—

" Already in the Confessor's time it paid geld for a hundred hides : that is, it paid ten times what the ordinary Cambridge-shire village would pay. Clearly, therefore, in the eleventh century it was not a vill of the common kind ; its taxable wealth did not lie wholly in its fields. But fields it had. It was cast in an agrarian mould." [3]   In this respect Cambridge stands at one end of the scale. At the other end is Maldon where one-twelfth of the burgesses had (in 1086) little more than half a hide of land apiece and the rest " nothing beyond their houses in the borough." [4]

---

[1] As at Chester (*D.B.* i. 262b, 1).
[2] As at Shrewsbury (*ibid.* 252a, 1).
[3] *Township and Borough*, p. 54.
[4] *D.B.* ii. 5b. For Professor Stephenson's later admission of some urban character in towns such as Norwich, see below, p. 131.

IV

THE BURGESSES AND THEIR TENURE

OVER-EMPHASIS upon the agricultural aspect of the Anglo-Saxon borough and inadequate appreciation of its character as a *port* are not the only questionable features in the picture which Dr. Stephenson has drawn from Domesday Book. With Professor Stenton he has been so much impressed by the apparent variety of condition among its burgesses disclosed in the survey as to deny that *burgensis* was a technical term or had any reference to personal status.[1] Professor Stenton sees nothing more definite in it than " dweller in a borough." [2] Dr. Stephenson would add " or contributory thereto," perhaps to cover the case of that very doubtful class (at this date) of *burgenses ruremanentes*.[3] He is in full agreement, however, with Professor Stenton's statement that " there may have existed as much variety between the different burgesses of a borough as existed between the different classes of free tenant upon a manor in the open country." [4] Indeed he would go much further, for in his opinion a burgess might be landless and economically dependent on a landowner or even personally unfree. The uniform burgage tenure of the twelfth century could not exist in such conditions and was in fact a Norman innovation.[5]

Professor Stenton's view, though insufficiently founded on the one case of the Stamford sokemen,[6] who are not clearly proved to have been reckoned as burgesses, has some support from the East Anglian boroughs, but the tenurial variations found there, inconsistent as they are with the neatness of later burgage tenure, do not exclude common features which distinguish the burgess not only from the country freeholder,

---

[1] *E.H.R.* xlv. 180; *Borough and Town*, pp. 77 ff.
[2] *Lincolnshire Domesday*, ed. C. W. Foster, Introd., pp. xxxiv-xxxv.
[3] I cannot find in Domesday evidence of those groups of " foreign " burgesses of which Miss Bateson made so much (*E.H.R.* xx. 148 f.).
[4] *Lincolnshire Domesday, loc. cit.*
[5] *Op. cit.* pp. 188-90.   [6] See p. 80.

but also from other inhabitants of the borough and so invalidate his definition of *burgensis*.

The more sweeping conclusions of Dr. Stephenson from the Domesday evidence are too largely based upon that portion of it which immediately applies to the state of things in 1086 after twenty years of baronial exploitation. A close investigation of what is definitely reported for the age before the Conquest will, I think, show that the most essential features of burgage tenure, free holding of building plots, with small agricultural appurtenances, at low and more or less uniform rents, subject to various public services, was substantially in existence at that date. Before entering upon this inquiry, however, it will be well to see what light Domesday and the Anglo-Saxon sources have to throw upon the personal condition of the pre-Conquest burgesses.

1. Social Status of the Anglo-Saxon Burgesses

As might be expected from their numbers and the severe condensation of the survey, especially in Great Domesday, burgesses are seldom mentioned by name. Even in the much more expansive Little Domesday, the list of some 276 king's burgesses of Colchester,[1] already mentioned, stands quite alone. Lists of this kind may indeed have been prepared in other cases and omitted in the final compilation. From such a list may very likely have been derived the names of the burgesses of Winchester and their holdings T.R.E. which are recorded in the survey of the city drawn up under Henry I.[2]

Even when one or two burgesses are subjects of specific mention they are not named except in Little Domesday and there but rarely. An Edstan is mentioned at Norwich as the only king's burgess who could not alienate his land without royal license.[3] Among the holders of churches at Ipswich in 1086 one Cullingus is distinguished as a burgess.[4] Another burgess of that borough, Aluric, is entered elsewhere as having inherited from his father Rolf, 12 acres in the neighbouring village of Thurlston.[5]

---

[1] See above, p. 73.   [2] *D.B.* iv. 531 ff.
[3] *Ibid.* ii. 116. He was an important person and very probably the king's reeve (W. Hudson, *Records of Norwich*, i. 1). His land was, it may be suggested, official reeveland.
[4] A distinction not easily reconciled with the explanation of *burgensis* proposed by Professors Stenton and Stephenson (above, p. 78).
[5] *D.B.* ii. 446. For two or three named burgesses of Lincoln, *cf.* p. 87, n. 5.

If the inclusion of Aluric's little rural holding in the *terra vavassorum* is to be taken as indicating his status, the case is of special interest as evidence that the English burgess was not always a simple freeman.   For in a legal collection not of later date than 1135 the *vavasseur* is identified with the " average " or " lesser " thegn of Anglo-Saxon times,[1] while Professor Stenton sees in the *vavassores* " the predecessors of the *milites* on whom the administration of royal justice had come to depend before the end of that (the twelfth) century." [2] This little piece of evidence fits in neatly with that which comes from Hereford where the burgesses who had horses in King Edward's day were subject to the lesser thegn's heriot of horse and arms.[3]   We are not entitled to infer, however, that this type of burgess was more than exceptional. London indeed had its *burhthegns*,[4] and Liebermann at least took the thegns of the Cambridge thegn gild to have been burgesses [5] and not, as Maitland suggested, merely members of a Cambridgeshire club.[6]   The Norman sheriff Picot exacted thegnly heriots, including horse and arms, from the Cambridge lawmen, but his English predecessor had taken only 20s. in money from each.[7]   Even this was much higher than the average country socager's heriot of a year's rent, but there is still some doubt whether the lawmen were ever reckoned as burgesses.   Those of Stamford are said to have shared the use of the borough fields with the burgesses.[8]   In any case, though highly privileged, they were not of thegnly rank, for their wergild was apparently that of the ordinary freeman.[9] Another privileged body in that borough whose inclusion among the burgesses remains doubtful, despite Professor Stenton's acceptance, was that of the sokemen who had seventy-seven messuages in full ownership (*in dominio*) free from all royal custom save the amends of their forfeitures, heriot, and toll.   These largely exempt tenements are clearly contrasted with the hundred and forty-seven of the preceding clause, which corresponds to the normal enumeration of royal

---

[1] II Cnut, 71, 2 ; Liebermann, *Ges.* i. 358, ii. 501 ; Chadwick, *A.-S. Institutions*, p. 82 n.   [2] *English Feudalism, 1066–1166*, p. 22.

[3] *D.B.* i. 179a, 1.   The three marks " relief " of the Derbyshire or Nottinghamshire thegn with six or less manors, " whether he dwells within or without borough " (*D.B.* i. 280b, 1) is a different matter.

[4] Liebermann, *Ges.* ii. 571, § 9a ; W. Page, *London*, pp. 219 f. ; below, p. 257.   [5] Liebermann, *loc. cit.*   [6] *D.B. and B.*, p. 191.

[7] *D.B.* i. 189a, 1.   [8] *Ibid.* f. 336b, 2.   See below, p. 87.

[9] So Liebermann (*Ges.* ii. 565, § 4a, 732, § 6a) ; but may it not have been that of their men ?

burgesses or houses in other boroughs, for these are expressly stated to have rendered all customs. The importance of the distinction will appear in the next section.

The mention at Nottingham of *domus equitum* contrasted with *domus mercatorum* [1] has been thought to reveal the presence among the burgesses there of members of that class of semi-military retainers of Anglo-Saxon nobles who were known as *cnihts*. The *cnihtengilds* of London, Winchester, and Canterbury, the last of which appears as early as the ninth century sufficiently attest the importance of the part they played in burghal history,[2] but the Nottingham identification is almost certainly mistaken. The *equites* only occur on the lands of the Norman barons, there is no mention of pre-Conquest *antecessores*, and there seems every probability that they were not Englishmen at all but the *milites* or armed French retainers of the barons.[3]

It will be noticed that the difficult passages we have been discussing all refer to boroughs which, save Hereford, had been settled or strongly influenced by Danes, and that burgesses of thegnly rank are only discerned with certainty at Hereford and perhaps, in one case, at Ipswich. Nor do we find them in the other western boroughs, for the heriot of 10s., which was exacted from the horseless burgess of Hereford, was universal at Shrewsbury and Chester. Its more advanced position against the Welsh may perhaps account for the special armed class of burgesses at Hereford.

Wergilds afford a simpler indication of social standing in Anglo-Saxon times than heriots do, but unfortunately Domesday throws no direct light upon burgess wergilds, unless indeed the Stamford lawmen were burgesses and this, as we have seen, is doubtful. Still, as they were apparently not thegns, we may safely infer that the less privileged burgesses were not. The first clear mention of a burgess wergild is that of the Londoners in Henry I's charter to the city. This sum of 100 Norman shillings was somewhat higher than the wergild of the ordinary West Saxon or Mercian freeman (*ceorl*) before the Conquest,[4] but far below that of

---

[1] *D.B.* i. 280a, 1.   [2] See below, pp. 120-22.

[3] For the use of *eques* for *miles* in the Norman period see Stenton, *English Feudalism*, p. 155, and Ballard, *An Eleventh Century Inquisition of St. Augustine's, Canterbury*, Introd., p. xviii (Brit. Acad. Records, vol. iv.).

[4] The 200 shillings of the English ceorl's wergild were only of 5d. in Wessex and 4d. in Mercia, and the sum was therefore equivalent to £4 3s. 4d. and £3 6s. 8d. Norman respectively.

the thegn.[1] Liebermann, in his glossary under London,[2] regarded its £5 wergild as pre-Conquestual and a southern equivalent to the £8 of the thegns of the Cambridge gild, whom he took to be the upper class of burgesses there, but in the article Wergild,[3] apparently realizing the difficulties which this suggestion raised, he seems to associate it with Norman alterations in wergilds. It is to be noticed that, whatever may have been the case before the Conquest, there was no distinction of wergild among the London citizens after it.

Although the mention in 1018 of the *witan* of the boroughs of Devon [4] is sufficient to show that the aristocratic organization of the borough community in the Norman age was no new thing, it is impossible to draw a clear picture of the upper class in the boroughs from such scanty and ambiguous evidence as we have been putting together. The most direct glimpse we get of it in Domesday is perhaps the statement that the twelve judges of Chester were taken from the men of the king and the bishop and the earl,[5] but it would be highly dangerous to make inferences from this even to other boroughs in which all three were interested.

As for the mass of the burgesses, their fully free status is clearly established by the evidence of Domesday, the almost complete absence of any private service for their tenements save rent, the frequent mention of their power to sell them and the rarer references to mortgages and in some East Anglian boroughs the striking correspondence of the terms in which their position is stated to those used of freeholders elsewhere, all this leaves no doubt that they must be classed, *mutatis mutandis* with the freemen who held by what came to be known as socage tenure, where that prevailed and with similar but more burdened freeholders elsewhere. Undue stress has been laid in criticism of this view upon the hunting and guard services required from the burgesses of Hereford and Shrewsbury during royal visits, the summer reaping on an adjacent royal manor by the former and the *merchet* payable on the marriage of their daughters by the latter. The demands made upon the freemen, within and without the boroughs, varied with local conditions. In the western frontier-land they were inevitably more onerous than, to go to the other

---

[1] Six times that of the *ceorl*.   [2] *Ges.* ii. 571, § 9a.

[3] *Ibid.* p. 732, § 5. The £5 *burhbrece* (more probably *borhbryce*) of Ethelred II's London law (*ibid.* i. 234) was not, as Miss Bateson supposed (*E.H.R.* xvi. (1901), 94), a wergild (see Liebermann, *op. cit.* iii. 165).

[4] Above, p. 42.   [5] *D.B.* i. 262b.

end of the scale, in Scandinavianized East Anglia. The services exacted were mostly of a public character ; the hunting and reaping services, which the Normans regarded as servile, were among those required from thegnly lords of manors in the land between Ribble and Mersey [1] and *merchet*, as Maitland showed long ago, was being paid in Northumberland as late as the thirteenth century by men who held whole vills in thegnage.[2]   It should be noted, too, that such services—though not apparently *merchet*—were laid upon the burgesses of Hereford indifferently, with no exception for those who had the horse and arms of the thegn.

More pertinent to the question at issue are the half-dozen cases collected from Domesday by Professor Stephenson of what he terms villein-burgesses, doing some sort of agri-cultural service.[3]   There are really only four in which work on the land is more or less clearly indicated, for the Tewkesbury burgesses at Gloucester " servientes ad curiam " were no more rendering agricultural service than the bishop of Worcester's forty-five demesne houses in that city which rendered nothing " nisi opus in curia episcopi," [4] and the *servitium* which Nigel's five haws at Arundel gave instead of rent is equally vague nor need their occupants have been burgesses.   We might almost deduct a third, for the Wichbold burgesses in Droitwich did only two days' boon work in the year on their manor besides " serving at court."   Such occasional agri-cultural service is indicative of free tenants not of villeins. The remaining three cases are stronger.   That of Steyning in Sussex is perhaps, however, capable of another interpretation than Professor Stephenson's.   In that borough, belonging to Fécamp abbey, it is said that 118 masures " ad curiam operabantur sicut villani T.R.E.," [5] but the Worcester " opus in curia " suggests a non-agricultural service in this instance also, while " sicut villani " need only mean " as villeins do." It was the duty of the West Derby thegns to build the king's houses " sicut villani," [6] but that did not make them villeins. The somewhat similar Tamworth passage is not, however, open to this explanation, for the eight burgesses belonging in 1086 to the king's neighbouring manor of Drayton (Basset) " ibi operantur sicut *alii* villani." [7]   Possibly we have here

---

[1] *D.B.* i. 269b, 2.   [2] *E.H.R.* v. (1890), 630 ff.
[3] *Ibid.* xlv. 189 *n.*   [4] *D.B.* i. 173b, 1.
[5] *Ibid.* f. 17a, 2.   [6] *Ibid.* f. 269b, 2.
[7] *Ibid.* f. 246b, 2.

a glimpse of a transition period in the conversion of a villein into a fully free burgess, when, if his manor was near, he did not immediately escape from all his customary duties there. The two Shrewsbury burgesses who were cultivating St. Julian's half-hide at Shelton [1] were certainly doing agricultural work, but they were paying rent and were clearly not of villein status.

It may be noted, in conclusion, that in all the six cases but one (Steyning) the service is stated as obtaining in 1086 only, and is not necessarily therefore of Anglo-Saxon origin. And even if it were, the freedom of these burgesses from the cultivation of (at least) manorial " yardlands " placed them in a position very different to that of the purely agricultural villein. They were, too, an almost negligible minority [2] among the thousands of burgesses enumerated in Domesday. It is unsafe to argue without further proof, as Dr. Stephenson does, that these cases are only casual records of a more widespread custom and further evidence that the Anglo-Saxon borough was, socially and tenurially, as lacking in uniformity as the countryside. It is evidence that burgage tenure in its fullest form had not been attained in the eleventh century, but an equal want of uniformity in its successor might be deduced from the emancipation of the burgesses of Lancaster from ploughing and other servile customs as late as 1193,[3] the release of the burgesses of Leicester by the earl their lord from a mowing commutation about the same date [4] and the reservation of a day's ploughing and a day's mowing every year by the founder of the new borough of Egremont c. 1202.[5]

The *villanus* even on his manor, and *a fortiori* in a borough, was personally a free man, but if Professor Stephenson's interpretation of a passage in Little Domesday holds good, a burgess might be a serf, and a serf in the eleventh century, though not a mere chattel, was " in the main a rightless being," a slave. The passage in question runs : " In the same borough [Ipswich] Richard [Fitz-Gilbert] has thirteen burgesses whom Phin had T.R.E. ; over four of these he had soke and sake, one of them is a *serf* (*servus*), and over twelve commendation only." The numbers, if not also the sense, have suffered from over-compression, but taking the wording

---

[1] *D.B.* i. 253a, 1.
[2] The total is 154, of which 118 (if each haw had its burgess) were at Steyning.
[3] *B.B.C.* i. 95.   [4] *Ibid.* p. 94.   [5] *Ibid.* p. 95.

as it stands, it is plain that the burgess, though a serf in 1086, had not been one or at least not known to have been one twenty years before, for a serf could not be subject to sake and soke or free to commend himself to a lord. If this is not merely an instance of that degradation of status which was so common an effect of the Norman Conquest, it may be the earliest recorded case of the reverse process, the enfranchisement of the serf in the free air of the town.

To sum up. There is little direct or unambiguous evidence about the personal condition of the burgesses before the Conquest. Yet it is not impossible to make some more or less general statements on this head. There were certainly men of thegnly rank among these burgesses in some boroughs, and the rest, the great majority, must necessarily, unless altogether unjustifiable inferences are drawn from the Ipswich " serf-burgess," have been ordinary free men. For there was no middle rank between thegn and ceorl. In this aspect there was no distinction between burgess and villein, their wergild was the same. Another kind of distinction was, however, drawn between them by their different relation to the land and this was reflected in their heriots. The agricultural villein's heriot was his best beast,[1] while even in those western boroughs which diverged most widely from later standards of borough freedom, money heriots only were required from the ordinary burgesses. This contrast, which was vastly accentuated by the deterioration of the villein's status under Norman manorialism, did not indeed extend to the rural rent-paying tenant, for his heriot was also a money one,[2] yet conditions peculiar to the boroughs had long been drawing other, though far less sharp, lines between the rental tenures which the Normans distinguished as burgage and socage. The very existence of the former before the Conquest has been denied, but the sceptics have allowed themselves to be so impressed by the developments of two centuries as to overlook completely the essential unity of a nascent and a fully organized system.

---

[1] *Leis Willelme*, 20, 3 ; Liebermann, *Ges.* i. 507. Liebermann strangely states that burgesses paid their best beast as heriot until released from it by the crown in the twelfth century (*ibid.* ii. 307 *s.v.* " Besthaupt ").

[2] A year's rent in the Norman period (*Leis Willelme*, 20, 4 ; Liebermann, *Ges.* ii. 507, 515, iii. 291).

2. THE "CUSTOM OF BURGESSES"

Recent scholarship insists that in the normal Domesday borough *burgensis* means no more than inhabitant of a walled town and has no reference to legal status. Domesday indeed mentions here and there besides burgesses classes with other names, lawmen, sokemen, villeins, bordars, cottars, and even serfs, but it is claimed that all these were burgesses, too, and that it is only the caprice of the compilers which usually reserves the name for the richer, landholding inhabitants.[1] This, however, is pure conjecture, for save in two ambiguous cases [2] Domesday never applies burgess and any one of these other terms interchangeably to a single person or group of persons. It is obviously risky to identify the " poor burgess " of one borough as of the same status as the villein or bordar of another. On the other hand, Domesday not infrequently distinguishes burgesses from some of these classes, from lawmen at Stamford,[3] from villeins at Nottingham,[4] from bordars at Norwich [5] and Huntingdon.[6] The same distinction is clearly implied in the statements that the bishop of Lincoln's houses in that city [7] and the abbot of Malmesbury's nine cottars (*coscez*) outside the walls of that borough [8] " gelded with the burgesses." It can be seen, too, in the singling out of two or three of the fifty odd baronial houses at Hertford as having formerly belonged to burgesses.[9]

Wherein lay this distinction ? The bishop of Lincoln's houses in his see town will give us a starting-point. They were exempt from all burghal " customs " and their tenants therefore did not rank as burgesses, though they were assessed with them to the (dane)geld.[10] No more did the abbot of Malmesbury's rural cottars or the hundred bordars at

---

[1] Above, p. 78.

[2] That of the " serf-burgess " at Ipswich (above, p. 84) and that of a lawman included among burgesses (below, p. 87, *n.* 5).

[3] Lagemanni et burgenses habent cclxxii acras sine omni consuetudine (*D.B.* i. 336b, 2).

[4] *Ibid.* f. 280 : fuerunt T.R.E. clxxiii burgenses et xix villani.

[5] *Ibid.* ii. 116b : modo sunt in burgo dclxv burgenses Anglici et consuetudines reddunt et cccclxxx bordarii qui propter pauperiem nullam reddunt consuetudinem.

[6] *Ibid.* i. 203a, 1 : In duobus ferlingis T.R.E. fuerunt et sunt modo cxvi burgenses consuetudines omnes et geldum regis reddentes et sub eis sunt c bordarii qui adjuuant eos ad persolutionem geldi.

[7] *Ibid.* f. 336a, 1.   [8] *Ibid.* f. 64b, 1.   [9] *Ibid.* f. 132a, 1.

[10] *Ibid.* f. 336a, 1. Remigius episcopus habet, 1 maneriolum . . . cum saca et soca et cum thol et theim super . . . et super lxxviii mansiones praeter geldum regis quod dant cum burgensibus.

Huntingdon who were under the burgesses (*sub eis*) and helped them in payment of the geld.

It would seem then that a burgess was not any resident in a borough, but one whose tenement was assessed to the borough customs or, as we should say, rates, though the eleventh-century customs cover a rather different range of payments. More direct statements of the burgess qualification come from Colchester and York. At Colchester, in 1086, Eudo *dapifer* was in possession of five houses which in 1066 had been held by burgesses, "rendering all custom of burgesses."[1] At York, apart from the archbishop, who had one of the seven "shires" of the city with all customs, it is noted that but one great thegn, four judges (for life only) and the canons had their houses on any freer terms than as burgesses (*nisi sicut burgenses*).[2] Here the customs had been little decreased by alienation. Even the bishop of Durham's house, for which full exemption was claimed in 1086, was declared by the burgesses not to have been more quit than a burgess house twenty years before, except that St. Cuthbert had the toll of himself and his men.[3] With these statements may be compared the Winchester evidence as to twelve persons dispossessed for the building of the Conqueror's new house; "these held houses and were burgesses and did (*faciebant*) custom."[4]

We seem now in a position to explain the distinction drawn at Stamford between the lawmen and the burgesses who shared 272 acres of arable land. The lawmen here as at Lincoln had extensive immunities.[5] So, too, had the sokemen who held seventy-seven *mansiones* here, and it may well be doubted whether they ranked as burgesses, despite Professor Stenton's opinion to the contrary.[6]

The number of burgesses could be depleted by inability to render custom as well as by special exemptions. The 480 *bordarii* at Norwich in 1086, who rendered nothing, had clearly once been burgesses, but were now impoverished cottagers.[7] The "minor burgesses" of Derby,[8] the "poor burgesses"

---

[1] *D.B.* ii. 106, 106b.   [2] *Ibid.* i. 298a, 1.
[3] *Ibid.*   [4] *Ibid.* iv. 534a.
[5] One of the three burgesses of Lincoln who, according to the Lincolnshire "Clamores" (*D.B.* i. 376a, 2), were mortgagees T.R.E. of land in Lawress hundred, was indeed Godred, a lawman of the city, but the others were not and a rural hundred court would not make fine distinctions.
[6] *The Lincolnshire Domesday*, ed. C. W. Foster and T. Longley (Lincs. Rec. Soc. 19), pp. xxxiv-xxxv.
[7] See p. 69; *borde*, "small house," "cottage" in Old French.
[8] *D.B.* i. 280a, 2.

of Ipswich,[1] and the burgesses rendering custom only from their heads of Colchester [2] had fared but slightly better, the latter rendering only a small poll-tax towards the king's geld, yet they had not wholly lost their burgess status. These were the wreckage of the Conquest and its sequel of castle-building, rebellion, heavy taxation and official and baronial extortion. Such losses of burgess customs are carefully noted in Domesday Book, for these customs formed an important part of the royal revenue and the diminished body of burgesses was struggling to avoid being forced to make up the deficiency. Nor was the king likely to make allowance for the compensation he was receiving in another direction. It was, as we have seen, one of the features which distinguished most old English boroughs from the ordinary vill that the king had to share their revenue with a high local official, almost always the earl, usually in the proportion of two to one.[3] These comital thirds, though not formally abolished, were by the escheat of earldoms practically crown revenue in most cases in 1086. Yet the formal distinction and the possibility of the creation of new earls must have stood in the way of any abatement of royal demands.

In holding that the burgess tenement rendering customs was the unit for the collection of this revenue in the eleventh as in the twelfth century, we have fortunately not to rely solely upon indirect inferences from Domesday data. The great survey itself incidentally supplies direct confirmation of this view. In its description of Chester it records an illuminating decision of the Cheshire county court that the land, on part of which the church of St. Peter in the market-place (de Foro) stood, had never, as its Norman grantee, Robert of Rhuddlan, claimed, been attached to an outside manor, was not therefore thegnland (teinland),[4] but belonged to the borough and had always been in the custom (in consuetudine) of the king and earl, as that of other burgesses was (sicut aliorum burgensium).[5] From this it may be concluded that

---

[1] D.B. ii. 290a.   [2] Ibid. ff. 106a, b.   [3] Above, p. 64.
[4] This was not the ordinary meaning of the term—" a plot carved out of the manorial territory for a special purpose " (Vinogradoff, English Society in the Eleventh Century, p. 371). The theinland at Winchester, on the bishop's fief, from which Herbert the Treasurer rendered T.R.H. the same custom as his antecessor T.R.E. (D.B. iv. 535a) perhaps belonged to this latter category.
[5] Ibid. i. 262b, 2. The manor in question was apparently West Kir[k]by in Wirral which Robert had given along with St. Peter's to the Norman abbey of Evroult. His gift was confirmed by William I and Henry I,

land in a borough which had long been recognized as not subject to this custom might be treated as part of a rural manor. Its inhabitants were not burgesses, and this seems to be confirmed by Robert's calling his three tenants on the land in dispute *hospites* in a charter executed before the decision and *burgenses* in one granted after it. The vital distinction in the early borough then according to this decision, was between customary land tenanted by burgesses and land free from custom which was not so tenanted.[1] The former was, strictly speaking, the only borough land. In two boroughs, remote from Cheshire, it seems possible to identify it as a definite area. A chance remark in Domesday that one of the messuages in Oxford held in 1086 by Walter Giffard had been granted to his *antecessor* by King Edward out of the eight virgates which were then *consuetudinariae* [2] carries back beyond the Conquest the " Octovirgate regis " from the custom of which twelfth-century kings made grants of landgable.[3] It is certainly no mere coincidence that at Wallingford King Edward had also eight virgates in which were 276 haws rendering gable and special service by road or water to four royal manors.[4] It would seem that in both cases this area represents the original lay-out of an artificial borough, the revenue from which was reserved for king and earl. In boroughs which had grown up within Roman walls, so simple a plan is not to be expected. Canterbury, for instance, was more an ecclesiastical than a royal city. The king received gable from no more than fifty-one householders, though he had jurisdiction over 212 more.[5] There seems to have been some hesitation locally as to whether the latter should be described as burgesses. The transcript of the original Domesday returns made for the monks of St. Augustine's calls them first *homines*, then *liberi homines* and perhaps finally *burgenses*, as Domesday Book does.[6] At Norwich and Thetford, probably too at Buckingham, there is evidence

as well as by Earl Ranulf I of Chester (Orderic Vitalis, *Hist. Eccl.*, ed. Le Prévost, iii. 19, v. 186 ; Davis, *Regesta Regum Anglo-Normannorum*, no. 140 ; Round, *Cal. of Docs. in France*, nos. 632, 636 ; *Chartulary of Chester Abbey*, ed. Tait (Chetham Soc.), pp. 288 ff.). It was not the ownership of the church and its land that was in dispute but the terms on which they were held.

[1] The territorial distinction is clearly expressed in a Thetford entry: abbas de Eli habet iii aecclesias et 1 domum liberae et ii mansuras in consuetudine, in una est domus (*D.B.* ii. 119a).

[2] *Ibid.* i. 154a, 1.

[3] H. E. Salter, *Early Oxford Charters*, nos. 66, 78, 96.

[4] *D.B.* i. 56a, 2. *Cf.* p. 17, *n.* 5.   [5] *D.B.* i. 2a, 1.

[6] *Inq. St. Augusta.*, ed. Ballard (British Acad. Record Series IV), 7, 9, 10.

that the burgesses, with few exceptions, were free to commend themselves to other lords but did not thereby transfer the king's customs to them.[1]

The customs lay upon the tenement or the house on it rather than on the burgess. These could be used interchangeably as in the extraordinary expression " 140 burgesses less half a house " at Huntingdon.[2] Norman magnates and religious houses appear in the list of king's burgesses at Colchester.[3] The burgess of Hereford who fell into poverty had to resign his house to the reeve, so that the king should not lose the service,[4] and this, though with perhaps less formality, happened elsewhere in hundreds of cases after the Conquest.

The rent—landgable or gable—of the house or tenement, was obviously the most fundamental of the " customs " rendered by the burgess, and in the Domesday description of Cambridge it is contrasted with the others grouped under the latter name.[5] As these rents were fixed and had been often usurped by the Norman barons, they are much more frequently mentioned separately than such variable customs as toll and judicial perquisites which are frequently concealed in the amounts of general or special farms.

There are cases of uniformity of rent either for the whole borough or for a particular class of tenement, as in later burgage tenure. Where, very exceptionally, Domesday states the amount of the gable per tenement, it is either a single figure, as at Malmesbury, where it was $10d.$,[6] and apparently at Lincoln, where it was $1d.$,[7] or two figures, as at Hereford, where masures within the walls paid $7\frac{1}{2}d.$ and those without $3\frac{1}{2}d.$, or three, as at Southampton, where they were $6d.$, $8d.$ and $12d.$ Where we have only the total amount of the gable and the number of houses no more than an average is possible. At Huntingdon some details point to a rate of $10d.$,[8] as at Malmesbury, but the totals do not confirm the suggestion, while at Exeter there are no separate totals, but frequent references to " king's custom " paid or withheld, which in

---

[1] See below, pp. 89, 92.   [2] *D.B.* i. 203a, 1.
[3] *Ibid.* ii. 104 ff.   [4] *Ibid.* i. 179a, 1.
[5] *Ibid.* 189a. 1.   De consuetudinibus hujus villae vii lib. et de Landgable vii lib. et ii orae et duo denarii.   [6] *Ibid.* i. 64b, 1.
[7] *Ibid.* f. 336a, 1 : de una quaque [mansione] unum denarium idest Landgable. This was taken by a privileged thegn, but $1d.$ was the general rate during the Middle Ages (Hemmeon, *Burgage Tenure*, p. 69).
[8] *D.B.* i. 203a, 1.   For wider variety in older towns, *cf.* p. 97.

every case but one was 8*d*.[1] The rate, uniform or average,
varies from the Lincoln 1*d*. up to what is almost exactly
16*d*., the ounce of the small mark, at Canterbury.[2] It was
15*d*. at Bath,[3] and within a farthing of that at Gloucester.[4]
An average of about 9½*d*. is observable at Wallingford,[5] and
(in 1086) in the Wiltshire boroughs of Calne [6] and Tilshead.[7]

The Lincoln rate continued to be the same throughout the
medieval period, and the total of the Cambridge hawgable
in 1485 was within a few shillings of that of the landgable in
1086.[8] That splitting of tenements and even of houses,
which made such rents generally lower in the later period,
had already begun. At Huntingdon there were no less than
139½ burgesses, *i.e.*, houses, on 80 haws or tenements.[9]

So far the evidence of Domesday and of the later Winchester
survey seems to confirm the broad distinction drawn by the
Chester judgement between land in the borough rendering
custom to king and earl, the tenants of which alone were
burgesses, and land which belonged to external manors and
was known as thegnland. The two surveys make it clear that
burgess houses normally rendered all customs and that there
were, even in 1066, other houses, varying in number in different boroughs, which were wholly or partially exempt.
The Norman compilers of Domesday, in accordance with their
feudal ideas, endeavoured to arrange the facts under two
categories (1) royal demesne (*dominium* or *terra regis*, (2)
baronial land (*terra baronum*).[10] But the loose Anglo-Saxon
system did not lend itself well to logical classification, the
compilers found themselves with many exceptions and cross-
divisions on their hands and their attempt to deal with these
is often far from clear. It was quite logical, indeed, to collect
under the second head the numerous cases of houses once
liable to all customs which the Norman barons had entered
upon with or without the king's license and were withholding
the customs. The burgesses of Hertford complained that

---

[1] *D.B.* i. 102a, 1 (Drogo of bp. of Coutances), 103b, 2 (abbot of Tavistock), 104a, 2 (Battle Abbey), 108b, 1 (Judhel), 110a, 2 (Wm. Chievre),
113b, 1 (Rich. (fitz Turold)), 115b, 2 (Tetbald), 116a, 2 (Alured (Brito)),
117a, 1 (Osbern (de Salceid)), 117a, 2 (Godebold).
[2] *Inq. St. August.*, p. 7.   [3] *D.B.* i. 87a, 2.   *Cf.* p. 111, *n.* 1.
[4] Ellis, *Introd. to Domesday*, ii. 446.   [5] *D.B.* i. 56a, 1.
[6] *Ibid.* f. 64b, 2.   [7] *Ibid.* f. 65a, 1.
[8] W. M. Palmer, *Cambridge Borough Docs.* I. lix.
[9] *D.B. loc. cit.*
[10] *E.g.* at Warwick : " the king has 113 houses in demesne and the
king's barons have 112 " (*D.B.* i. 238a, 1).

tenements formerly tenanted by burgesses had been unjustly taken from them (*sibi injuste ablatas*) by such aggressors,[1] which means that they had ceased to contribute to the customs for which the king held the burgesses responsible. At Gloucester some twenty-five houses which had rendered custom in 1066 were paying none twenty years later,[2] at Colchester only two out of sixty-six rendered full custom,[3] and at Exeter there is frequent mention of custom withheld (*retenta*).[4] Such cases were put on record at the instance of the burgess jurors who no doubt hoped that the king would be stirred up to reclaim his rights.[5] Norman usurpation, however, will not account for facts which conflict with that sharp distinction between *terra consuetudinaria* and thegnland which the Chester county court drew after the Conquest. Most of the Colchester houses on the *terra baronum* in 1086 had been held by external lords, thegns and others, in 1066, and a third of the number are expressly recorded to have been appurtenant to rural manors, yet they had, without exception, rendered all customs of burgesses. They had either been granted to these lords on condition of continued payment of customs or perhaps more probably the burgesses had merely commended themselves to them, and commendation, as we have seen in the cases of Norwich and Thetford, left the king's customs practically unaffected. This is what seems to have happened at Buckingham where the barons of 1086 had burgesses who were still rendering to the king money payments averaging about 3*d*. as well as larger rents to their Norman lords, as they had done to King Edward and the English thegns whom the Normans succeeded.[6] They are usually described as the "men" of the thegns, and this distinctly points to commendation. An absolutely clear instance is that of the twelve burgesses of Ipswich over whom the thegn Phin had nothing T.R.E. but commendation, and who "dwelt on their own land and rendered all custom in the borough."[7] Such tenements in the pre-Conquest borough formed a middle term

---

[1] *D.B.* i. 132a, 1.   On the other hand, a house, once a burgess's, given by the king to Harduin de Scalers, still rendered all custom.   For a transfer of a tenant by Henry I "de consuetudine regis in terram Rad. Roselli" see *Liber Winton.* in *D.B.* iv. 535a.   The record of a gift of houses in Exeter by William I to Baldwin the sheriff (*ibid.* i. 105b, 2, iv. 293) says nothing of the custom.   [2] *Ibid.* i. 162a, 1.

[3] *Ibid.* ii. 106b, 107.   [4] See p. 91, *n.* 1.

[5] Nor were they wholly disappointed, for the expressed purpose of the survey of Winchester ordered by Henry I was the recovery of such lost revenue (*D.B.* iv. 531a).   [6] *Ibid.* f. 143a, 1.   [7] *Ibid.* ii. 393a.

between land over which the king alone had lordship, *dominium* in the Norman sense and thegnland·free of custom as defined in the Chester ruling, but by 1086 it had been almost eliminated,[1] either by royal grants of exemption or, much more commonly, by baronial non-payment of customs.

In the case of commended tenements, then, there is no need for surprise when we find burgesses on the land of thegns, rendering customs to the king, even, exceptionally, in 1086. The " thegnland " of the Cheshire doomsmen,[2] on the contrary, was land for which it was claimed that it was not " customary " and therefore not borough land, though locally in the borough. In other words, Robert of Rhuddlan had maintained that the land in dispute did not merely " belong " to his manor of West Kir[k]by in the usual sense that it yielded a revenue to it, but was actually part and parcel of it, manorial not burghal land. Such a pretension was probably a novel Norman attempt at encroachment.

More difficult, at first sight, to reconcile with the Cheste ruling that the burgess was one who rendered custom to th$_s$ king and earl is the presence of burgesses upon land in borough$_s$ which was legally quit of such custom. The two great churche$_s$ of Canterbury, for instance, had large numbers of burgesse in the city, appurtenant to rural manors,[3] though by ancient privilege they took all customs on their land, the king receiving nothing.[4] The explanation seems to be that when burgess tenements were granted to churches and lay magnates along with the customs due from them, the customary tenure was not altered and the tenants would remain burgesses. An interesting confirmation comes from Lincoln. In 1086 the bishop's *maneriolum* and eighty-one houses were quit of all custom save danegeld.[5] But the " little manor " of Willingthorpe or Westgate is described as " *burgum* de Willigtorp " in a papal bull of 1126,[6] and this was no mere slip, for some forty years later the bishop's court decided that four *mansiones* there were free of all service " preter burgagium." [7] Clearly

---

[1] See p. 92.

[2] See above, p. 88.

[3] *E.g.* ninety-seven belonged to the Christ Church manor of Northwood (*D.B.* i. 5a, 1).

[4] Ipsae aecclesiae suas consuetudines quietas habuerunt R.E. tempore (*ibid.* f. 2a, 1 ; *Inq. St. August.*, p. 7).   [5] *D.B.* i. 336a, 1.

[6] *Reg. Antiquiss.*, ed. C. W. Foster (Lincs. Rec. Soc.), i. 188 ff. Domesday speaks of the " bishop's borough " at Chester which gelded with the city (*D.B.* i. 262b, 1).

[7] F. M. Stenton, *Danelaw Charters* (Brit. Acad.), p. 343.

H

some part, at least, of the " manor " was held of the bishop
by burgage rent.   All this may seem to conflict with the statement of Domesday that the bishops' houses merely gelded
with the burgesses, which almost seems to imply that their
tenants were not burgesses.   But here, as in the Chester
judgement, burgesses must be taken in the restricted sense of
royal burgesses whose customs formed the king's revenue.
The borough jurors and the Domesday commissioners were not
specially interested in houses or burgesses which by privilege
did not contribute to that revenue, which were not " in
consuetudine regis."   If the king's custom was being illegally
withheld, it was another matter.

Such complete exemptions as were enjoyed by the
Canterbury and Lincoln churches and by the archbishop of
York,[1] who had all the customs in one of the seven " shires "
of the city, and a third of those of a second, were of course
exceptional.   Not all churches were so highly favoured.
Of Ramsey abbey's thirty-two burgesses at Huntingdon,
twelve were indeed quit of all custom save (dane)geld, but the
rest paid 10d. each yearly to the king, all the other customs
going to the abbot.[2]   The abbot of Peterborough's privileges
in the Northamptonshire ward of Stamford included landgable and toll, but the other customs were the king's.[3]   Great
thegns like Merlesuain at York and Tochi at Lincoln might
have their halls quit of all custom, but the full privilege did
not extend to any other houses they might possess.   Tochi
had landgable from thirty, but the king retained toll and
forfeiture, if the burgesses swore truly in 1086.[4]   On the other
hand, three thegns of Kent shared with Queen Edith and the
great churches the right to all customs on their tenements
in Canterbury.[5]   The Queen also had seventy houses in Stamford free of everything except baker's custom ((consuetudo)
panificis).[6]

In all these cases, the tenure of the houses remained customary burghal tenure whether the whole or only part of the
customs were alienated by the crown.   The houses might
revert to it, Queen Edith's being held only for life were certain
to do so.   The revenue from the houses was assigned towards

---

[1] D.B. i. 298a, 1.   [2] Ibid. f. 203a, 1.

[3] Ibid. f. 336b, 2.   For burgesses rendering full customs to the king
though on the abbot of Winchester's demesne in that city, see D.B. iv. 534a.

[4] Ibid. i. 336a, 1.   [5] Ibid. f. 2a, 1 ; Inq. St. August. p. 9.

[6] D.B. i. 336b, 2.

her dower, just as two-thirds of the revenue of Exeter was earmarked for it.[1]

To trace an institution beyond the Norman Conquest is to find oneself in an atmosphere of dimmer conceptions and less well-defined boundaries than prevailed afterwards, but it is at least clear that the division of really practical importance in the pre-Conquest borough was not between king's land and land held by churches and thegns, but between land which paid custom in whole or in part to the king and earl and land that was wholly exempt. King's land might be, though it rarely was, exempt [2] and, as we have seen, land held by subjects quite commonly rendered full customs. Domesday's sharp distinction between *terra regis* and *terra baronum* in boroughs was a result of the Conquest. The Anglo-Saxon king, like his Norman successor, was chiefly interested in the land that rendered custom to him, but in his time the land " in consuetudine regis " was not, as it had virtually become by 1086, identical with the land over which he had sole lordship, the land of his demesne, in Norman language.

As the whole administration of the Anglo-Saxon borough turned upon the customs and these were " the customs of the burgesses," who are distinguished from episcopal tenants and other classes of men living in some boroughs, it is impossible to agree with Professors Stenton and Stephenson that *burgensis* before the Conquest had no technical meaning. In maintaining that the term was without reference to legal status, Dr. Stephenson relies chiefly on the mention in some Domesday boroughs of considerable numbers of landless burgesses, poor men, villeins and bordars, even a serf. But, as we have seen,[3] none of these, save a few villeins,[4] existed before the Conquest. They were mostly the result of disturbances set up by that great change. Nor are they called burgesses in 1086, unless they contributed something to the king's custom, if it were only a penny on their heads. In one case this element was actually created by the rapid growth of a borough after the Conquest. Dunwich with its 120 burgesses in 1066 had

---

[1] *D.B.* i. 100a, 1.

[2] There were two such houses at Winchester: one held T.R.E. by Stenulf the priest, and the other by Aldrectus frater Odonis (*D.B.* iv. 533b).

[3] Above, pp. 84, 88.

[4] The nineteen villeins at Nottingham in 1066 are distinguished from the burgesses and were probably the predecessors of the eleven villeins who were cultivating in 1086 the ploughland once belonging to King Edward (*D.B.* i. 280a, 1), the nine villeins mentioned at Derby (*ibid.* col. 2) were on the adjacent royal manor of Litchurch.

grown in the next twenty years into a town of 236 burgesses and 178 " poor men." [1]   Of course such a class of non-burgesses is found in most, if not all, boroughs throughout the Middle Ages and later.

It is even more misleading to convert the great majority of the burgesses of Maldon into such poor burgesses, because (in 1086) they " held nothing beyond their houses in the borough." [2]   This was a case of a borough with a very small appendage of agricultural land, and houses of course stand here for messuages in the town.   Maldon was an early case of a borough with practically no agricultural " shell." [3]   It is therefore on late and irrelevant evidence that Professor Stephenson arrives at his conclusion that *burgensis* in the Anglo-Saxon period " meant nothing more than an inhabitant or contributory to a borough." [4]   This period, so far as the Domesday evidence relating to it goes, knew no burgesses who were not holders of messuages either rendering customs to the king or some other lord or to both or in rare cases expressly exempt from payment.

3. Tenure by Customs and Burgage Tenure

If the pre-Conquest burgess was a freeman who held a messuage and house in a borough, with or without a share in its fields, by the render of customs of which a money-rent or landgable was the most vital, the general likeness of his tenure to the burgage tenure of the twelfth century seems sufficiently obvious.   Dr. Stephenson, however, with his conception of the ordinary Anglo-Saxon borough as only a piece of the countryside walled off and exhibiting the same patchwork of tenure, refuses to see any resemblance save in a few exceptional boroughs.   Burgage tenure, in his opinion, was as French in origin as in name.   He rejects the late Dr. Hemmeon's argument from the continuity of the landgable in burgage tenure on the ground that it was equally the rent payable by the *geneat* of the *Rectitudines* who was subject to all kinds of onerous services as well as the gable.   " Really to mark burgage tenure," he says, " landgable must be a heritable money rent in return for all service." [5]   If that be

---

[1] *D.B.* ii. 311b.   [2] *Ibid.* f. 5b.
[3] See above, p. 71.   [4] See p. 78.
[5] *E.H.R.* xlv (1930), 186.   Hemmeon did not claim that the fully developed burgage tenure existed before the Conquest, but insisted on the presence of its most essential feature in the landgable : " the lands

so, there was as little real burgage tenure in the early years of the twelfth century as before the Conquest. The Winchester survey of Henry I notes no change in the several *consuetudines*, in addition to landgable, for which the burgess was liable under Edward the Confessor. It was the king's expressed intention to have them all enforced.[1] They included other monetary dues than the landgable, the *brugeld* or brewing money [2] and the *fripeni* [3] together with personal services, not merely the town watch (*wata*),[4] but carrying duty (*avra, avera*) [5] and feeding prisoners (*pascere prisonem*).[6] The landgable itself was paid, if paid at all, not at the uniform rate characteristic of new Norman boroughs, but at the various rates which had obtained in 1066, of which 6*d*. per house is the most prominent. In other respects, too, there was actually less uniformity than there had been half a century before, at any rate in the heart of the city. Two-thirds of the houses in the High Street which had been inhabited by burgesses rendering full customs had passed into other hands and were paying nothing. " Boni cives," it was complained in some cases, had been replaced by " pauperes." [7] Nothing had been done and nothing of course could be done to get rid of the old church sokes which were the greatest obstacles to the unitary development of the city. Still, untidy as were Winchester arrangements under Henry I, judged by the standard of small Norman *bourgs*, there is every reason to believe that it could already be described as having burgage tenure. There is no likelihood that contemporary York showed more uniformity and fewer survivals of the past, yet Henry in the last decade of his reign confirmed to the men of Beverley " *liberum burgagium*

in the boroughs were held not by leases nor in base tenure, but by this fixed heritable money rent and seldom by any additional services. This is burgage tenure " (*Burgage Tenure in England*, p. 162).

[1] Henricus rex uolens scire quid rex Edwardus habuit omnibus modis Wintonie in suo dominico . . . volebat enim illud inde penitus habere (*D.B.* iv. 531).

[2] This was a Hereford custom in 1066 (*ibid.* i. 179a, 1). It was closely associated with the landgable (*ibid.* iv. 531a, 539b). It appears (as brugable) in the same association at Oxford under Stephen (Salter, *Early Oxford Charters*, no. 66) and as brugavel and brithengavel at Exeter throughout the Middle Ages (J. W. Schopp and R. C. Easterling, *The Anglo-Norman Custumal of Exeter* (1925), pp. 21, 30). It was abolished at Marlborough in 1204 (*B.B.C.* i. 151). *Cf.* the aletol of Rye (*ibid.* p. 97).

[3] The tithing penny of the frankpledge system. See N. Neilson, *Customary Rents*, pp. 170-1 (Oxford Studies, ed. Vinogradoff).

[4] *E.g. D.B.* iv. 534b.   [5] *Ibid.* p. 533a.

[6] *Ibid.* p. 537b. Henry I exempted the citizens of Rouen from this (Round, *Cal. of Docs. in France*, p. 32).   [7] *D.B.* iv. p. 532.

secundum liberas leges et consuetudines burgensium de Eboraco . . . sicut Turstinus archiepiscopus ea eis dedit." [1]

Some old English boroughs of less importance than these were subject to more burdensome " customs " and only slowly obtained release from them. The special favour of Henry II indeed acquitted the burgesses of Wallingford as early as 1156 from " work on castles, walls, ditches, parks, bridges and causeways, and from all secular custom and exaction and servile work." [2]   It has already been mentioned that agricultural services or their equivalent in money were exacted from the burgesses of Lancaster and Leicester respectively down to nearly the end of the twelfth century. [3] Leicester had been mediatized after the Conquest and its mowing service may have been imposed by its new lords, and Lancaster, though a royal borough when freed from its service, may have owed it to their Norman lord of Conquest date, Count Roger of Poitou.   If so, Norman influence did not always make for greater simplicity and freedom.   As late as the beginning of the thirteenth century, the founder of the borough of Egremont reserved certain agricultural services from his burgesses. [4]

Even the " villanous " *merchet* was not immediately rooted out by the Conquest from boroughs in the regions where it was prevalent.   Had it been, it would hardly have been necessary for those who drew up the customs of Newcastle-on-Tyne under Henry I to affirm so stoutly that " in the borough there is no merchet." . . . [5]   It was forbidden in charters which, like those of Durham and Wearmouth, incorporated Newcastle customs, but the reactionary Egremont charter retained it, at least in the case of a burgess who married the daughter of a villein. [6]

Peterborough burgesses were liable to merchet for over 150 years, [7] and heriot or relief, which was excluded with it, under the former name, from Newcastle and its daughter boroughs, [8] is not uncommon down to the very end of the thirteenth century in the charters of boroughs founded by Anglo-Norman lords, even when they contained a formal

---

[1] *Early Yorkshire Charters*, ed. Farrer, i. 92.
[2] *B.B.C.* i. 94.   [3] Above, p. 84.   [4] *B.B.C.* i. 95.
[5] *Ibid. Archæologia Aeliana*, 4th series, Vol I (1925). Yet merchet was not a mere villein custom in the north. See p. 83.
[6] *B.B.C.* i. 95.   [7] *V.C.H. Northants*, ii. 425 and Addenda above.
[8] And as " heriot or relief " from Tewkesbury and Cardiff between 1147 and 1183 (*ibid.* pp. 75-6).

exemption from all customs and services.[1]   Normally a money payment, a year's rent not infrequently, but sometimes double that or even more, it is only in the Salford group of boroughs that it appears in the original heriot form of arms—sword or dagger or bow or lance.[2]   With one notable exception, it never occurs in the charters of royal boroughs.   Henry II, however, reserved a relief of 12d. in his charter to Pembroke,[3] which contrasts strangely with Earl Robert de Beaumont's earlier abolition of relief in his mesne borough of Leicester.[4] In the demesne boroughs generally it was doubtless abolished, where it had existed, without written authority or at least any that has survived.   Yet as late as the first quarter of the fourteenth century the heir of certain tenements at Hereford, which were held in free burgage, was charged with relief by the Exchequer on the ground that he had done fealty to the king.   In the end the king ordered that if such tenements were by custom free from relief, the demand was to be relinquished, notwithstanding the fealty.[5]

Further evidence that the Norman Conquest was far from effecting a revolutionary change in the system of burghal tenure in the ancient boroughs of the realm is afforded by the persistence of eleventh-century nomenclature.   The concrete use of the term burgage for the tenement of the burgess which readily suggested itself in new boroughs cut into approximately or even exactly equal land shares never got any real hold in the older cities and boroughs, with their more irregular lay-out.[6]   For them burgage had for the most part its original abstract sense of " borough tenure."   [7]   The old English word haw for the burgess's holding did not wholly die out and the more common French terms by which it was now designated, mansion—akin to the *mansa* of the Anglo-Saxon charters—

---

[1] Relief is reserved in the charters of Bradninch and Lostwithiel which both have the formula.   Cf. *B.B.C.* i. 46, 48, with *ibid.*, p. 76.   Both heriot and relief were exacted from the burgesses of Clifton-on-Teme (1270). See R. G. Griffiths's history of the town (Worcester, 1932), ch. v. p. 47.
[2] *B.B.C.* ii. 95.   [3] *B.B.C.* i. 76.   Between 1173 and 1189.
[4] *Ibid.* p. 117.   Between 1118 and 1168.
[5] Madox, *Firma Burgi* (1726), pp. 257-8.
[6] In Dr. Veale's calendar of 226 Bristol feet of fines (*Great Red Book of Bristol*, Introd., Part I, pp. 180 ff.) burgage in this sense occurs but once, in 5 John (p. 180).
[7] Bourgage (*burgagium*) seems to have developed its several meanings in the following order : (1) Tenure in a *bourg* or borough ; (2) the area over which the tenure extended, the *bourg* or borough in a topographical sense ; (3) the normal tenement in it ; (4) the rent of the tenement (for this see the deed quoted above, p. 93 : " all service but burgage ").

messuage and tenement were older and more general in sense than *bourgage*.

Having traced the survival, long after " free burgage " became the recognized description of borough tenure everywhere, of features found in the Anglo-Saxon borough which we are asked to regard as quite incompatible with that form of tenure and in the case of heriot identified with a feudal impost in some of the newest and freest boroughs, we will reverse the process and inquire how far the essential characters of burgage tenure were present in the pre-Conquest boroughs. The inquiry has been in part anticipated in earlier sections, but it will be convenient to give here a brief summary of the evidence as a whole :—

(1) The typical tenement in an Anglo-Saxon borough was that of the freeman burgess who rendered all local and general " custom(s) of burgesses." The most fundamental of the local customs was the money rent, that landgable or hawgable which continued to be the central feature of " burgage tenure " and can be proved in some cases to have remained at the same figure after as before the Conquest. Tolls and judicial forfeitures were the most important of the other local customs and these too were permanent charges. Here and there the burgess was subject to personal services, other than the watch, which were gradually abolished or commuted in later times, but none of these, in the important royal boroughs at any rate, carried any stigma of unfreedom at the time and in the place where they were customary. Professor Stephenson himself is willing to admit that exemption from such services may have been already obtained in certain boroughs before the Conquest. The cases he adduces [1] do not, however, prove his point. The Winchester burgesses, as we have seen, were not free from services of this kind under Henry I, their " fee farm rents " under Edward the Confessor did not therefore differ from the landgable and other customs of the boroughs generally. For Southampton the only evidence adduced is the mention in Domesday of three rates of landgable in 1066 and the backward Hereford had two.[2]

---

[1] *E.H.R.* xlv. (1930), 190. The inference seems to be withdrawn in his book (p. 93).

[2] The Southampton entry in Domesday (i. 52a, 1) is very brief, but it leaves no doubt that other customs than gable were exacted. The statement that ninety-six new settlers since the Conquest, French and English, rendered £4 0s. 6d. " de omnibus consuetudinibus " would imply that, even if Professor Stephenson were right in translating " in return for

The burgess customs, so far as they were paid in money, formed the bulk of that *redditus* of the borough which normally before the Conquest and in certain cases after it was shared between king and earl.

(2) The heritability of the burgess tenement is sufficiently established by casual evidence in Domesday and elsewhere. It is implied in the mention of heriots at Chester, Shrewsbury, Hereford and Ipswich, and by the record of their absence at York.[1] For London it is distinctly stated in the Conqueror's brief charter.[2] The rights of the kin are alluded to in Domesday at Chester,[3] and specifically affirmed at Lincoln (see below).

(3) The right of the royal burgess to give or sell his tenement with or without license, is attested by Domesday evidence from widely separated regions. Whether the same freedom was enjoyed by the burgesses of other lords than the king, is usually uncertain, but we are told that Harold's burgesses at Norwich had it.[4] The leave of the king or his reeve was sometimes required, but at Norwich with its 1320 burgesses, it was only necessary in two cases, where the tenements were perhaps official *reveland*, and at Thetford with 943 burgesses in thirty-six,[5] if the right to do homage to other lords here implies that of sale, while at Torksey the burgess could sell his holding and leave the town without even the knowledge of the royal reeve.[6] At Hereford, on the other hand, a frontier town where unusual personal services had to be rendered, the reeve's licence must be obtained and a buyer found who was willing to perform these services. The reeve was also entitled to take a third of the purchase price.[7]

The Domesday commissioners were less directly concerned with the restrictions on sale or gift imposed by family law which figure so largely in the later burgage tenure, but that they already existed is accidentally revealed in an interesting

all customs," whereas it can only mean " from all customs." His version would require " pro " instead of " de." King William gave to certain barons "the custom(s) of their houses " (consuetud' domorum suarum).

[1] *D.B.* i. 298a, 1.

[2] Stubbs, *Select Charters*, ed. Davis, p. 97 ; *B.B.C.* i. 74, incorrectly placed under Intestate Succession. See Liebermann, *Ges.* ii. 391, § 12a, iii. 276.

[3] *D.B.* i. 262b, 1. Qui terram suam uel *propinqui sui* releuare uolebat x solidos dabat.

[4] *Ibid.* ii. 116a.   [5] *Ibid.* ff. 118b, 119a.

[6] *Ibid.* i. 337a. 1. *Cf.* the Newcastle privilege under Henry I, except when the ownership was in dispute (Stubbs, *Select Charters*, ed. Davis, p. 134; *B.B.C.* i. 64).   [7] *D.B.* i. 179a, 1.

passage in the survey of Lincoln. A certain Godric, son of Gareuin, on becoming a monk of Peterborough, had conveyed his church of All Saints and its land to the abbey. The burgesses in 1086 protested that the abbot had it unjustly because neither Gareuin nor his son nor any other could give it out of the city or out of their kin without the consent of the king. Godric is not said to have been a burgess nor the property a landgable tenement, but the rule is laid down quite generally.[1]

In burgage tenure restrictions on the alienation of land, protecting the interests of the kin were commonly and by ancient tradition[2] confined to inherited tenements, those purchased by the burgess himself being left to his free disposition. It is significant therefore that in a second survey of Gloucester, made within a quarter of a century of Domesday, the " mansions " of the royal burgesses are enumerated in these two categories, though without any overt reference to capability of alienation.[3]

(4) The Anglo-Saxon burgess could also mortgage his tenement. This is revealed by the complaint of burgess jurors in 1086 that king's custom was being withheld by certain mortgagees. At Exeter the abbot of Tavistock had one house in bond (*in vadimonio*) from a burgess [4] and Walter de Douai two,[5] from neither of which was custom rendered. A house at Lincoln, for which the abbot of Peterborough was called to account for not paying geld, had been held in bond by one Godred [6] and may have been a burgess tenement, though this is not definitely stated.[7]

In the tenurial system thus fragmentarily bodied forth in Domesday Book the essential features of the burgage tenure of the twelfth century, a fixed money rent, heritability and ease of transfer either as security or outright, are sufficiently recognizable. They are not seriously obscured by occasional personal services in addition to the rent, by heriots and a rare due on marriage or by many exemptions ranging from the individual quittance of custom to the wide church soke. There is, no doubt, a striking contrast between arrangements so deficient in neat uniformity and the burgage tenure of the

---

[1] *D.B.* i. 336a, 1.

[2] For this distinction in early Teutonic law abroad, see *E.H.R.*l. (1935), 2.

[3] Ellis, *Introd. to Domesday Book*, ii. 446. The date is between 1096 and 1101.

[4] *D.B.* i. 103b, 2.   [5] *Ibid.* f. 112a, 1.   [6] *Ibid.* f. 336b, 1.

[7] The clear cases are late, but for A.-S. mortgages *cf.* pp. 42, 87 *n.* 5.

late Middle Ages, when personal services of a non-civic kind had entirely disappeared and the traffic in tenements, along with some fall in the value of money, had reduced the landgable to a mere quit-rent, often unleviable owing to subdivision. It was only very gradually, however, that this stage was reached and some irregularities, especially the church sokes, still persisted. Much of the Anglo-Saxon disorderliness had, as we have seen, survived into the twelfth century, and even the thirteenth. And by the time it had been pruned away burgage tenure had itself become something of a survival for new avenues to citizenship, membership of merchant gilds, apprenticeship and purchase had diminished the importance of the house and levelled the distinction between the tenement which paid landgable and that which did not.

In this evolution the Norman Conquest and the French *bourgage* undoubtedly played a very important part, directly or indirectly, though the immediate effect of the Conquest was greatly to decrease the uniformity of tenure in the old borough. But Dr. Stephenson, confining his attention almost entirely to the evidence of Domesday on borough tenure and to those features which differ most from pure burgage tenure, insists that the Conquest was the starting-point of a wholly new system. Had he carried on his inquiry into the twelfth-century sources, he would probably have been more disposed to recognize a development where he sees only a revolution.[1] It is immaterial, for instance, that landgable was a term used for other than burghal rents. A general term may always take on a more technical sense in special circumstances and, as it happens, the *gabelle* of the French *bourgage* was also, as is well known, in general use outside the *bourgs*.[2] The process of specialization in towns everywhere had necessarily to begin from the general level, and it might be the effect of changes without as well as within. Thus that most characteristic feature of fully developed burgage tenure, freedom of bequest of land by will, was entirely due to the prohibition by the common law of what was general custom down to the end of the twelfth century.

Irrelevant is a fair description of the argument Dr. Stephenson attempts to draw from the mention in Domesday

[1] This to some extent he now does, chiefly on consideration of the considerable populations of the larger pre-Conquest boroughs (*Borough and Town*, p. 212).

[2] See below, p. 110.

of holdings in neighbouring manors by burgesses of Bedford, London, and Norwich. "This," he says, "is not burgage tenure." [1] It certainly is not, but who has ever claimed it as such ? The investments of later citizens in rural land might with equal reason be used as evidence that they did not hold their town houses by burgage tenure.

More plausible is Dr. Stephenson's deduction from a well known and much disputed set of entries in the Domesday survey of the rather abnormal borough of Canterbury.[2] In these he sees evidence of three different forms of tenure by burgesses, and concludes that uniform burgage tenure did not yet exist. These difficult entries will be best discussed in the next chapter. All that need be said here is that the " bookland " was apparently held by a gild not by individual burgesses and that tenure *in alodia* was not incompatible with rendering of the royal customs, as we have seen in the case of the Ipswich burgesses who " lived on their own land and rendered all custom in the borough." [3] The Canterbury *alods* are indeed expressly said to have been held of the king. It must be kept in mind that before the Conquest the king's customs were not merely exigible from royal demesne in the Norman sense of the term, but in fact or in theory from all land which had not received exemption from them. Liability to these customs on the part of the *alodiarius* on the one hand and the tenant of a church or thegn on the other, practically established a double tenure of which the tie with the king was the early form of burgage tenure. Burgage tenure itself, as every collection of medieval town charters shows, was, as the result of more or less free sale and devise, combined with fee-farm and lease tenures, under which economic rents for larger than the landgable were paid to others than the king.[4] The landgable had become merely a quit rent on land which was accounted royal demesne in the Norman settlement, but in the eleventh century, combined as it was with the other customs, it was more than an ordinary rent, it had a wider and public aspect and in practice was exacted by the king not as landlord in the strict sense but as lord of the borough.

---

[1] *E.H.R.* xlv. (1930), 186. One of the Bedford burgesses' holdings at Biddenham is noted to have been purchased after the Conquest (*D.B.* i. 218).

[2] *Ibid.* i. 2a, 1. [3] Above, p. 92.

[4] As early as the Winchester survey of 1107–15 the former was sometimes distinguished from the landgable as *renta* (*D.B.* iv. 536a, 1—Gardini). The rent as well as the landgable might be the king's (*ibid.* 532a, 1—Hugo Oilardus). Professor Stephenson notices these entries (p. 190), but the volume number is misprinted.

With Dr. Stephenson's more speculative argument against the existence of anything like burgage tenure before the Conquest, based upon his conception of the normal Anglo-Saxon borough as almost purely agricultural and of its burgesses as in the main cultivators of the land of a rich minority, we have already dealt.[1] Burgage tenure he considers to have been almost entirely [2] a new development in England due to the commercial energy and urban experience of the new Norman lords of the land.

Except in the case of Norwich, Domesday unfortunately tells us little about the communities of French settlers established in various towns or round new castles before 1086. It was only natural that they should be treated with special favour. At Shrewsbury, they were exempted, as the English burgesses bitterly complained, even from the danegeld.[3] At York nearly 150 tenements occupied by them had ceased to render customs.[4] This was no doubt in large part a temporary state of things and, as Hemmeon correctly noted,[5] the general tendency later was towards assimilation of these settlements in the old boroughs to the model of their English neighbours and not the reverse, but their influence and that of the new castle-boroughs may certainly have tended towards the disappearance of personal services of the kind which was occasionally required from the burgesses in some Anglo-Saxon boroughs.[6] The 1d. custom of the " new borough " (Mancroft) at Norwich, which covered everything but forfeitures,[7] un-

---

[1] Above, p. 78.
[2] For exceptions allowed by him, see pp. 96, 100.
[3] *D.B.* i. 252a, 1.   [4] *Ibid.* f. 298a, 1.
[5] *Burgage Tenure in England*, p. 168. He refers particularly to devise of land.
[6] On the other hand, we find the abbot of Battle exacting light manorial services as well as rent from his new burgesses there (*Chron. Mon. de Bello*, pp. 12 ff.; *E.H.R.* xxix. 428 f.) and the Conquest brought with it some danger of feudal burdens, especially in small mesne boroughs. The three aids were customary in the thirteenth century at Egremont (*B.B.C.* i. 91), and at Morpeth (*ibid.* ii. 119), all but ransom at Saltash (*ibid.* p. 116). Special grants of liberty of marriage were found necessary in the twelfth century (*ibid.* i. 76 ff.). Nor were the new burgesses all French. Of over 100 at Battle, t. Hen. I, about three fourths were English. At Baldock, Herts, where also the names and holdings of the burgesses are recorded, old English names were rare in 1185 (Lees, *Rec. of Templars*, 66 ff.). From the fact that only the first in the list is said to hold *de burgagio*, Miss Lees infers that it was the only such tenancy (p. cxxxviii.). The words were of course understood in all the following cases.
[7] *D.B.* ii. 118a. Professor Stephenson's suggestion that there was a rent at Southampton " for all customs " seems untenable. See above, p. 100, n. 2.

doubtedly anticipates the mere landgable of burgage tenure, but in these very free eastern boroughs where before the Conquest we find the 1d. landgable at Lincoln and a possibility of it at Norwich itself, there is not much evidence of onerous custom. It is noteworthy that the 1d. at Mancroft was due not only from the burgesses on the demesne reserved for the king and earl, but also from the knights to whom lands were assigned and who had burgesses under them. This was a recognition of the ownership originally of the earl alone and later of king and earl jointly. Dr. Stephenson invokes the authority of Miss Bateson for his view. He seems, however, to put something of a strain upon her *obiter dictum* as to the influence of the Anglo-Norman seignorial boroughs " in reshaping the older conception of the borough " when he says that she was inclined to believe that burgage tenure was, at least in large part, a French importation.

Her actual words were that the term burgage tenure could only have arisen in the boroughs with real unity of tenure under a single lord, and from them the *term* might easily spread to those other boroughs where already in the king's " gafol " there was a low payment made by each house which could not easily be differentiated from a rent.[1] This is not altogether clear, but it surely suggests that a new name was applied to an old state of things, having a strong resemblance to the later development, not that any really vital alteration was introduced. It may even be doubted whether Miss Bateson's premiss is sound. She was clearly thinking of a uniformity consisting in tenure of urban houses by fixed and more or less equal rents, not of the wider privileges understood by burgage tenure in its full sense. Yet it was precisely in this wider sense that the term *burgagium* seems to have been first applied both to the older boroughs and the new. The " free burgage " which Archbishop Thurstan bestowed upon the men of Beverley and which Henry I confirmed is defined not in terms of tenure but as " the free laws and customs (not in the Domesday sense of course) of the burgesses of York." [2] In similar terms Henry II granted "free burgage " to William, earl of Albemarle, for his burgesses of Hedon, York or Lincoln to serve as model.[3]

---

[1] *E.H.R.* xvi. 344-5. Hemmeon, from his different point of view, also regards the passage as asserting that burgage tenure was an institution of Norman origin (*op. cit.* p. 167).

[2] *Early Yorkshire Charters*, ed. Farrer, i. 92.

[3] *B.B.C.* i. 38 (where the heading " Grants of Burgages " is misleading in such cases as this).

Abbot Richard of Whitby granted that town in " free burgage " and to its burgesses " libertatem burgagiae et leges liberas liberaque jura." [1] No doubt the free tenement was at the root of this abstract conception of " free burgage," but it was only derivatively and gradually that " burgage " came to be used concretely for " tenement " and then almost exclusively in new boroughs. As the old English borough already possessed a large measure of uniformity in its group of burgesses enjoying greater advantages and rendering less onerous, because mainly pecuniary, customs than the inhabitants of the agricultural vill, it seems unnecessary to suppose, with Miss Bateson, that the newcomers could not find a word to express its nature except in the new boroughs under single lords. It was only, it would seem, by assuming that the original meaning of *bourgage* was " tenement " not " borough status " that she reached this conclusion. As a matter of fact, there is a long chain of evidence to show that tenure of land from the crown in the ancient boroughs was for three centuries after the Conquest known by a term of old English origin, socage.[2] Nor was the absence of a single lord in the old borough so fatal to uniformity as she supposed. There were indeed usually other lords than the king, but this did not necessarily exempt the tenants of these lords from rendering the royal customs or exclude them from the burgess community. It was the Conquest itself which for a time drew a much sharper line between *terra regis* and *terra baronum*. Yet Domesday makes it clear that the burgesses rendering custom to the king were still the normal element in the borough, the others the exception. The effacement of this line of division was, as we have seen, a very slow process. The survey of Winchester under Henry I shows it still as sharp as, or sharper than, in 1086. Nevertheless, this did not prevent contemporaries from

---

[1] *B.B.C.* i. 39.

[2] In the list of St. Paul's rents, *c.* 1130, the royal quit-rent is described as *de socagio* (*Essays presented to T. F. Tout*, p. 56). The same term is applied to the landgable in an early thirteenth century London list of city rents (*E.H.R.* xvii. (1902), 484, 495). As late as 1306 the mayor and aldermen informed Edward I that all tenements in the city were held in chief of the king *in socagio* (*Rot. Parl.* i. 213 b.). It was only later that *in libero burgagio* was substituted in such returns. At Worcester a landlord acquits a tenant's holding against the king's reeves " de iiii denariis et obolo qui sunt *de socagio domini regis*" (*Worcester Cartulary*, no. 395). At Bristol in 1355 tenements are mentioned as held of the king in chief " by socage after the custom of Bristol " (E. W. Veale, *Great Red Book of Bristol*, I. i. 167).

speaking of the free burgage, the free laws and customs, of such boroughs.

The ancient English boroughs, then, exhibit no very neat system of " burgage tenure " in the Norman period. It is possible, however, to assume too strong a contrast in this respect with the new foundations of French type. Unluckily, owing to lack of evidence, a direct comparison with these is precluded, but fuller information from Normandy itself does not reveal so acute a contrast or a burghal system of the advanced type which Dr. Stephenson regards as alone entitled to be called burgage tenure.

4. BURGAGE TENURE IN NORTHERN FRANCE IN THE ELEVENTH CENTURY

There was no Domesday Book on the other side of the Channel, but contemporary charters contain material which, interpreted in the light of later evidence, discloses the general features of the eleventh-century *bourg*. This, whether a trading appendage to an ancient *civitas* or founded on a rural *villa* to encourage similar settlement, was a newer development than the English borough and allowed of much greater uniformity from the outset. As feudalism was already highly developed in the open country, the line between *bourg* and *ville* was drawn far more firmly than in England. This appears very clearly in M. Henri Legras's valuable study [1] of burgage tenure in the ducal *bourg* of Caen, first mentioned in 1026, and the two ecclesiastical *bourgs* of St. Stephen's and the Trinity founded by the Conqueror himself with the same constitution. There is no class corresponding to the sokemen of some English boroughs and in the ducal *bourg* no *terra baronum*, though the bishop of Bayeux takes the *census* and custom of certain houses, doubtless by some unrecorded grant.[2] There are *manentes* paying rent (*merces*) who are not burgesses, but, M. Legras supposes, traders belonging to other towns.[3]

The burgesses of Caen, like their English contemporaries, had to perform personal services which were incidental to their tenements, watch and ward, cleansing and repair of the ditches of the castle and upkeep of public roads,[4] but there is no word of carrying service or of the provision of guards for

---

[1] *Le Bourgage de Caen* (Paris, 1911). [2] *Ibid.* pp. 52 ff.
[3] *Ibid.* pp. 44 ff. [4] *Ibid.* pp. 59 ff.

the duke and his officers, still less of the hunting services of Shrewsbury or the boon reapings of Hereford. This is the difference between a system which has been created at a comparatively late date and one which has grown irregularly from diverse beginnings. On the other hand, the Caen burgesses were not wholly free from feudal burdens. The duke had oven-right, for which there is no evidence in the old English borough, and M. Legras is of opinion that the later transfer due paid when houses changed hands implies an original relief and thinks it probable that the burgesses were subject to the three feudal aids. However this may be, there is no question here of that burgage tenure by payment of a rent " pro omni servitio, consuetudine et demanda," which becomes common in England by the thirteenth century. For contemporary charters speak of " gablum (censum) *et consuetudinem*," [1] and this custom is once defined as " omnis consuetudo omnium domorum." [2] As in England, there were houses that were subject to custom (*consuetudinariae*) and houses that were exempt. M. Legras takes this custom to have been limited to dues on trade and industry. There is early mention of a *consuetudo culcitrarum*, a custom on coverlets, and of *consuetudines in foro*. [3] In the fifteenth century when customary houses had come to be exceptional, traders avoided them. If this was the only kind of 'custom' in Caen, the term was used in a much narrower sense than it has in Domesday. The *consuetudines* of an English borough included the gable and not only tolls and baker's custom, [4] but heriots, local money dues such as the two marks a year rendered after Easter by the royal burgesses of Colchester and their 6*d*. yearly for the military needs of the crown, [5] even personal services like carrying duty and feeding prisoners. [6] Indeed the danegeld itself could be brought under this comprehensive term. It will be seen that duties such as work on the castle ditches and payment of relief, which M. Legras distinguishes from *consuetudines* as falling

---

[1] Legras, *op. cit.* p. 52. This distinction is made exceptionally in the Domesday account of Cambridge (above p. 90).

[2] *Ibid.* Cf. the " consuetud' domorum " at Southampton (above, p. 100, *n.* 2).　　　　[3] Legras, *op. cit.* pp. 52, 74 ff.

[4] The " (consuetudo) panificis " of Stamford (*D.B.* i. 336b, 2), and the later attested " bacgavel," "baggabul " of Exeter (Schopp, *Anglo-Norman Custumal of Exeter*, pp. 21, 30) and "backstergeld" of Lincoln (*Reg. Antiquiss.* iii. 303, a. 1263).

[5] *D.B.* ii. 107a. The 6*d*, though described as annual, was taken only if the king had hired troops or made an expedition, and only from houses that could pay it. It was therefore not included in the king's farm.

[6] See above, p. 97.

I

upon the burgess by the mere fact of his holding of the lord's soil, are all placed in the same category in the Anglo-Norman documents. It is possible that the original *consuetudines* of Caen may not have been so exclusively customs on trade and industry as they seem to have been later. Were the burgesses not liable to such state requisitions as had to be formally renounced in some Flemish cities ? Count William of Flanders in his charter of 1127 to St. Omer applies the term *consuetudines* to these alone : " ab omni consuetudine liberos deinceps esse volo : nullum scoth, nullam taliam, nullam pecunie sue petitionem eis requiro." [1]

In any case, the difference between the Anglo-Saxon borough and the North French *bourg* in regard to tenure was a difference in detail, not in kind. The Normans found it sometimes difficult, but never impossible to apply the terms with which they were familiar to the description of English towns. It is particularly noteworthy that at Caen one of the terms in use for the house rent in which Professor Stephenson finds so strong a contrast to the borough rents of Anglo-Saxon England was that very " gable " (*gabulum, gablum*) by which these were usually designated, and if a technical meaning is to be denied to the English (land) gable because it was also applied to country rents, it must be equally refused to the French *gabelle*, for that, too, had its more general application. So, too, had *census* [2] which is used as equivalent to gable in the Caen documents, as it is in the Domesday descriptions of Derby and Nottingham.[3] What was normally distinctive of these burghal rents was their lowness and their equality for all tenements of equal size in the same town as compared with the more economic and varied rents of agricultural land, where they are found. These features were naturally more pronounced in French *bourgs* of recent foundation, to which traders were attracted by comparatively light recognition of the lordship of the soil, than in the older English boroughs, but they can, as we have seen, be discerned in Domesday. The original gable at Caen seems to have been 3*d*. or 1½*d*. according to the size of the tenement.[4] The larger figure may be compared with the 3*d*. of Winchcombe [5] and the

---

[1] Giry, *Hist. de Saint-Omer*, p. 373.   [2] Legras, *op. cit.* p. 52.
[3] *D.B.* i. 280.   [4] Legras, *op. cit.* p. 56.
[5] Madox, *Firma Burgi*, p. 22. The local tradition in the fifteenth century that the 3*d*. was " pro Walgauell " is interesting, but too late and too isolated to throw serious light on the origin of borough gable.

3¾d. of Bristol.[1] At Hereford, where there were also two rates, but decided by situation not by size, the figures were rather more than double those of Caen. On the other hand the 1d. of Lincoln and (probably) Norwich was lower than the smaller rent in the Norman *bourg*. In twelfth-century foundations in both countries higher rents were demanded, the shilling rent being very common, but this was doubtless partly a set-off to quittance of custom.

If the fundamental features of the Anglo-Saxon borough did not differ essentially from those of the French *bourg* of the eleventh century, the rights of the burgess over his tene-ment were often greater in the former. The burgess of Norwich or Torksey, for instance, could sell his tenement and leave the borough without licence, but at the end of the eleventh century leave to sell was indispensable at Caen and the buyer was usually the lord.[2] Not until a century or so later was full freedom of alienation attained. Again, the right to devise the burgess tenement by will enjoyed in English boroughs, originally by the common law and from the latter part of the twelfth century as a distinctive burghal privilege, never existed in Caen or in any other Norman borough. Burgage tenure of land in England was in fact a development rooted in old English law and on the legal side owed little to Norman precedents. Where French burgesses established themselves at the Conquest alongside English borough com-munities, as at Shrewsbury and Nottingham, it was in the main the English customs which ultimately prevailed.[3]

In view of these facts, we cannot see our way to agree with Dr. Stephenson that the history of burgage tenure in England begins practically at the Norman Conquest. The formative influence of the French *bourgage* on the English borough was neither so great or so immediate as he suggests. Its greater simplicity as developed in Normandy and in Norman foundations on this side of the Channel doubtless had reactions upon the older boroughs which were not confined to the name, but it is easy to exaggerate the influence of these small seignorial creations upon the ancient and far greater

---

[1] E. W. W. Veale, *Great Red Book of Bristol*, Introd., Part I, pp. 137 ff., 296 ff. (Bristol Record Soc., vol. II). Was this curious sum originally a fourth of the 15d. we find as average rate at Bath and nearly so at Gloucester (above, p. 91, *n.* 3) ?   [2] Legras, *op. cit.* p. 58.
[3] Primogeniture is no exception. " It is by no means certain," says Maitland, " that in 1066 primogeniture had gone much further in Normandy than in England " (*Hist. of Eng. Law*, ii. 264).

royal cities and boroughs. Although *bourgage* (*burgagium*) gave a name to the tenure, it did not drive out in these towns more general terms for the burgess holding, the English *haw*, old French words derived ultimately from the Latin manere, " to dwell," and akin to the *mansa* of Anglo-Saxon charters : *mansion* (common in Domesday as *mansio*), *mesuage* and the feudal *tenement*. Nor is this conservatism surprising since we find that even in France it was long before *bourgage* was applied to the tenement as well as the tenure, and that terms such as *area* and *mansura* (a frequent alternative to *mansio* in Domesday) are used not only in documents relating to the old *civitates* but in those of *bourgs* such as Caen.[1]

The real change which the Normans wrought in the English boroughs did not consist in the transformation of their tenurial groundwork, though that, after the first disorganization following the Conquest, was gradually simplified, but in the new spirit which they brought into town life. Their racial energy and commercial enterprise speedily made themselves felt in the rapid development of merchant gilds, and these in turn stimulated communal self-consciousness and provided a new and more effective organ, alongside the borough court, through which the boroughs secured from needy kings confirmation and extension of their freedom over against a now more deeply manorialized countryside and ultimately a large measure of municipal autonomy. Judged by such a standard, the Anglo-Saxon borough, so far as it is revealed to us, seems a dull and lifeless place, but we must not hastily assume that it was normally devoid of communal organization and feeling. Some glimpses of these may be obtained even from the arid legal and financial records which are almost our only sources.

[1] Legras, *op. cit.* p. 43.

V

THE BOROUGH COMMUNITY

IF the burgesses of an Anglo-Saxon borough were not a hap-
hazard and heterogeneous population exhibiting every variety
of status found in the rural world without its walls and no
others, but had this in common that they held their tenements
by render of landgable and other customs, an early form of
burgage tenure, we may expect to discover, even in the
financial details of Domesday, some evidence of common
interests, organization and action. Alienation of customs by
the crown had indeed marred this tenurial uniformity, but,
in favour of laymen at least, to a far less extent than the
greed of Norman barons in the first twenty years after the
Conquest. The burgesses had not yet suffered the heavy
losses in numbers and status which it brought about, and as
they were more numerous, more prosperous and, we may add,
less subject to financial oppression, they may be presumed to
have been not less but more alive to their interests as a community than they could be under the Normans until their
revival in Henry I's time.

It will be vain, of course, to look for more than the germs
of that municipal development which only reached its zenith
in the thirteenth and fourteenth centuries. Resistance to
the Danes must, indeed, have aroused communal spirit in the
burgesses, but they lacked the incentives to co-operation which
the pressure of feudalism and a more advanced commerce
gave to their continental fellows. It was in the ordinary
routine of their lives that the seed of municipal self-consciousness lay, in the making and enforcement of by-laws for
their participation in the common fields, meadows and pastures, in the regulation of trade in the borough market and in
the conduct of their financial relations with the king or rather
his local representatives, the portreeve and the sheriff. Then,
as afterwards, their progress was not uniform. It was naturally

113

more rapid in the regions which had long been in touch with the opposite coasts of the mainland.

1. The Burgesses as Agricultural Community

In an earlier chapter it has been seen that the agricultural economy of the vill (or vills) out of which the borough had grown had been to a considerable extent transformed by its urban growth. Increased trade and population made agriculture merely a subsidiary means of livelihood, often insufficient to feed the people. Churches and magnates were permitted by the king to encroach upon the fields and pastures. In towns such as Canterbury, Ipswich, and Norwich the burgesses retained a mere fragment of the original agricultural appurtenances. Maldon was perhaps not alone in having apparently been created with only enough land for a small minority of its burgesses. Boroughs which still kept great stretches of arable land were sometimes content to leave its cultivation to a few of their number. This seems to have been the case at Derby, Nottingham, and probably at Huntingdon.

On the other hand, there were some large boroughs where, so far as we can see, the burgesses still utilized the whole of their ancient fields, without such delegation. Colchester was one, Exeter perhaps another, though this has been disputed. Its arable land is briefly described in the following lines of Domesday : "Burgenses Exonie urbis habent extra civitatem terram xii carucarum quae nullam consuetudinem reddunt nisi ad ipsam civitatem."[1] The Latin *burgenses* is, of course, ambiguous, but its wider meaning here is established by the entry later of the bishop's $2\frac{1}{2}$ acres " which lie with the land of the burgesses " (*jacent cum terra burgensium*).[2] Had a few burgesses only been in question, Domesday would, no doubt, have given their number, as it does at Derby, Nottingham, and Thetford.[3]

At Colchester and Exeter the whole management of the common cultivation would be in the hands of the burgesses as a body, though the details, fortunately preserved in the former case, show that the individual's interest must have

---

[1] *D.B.* i. 100a, 1. [2] *Ibid.* f. 101b, 2.
[3] At Lydford in Devon Domesday makes it quite clear that the whole burgess population shared in the arable (*ibid.* f. 100a, 2). But Lydford was a small borough, with only two carucates of land.

been quite subordinate to other means of subsistence. And even where the town fields were of small extent, the burgess community would still be responsible for the observance of its by-laws. Where the fields were leased, their control would be less direct and at Huntingdon the leases were granted by the officers of the king and earl.

Apart from any manorialization in the fields, the burgesses had not always the sole enjoyment of them. The churches of the borough had usually shares of varying area. At Ipswich the many churches held among them double the number of acres that belonged to burgesses.[1] At Stamford [2] and Lincoln [3] the lawmen also had their portion, but at Lincoln perhaps only took custom or rent from burgesses who actually cultivated the land.

The description of the Lincoln fields is by far the fullest in Domesday, but is not easy to interpret. Of the $12\frac{1}{2}$ carucates the king and earl are said to have held 8 " in demesne," the lawmen held three and two churches the rest. In what sense did they hold them? There is some evidence that the fields of boroughs were normally subject to custom separately from the tenements within the town.[4] At Exeter this custom was left, doubtless by some unrecorded grant, to the burgess community (*ad civitatem*), clearly to use for its own purposes ; [5] at Stamford none was exacted.[6] The explanation of the tenure of the Lincoln carucates that first suggests itself is that the king and earl had released their custom over some third of the arable to lawmen and churches, but retained it over the other two-thirds, and this fits in with another statement in Domesday which implies that besides thirty crofts in the city, the churches and burgesses had the use of the twelve and a half carucates. The chief difficulty in accepting this interpretation is that the king and earl's portion was so dominical that King William had exchanged one carucate for a ship and, the purchaser being dead, no one had this carucate, unless the king granted it. But the conveyance of land when only profitable rights in it are transferred is a common enough feature of Anglo-Saxon practice. Moreover, this land is

---

[1] *D.B.* ii. 290a, b.   [2] *Ibid*. i. 336b, 2.   [3] *Ibid*. f. 336a, 2.
[4] At Cambridge hawgable and landgable were still distinguished in the thirteenth century, though they had both been comprised under landgable in Domesday (Maitland, *Township and Borough*, pp. 70, 180). At Bury St. Edmunds there was a separate *landmol* on the arable appurtenances (M. D. Lobel, *The Borough of St. Edmunds* (1935), p. 56).
[5] Above, p. 114.   [6] " Sine omni consuetudine."

carefully distinguished in Domesday from 231 acres of arable *inland* and 100 acres of meadow in Lincoln which also belonged to the king and earl, but in a more fundamental sense. If the suggestion made above be correct, the burgesses were the actual holders of the 12½ carucates and upon them as a community would fall the regulation of its common cultivation. The only difference between them and the burgesses of Exeter and Stamford would be that they had still to render custom either to king and earl or to their grantees.

It is in favour of the view here advanced that from the arable and meadow land which belonged to Huntingdon there was a *census* divided between king and earl.[1] Here, however, a further piece of information is given. The burgesses took it on lease from (*per*) the officers of the king and earl. In this case *burgenses* must probably mean certain burgesses, the limited extent of the arable, apparently 280 acres, not providing sufficient land for more than a minority of the population of a town which in 1066 seems to have contained nearly 400 houses.

The most urban stage reached by any burgess community in its relation to the agricultural appurtenances of the borough, so far as our sporadic information goes, was that of the burgesses of Exeter, who were not merely excused payment of the land custom to the king, but authorized to collect it for their own communal use. They had at their disposal an income independent of the sums they had to render to the lady of the borough.[2] The definite statement that the custom went to the city discourages any suggestion that they divided it between themselves as the burgesses of Colchester did a more occasional windfall.[3]

It was not, however, in the agricultural " shell " of the borough, an urbanized survival of a rural past, that the burgesses were getting the training in communal action which was most valuable for their municipal future.[4] Much more important in this respect was their growing market. The market was the centre of their interests and in the develop-

---

[1] *D.B.* i. 203a, 2.
[2] The germ of the later distinction in all royal boroughs between the income of the town treasury (*camera*) and that of the king's reeve's office (*prepositura*). See below, pp. 125, 225.   [3] See below, p. 129.
[4] The leasing of the town arable to a few burgesses in certain boroughs is evidence of the comparative unimportance of the agricultural appurtenance of the urban tenement, not of an urban land-owning aristocracy (see above, p. 69).

ment and enforcement of rules and regulations for traders they were learning to act together as a really urban community. The *port* had gone far towards obliterating the underlying *villa*. Its royal governor was not a *tun-* but a *portgerefa*.[1]

2. The Burgesses as Trading Community

Apart from its record of the profits of tolls and markets Domesday Book, as concerned only with revenue, throws little direct light upon pre-Conquest trade, and this has led to over-emphasis on the agricultural aspect of the Anglo-Saxon borough. How misleading its silence is may be realized from the fact that the only borough to which it gives the name of *port* is Hereford, which Dr. Stephenson singles out as the least truly urban of all the larger boroughs. Yet *port* in " portway " is fairly common in Anglo-Saxon charters and the former in place-names.

The unusual fullness with which the customs of Chester are recorded in Domesday provides some details as to its external trade, its chief import being marten skins,[2] which, we learn from other sources, came from Ireland.[3] The Gloucester render of iron as part of its farm [4] records an industry that is still kept in memory in the city arms. The ancient salt industry of Droitwich is noticed.[5] Other forms of trade may be inferred from the Domesday statistics. The number of burgesses at Dunwich, Maldon, and Yarmouth [6] bespeaks important fisheries, as do the ships of the Kentish ports mentioned as doing naval service, in return for financial concessions. The burgesses of Dover, perhaps of all the Cinque Ports, enjoyed exemption from toll throughout England,[7] and it seems unlikely that London at least did not possess this privilege. The large populations of the greater boroughs in the eastern counties can only be explained by considerable trade, which may have been wholly local or in part a share in that commerce with the Continent which is attested from the beginning of the eleventh century. It is known, from a

---

[1] Had its walls been the only distinctive feature of the Anglo-Saxon borough, as Professor Stephenson suggests, why was he not called *burh-gerefa* ?

[2] *D.B.* i. 262b, 1. Part of the farm was paid in these skins (*ibid.* col. 2).

[3] Round, *Feudal England*, p. 467.

[4] *D.B.* i. 162a, 1.   [5] *Ibid.* f. 172a, 2.

[6] *Ibid.* ii. 312b, 48a, 118a.   [7] See below, p. 127.

foreign source, that English cheese was exported to Flanders as early as 1036.[1] Further north some intercourse with Scandinavia seems probable.[2] The merchants who frequented York at the end of the tenth century are said to have been chiefly Danes,[3] but may have come from other parts of the Danelaw. In the south-west the burgesses of Exeter, when preparing to defend themselves against the Conqueror in 1068, enlisted the aid of certain foreign merchants,[4] skilled in war, who happened to be in their city.

A picture that does not include the two cities, the weights and measures of which had some claim to be considered the norm for the whole kingdom,[5] is of course very imperfect. But fortunately the omission in Domesday Book of any description of either London or Winchester is more or less compensated by the survival of an older London record and a later Winchester one probably based upon the original Domesday returns. The Liber Winton is not much more informative on the trade of the city than a more succinct survey in Domesday Book would have been, but the summary of customs in the port of London about 1000 A.D., which is contained in the fourth law of Ethelred II,[6] shows already in existence that active trade with the southern coast of the Channel from Flanders to Normandy, with the cities of Lower Lorraine along the Meuse and with the " men of the emperor " generally which is recorded in a London document of about 1130,[7] often in similar terms, and by other post-Conquest evidence. The chief defect of the earlier record is that while telling us much about imports, it is silent about exports. Yet English merchants still, as in Offa's day, made their way far into the Continent. Cnut in 1027 obtained from the

[1] G. W. Coopland, " The Abbey of St. Bertin, 900–1350 " (*Oxford Studies*, ed. Vinogradoff, vol. IV), p. 51. For the participation of Anglo-Saxon merchants in international trade at Bruges and Tiel in the period on either side of 1100, see Pirenne, *Hist. de Belgique*, i. 2ᵉ livre, § 1.

[2] *Cf.* F. M. Stenton, *The Danes in England*, Proc. of Brit. Acad. xiii. (1927), p. 233. The direct evidence does not go back beyond the reign of Henry I, but earlier intercourse may not unfairly be presumed. Alex. Bugge in an article on North European trade routes in the Middle Ages (*Vierteljahrschrift für Social- und Wirtschaftsgeschichte*, iv. (1906), 255 ff.) is less cautious.

[3] *Vita S. Oswaldi* (*Hist. of York*, Rolls Series, i. 454).

[4] " Mercatores advenas, bello habiles " (Freeman, *Norm. Conq.* iv. 140, *n.*) For extranei mercatores at Canterbury, *D.B.* i. 2a, 1.

[5] Liebermann, *Ges.* i. 204, iii. 137.

[6] *Ibid.* i. 232-5. The heavy penalty of £5 for evading toll is noticeable.

[7] *E.H.R.* xvii. (1902), 499 ff.

masters of the Alpine passes protection for his subjects,
"*merchants* or pilgrims," going to Rome.[1]

The Winchester survey, though full for its particular object,
which was to ascertain what "customs" were due from the
tenements of the city, yields nothing to the present purpose
save the occasional mention of burgess occupations, for
which we look in vain to the Domesday notices of pre-Conquest
boroughs. There is no hint of the vigorous cloth industry
which flourished at Winchester in the thirteenth century.
The burgess population was probably mainly occupied in
providing for the needs of an important administrative and
ecclesiastical centre and its surrounding district. But intensive industry and commerce in the larger sense were not
invariable features even of the later medieval country boroughs.
It was in their borough courts that the burgesses must have
enforced and, if need were, enlarged their borough usages
in matters of trade, besides exacting the penalties imposed
by the king and his witan on those guilty of the more serious
offences to which it was exposed. The London pound was,
as we have seen, known as the pound of the husting.[2] The
Londoners secured from Ethelred a confirmation of their
customs and sought his permission to exact a special fine of
30s. for breach of the borough peace from those who resorted
to violence in their disputes instead of seeking legal redress :
" If he cares for the friendship of this port, let him make
emends with thirty shillings, should the king allow us (to take)
this." [3]

Whether the gilds in which the English were fond of combining, in boroughs as elsewhere, were ever formed or used
for the promotion of trade, like the merchant gilds which
sprang up after the Norman Conquest, is disputable. Such
descriptions of thegn gilds and cniht gilds in boroughs as
have survived do not suggest that they were, and indeed the
ninth century cniht gild of Canterbury is distinguished from
the burgesses within the city.[4] Yet two centuries later
Domesday definitely records gilds of burgesses at Dover and
Canterbury in 1066.[5] The " gihalla burgensium " in the former
town does not admit of dispute, but the evidence for the
Canterbury gild has been called in question. Gross maintained

---

[1] Liebermann, *Ges.* i. 276, 6.   [2] Above, p. 40.
[3] Liebermann, *op. cit.* i. 234, 4, 2. To be additional to the king's
own fine of £5 for breach of his peace. *Cf. ibid.* iii. 165, *n.* 3 on 4, 1. It
was the same penalty as for disobedience to the hundred.
[4] *Cart. Sax.* ii. 128, no. 515.   [5] *D.B.* i. 1a, 1 ; 2a, 1.

that the 33 acres which, according to Domesday Book, *burgenses* of Canterbury had " de rege " T.R.E. " in gildam suam " and which Ranulf de Columbels held in 1086, with other property once belonging to burgesses,[1] were merely land that was in geld with the borough, in its geldable, as it was later expressed.[2]   But in this, as in another case in the next century,[3] he resorted to this strained interpretation where " gild " in the sense of association was awkward for his argument.   The Inquisition of St. Augustine's,[4] which was unknown to him, has a variation from Domesday Book in this passage which leaves no doubt that a gild is meant : " adhuc tenet idem Ranulfus xxxiii agros terre quos burgenses semper habuerunt in gilda eorum de donis omnium regum."   Further evidence has also been fatal to Gross's like interpretation of another Canterbury entry in which tenements are recorded as held by clergy (*clerici*) of the town " in gildam suam." [5] The Holy Trinity (Christ Church) version of the Domesday returns, corresponding to the Inquisition of St. Augustine's, identifies this gild with the convent of secular canons at St. Gregory's, founded by Lanfranc in 1084.[6]

The Dover gild shared the fate of most English associations of the sort at the Conquest, but there is some reason to believe that the Canterbury burgess gild, may, like the Cnihtengild at London, have been more fortunate and survived, if only for a time.   Without questioning the general truth of Gross's contention that the merchant gild in our boroughs was a Norman introduction, it seems impossible to see a gild of purely Norman origin in the body which made an exchange of houses with the convent of Christ Church, Canterbury, by a document written in Old English not later than 1108.[7] The lay party to the deed is described as the cnihts, at Canterbury, of the merchant gild (*cepmannegilde*).   The agreement is witnessed by Archbishop Anselm and the convent on the one part and by Calveal,[8] the portreeve, and the elders

---

[1] *D.B.* i. 2a, 1.
[2] *Gild Merchant*, i. 189, *n.* 6.   Similarly the land in Eastry hundred " quod jacuit in gilda de Douere " ((*D.B.* i. 11b, 1) gelded, he thought, with the town.
[3] Below, p. 223.   [4] Ed. Ballard, p. 10.
[5] *D.B.* i. 3a, 1 ; Gross, *loc cit.*
[6] *Inq. of St. August.*, p. 15 ; *E.H.R.* xviii. 713.
[7] Gross, *Gild Merchant*, ii. 37-8.
[8] He was very likely the Calvellus from whom, according to a charter of Malling nunnery, Archbishop Ralph d'Escures bought two mills which he granted to his sister Azeliz between 1114 and 1122 (*Cal Ch. R.* v. 52).

(*yldesta men*) of the society (*heap*) on the other. It is noteworthy that the names of the tenants of the houses which
the gild took in exchange and possibly that of the portreeve
are English and that the reeve of the city is the head of the
gild.

The lack of any later mention of this gild and the consequent
probability that, like the London gild, it soon after ceased to
exist, strengthen the suggestion that it was the gild briefly
mentioned in Domesday. It differs from the other recorded
gilds of cnihts in being described as a merchant gild. The
name may be new and show Norman influence, but everything
else, not least the presidency of the portreeve, suggests the
identity of the " heap " with the gild of burgesses that
appears in Domesday. If so, the latter was also an association of leading merchants, though perhaps under a different
title, most probably Cnihtengild, as at London. In both towns
then at the end of the eleventh century the leading burgesses
were known in English as cnihts. But in a remote past the
cnihts in a borough may not have been burgesses, at least not
king's burgesses. The ninth century charter which is witnessed
by the " cniahta geoldan " (*sic*) of Canterbury distinguishes
them from another body of witnesses, the burgesses within
the city (*innan burgware*).[1] It is not clear how this is to be
reconciled with the mention of three *geferscipas* of inner and
outer (*utan*) burgesses in a charter of *c*. 950.[2] Were the cnihts
now reckoned as burgesses and their gild as one of the three
societies ? Or was the gild still distinct from them ? Professor
Stenton has recently suggested an explanation of the application of the term cnihts to the independent merchants of the
eleventh century. As the essential meaning of cniht is
" servant," " minister," " retainer," he would trace these to
the ministers of rural landowners who managed their burghal
properties in early times and formed a link between their

[1] *Cart. Sax.* ii. 128, no. 515.
[2] *Ibid.* iii. 213. I have assumed that " inner " and " outer " mean
within and without the walls, a distinction found in later times (*e.g. D.B.*
i. 179a, 1 (Hereford)) ; a possible suggestion that the outer burgesses of
this charter were those who " belonged " to rural estates and represent
the cnihts of a century earlier encounters at once the objection that the
" innan burgware " of *c*. 860 implies " utan burgware " distinct from the
" cniahta geoldan." Gross absurdly adopted a post-Conquest identification of the three *geferscipas* as the convents of Christ Church, St. Augustine's
and St. Gregory's, although the last was not founded until 1084 (*Gild
Merch.* i. 189) *Fership* was used as late as the fourteenth century of the
society which owned passenger ships at Dover (S. P. Statham, *Dover
Charters*, pp. 35, 53).

lords' upland estates and the borough market.[1] An obvious
objection to the theory is that in the origin of the eleventh
century Cnihtengilds it finds no place for those king's burgesses
who formed a majority in most towns. True, as Professor
Stenton remarks, these gilds had evidently a long history and
may have undergone many changes before the eleventh century. It might even be significant that they are only recorded
in cities, Canterbury, London, and Winchester, where great
churches had large properties which at Canterbury at least
were connected with their rural estates. In these towns the
number of cnihts in the original sense would have been
unusually large.

Possibly, however, the theory has too narrow a basis.
A burgess under certain conditions could become a king's
thegn. There were also civic thegns of lesser rank, *burhthegns*.
They are only certainly recorded in London and at the very
end of the Anglo-Saxon period, but in view of the extreme
imperfection of our evidence too much stress should not
perhaps be laid upon that. It should be noted, however, that,
with the exception of the Cinque Ports, London alone had
" barons " in the post-Conquest age.[2]

However this may be, the Canterbury and London evidence
affords clear proof of the existence of gilds of burgesses before
the Conquest and practical certainty that their members
were the leading traders of their towns. These societies must
have made for a stronger sense of community and their presence weakens the suggestion that the burgesses of an Anglo-
Saxon borough were a mere fortuitous collection of disparate
elements, with no real bond of union.[3] But these gilds,
fostered though some of them were by the English kings,
had perhaps a more or less private character. At any rate,
Calveal the portreeve's headship of the Canterbury gild is the
first evidence of that close connexion with the government of
the borough which made the Norman merchant gild so vital
a factor in municipal growth. The germs of the municipal

---

[1] *The First Century of English Feudalism* (1932), p. 134.
[2] See below, pp. 256-9. Liebermann (*Ges.* ii. 571, 9a) agreed with
Ballard (*Domesday Boroughs*, p. 112) in regarding the burhthegns of some
of the Confessor's writs to London as a patriciate and supported the view
by comparing the London wergild of £5 with the £8 wergild of the thegns
of the Cambridge gild (*D.B.* i. 189a). But it is not certain that these were
borough thegns, and elsewhere Liebermann seems to consider the London
£5 as a Norman innovation (*Ges.* ii. 732, § 5).
[3] Canterbury is not one of the exceptions which Dr. Stephenson allows.

corporation must rather be looked for in the borough farm and the borough court.

3. THE BURGESSES AS REVENUE-RENDERING AND ADMINISTRATIVE COMMUNITY

That the burgess was not merely responsible as an individual for the burdens assessed on his own house is well known, so far as the danegeld is concerned, from the complaint of the English burgesses at Shrewsbury in 1086 that, though a great many houses had been destroyed for the castle or given free of geld to the new abbey or to Frenchmen, they were still held liable for the whole of the original assessment. The zeal with which burgess jurors in some towns reported baronial absorption of burgess houses and the loss of royal custom, which almost always resulted, points to a similar communal responsibility for this ordinary revenue. Such responsibility seems inherent in the system of collection which was in use. The usually round numbers of the amounts paid over to king and earl would suggest that these revenues, at any rate the variable element, *e.g.* tolls, were farmed, even if there were not occasional mention of the " king's farm." The sheriff would normally be the king's farmer, as he was after the Conquest until from the twelfth century onwards the boroughs themselves gradually obtained the privilege of farming the town revenues from the crown and paying them direct into the exchequer.[1] The exceptional farming of the revenue of Hereford by the town reeve [2] was of course not a case of such farming by the burgesses, for he, like the sheriff, was a crown official and his farm a private speculation. Farming by the burgesses from the sheriff is not recorded in Domesday until 1086 and then only in one borough, Northampton.[3] But the silence of Domesday is not safe evidence and even if the pre-Conquest sheriff did not adopt this course, he would naturally leave the actual collection of borough revenue to the reeve and burgesses as a cheaper and more effective method than levying it by officials of his own.

It is a defect of the farming system that allowance for loss of rateable tenements can only be secured by special concession from the ultimate recipient, and this is not usually easy to obtain. Hence the lament of the burgesses of Hertford

---

[1] See below, chapter vi.
[2] *D.B.* i. 179a, 1.
[3] *Ibid.* f. 219a, 1.

that houses once inhabited by burgesses had been wrongfully taken away from them (*sibi injuste ablatas*),[1] and the Colchester complaint that similar houses, which had rendered the *consuetudo regis* in King Edward's time, had ceased to contribute their share.[2]   Hence, too, the claim of the latter borough that five hides at Lexden, within the burghal hundred, were liable to custom and to account with the city (*ad consuetudinem et compotum civitatis*),[3] or, as we should say, were rateable with it.   The result of their claim is not given, but the men of Southwark put on record, apparently with some self-satisfaction, that they had recovered from Count Eustace of Boulogne a haw and its toll for the farm of Kingston (on Thames) in which the revenue from the borough was included.[4] This stimulus to common interest and common action was doubtless much more seldom felt before the Conquest, but it must have existed.

The burgesses were more directly and more constantly trained as a community, however, by participation in the government of the borough.   The king's reeve was indeed and long remained an official over whom they had no direct control. They did not appoint him, but he had to work with the burgess community in its court and more particularly with their "eldest men" (*seniores*, *senatores*) or "witan" (*sapientes*), just as the king himself had to consult with his "witan." For these nascent borough councils were not the mere personal advisers of arbitrary reeves.   They had a separate standing of their own.   It was they who drew up the list of London usages embodied in the fourth law of Ethelred II.[5]   The royal draughtsman has left the " We " of the original standing. It was to the witan of the four Devon boroughs, without mention of their reeves, that Bishop Eadnoth of Crediton, some twenty years later, sent official notice of a mortgage of part of his land.[6]   In the Danish boroughs the lawmen, though primarily judges, may have occupied a similar position.[7]

---

[1] Above, p. 92.   [2] *D.B.* ii. 106b.
[3] *D.B.* ii. 104a.   *Compotum* seems a certain emendation of the MS. *cootum.*   For the inclusion of Lexden and three other agricultural vills in Colchester hundred, see above, p. 48, and for the admitted rateability of Milend in the twelfth century, D. C. Douglas, *Feudal Documents from the Abbey of Bury St. Edmunds* (1932), p. 144.
[4] *Ibid.* i. 32a, 1.   See above, p. 58.
[5] See above, p. 118.   [6] Above, p. 42.
[7] Liebermann, *Ges.* ii. 565.   In 1106 a lawman of York was described as hereditario iure lagaman civitatis quod Latine potest dici legislator vel iudex (*ibid*).   Alex. Bugge somewhat exaggerated the self-government of these boroughs (*Vierteljahrschrift für Social. u. Wirtschaftsgeschichte*, iv, 257).

Already, too, there is a faint adumbration of the borough treasury (*camera*) of the future, a repository of revenue available for local purposes, as distinguished from the reeve's treasury (*prepositura*) into which went the revenue due to the king.[1] The borough " accounts " (*compotus*) of Colchester were confined to royal revenue, though, as we have seen, the burgesses, for personal reasons, were keenly interested in them. But when the Londoners asked King Ethelred to allow them to inflict a special penalty for breach of the peace of their " port," in addition to his own much heavier fine, they must either have had a city chest [2] or have been prepared to start one. The provoking ambiguity of the Latin in the statement of Domesday that the church of St. Mary at Huntingdon had belonged to the church of Thorney until the abbot " inuadiauit eam burgensibus " [3] leaves us in doubt whether the community or a group of burgesses were the mortgagees, but a borough *camera* is clearly implied in a well-known series of entries under Kent. Edward the Confessor's release of sake and soke to the burgesses of Dover, recorded on the first page of Domesday Book, was a grant of the profits of justice in their court. This revenue was indeed only a set-off against a new personal service required by the king, but provision must have been made for the safe keeping of the money until it was needed. Other entries show that the same release was conceded to Sandwich, Romney, and Fordwich.[4] The arrangement of which it formed part was in fact the origin of the liberty of the Cinque Ports, though Hastings and Hythe are not credited with the release in Domesday.[5] The fullest account of it is in the case of Romney where the burgesses of the archbishop and of Robert de Romney (*Romenel*) had, it is stated, all the forfeitures except the three highest, usually reserved to the crown, but here belonging to the archbishop.

The record indeed goes further and says that the burgesses had *all customs* as well as the lower forfeitures.[6] This would seem also to have been the case at Sandwich according to a brief allusion to the grant which is found only in the Holy

---

[1] See above, p. 116 *n*. and below, p. 225.

[2] Liebermann makes this inference (*Ges.* iii. 165, on IV Ethelred, 4, 2).

[3] *D.B.* i. 208a, 1.

[4] *Ibid.* i. 3a, 1 ; 4b, 1 ; 10b, 2 ; 12a, 2. For the evidence of the St. Augustine's inquisition, see below, p. 126.

[5] Hythe is given only a few words (*ibid.* 4b, 1), and Hastings is not described at all.   [6] *D.B.* i. 4b. 1.

K

Trinity and St. Augustine's transcripts of the Domesday returns : " homines illius ville antequam rex [Edwardus] eis dedisset suas consuetudines reddebant xv lib."[1] But the form in which the concession to Dover is stated can hardly be interpreted so widely. It is true that sake and soke, though generally quite clearly distinguished from non-judicial custom,[2] occasionally appears to include other custom, but this may be due to over-condensation.[3] As a matter of fact the full description of the borough in Domesday makes it clear that the king was still drawing custom from most of its tenements. Perhaps the judicial revenue of Dover was in itself sufficient compensation for its share in the naval service (*servitium maris*) which the ports were called upon to render : " Burgenses dederunt xx naues regi una uice in anno ad xv dies et in una quaque naui erant homines xx et unus."[4] Except that it was one ship less, this is exactly Dover's contingent in later times,[5] clear evidence that, though formal confederation was still in the future, its essential basis was already in existence before the Conquest.[6] The only other light on this early phase is concealed by over-abbreviation in Domesday Book, but clearly given in the St. Augustine's version : " Ibique [Fordwich] habet archiepiscopus vii mansuras terre qui in mari debent seruire cum aliis burgensibus sed a modo eis aufert inde seruicium."[7]

The ship service of the south-eastern ports did not stand absolutely alone. Maldon, in Essex, had to provide one ship,[8] and this obligation was still in force as late as 1171.[9] The period of service was then longer than in Kent, forty days, in which feudal influence is apparent. They were, however, excused all other " foreign " service.

---

[1] *Inq. St. August.*, ed. Ballard (Brit. Acad., Rec. IV), p. 20.

[2] *E.g.* " socam et sacam et consuetudinem " at Norwich (*D.B.* ii. 116a) ; in burgo de Gepewiz [Ipswich] habuit Stigandus ii burgenses T.R.E. cum soca et saca et rex habebat consuetudinem (*ibid.* f. 289a).

[3] *E.g.* " cum saca et soca preter geldum regis " at Huntingdon (*ibid.* i. 203a, 1) ; inde . . . sacam et socam nisi commune geldum in villa uenerit unde nullus euadat (*ibid.* f. 30a, 1).   [4] *Ibid.* f. 1a, 1.

[5] *Black Book of St. Augustine's*, ed. Turner and Salter (Brit. Acad.), i. 144.

[6] For its origins see K.M.E. Murray, *Constitutional History of the Cinque Ports*, (1935), pp. 9 ff.

[7] *Inq. St. August.*, p. 18.   Comparison with the thirteenth-century list quoted in note 5 shows a subsequent change of assessment, for the members of Sandwich (including Fordwich) and Dover are said to be charged " non de solo sed de catallis."

[8] *D.B.* i. 48a. For naval services other than the provision of ships, see Ballard, *Domesday Boroughs*, p. 80.   [9] *B.B.C.* i. 90.

Another and more welcome privilege which Dover owed to Edward the Confessor, more welcome because not apparently a *quid pro quo*—there is no sign that it was part of the ship-service bargain—was that of exemption from toll throughout England.[1] As far as the Domesday evidence goes, it was only granted to Dover, but it was certainly enjoyed by all the Cinque Ports as early as the reign of Henry I,[2] and they do not seem to have had any Norman charter for it.[3] Incidentally, the Domesday account of the exemption at Dover confirms the view expressed in the last chapter[4] that the payment of royal custom was the test of burgessship, for it was confined to the permanent resident who rendered the king's custom.[5] Domesday supplies further evidence of the communal activities of the burgesses of Dover in recording their responsibility for providing the king's messengers crossing the channel with a steersman and helper.

It is obvious of course that at Dover and more or less similarly in the other Kentish ports, the borough community was of an advanced type for the period. The grant of sake and soke and of general exemption from toll, indeed, anticipate two of the most important clauses of the borough charters of the twelfth and thirteenth centuries.[6] But, leaving out of account probable privileges of London and Winchester, on which we have no information, they do not stand quite alone. By some lost or more probably unwritten grant, Exeter had the privilege of gelding only when those two cities and York gelded, and then only the nominal sum of half a mark.[7] The city, it may be suggested, perhaps owed this highly favourable assessment to its being a dower town of Queen Edith and possibly of her predecessors. It is this exceptional status probably, and not any such plans for setting up an aristocratic republic as Freeman imagined, that contains the true explanation of Orderic's statement that the *majores* of the city in 1068 refused to take an oath to the Conqueror or to admit him within the walls, though they were willing

---

[1] *D.B.* i. 1a. [2] *B.B.C.* i. 184.
[3] Their " members " were in a different position. Folkestone first received the privilege from Henry I or Stephen. (Murray, *op. cit.*, pp. 15, 45.) Lydd and Dengemarsh had it under Henry I, but their charter has not survived. [4] See above, p. 87.
[5] " Quicunque manens in villa assiduus reddebat regi consuetudinem."
[6] *B.B.C.* i. 113, 180; ii. 147, 254.
[7] *D.B.* i. 100a, 1. Palgrave drew the strange conclusion that no taxation could be levied upon them, unless they jointly assented to the grant (*Normandy and England* (1921), iii. 195).

to render to him "tributum ex consuetudine pristina."[1] At the same time, we may accept the Exeter privilege as evidence that the city ranked among the greatest of the realm. The smaller boroughs of Devon had shared to a lesser extent in her good fortune. Totnes and perhaps Barnstaple and Lydford, though Domesday is silent as to them, gelded when Exeter did, at half her rate,[2] and all three rendered jointly the same amount of military and naval service as the county town.[3]

Royal concession to a burgess community might in other cases take the form not of a low assessment for taxation but of liberty to commute a personal obligation for a money payment. Thus Oxford was free to pay £20 instead of sending twenty burgesses to the king's wars.[4] This in itself required communal action.

Lastly, it seems possible that a release of revenue to burgesses, similar to that at Dover, but of gable not of sake and soke, is the true explanation of a difficult passage in the Domesday description of Canterbury : "Burgenses habuerunt xlv mansuras extra civitatem de quibus ipsi habebant gablum et consuetudinem ; rex autem habebat sacam et sacam."[5]

These messuages, it was complained, had been seized by one Ranulf de Columbels. Owing to the absence of the article in Latin, this entry has been claimed by some as evidence of communal property and by others as merely referring to the private property of a few wealthy burgesses. The ownership of a number of tenements by the borough community as such at this early date is certainly very unlikely,[6] and it is, moreover, impossible not to connect these with the 212 burgesses over whom, we have been previously told, the king had sake and soke, but by implication not gable. Now, they are particularly described in the Inquest of St. Augustine's as *liberi homines*,[7] and that generally means owners of their own land. But the fuller transcript of the Domesday returns in the Inquest strongly suggests that it is not ownership but revenue which is in question here : "Item [after recording the king's loss of gable from two burgess houses] demonstrant burgenses civitatis xlv mansiones terre unde habebant liii solidos de gablo T.R.E. et ipse rex habebat inde sacam et socam."[8]

---

[1] Freeman, *Norman Conquest*, iv. 146 ff. ; *cf.* Round, *Feudal England*, pp. 431 ff. [2] *D.B.* i. 108b, 1.
[3] *Ibid.* f. 100a, 1. [4] *Ibid.* f. 154a, 1. [5] *Ibid.* f. 2a, 1.
[6] Ownership by a gild of burgesses is, of course, a different matter. See above, p. 120.
[7] *Inq. St. August.*, ed. Ballard, p. 9, *cf.* p. 7. [8] *Ibid.* p. 10.

It is clear from this and from the " Item dicunt burgenses " of the next paragraph that it is the burgess jurors who are speaking and that they are complaining of a double loss, of an income of £2 13s. to their community and of sake and soke to the king. There is nothing to show in what circumstances the gable, and, according to Domesday Book, other custom, of these tenements and presumably of the rest held by the 212 burgesses came to be rendered to the community, but that such a diversion of revenue was possible is proved not only by Domesday's very clear account of what happened at Dover, but also by its record of the payment of the custom from the fields of Exeter to the city.[1]

An instance of communal property has been claimed for Colchester which at first sight appears more plausible than that at Canterbury. Besides the shares of the individual burgesses in the fields of the borough, there were common to the burgesses (*in commune burgensium*) 80 acres of land and about the wall 8 perches, from all of which the burgesses had yearly 60s., for the king's service if need were and if not they divided it among themselves (*in commune*).[2] This seems a case, however, not of true communal ownership, but of communal use of crown land with occasional enjoyment of the profits. The inclusion of the eight perches around the wall is significant for they would certainly come under the royal claim, of which there is so much evidence later, that vacant places in boroughs belonged to the crown. It may not be accidental, indeed, that the entry immediately follows the description of the agricultural demesne which the king had in Colchester and which, it is added, was included in his farm. The 60s. evidently was not included, being treated as a reserve against extraordinary expenditure.

The division of this revenue among the Colchester burgesses, when it was not required for the king's service, does not suggest that as yet they had a permanent borough chest such as must have been called into existence by the concession of part of the royal revenue to the burgesses of the Cinque Ports and perhaps of Canterbury and Exeter.

[1] Above, p. 115.
[2] *D.B.* ii. 107a. Round took the first " in commune " as referring to common of pasture (*V.C.H., Essex*, i. 577), but the description of the 80 acres is that of arable not pasture, and he himself admitted that the 60s. was a surprisingly high return from pasture.

VI

SUMMARY AND GENERAL CONCLUSION TO 1066 [1]

IF the foregoing reconsideration of the evidence leaves no
room for the old idea, which was still held by Miss Bateson,
that a specially created urban court formed a universal legal
criterion of the early borough,[2] it does not bear out Dr.
Stephenson's contention that his own criterion of mercantile
settlement was generally absent, and the normal borough
merely an agricultural group much of the usual manorial
type. Every borough had a market [3] and every borough was
a *port*, a place of trade. The early trade even of the more
considerable of these ports must not be judged by the standard
of the great cities of the Netherlands,[4] which, with rare exceptions, they never reached. Yet by the end of the Anglo-
Saxon period, many of them were evidently prosperous. Of
the thirty-five for which Domesday gives statistics of population in 1066, twenty-one had more than 200 burgesses and five
of these (not including unsurveyed London and Winchester)
more than 900, involving total burgess populations of from
about 1000 to about 9500. In a large proportion of these
cases we should feel sure that the burgesses had some other
means of support than agriculture, even if Domesday did not
tell us that the 1320 burgesses of Norwich had only 180
acres of arable and the 538 of Ipswich (which had eight parish
churches) only forty, and that among the vast majority of the
burgesses of Colchester the average share of the individual
was only a little more than a quarter of the villein's yardland.

In his article of 1930 Dr. Stephenson recognized no real

---

[1] As this study was written before the appearance of Dr. Stephenson's
fuller and somewhat modified statement of his views in his book *Borough
and Town* (1933), I have thought it best to use for this purpose, with some
slight revision and additions, part of my review of that work in *E.H.R.*
xlviii. 642 ff.   [2] See above, chapter II.
[3] Except perhaps the abnormal Seasalter (above, p. 67). *Cf.* p. 207.
[4] For Professor Pirenne's study of the origin of these cities and its
supposed bearing on the English problem, see above, p. 5.

towns outside the seaports of the south-east, but since then he has been impressed by some of the population figures and in his book *Borough and Town*,[1] admits a considerably wider extension of urban trade. In his concluding chapter the large populations of York, Lincoln and Norwich—he might also have added Thetford with its 943 burgesses—are recognized as evidence of Scandinavian trade. The fisheries of Dunwich and the salt industry of Droitwich are noted. He is even ready to allow that the beginnings of municipal privilege may have extended beyond the south-eastern seaports, though evidence of this is wanting, and that the Norman Conquest only speeded up a process which was well under weigh. But he still maintains that it had not touched the ordinary borough and the line between the ordinary and the extraordinary is left exceedingly vague. The Irish-Scandinavian trade in furs at Chester is obscurely alluded to elsewhere, but nothing is said of the journeys of their cloth merchants as far as Cambridge, of the iron industry of Gloucester, of the presence of *mercatores advenae* at Exeter in 1068. The well-attested activity of Anglo-Saxon merchants from Iceland in the north to Rome in the south, the export of English cheese to Flanders, the testimony of William of Poitiers to the skill of their artificers in metal, are not taken into account. Even where mercantile settlement is finally admitted, some inconsistency with earlier arguments is occasionally observable. Not far short of half the population of English Norwich in 1086, for instance, is classed as dependent cultivators and the municipal growth of the city is derived entirely from the settlement of 125 French burgesses in a new borough, the later Mancroft ward, under William I.[2] In this, as in two or three other such new foundations, as at Nottingham and Northampton, there is a certain likeness to the *poorts* of the Netherlands which grew up outside feudal *burgs*, but at Norwich at least the old borough was of a type very different from the *burg* of that region and it is significant that its French neighbour was known as Newport. Dr. Stephenson is inclined to claim cispontine Cambridge as another of these French boroughs, reviving the old theory, combated by Maitland, which packed

---

[1] P. 212.

[2] It is claimed as significant that when here and elsewhere the old and the new boroughs were amalgamated, the common centre was fixed in the latter, but it is an error to assert that this was the case at Northampton, and other considerations, such as central position, may have determined the choice elsewhere.

400 houses into 28 acres north of the bridge. Not the least of the objections is the apparent continuity of the royal tenement rents from 1066 to 1483.[1]

To such foreign mercantile settlements, Scandinavian in this case, Dr. Stephenson would ascribe even the limited urban development which he now allows to the great Danelaw boroughs at an earlier date. Little or no allowance is made for a like native development in the English boroughs, because he has convinced himself that they were predominantly agricultural. This under-estimate of English trade and urban growth results partly from failure to distinguish always between what Domesday reports for 1066 and what for 1086, and partly from a tendency to interpret ambiguous evidence in the light of a theory. The villeins and bordars and minute or poor burgesses mentioned in a few boroughs were either on *enclaves* of royal or private arable or, in the great majority of cases, obvious victims of Norman devastation, a depressed class of former full burgesses. The 480 *bordarii* at Norwich in 1086 were reduced to the status of " cottagers " because they were unable to pay any customs, *i.e.*, dues, with the burgesses, but it is most unlikely that they had anything but the name in common with the rural bordars. They probably got a precarious living in minor urban occupations. The misunderstanding is the more unfortunate because it is used to support a theory that the mass of the Anglo-Saxon *burgenses*—a term meaning, it is held, no more than " borough people " and covering various classes—were mere cultivators of borough arable which was in the hands of a few rich men. This theory seems to have been suggested mainly by the division of the arable land at Derby and Nottingham between a small number of burgesses. But the arrangement may be more probably explained by a system of leases, such as obtained at Huntingdon, and not as a manorial relation. It may even mean that the " agricultural shell " of the borough was becoming unimportant for the mass of the burgesses. In accordance with his view Dr. Stephenson sees only a small number of individual landowners in the passage : " Burgenses Exonie urbis habent extra civitatem terram xii carucarum." This is grammatically possible, but it is equally possible and

---

[1] Above, p. 91, *n*. In *Proc. Cambr. Antiq. Soc.*, vol. xxxv. (1935), pp. 33-53, Miss Cam reviews the whole evidence, including archæological discoveries not taken into account either by Maitland (*Township and Borough*, p. 99) or by Dr. Stephenson (*Borough and Town*, pp. 200 ff.) and decides that its weight is against the theory in question.

more probable that the borough fields of Exeter were divided, as they certainly were at Colchester, between, at any rate, a considerable proportion of the burgess body.

The small borough, especially in the south-west, has a deceptively agricultural look in Domesday. It was often seated in the *caput* of a large royal manor and the revenue from market and burgess rents was included with that of the manor in a single farm. The compilers of the survey were, therefore, not always careful to enumerate the burgesses separately from the villeins and bordars, but the limitation of the earl's third to the borough revenue shows that borough and manor were distinct entities. Where burgesses were few, the borough might sooner or later disappear, as it did for instance, at Bruton in Somerset. On the other hand, a more favourable position for trade already marked out Ilchester, with its 108 burgesses in 1086, for municipal growth. The same variety of fortune befell the similar little groups of burgesses round markets which Norman lords established at their manorial centres after the Conquest. In Hertfordshire, Ashwell and Stansted failed to maintain the urban character which St. Albans retained and extended. Even the smallest Anglo-Saxon boroughs were not essentially different from " mercantile settlements " like these.

In the agricultural borough pictured by Dr. Stephenson, the burgage tenure of the twelfth century could not exist. It came, he holds, with mercantile settlement. Yet we find the essential features of the tenure already present. The tenement is hereditable at a money rent, the landgable or " custom of burgesses " ; subject to some varying restrictions, it may be sold or mortgaged. Inability to render any custom or exemption from custom excludes from the class of burgesses. Villeins and bordars are usually carefully distinguished from them. Their rents formed a leading item in the fixed farm of the borough, and in 1086 they were complaining that they were held responsible for rents and taxes withheld by Normans who had dispossessed burgesses. The burgage rents were still called landgable. Identities of amount can be proved, as at Cambridge. The rateable area at Oxford was known both before and after the Conquest as the king's " Eight Virgates."

Had the borough been primarily agricultural, the unit of assessment would have been acres in the arable fields ; actually it was the house (*domus*) within the ramparts and many burgesses had no share in the fields.[1] As a source of revenue burgess and house were convertible terms. It is true that otherwise land tenure in the boroughs, differed little, if at all, from free tenure outside them, but the peculiarities of the later burgage tenure, especially that of devise of land, were not due to foreign innovation but to changes in the common law from which they were protected by their charters. Just as borough law was merely an evolution from general law, burgage tenure of land in England cannot historically be dissociated from the common freehold tenure which came to be known as " socage." As late as 1306 the mayor and aldermen of London reported to the king that all tenements in the city were held *in socagio*,[2] and it was half a century before *in libero burgagio* replaced it in the conservative city.

For long after the Conquest *liberum burgagium* comprised not merely land tenure, but the whole body of burghal privilege, the status of a borough. Thus Henry I granted it to Beverley " secundum liberas leges et consuetudines burgensium de Eboraco." It is not possible to take these " laws and customs " as wholly of Norman introduction. The Domesday surveyors would hardly have devoted a column and a half to the *leges* of Chester before the Conquest, had they become altogether obsolete. Henry I's survey of Winchester shows no radical change there nearly sixty years after that event. The rather irregular landgable rents of 1066 were still in force, and even a few of those occasional personal services which were required from royal burgesses in some Anglo-Saxon boroughs and which Dr. Stephenson regards as inconsistent with real burgage tenure. None of them, however, were servile according to English ideas and they occasionally lingered on to the eve of the thirteenth century.[3] That Norman castle-building and mere ravaging made gaps in certain boroughs, which en-

[1] More than half the whole body at Colchester, over nine-tenths at Maldon.

[2] See above, p. 107, *n.* 2. In the twelfth century the tenements then held of the crown were known collectively as the king's soke (Page, *London*, p. 117). *Cf.* the payment *de socagio* to the king in the St. Paul's rental of *c.* 1130 (*Essays presented to T. F. Tout* (1925), p. 56).

[3] By a fortunate chance we are able to give a lower limit of date for their disappearance at Chester. About 1178 Earl Hugh granted a charter in which its citizens are described as *liberi custumarii* and as having *consuetudinariam libertatem*, rendering only rent *pro omni servitio*. Several of the customs from which they were free are specified : tolls, arresting and guarding prisoners, taking distresses, carrying writs and keeping night watch (*Chester Archæological Society's Journal*, x. p. 15). *Consuetudines* is here, of course, used in another sense than in the Beverley charter.

tailed some early changes, is not to be denied, but they were changes of detail not of principle. The Winchester burgesses of *c.* 1110 seem to have thought that the chief result was too often to substitute *pauperes* for *boni cives*. They certainly did not regard themselves as better off than their Anglo-Saxon predecessors.

York, indeed, and perhaps Winchester, Dr. Stephenson allows to be an exception to his general idea of the Anglo-Saxon boroughs. But a re-examination of the Domesday evidence for the " ordinary " borough of that date points to a substantial continuity with later conditions which the small and lifeless *burg* of the Netherlands, with which he compares it, never exhibited. If absorbed in the *poort*, which did not always happen, the *burg* became a mere fraction of an entirely new organism. In England, on the contrary, the beginnings of urban life were worked out within the walls of its *burhs* not without them. The universal features were a market and a free burgess tenement of urban type, held at a low rent and within certain limits, which were enforced also after the Conquest, transferable. A purely urban court was less general. The London *husting* was then exceptional and, at the other end of the scale, the minuter of the boroughs of the south-west could have had no other court than those of the hundreds in which they lay. It may, indeed, be conceded to Dr. Stephenson that the court of most boroughs was in origin an ordinary hundred court and that the hundred did not always, as it did at Sandwich, for instance, coincide exactly with the urban area. But the addition of three or four rural vills to such an area, to make up a full taxative hundred or half-hundred, left the court predominantly urban. The needs of traders involved specialization and the tract *Episcopus*, written before 1050, distinguishes between *burhriht* and *landriht*. The appendant vills, the " liberties " of the later municipal boroughs, were a wholly secondary element in their judicial as in their administrative organization. No argument against the urban character of the pre-Conquest borough can fairly be drawn from the antecedents of a court which persisted into the age of self-government, not infrequently, as at Colchester, under its original name.

In these urban courts, which were administrative as well as judicial, and in their ultimate responsibility for the borough farms, the burgesses could not fail to develop some communal spirit. Its scope was limited, no doubt, before, as for long after, the Conquest by the presidency of a reeve appointed by the king, but it is not unlikely that trading interests were already stimulating communal feeling outside the courts. It may well be that Gross drew too sharp a line between the Anglo-Saxon cnihtengilds of London, Canterbury and Winchester, and the Anglo-Norman merchant gilds. The London cnihtengild continued for half a century after the Conquest to be composed of the leading English merchants and the chapmangild of Canterbury, whose members were *cnihts*, though first mentioned by that name about 1100, has every appearance of a pre-Conquest origin. It was probably indeed, the gild of burgesses which appears in Domesday.[1] Its head significantly was the portreeve of the city, and from his name possibly an Englishman. Dover, too, had its English *gihalla burgensium*. Such gilds are not, indeed, attested elsewhere, but, except at London, they are only casually mentioned and even the later merchant gilds are found only in a minority of boroughs.

The active element in the medieval borough court was naturally its wealthiest and most experienced members. A casual record reveals the existence of this practical aristocracy nearly fifty years before the Conquest in a group of boroughs far remote from the Channel ports. When a bishop of Crediton in 1018 wished to secure full publicity for a mortgage of part of his lands, he sent a formal intimation of it to the witan (*burhwiton*) not merely of the county town, but also of the three smaller boroughs of Devon.[2] This was clearly a recognition of the boroughs as communities, for otherwise he would have sent his notice to the king's reeves of the respective boroughs.

That the Norman Conquest ultimately gave a great impulse to English trade and urban development is not in dispute. The questions at issue are how far it made a new start in this development, and whether the old English borough-port from the first did not contain a germ of urban growth which might indeed come to little or perish, as it did in not a few small " free boroughs " of post-Conquest creation, but which marks it as essentially different from the *burg* of the Low Countries. On this latter point Dr. Stephenson adheres to the view he expressed in his article of 1930. On the first he has yielded a good deal of ground. He no longer maintains that

---

[1] See above, p. 120.   [2] See above, p. 42.

there was no urban continuity between the Anglo-Saxon borough and the Anglo-Norman " town," except in a few seaports of the south-east.   But he regards this urban growth before 1066 as quite recent, and he still leaves us with a large and indefinite class of " ordinary " boroughs, agricultural, save for insignificant local trade. Unfortunately, some of the evidence he adduces for this is equally applicable to larger boroughs in which he now admits trading settlement.   This seems to be due to insufficient reconsideration of certain conclusions from Domesday in his original article.   His study of the Anglo-Saxon borough began with the survey of 1086, and he was too much impressed by features which seemed capable of a non-urban interpretation.

It would be idle to deny that the Anglo-Saxon borough, even in the middle of the eleventh century, had features which were not in harmony with autonomous municipal organization : ecclesiastical and lay immunities, the sokes of the larger towns, burgesses dependent on rural estates, differences of rank, in some cases personal services in addition to money rents. Municipal autonomy, however, lay in a somewhat distant future.   The Norman kings took over the boroughs from their predecessors, subject to rights, partly flowing from land ownership, partly from sovereignty, yielding, relatively to area, a larger revenue than their rural domains. If in some respects the borough system before long became a little more orderly, thanks partly to the influence of the new Norman foundations, in others the disorder was retained and even extended.   Feudalism increased the number of sokes and preserved the Anglo-Saxon heriot in some boroughs as a feudal relief.   At Norwich, Northampton, and Nottingham, English and French boroughs, with different customs, lived uneasily side by side.   The gild merchant while preparing the way for the communal movement and incorporation, which ultimately swept away the relics of a disorderly past, introduced a further conflict of ideas and occasionally severe friction in practice.

If it is not possible to draw a perfectly sharp line of demarcation in the development of the borough at the Norman Conquest, it is equally difficult to draw such a line at the settlement of the Danes in the northern boroughs or indeed at any earlier date after the permanent re-occupation of the old Roman towns.   It is all one story.   A study of its various phases certainly discourages the old quest of a neat legal definition of the borough, applicable at all periods. Government officials in the fourteenth century found this no easier than does the student of the Burghal Hidage and Domesday Book. Yet, if, with Dr. Stephenson, it is preferred to find the common thread in the gradual development of a trading community, why should its humble beginnings be ignored ?

THE POST-CONQUEST PERIOD

VII

THE FIRMA BURGI AND THE COMMUNE, 1066–1191 [1]

THE outstanding features in the history of the English boroughs in the century and a half after the Norman Conquest are the growth of merchant and craft gilds, the evolution of the conception of " free borough " (*liber burgus*), the gradual acquisition by some of the more important boroughs of the privilege of farming the revenues which the Crown drew from them and the influence exercised upon them by the communal movement on the Continent. Of these developments, the third, though it was almost peculiar to England, has received the least attention. Madox in his well-known treatise, *Firma Burgi*, studies only the fully developed fee farm system of the thirteenth century onwards. The student of the dynamic side of borough growth will look in vain in his pages for an account of the early hesitation of royal policy between temporary and permanent concession of the farming privilege which the money needs of Richard and John ended in favour of the fee farm or perpetual lease. The comparative neglect of this aspect of municipal development has not been due to lack of material, for the long series of Exchequer Pipe Rolls contains the fullest and most exact information for nearly the whole of the period in which the way was being paved for the shower of fee farm grants to towns which descended in the reigns of Henry II's sons. But until recently the rolls for this period were only partly in print. Now that they are published down to the great crisis when the citizens of London recovered the farm of their city and county, which Henry I had granted and his nephew and grandson had withdrawn, and were allowed to set up a commune, the time seems come to

[1] Reprinted from *E.H.R.* xlii. (1927), 321-60.

see what light they can be made to throw upon the farming system of the twelfth century. Their most striking revelation is that this London crisis was not a single one, as has hitherto been generally assumed,[1] but fell into two parts, the farm being obtained in 1190 and the commune a year later. This is only a negative contribution to the history of the London commune, but earlier Pipe Rolls, we shall see, record similar but abortive attempts at Gloucester and York.

The earliest known case of a borough being farmed by its burgesses directly from the Crown occurs in 1130, when the men of Lincoln secured this privilege, and in all probability this was the first grant of the kind. Nearly fifty years before, as we learn from Domesday Book, the burgesses of Northampton were farming their town, but they were farming it from the sheriff of the county, who alone was responsible to the Crown. How far was this a typical case in 1086, and to what extent had the Normans taken over the old English system? The details given in the invaluable descriptions of boroughs in the great survey supply a fuller answer to the first than to the second of these questions, but the pre-Norman data, though somewhat scanty, are occasionally illuminating. They are well known, but studied from this particular angle they suggest conclusions which do not wholly accord with current views of the sheriff's official relations to the towns before the Conquest.

1. THE FIRMA BURGI IN 1066

At the date of the Norman Conquest, the contrast between England and the much more highly feudalized region from which the invaders came was nowhere more marked than in the status of the towns. With the partial exception of Durham, there was nothing corresponding to the great cities held by feudatories of the French and imperial Crowns. The Confessor had indeed granted all his profits from Exeter,[2] Bath,[3] Ipswich,[4] and Torksey [5] to his wife, Queen Edith, but this was part of her dower and would lapse to the Crown at her death. Apart from Durham, and Dunwich in Suffolk, the permanently mediatized borough occurred only in Kent and was comparatively unimportant. Sandwich,[6] Hythe,[7] and

---

[1] Mr. Page is an exception, but he hardly realizes the importance of his correction. See below, pp. 181-2.

[2] *D.B.* i. 100.

[3] *Ibid.* iv. 106.

[4] *Ibid.* ii. 290.

[5] *Ibid.* i. 337.

[6] *Ibid.* i. 4.

[7] *Ibid.* i. 4b ; *Mon. Angl.* i. 96-7.

Seasalter[1] belonged to the see of Canterbury and Edward had recently granted all his rights in Fordwich to the abbey of St. Augustine.[2]

An overwhelming proportion of English boroughs were therefore still directly subject to the authority of the national monarch and a source of profit to him. Their reeves were royal officers appointed by the king. In most of them, he was the largest landowner. Despite extensive immunities and a deduction of one-third (*tertius denarius*) for the earl, the total sum flowing into the royal treasury from their judicial amercements, tolls, mints, customary payments, rents, and escheats formed no inconsiderable part of the modest state revenue of a somewhat unprogressive age.

The earl's third penny of borough revenue deserves some attention because, rightly understood, it seems to give a clue to the old English methods of dealing with this revenue. A brief summary of the Anglo-Norman system will make the exposition clearer. One result of the Conquest and the resultant forfeiture of most of the English earls was the resumption of their borough third penny by the Crown. In new creations, it was seldom granted with the third penny of the pleas of the shire. When the Pipe Rolls begin in 1130, the whole revenue from royal towns, save a few which were separately farmed, is included in the farm of the sheriff of the county in which they lie. An exceptional grant of the third penny of a borough to a new earl (or other magnate) would only mean a payment by the sheriff for which he received allowance in his annual account at the exchequer,[3] just as he did for the third penny of the county pleas in the case of a number of earls. The third penny was merely a mark of dignity, the earl as such having no official position in town or county, but in the days before the Conquest when he was the highest of local officials and an overmighty one, when, too,

---

[1] *D.B.* i. 4.   [2] See below, p. 143.

[3] But the allowance might be concealed on the earliest Pipe Rolls by some adjustment of the county farm and at any date if made on the farm of some manor to which the third penny was attached (see below, p. 142). Even the third penny of the county does not always appear on the Pipe Rolls when granted to an earl. See Round, *Geoffrey de Mandeville*, App. H. The third penny of Ipswich granted to Count Conan of Brittany before 1156 was allowed to the sheriff of Suffolk in that year (*P.R.* 2 Hen. II, p. 8), but, perhaps owing to the union of the farms of Norfolk and Suffolk in 1157, does not appear again until Count Conan's fief escheated in 1171 (*ibid.* 18 Hen. II, p. 5). The third penny of Norwich granted to Hugh Bigot with the earldom of Norfolk (1155) does not appear on the rolls with the third penny of the county.

apart from the profits of royal estates, there was little revenue that went undivided to the king, the earl's third was actually a share and a share the amount of which, in so far as it proceeded from unfixed sources let to farm, he was not without means of influencing. Such expressions as " the borough of Y renders z pounds between king and earl " are common, but it was not apparently because it was a borough in which no earl had a share that Stamford is exceptionally described as *burgum regis*.[1]

The reality of the earl's third is reflected in a system of accounting which differs from that with which we are familiar in the Pipe Rolls. The king's share alone appears in the account of the sheriff or other responsible officer. The earl's share is kept distinct and generally attached to some comital manor, which in more than one case was adjacent to the borough. It was not affected by the mediatization of a town. The king could not grant away more than his own two-thirds.

The Old English method of accounting is best illustrated in the case of Warwickshire. Although the sheriff's render in 1066 included all the items of the later county farm, the borough revenue, which forms one of them, was not the whole issues of Warwick but the king's two-third only.[2] For, as Dr. Round has pointed out, the profits from the borough which, with the third penny of the pleas of the shire, were included in the render of Earl Edwin's adjoining manor of Cotes were evidently the third penny of the burghal issues to which the earl was entitled.[3] Ipswich provides a close parallel to this arrangement. Earl Gurth, like Eadwine at Warwick, had a manor (*grange*) near by which with the third penny of the borough was worth £5 and with two hundreds was farmed (*liberatum*) at £20.[4] In other cases, Domesday Book only tells us that the king had so many pounds from the borough and the earl[5] so many, but the description of the change effected at Worcester by the Conqueror reflects light upon the earlier system. " Now king William has in demesne

---

[1] *D.B.* i. 336. Dover is similarly described in *An Eleventh Century Inquisition of St. Augustine's, Canterbury* (Brit. Acad. Records of Social and Economic Hist. IV), p. 23, and the earl had his third penny there.

[2] *D.B.* i. 238. [3] *V.C.H. Warwickshire*, i. 290. [4] *D.B.* ii. 294.

[5] At Shrewsbury, however, the third penny went to the sheriff (*ibid.* i. 252), and at Worcester there was an even more irregular arrangement. See next note. At Lewes king and earl each took half the revenue (*ibid.* 26).

both the king's part and the earl's part. Thence the sheriff renders £23 5s. by weight from the city."[1]

Charter evidence from Kent brings an interesting confirmation of this dualism. Domesday Book records that King Edward had given his two-thirds of the little borough of Fordwich to St. Augustine's at Canterbury, and that many years later, after the Conquest, Earl Godwine's third part was obtained by the abbey from Bishop Odo of Bayeux (his successor as earl of Kent) with the consent of King William.[2] The text of both charters has survived and it is noteworthy that neither mentions the other portion. Edward grants so much land as he has in Fordwich,[3] and Odo all his houses in the borough and the customs he has by right.[4] Of course, the earl's rights must have been saved by the king's qualification, but the charters nevertheless illustrate very strikingly the conception of the earl's third penny as a separate estate.

If the pre-Norman sheriff (or other officer of the king) was only responsible to the Crown for a proportion of the revenue of a borough, how was the collection and division between king and earl managed? It is known from Domesday that the farming system was applied before the Conquest to borough revenue as well as to others, and the term *firma burgi* is used in the description of Huntingdon. How far did the early eleventh century *firma burgi* correspond with that of the twelfth and by whom were borough issues let to farm? There is one case on record which in some respects anticipates twelfth-century practice. At Hereford the royal officer apparently farmed the whole of the issues (though *census* not *firma* is the term used) and from his farm paid to king and earl their respective shares.[5] This officer, however, was not the sheriff, but the king's town reeve and even if he paid the king's share to the sheriff, which is by no means certain, the case is not on all fours with later usage since a twelfth-century sheriff would have received the whole *firma* from the reeve and paid the earl (if any) himself. It is unfortunate that information of the Hereford kind is rarely vouchsafed in Domesday. The Huntingdon and Chester entries, however, show that the earl was not always the passive recipient that he seems to be at

---

[1] *D.B.* i. 172. In 1066 the king had £10 besides the landgable, the earl £8 and the bishop a third penny of £6 (*ibid.* 173b). In 1086 the bishop had £8. For the origin of the episcopal share, see above, p. 20.
[2] *Ibid.* i. 12.   [3] *Mon. Angl.* i. 142.
[4] Davis, *Regesta Regum Anglo-Normannorum*, nos. 99, 100.
[5] *D.B.* i. 179.

Hereford. He might have his own officials in the borough taking an active part in arranging the farm and collecting the various items of revenue.   From these entries, too, we learn that the *firma burgi* at this date could have an unexpectedly limited connotation. The total render of the borough of Huntingdon from landgable, mills, moneyers, tolls, and judicial profits was in 1066 £45, of which the king's share was £30.[1] It was only the two last-mentioned items of revenue which were let to farm, and this was done, it is implied, by the king and earl jointly, through their officers (*ministri*) no doubt, who are said later in the passage to have joined in letting land outside the borough to burgesses. The *firma burgi* is here the farm of the fluctuating revenue only, the rest being more or less fixed returns. Its amount in 1066 was £30,[2] but it is noted, if we rightly interpret a somewhat difficult sentence, that the king and earl might sometimes get more or have to take less from the farmer.[3] Nothing is said as to the collection and distribution of the fixed issues, but light may perhaps be gained from Chester where the earl's reeve (*prepositus*) joined with the king's in the collection of tolls and forfeitures,[4] and probably also, in letting the farm of which these issues were the chief, though here apparently not the only, subject.

Although the king's and the earl's shares of the borough revenues were separate estates which could be alienated, *e.g.*, to a religious house, in the earl's case perhaps not without royal licence, and though it is clearly proved that in some instances at any rate the earl's officials took part in the raising of the revenues which were to be divided, it would be dangerous to generalize freely from these facts. Domesday Book is not only reticent, but its concise language is often difficult to interpret and sometimes apparently inconsistent, partly, perhaps, from lack of editing but more, probably, from reflection of differences of usage and want of clearness in contemporary

---

[1] *D.B.*, i. 203.

[2] Not to be confused, of course, with the king's share of the whole revenue from the town including the farm, which happens to be the same amount.

[3] Preter haec habebat rex xx libras et comes x libras de firma burgi, aut plus aut minus sicut poterat collocare partem suam. The last words cannot really mean that king and earl farmed their shares separately. It is merely an awkward way of saying that the sums realized from their shares might be proportionately greater or less than the figures given for 1066, according to the terms of their common bargain with the farmer.

[4] *Ibid.* i. 262b.

thought. In the nature of the case, it cannot be construed so
strictly as the report of a modern royal commission. Thus,
for example, it is provokingly unsystematic in its statement
of the renders of boroughs and their division between king and
earl. Normally, indeed, the total amount is given and the
earl said to take a third or the amount of both shares is stated,
but at Huntingdon the king's share alone is given and save for
the details supplied in an earlier part of the entry it would
probably have been mistaken for the total render.

A real indefiniteness in the English conception of the
relation of king and earl in the borough may be responsible
for some of our difficulties. It was no doubt essentially a
money relation. Tolls and forfeitures in towns where others
than king and earl held land could only be divided in cash.
Nor is there any proof that the demesne houses were ever
actually apportioned between king and earl. The comital
houses which are mentioned at Stafford [1] and Oxford [2] may
at first sight suggest such an apportionment, but as at Stafford
they were not far short of double the number of the demesne
houses, the supposition is on this account alone obviously
inadmissible. The actual division of large stretches of arable
land outside the inhabited area at Thetford [3] between king
and earl does not invalidate these conclusions nor was it the
universal practice. At Huntingdon, as we have seen, such land
was under their joint control.

When the king has granted out his share, the gift or its
result may be referred to in terms which would now imply
an actual splitting up of the borough. King Edward gave
two-thirds of the borough (of Fordwich) to St. Augustine.
Queen Edith had T.R.E. two-thirds of the half-hundred of
Ipswich and of the borough, and Earl Gurth had the third
part. But this was only the concreteness of an age which
identified profitable rights with the local group in which they
were exercised.

Although the earl's share must have been originally derived
from the king, it was inevitable that they should often be
regarded as joint holders of the borough profits and even in
some sort of the soil where they accrued. Borough land, as
distinguished from land belonging to manors without the city,
was defined at Chester in 1086 as " that which had always
paid custom to king and earl." [4] At Norwich, except for the

---

[1] *D.B.* i. 246.   [2] *Ibid.* i. 154.
[3] *Ibid.* ii. 118b.   [4] *Ibid.* i. 262b. See above, p. 88.

small immunities of Archbishop Stigand and Earl Harold, it seems to have been a matter of indifference whether the citizens or the lands on which they lived were described as " in the soke of king and earl." Very instructive from our present point of view is the record of the foundation of a new French borough (the later Mancroft) by Earl Ralph after the Conquest. In obvious imitation of the old system, he gave land to the king in common (*in commune*) to make a borough between him and the king, the profits of which were divided in the ancient proportion. At the date of Domesday there were forty-one burgesses " in the demesne of king and earl." [1]

In this interesting arrangement the idea of joint holding was indeed more clearly developed than in the old boroughs where the derivative character of the earl's rights was never wholly lost sight of. The borough " custom " is sometimes referred to as the king's custom only,[2] and the same lack of precision may explain an apparent inconsistency in the description of Huntingdon, if it be not a mere error. In the enumeration of the houses in the borough, twenty are recorded to have been destroyed in making the castle " which had rendered 16s. 8d. to the king's farm." [3] Lower down, in the analysis of the borough revenue, this lost rent is described as " between the king and the earl." What was the king's farm in question ? Not the *firma burgi* because that did not include house rents (landgable) and presumably not the king's two-thirds since only a proportion of the loss fell on that. Is it possible that the term is here applied to the whole revenue of the borough before the separation of the earl's third ? King William does not seem to have been drawing the latter in 1086, so a reunion with the royal share is not the explanation.

The incompleteness, no less than the want of precision, of Domesday Book prescribes caution in generalizing. It is unsafe to assume that because the earl's reeve took part in raising the revenue in some boroughs, it was not finally divided between king and earl by the king's reeve as at Hereford. There is equal danger in arguing from the silence of Domesday that the earl's reeve did not participate in the handling of the revenue before division at Hereford and other boroughs where he does not happen to be mentioned.

The division of the borough revenues (of which the *firma burgi* in this period might only form a part) between

---

[1] *D.B.* ii. 118. There was not actually an earl at this date.
[2] *Ibid.* ii. 290.   [3] *Ibid.* i. 203.

king and earl may be thought to have favoured farming by
the burgesses themselves, but the casual references in
Domesday do not include any indication of this procedure.
There is evidence, however, of sufficient communal consciousness, in the larger towns at any rate, to make it possible that
London, Winchester, York, and Exeter [1] had been able to
obtain for themselves from the Crown some relaxation of taxation, though this certainly did not amount to " the right of
granting their own taxes." [2]   Dover secured from the Confessor exemption from toll throughout the kingdom and, along
with Fordwich, Romney, and Sandwich, the profits of jurisdiction within the town.[3]   The mixed motives which induced
the Crown to grant charters of privilege so freely to the towns
in the twelfth century were already at work.   A willingness
to show favour to communities with which it had close relations and whose support at times was valuable was perhaps
generally accompanied by more immediate considerations.
The price of their judicial privilege to the seaports of Kent,
for instance, was an annual sea service.

From the evidence offered above, incomplete as it is, we
seem entitled to infer that, at all events in boroughs where
the regular issues were shared between king and earl, the pre-
Norman sheriff did not occupy the same dominant position
as his successor in the period of the early Pipe Rolls.[4]   Even
at Warwick, where (and where alone) borough revenue is
distinctly stated to have been included in the sheriff's farm in
1066, he was only responsible for the king's share.   It is not
certain that this itself was always comprised in the county
farm.   Twenty years later, despite a notable extension of the
sheriff's authority after the Conquest, this was not so in every
case.   The king's two-thirds at Malmesbury were in the hands

[1] *D.B.* i. 100.

[2] As suggested by Dr. Stephenson in *American Historical Review*,
xxxii (1926), 19.

[3] *D.B.* i. 1.   See above, pp. 125-7.

[4] Dr. W. Morris seems to regard the pre-Conquest town reeve as normally the sheriff's subordinate (*E.H.R.* xxxi. 34) but the Wallingford part of
his evidence is based on an error (corrected in his book *The English Sheriff*,
p. 32), the lumping of judicial income from hundreds with the farm of
boroughs was rare and not necessarily decisive, and it is not the case that
" at Chester a certain *forisfactura* collected by the reeve was made over
to the *minister regis* within the city."   The passage in question runs :
malam cervisiam faciens aut in cathedra ponebatur stercoris aut quatuor
solidos dabat prepositis.   Hanc forisfacturam accipieb[ant] minis[tri]
regis et comitis in civitate in cuiuscunque terra fuisset (*D.B.* i. 262b).
The ministers of the king *and earl* are presumably the reeves of the preceding
sentence.

of a farmer who was not the sheriff of Wiltshire, and at Dover the royal reeve farmed both the king's and the earl's share. It seems not unlikely that these are instances of the retention of pre-Conquest arrangements, and the suggestion gains some support from the fact that only for a brief period towards the middle of the twelfth century is Dover known to have been included in the county farm and from 1154 at least no sheriff of Kent ever farmed the borough in our period. In the light of such cases, it is quite possible that the king's reeve at Hereford in 1066 was paying the royal share of the borough issues to the king directly and not through the sheriff. Nor need Hereford have been an entirely exceptional case.

In boroughs where no earl had a share, such as Gloucester, Stamford, and Wallingford, and in smaller towns which (unlike these) were wholly on royal land, the sheriff might be expected to appear as the farmer of the whole, anticipating the normal post-Conquest usage. But the statement in the Domesday account of Wallingford that the reeve was forbidden to provide food out of the king's *census* for burgesses doing carrying service to royal manors [1] suggests that he was farming the town and comparison with a similar but more onerous service at Torksey in Lincolnshire, where the burgesses were fed by the sheriff out of his farm,[2] seems to exclude the possibility that the Wallingford reeve was the sheriff's farmer. The position of the town on the eastern border of Berkshire and its close relations with Oxfordshire may have dictated direct relations with the king. Such a suggestion gathers strength from its subsequent history. As soon as the extant Pipe Rolls begin, it is found to be farmed separately from the county and though, as we shall see, the farmers varied, they were never (in our period) the sheriffs nor did the sheriffs ever receive the allowance which was their due when an ancient farm was withdrawn from them.

2. THE FIRMA BURGI IN 1086

Twenty years after, important changes had come about in the administration of the English boroughs. For the sake of clearness, these have to some extent been anticipated in the preceding section and need not delay us long. In the main, they were the result of the general disestablishment of the earl as an administrative officer and the consequent

---

[1] *D.B.* i. 56.   [2] *Ibid.*, p. 337.

enhancement of the local authority of the sheriff. Official earls remained only on the Scottish and Welsh borders where the Conqueror retained or created semi-regal jurisdictions, an incidental effect of which was the mediatization of Chester and Shrewsbury.[1] Everywhere else, except possibly at Northampton, if the Countess Judith's £7 from the issues of the borough in 1086 had belonged to her late husband, Earl Waltheof, the earl's third penny of the borough, unless it had been previously alienated, as at Fordwich, escheated to the Crown, and though it was in several cases granted out again,[2] the old dualism was effectually ended and the revenue and power of the king were substantially increased.

The new Norman sheriffs, men of superior rank to their English predecessors, were now the chief officials of the Crown in the counties. At an early stage of the Conquest most of the royal boroughs were placed under their control, which was all the more effective because they were usually constables of the castles erected in or just without their county towns. Domesday Book, which has so little to say on the relation of the pre-Conquest sheriff to the borough, affords abundant evidence here. When an intermediate date for an estimate of the value of a borough between 1066 and 1086 is chosen, corresponding to that of the first acquisition of a rural manor by a Norman holder, it is normally: " when X the sheriff received it " or some equivalent phrase.[3]

The sheriff's responsibility to the Crown for borough issues is occasionally recorded. From Worcester, for instance, the sheriff rendered £23 5s., and it is distinctly stated that this included both the king's part and the earl's part.[4] From a local inquest slightly later in date than the great survey we learn that Gloucester had rendered £38 4s. de firma in the time of Sheriff Roger (de Pistri), i.e., c. 1071-83.[5] In this case, the sheriff may have farmed it out as in 1086 Haimo was

[1] William also gave Totnes to Judhel with 20s. which it had rendered to the farm of the royal manor of Langford (ibid. pp. 101, 108b).

[2] To the sheriff at Exeter (ibid. 100), unless this was a pre-Conquest arrangement, and at Stafford, where, however, the king gave half of his own share instead, perhaps to preclude a claim to the earldom (ibid. 246). At Leicester, Hugh de Grentmesnil had the third penny of the £20 received yearly from the moneyers (ibid. f. 230). A third of the custom of the king's burgesses at Barnstaple was given to Bishop Geoffrey of Coutances (D.B. i. 100).

[3] E.g. quando Haimo uicecomes recepit (Canterbury), D.B. i. 2.

[4] See above, pp. 142-3.

[5] Ellis, Introduction to Domesday Book, ii. 446. By the date of the inquest (c. 1096-1101) its render had been increased to £46.

doing at Canterbury,[1] Roger Bigot at Ipswich,[2] the sheriff of Berkshire at Reading,[3] and the sheriff of Northamptonshire at his county town.[4]   It was natural that the sheriff, who had so much to do, should set the borough for which he was responsible to farm and probably this happened oftener than Domesday records.   A single farmer was perhaps the rule at present, as at Canterbury and Rochester, but the line of future progress was indicated by the arrangements at Northampton where the burgesses charged themselves with the payment to the sheriff of a fixed sum for the issues of their borough, which, it is added, formed part of his (county) farm.[5]

The sheriff had power to increase or reduce the sum raised from a borough.   In the first days after the Conquest the render of Winchcombe with its hundred had been fixed at £20 per annum.   Sheriff Durand (c. 1083–96) put on £5 and Roger d'Ivri a further £3.[6]   Roger Bigot, sheriff of Suffolk and keeper of the borough, gave the issues of Ipswich at farm for £40 at Michaelmas.   " Afterwards (continues the record) he could not have the rent (censum) and pardoned 60s. of it.   Now (1086) it renders £37." [7]   Some boroughs now give substantial money gifts [8] to the sheriff, a practice of which there is no earlier mention.

In the short period of fifteen years which had elapsed since the completion of the Conquest, the reorganization of local administration had not been completed in every detail. Domesday clearly reflects a stage of transition.   The earl's third part was now indeed in the hands of the Crown and accounted for by the sheriff, but it was by no means always consolidated with the king's part, as it was at Worcester.

---

[1] *D.B.* i. 2a.   [2] *Ibid.* ii. 290b.   [3] *Ibid.* i. 58.

[4] *Ibid.* i. 219.   Besides the farm, £7 were, as we have seen, paid to the Countess Judith, widow of Earl Waltheof.   This was perhaps the third penny of the borough.

[5] Perhaps, with Mr. Eyton (*Somerset Domesday*, p. 50), we should place Bath by the side of Northampton as a borough farmed by its burgesses. Domesday Book, it is true, merely states that the borough rendered the farm, and the mint £5 in addition, but the Exon Domesday (*D.B.* iv. 106) says " Besides this £60 and mark of gold, *the burgesses* render 100s. from the mint."

[6] *D.B.* i. 162b.   Cf. Ellis, *Introd. to Domesday*, ii. 446-7.

[7] *D.B.* ii. 290b.   For an explanation of Roger's keepership, see below, p. 151.

[8] *De gersuma* in *D.B.*, *de rogatu* in Ellis, *loc. cit.*   Ranging from 12s. (Winchcombe) to £5 10s. (Canterbury).   The burgesses of Yarmouth recorded that their *gersuma* was given freely and out of friendship.   It is doubtful whether these payments were ever premiums for the farm.

In a considerable number of cases, it was still attached to forfeited comital manors. The third penny of Bath was not even accounted for by the sheriff of Somerset, but by Edward of Salisbury, the sheriff of Wiltshire,[1] perhaps, as already conjectured, because included in the farm of some manor in that county. In many boroughs the division between king and earl still appears as the existing arrangement, though there was no earl, whether from the traditionalism which recorded Queen Edith as lady of Exeter twelve years after her death or in view of a possible revival of the earldom with the third penny, but without administrative powers.

There were exceptions to the rule that the royal boroughs passed into the undivided control of the sheriff, for absolute uniformity in this respect never became the policy of the Norman kings. The farming of Gloucester by William fitz Osbern, earl of Hereford (d. 1071) was doubtless a temporary expedient of the Conqueror's early years, but more permanent reasons of national defence dictated the committal of Dover to Bishop Odo of Bayeux, quasi-palatine earl of Kent and constable of its all-important castle. As earl the third penny of the borough went to him. It was probably because he was in prison in 1086 that the town was then farmed by the (king's) reeve.[2] Odo's predecessor, Earl Godwine, may have farmed the town, for the same reasons. It is less obvious, though here again a pre-Conquest arrangement may have been continued, why two of the Wiltshire boroughs, Wilton and Malmesbury (king's share), should have been withheld from the sheriff, who accounted for the third penny of the latter. Wilton was received *ad custodiendum* by Hervey de Wilton, a king's serjeant and small tenant-in-chief,[3] Malmesbury was farmed by Walter Hosed (*Hosatus*), a tenant of religious houses in Somerset.[4] In the next century a borough (or manor) was said to be in custody when it was not at farm, the *custos* being responsible for all receipts and usually receiving a salary. There is no difficulty in assuming that this was the arrangement at Wilton, but the statement that Roger Bigot (the sheriff of Suffolk) had Ipswich in custody seems to be contradicted by the subsequent record that he had let the town at farm. The explanation will perhaps be found in the Domesday division of the Suffolk *Terra Regis*, to which the description of Ipswich is attached, between Roger and others,

[1] *D.B.* i. 64b, 87.   [2] *Ibid.* i. 1.   [3] *Ibid.* 64b, 74b.
[4] *Ibid.* i. 64b ; Eyton, *Som. Domesday*, i. 119 ; ii. 13, 17, 25.

apparently as the result of Earl Ralph's forfeiture, each section being headed " quod servat (custodit) Rogerus (Godricus, etc.)." If so, *servare* (*custodire*) may have been used in a special sense.

While the royal revenue from many boroughs was increased after the Conquest by the confiscation of the earl's third penny, it was further augmented by a general raising of the total renders. A comparison of the figures for 1066 and 1086 (where both are given by the Domesday compilers) in the Table at p. 184 shows that in only two cases (Huntingdon and Malmesbury) was the Edwardian assessment retained without change (and at Huntingdon this was really an increase owing to loss of revenue from houses and mint), that in about a dozen instances the increment was slight or at least less than 100 per cent., but that double, treble and even higher figures were equally common. The farmer of Rochester actually paid eight times the value of the borough twenty years before, but it was noted that this farm was double the real value in 1086. This is an extreme case, but Colchester's assessment was more than five times that of 1066, those of Lincoln and Hereford over three times as much and that of Norwich only slightly less. Nor does this comparison disclose the whole of the extra burden borne by some boroughs. For it does not include the heavy *gersuma* exacted by certain sheriffs nor the revenue from the local mints which seems to be usually comprised in the Edwardian figures. Mesne lords were not slow to follow the royal example. The archbishop of Canterbury, for instance, was receiving from the farmer of Sandwich more than three times what it had paid to King Edward before he gave it to Holy Trinity and in addition 40,000 herrings.[1]

These increases are the more impressive because of the great destruction of houses in many boroughs by war, rebellion, and castle-building. Probably the pre-Conquest assessments were traditional and too low. A good deal must also be allowed for the stimulation of trade and industry by the new masters of the country. Indications are not wanting in Domesday, however, that protests were occasionally raised against the sums exacted as excessive. At Wallingford,[2] Chichester,[3] and Guildford,[4] as well as at Rochester,[5] the farms or renders are stated to have been higher than the true value. The case of Ipswich quoted above in a different connexion,[6] where the

[1] *D.B.* i. 3.   [2] *Ibid.* i. 56.   [3] *Ibid.* f. 23.
[4] *Ibid.* f. 30.   [5] *Ibid.* f. 3.   [6] P. 150.

sheriff had to lower the amount he demanded for the farm, because no one would give it, is significant. The fact that the reduction was only £3 in £40 seems to show that the sheep were being pretty closely shorn.

Stafford was the only borough which was rendering less to the king in 1086 than in 1066, but it had evidently suffered severely in the last rebellion of Earl Eadwine and many houses were lying waste.[1]

The values of boroughs when first taken over by the Normans are too rarely given to generalize from, but it is worth noting that only in one instance is the figure higher than that of 1086. What led to the reduction of the render of Maldon[2] by one-third to little more than the Edwardian figure we do not know.

Of the borough renders T.R.E. the only two that are distinctly said to have been *de firma* as a whole are those of Winchcombe and Chester,[3] but the *census* mentioned at Hereford and Wallingford may have been a farm and even where the whole was not farmed the details of the Huntingdon render have made it clear to us that the unfixed part of the borough issues, the tolls and forfeitures, might be, and probably usually was, let to farm and known as the *firma burgi*. It is not necessary to suppose, however, that when Domesday speaks only of a " render " there was not an inclusive farm behind it. The Norman administrative changes certainly favoured such farms, yet in the Domesday statistics for 1086 a farm is only definitely mentioned in some half a dozen cases. " Reddebat " may sometimes, perhaps often, be short for " reddebat in firma." Some confirmation of this conjecture is probably to be found in the disappearance of many of the payments in kind of twenty years before. At Norwich, for instance, no more is heard of the six sextaries of honey and the bear and six dogs for the bear of 1066.[4] Unless they were exchanged for the hawk of 1086, their value must be included in the largely increased money render. Gloucester is an even better case, for here there was nothing but money in 1086 to represent the honey and iron of King Edward's day.[5]

---

[1] *D.B.* i. 246.

[2] *Ibid.* ii. 6.   The figures are 1066 £13 2s. ;   quando Petrus (de Valognes) recepit £24 ; 1086, £16.

[3] *Ibid.* i. 162b. 262b.   The king's two-thirds at Malmesbury were included in a farm (*ibid*. i. 64b, 1).

[4] *Ibid.* ii. 117 f.   [5] *Ibid.* i. 162.

Among minor points of interest in these borough renders is the appearance even before the Conquest of payments that anticipate those *elemosynae constitutae* which figure so prominently in the sheriffs' farms in the Pipe Rolls. Small sums were being paid in 1066 by Norwich[1] and Ipswich[2] " ad prebendarios."

The amounts of the borough farms or renders in 1086 can only be used as an index of the relative size and wealth of English towns at that date with a warning that the royal demesne, from which the item of rents came, was a variable quantity and that though the number of burgesses or inhabited houses seems at times to show a rough correspondence with the renders, it is subject to startling exceptions. Unfortunately London, and Winchester are omitted from Domesday, but the farm of London is known from later sources to have been £300 in the time of the Conqueror.[3] Next come York and Lincoln with £100 each. The figure at Norwich was £90, but payments to the sheriff, etc., brought it up to much the same amount. Colchester paid £82, besides £5 to the sheriff. Chester and Thetford were charged with £76 apiece, Gloucester, Hereford, Oxford with £60, and Wallingford ought to have been according to the jurors, though it rendered £80.

The boroughs with the lowest renders were Stafford (£7), Pevensey (£5 19s.), Reading (£5), and Barnstaple (£3). It is noted that the farmer at Reading was losing 17s.[4]

3. The Firma Burgi and the Commune, 1086–1154

But for the accidental preservation of the Pipe Roll of 1130,[5] the seventy years which followed the great survey would be an almost barren period in the history of the borough farms. It is true that the age of royal charters to boroughs begins with the reign of Henry I, but, with the notable exception of the great charter to London, his grants did not touch the financial relations of the towns to the Crown.

As regards these, the reign of William Rufus is a blank, except in so far as further mediatization of boroughs diminished the royal revenue from this source. Rufus gave Bath, which had escheated to the Crown after Queen Edith's death, to the

---

[1] *D.B.* ii. 117b.   [2] *Ibid.* f. 290b.
[3] Round, *Geoffrey de Mandeville*, p. 352.   [4] *D.B.* i. 58.
[5] It seems to have been mistaken for the lost roll of 1 Hen. II. See Stevenson's preface to the earlier roll, p. vi.

bishop of Wells,[1] and it was he apparently who rewarded the loyalty of Henry of Newburgh and Simon of Senlis with the earldoms of Warwick and Northampton and the lordship of those towns.[2] Simon as the son-in-law of Waltheof had a hereditary claim to the earldom, though not to the town. One of his charters to his abbey of St. Andrew is addressed to his prefect of Northampton and all his men dwelling there, exempting the monks' land " ab omnibus consuetudinibus que ad burgum pertinent, a geldo scilicet (MS. set) et a gilda et ab omnibus aliis de quibus eos quietare possumus." [3] There is some evidence that Henry I granted the earldom of Northampton as well as that of Huntingdon to David of Scotland, the husband of Simon's widow, but he kept the lordship of the town in his own hands and it was being farmed from the Crown in 1130. Colchester was given by Henry with all its customs to Eudes the Sewer in 1101, but escheated on his death in 1120 and was not granted out again.[4] On the other hand, it was under Henry I that the count of Meulan, elder brother of the earl of Warwick, acquired the lordship of Leicester which he transmitted to the earls of Leicester, his descendants, and Henry gave Reading to his new abbey there.[5]

In the first extant Pipe Roll then, in 1130, the ancient issues of Bath, Warwick, Reading, and Leicester, along with those of Chester, were not included, because they were in the hands of subjects. Against this, however, was to be set the escheat of Shrewsbury by the rebellion of Earl Robert in 1102 and the vacancy of the bishopric of Durham during which the city was in the hands of the Crown.

Of the boroughs which remained chargeable to the king, the greater number would not have appeared by name in the roll, since their issues were incorporated in the county farms, were it not that gild fines, penalties in pleas of the Crown and the borough aid were *extra firmas*. Except in the methods of dealing with the problem of a depreciated currency, the transitional features observable in 1086 have disappeared and the local system of administration disclosed

---

[1] Davis, *Regesta Regum Anglo-Normannorum*, no. 326.

[2] It has been doubted whether Simon received the earldom before Henry I's time (Farrer, *Honors and Knights' Fees*, ii. 296), but he attests a charter of the previous reign as earl (Davis, *op. cit.*, no. 315) and was already earl at Henry's coronation.

[3] MS. Cott. Vesp. E. xvii, f. 5b. I owe this reference to Professor Stenton.

[4] Farrer, *Itinerary of Henry I*, no. 32.   [5] *Mon. Angl.* iv. 40.

by the roll differs in no essential respect from that which lies behind the early Pipe Rolls of Henry II.

Eight boroughs were at this date farmed separately from their counties and, with the exception of London and Lincoln,[1] six of these [2] are the only towns the amount of whose farms in 1130 is known. Malmesbury and Dover certainly and probably Canterbury and Wallingford had had this status in 1086. Colchester and Northampton were escheats. Dover and Canterbury were farmed by the sheriff of Kent, Malmesbury by the (royal) reeve of the town and the others by local barons, Brian fitz Count, the king's Breton protégé at Wallingford,[3] Robert Revell at Northampton and Hamon de St. Clare at Colchester. Since the sheriffs of Essex and Northamptonshire received no allowance for the loss of these borough farms, as they would have done in Henry II's time, we may perhaps infer that their county farms had been adjusted to meet the loss and that the amounts of farms in general were not yet so fixed as they afterwards became. Of the six borough farms with which we are dealing, only two, so far as we know, those of Colchester (£40 blanch) and Northampton (£100 by tale) remained exactly the same under Henry II. The Colchester farm of 1130 was just about half its render in 1086 but that of Northampton, on the other hand, showed a remarkable increase, being more than three times what the burgesses had paid to the sheriff in 1086. Was this the result of Simon de Senlis's régime? The other farms show similar variations in both directions. That of Canterbury had been reduced by almost exactly 50 per cent., from £54 to £27 8s. 10d., Wallingford's from the oppressive £80 of 1086 to £9 less than the £60 which had been given as its true value at that date. On the other hand, Malmesbury's farm had risen from £14 to £20, Dover's from £54 to £90 9s. 9d., and London's (with Middlesex) from £300 to £525 0s. 10½d.[4] In the last case only were there really serious

---

[1] *Red Book of Exchequer*, ii. 657; Ballard, *British Borough Charters*, i. 221 (the date must be 1154 or 1155, for the farm was raised from £140 blanch to £180 tale at Michaelmas 1155; unless we suppose that the latter was " the farm customary in the time of King Henry my grandfather " and had been reduced by Stephen.)

[2] Owing to mutilation of the roll, the farms of Winchester and Southampton are not known.

[3] His court influence is seen in the cancelling of three years' arrears of borough aid (£45) " on account of the poverty of the burgesses " (*P.R.* 31 Hen, I, p. 139).

[4] In this comparison, I have not taken into account any differences in the mode of computation. That is hardly possible at this period, except for blanch and tale payments, and in any case would not disturb the general impression.

arrears when the account was closed at Michaelmas 1130. The four sheriffs were left owing more than £310. It is not surprising that they were ready to pay a considerable sum to be relieved of their onerous office,[1] but they do not seem to have succeeded. Their enormous debt may very well have been one of the reasons which induced Henry not long after to issue his famous charter granting the farm to the citizens in perpetuity at the earlier and more equitable figure. This involved the concession of the right to elect the sheriffs who were the actual farmers and who had hitherto been appointed by the king. Already in 1130 the Londoners had proffered 100 marks for this right and had paid nearly half of that sum, but the smallness of the fine suggests that they were only paying for a temporary possession of the farm.[2]

The acquisition by the citizens of the right to pay their own farm into the exchequer with the other privileges conferred by Henry's charter, although it was in a few years lost again for half a century, forms the first great landmark in the development of self-government in the English boroughs. They were not, however, the first in the field, for the roll of 1130 records that the men of Lincoln proffered 200 marks of silver and four of gold " that they might hold the city of the king in chief " (in capite).[3] They had the additional stimulus that the sheriff farmers were not citizens as at London but external officials. It is not certain that they secured a grant of the farm in fee (feodi firma) or, in looser modern phrase, perpetual lease, but comparison of the sum they offered with the London one makes it not impossible. If they did, Lincoln can claim to have been the first borough to obtain such a grant. However this may be, she was certainly more fortunate than London in retaining her privilege, whether it was granted to them and their heirs or only to themselves. Stephen and Mathilda in their rival bids for the support of Geoffrey de Mandeville ignored Henry's charter to London and regranted its sheriffdom to him as it had been held by his father and grandfather. The only consolation of the Londoners was that the traditional farm of £300 was thereby confirmed. Lincoln, on the other hand, would seem to have continued to farm her own revenues, for at Michaelmas, 1155, Aubrey its reeve accounted for a whole year's farm, £140, including the last weeks of Stephen's reign, the amount being credited to the sheriff in the county farm.[4]

---

[1] P.R. 31 Hen. I, p. 149.   [2] Ibid. p. 148.
[3] Ibid. p. 114.   [4] Red Book of Excheq. ii. 657.

M

The proffers of London and Lincoln for their farms in
1130 are the first signs that the leading English boroughs
at least were no longer content to remain mere reservoirs of
revenue of which royal officials were the conduits, but had so
far developed a communal spirit as to aim at collecting the
borough issues themselves, putting an end to intermediate
profits and extortions and getting rid of distasteful interference.
They aspired, in fact, to secure the emancipation of the borough
from the shire in finance as well as in justice. That Henry I
was prepared to go some way in satisfying this ambition is
shown by his acceptance of their proffers and by his subsequent charter to London which not only allowed the citizens
to farm the city and the small county in which it lay, at a
greatly reduced rate, but placed them in a more favourable
position than the citizens of Lincoln in the power to elect the
justiciar who tried the pleas of the Crown arising in the city.[1]

These concessions may not have been entirely induced
by the sums which the boroughs were ready to pay for the
privilege and by Henry's desire to secure their support for his
settlement of the succession to the Crown. His other town
charters show him favourable to their liberties and if he kept
a strict control on the formation of craft gilds, he was probably meeting the wishes of the governing class in the boroughs.
He had shown his confidence in the higher business qualities
of townsmen by letting the farm of the silver mine of Alston
to the burgesses of Carlisle.[2] As a statesman, he may have
thought that the best way to exclude the violence of the
communal movement on the other side of the channel was to
remedy grievances, bring the towns into more direct relations
with the Crown and satisfy reasonable aspirations. Even the
less liberal policy of the French kings was successful in excluding the commune, essentially an uprising against mesne
lords of towns, from the cities of the royal domain. In England
where mesne towns were rare and recently mediatized and
where the royal power was normally much stronger than
in France and still more than in the Empire, the influence of the
continental movement never became really disturbing save
at times of political crisis.

The phrasing of Henry I's grants to Lincoln and London,

---

[1] The bishop seems to have been *ex officio* justiciar of Lincoln and
Lincolnshire (*Registrum Antiquissimum of Lincoln Cathedral*, ed. C. W.
Foster (Linc. Rec. Soc., no. 27), i. 63, *cf.* 60).

[2] *P.R.* 31 Hen. I, p. 142.

especially that to Lincoln as it is to be inferred from the Pipe Roll entry, suggests at first sight a close parallelism to the French commune as defined by Luchaire, a *seigneurie collective populaire*.[1] Formally, indeed, the English grants are in stricter feudal form than the French, for while Henry conceded to the citizens of Lincoln to hold their city in chief of the Crown and to those of London and their heirs to hold Middlesex [and London] of himself and his heirs, the communal charters merely grant the right to have a commune without any such security for permanence as at London, and defining its relation to the lord only by specific clauses similar to those in charters granted by Anglo-Norman lords to new boroughs in England and often containing severe restrictions on the independence of the commune. Henry's grants are, so far as we know, made without express restrictions and his concessions, like the communal grants, allowed the election of municipal officers by the citizens, though by making royal officers elective, not by allowing the creation of new popular officials. The burgesses of English royal boroughs already enjoyed the elementary rights which the communes were formed to secure, freedom of person and protection of their possessions against the arbitrary power of feudal lords and officials, with, normally, a court for all but the most serious cases arising within the boundaries of the town. It might seem that when they had obtained a lease of their farm, they had nothing to envy the continental commune.[2] Yet we shall find London and at least one other town which occupied this privileged position attempting to set up a commune, and in the case of London perhaps for a moment succeeding.

What did the greatest English boroughs lack which continental communes possessed? In the first place, it must be remembered that a strong monarchy, which drew a large part of its revenue from this source, kept them normally under strict control. Even in France, as we have seen, the French kings, while usually favouring the communal movement in towns belonging to other lords, did not allow communes in the more important cities of their own domain. Neither

[1] We need not commit ourselves to the extreme form in which this conception was finally stated. Cf. Stephenson, *Borough and Town*, pp. 215 ff.

[2] There seems no evidence of French communes obtaining farming leases until the grants of Philip Augustus to Pontoise, Poissy, Mantes, and Chaumont (Hegel, *Städte und Gilden der germanischen Völker*, ii. 68). It is possibly significant that these were all in or adjoining the French Vexin, on the Norman border. *Cf.* Madox, *Firma Burgi*, p. 3.

Paris nor Orleans, for instance, ever attained the communal status.

Maitland has warned us that the privilege conferred by a lease of its farm to a town was not so wide as the terms of some grants might suggest. The retention by the Crown of direct relations with its tenants in the boroughs and of its property in their unoccupied spaces shows that what the burgesses were enfeoffed with was not a mesne tenancy of the town.[1] His conclusion that the grant of a town in farm to its burgesses was merely a grant of the sheriff's bailliwick in the town is borne out by the terms of Henry II's charter to Cambridge in 1185.[2] The borough reeve or bailiff, though elected by the burgesses, when they became responsible for the farm, to represent them in the collection and payment thereof, remained in some sense a royal officer.

The continental commune, though its status was one of vassalage in place of previous subjection, does not itself seem to have obtained a mesne tenancy of the soil of the town. The rights of the lord over his tenants, though severely abridged and regularized, were carefully guarded. Nevertheless, the communal movement had inevitably a powerful attraction for the more restless and ambitious elements in English boroughs. (1) In its early and most striking phase, it was a revolutionary movement, and where it triumphed, its success was primarily due to a sworn confederacy of the citizens, though it was favoured by the quarrels of feudal lords and the self-interested sympathy of the king at Paris. (2) Between a self-governing community of this type created *de novo* and the slowly developing *communitas* of the English borough, comparison doubtless seemed all in favour of the " commune." It had the strongest bond of union, cemented by oath and sanctioned by charter. While the borough was painfully adapting an organization mainly judicial to growing administrative needs, the communal charter provided a council for both purposes.[3] Instead of a municipal head who even in rarely favoured towns was, though elective, still practically

---

[1] *Hist. of English Law*, i. 650 f.

[2] " Sciatis me tradidisse ad firmam burgensibus meis de Cantebruge villam meam de Cantrebruge, tenendam de me in capite per eandem firmam quam vicecomites mihi reddere solebant, et ut ipsi inde ad scaccarium meum respondeant " (Stubbs, *Select Charters*, ed. Davis, p. 196). This was a terminable lease, not a grant in fee farm.

[3] For the distinction of *consules* or *consultores*, usually twelve in number, from or among the *scabini* see K. Hegel, *Städte und Gilden der germanischen Völker*, passim.

an officer of the royal lord and in the rest was subordinate to the royal sheriff, the commune chose a mayor whose obligations were to it alone.[1]   It is not surprising that these features should have made a strong appeal to discontented or aspiring burgesses in England.who did not know how seldom the full ideal of communal independence was realized, how many compromises had to be made and what poor security for permanence the strongest of the communes possessed.

I have suggested that Henry I's concessions to Lincoln and London may have been in part dictated by a statesmanlike policy of keeping the influence of the communal idea within bounds, but it is no more than a suggestion.   The anarchy of Stephen's reign was much more favourable to the spread of the contagion, especially in London which was fully alive to the importance of its support in the succession strife.   Dr. Round has noted the likeness of the *pactio . . . mutuo juramento* between Stephen and the city in 1135 and the bilateral oaths of the French communes and their lords. He is inclined to see a definite adoption of French precedent in the *communio quam vocant Londoniarum* which in 1141 sent to the Empress Matilda to pray for the king's release and into which barons of the realm had been received, a well-known practice of foreign communes.   The parallel of sworn " conspiratio " is exact enough, but as there is no mention of municipal liberties demanded, its only object may have been the expulsion of the empress [2] and in any case it was short-lived.   As we have seen, even the concessions of Henry I were sacrificed to Stephen's need of the support of Geoffrey de Mandeville.   After Geoffrey's desertion to the empress, who confirmed Stephen's grant, he still kept a garrison in the Tower.   Its surrender in 1143 left it open to the king either to revert to the commune if there had been a communal constitution or to Henry I's constitution, but unfortunately we have no hint as to how London was governed in the last decade of the reign.

[1] In the Anglo-French communes this was not always so.   The burgesses of La Rochelle used to present three of the more discreet and better burgesses to King John for him to elect one of them as mayor (*Rot. Litt. Claus.*, p. 535).

[2] Petit-Dutaillis, *Studies Supplementary to Stubbs' Constitutional History*, i. 95.

4. Revocable Grants of Firma Burgi; Attempted Communes 1154–91

From the very beginning of his reign, Henry II repressed the more ambitious aspirations of the burgess class in the English towns. He might grant or confirm " communes " in his domains in France where the movement had been brought under control by politic lords and their concessions did not go much beyond what the English borough enjoyed by custom or charter, but in England the name was still the war-cry of extremists and we may see a substantial truth in Richard of Devizes' often-quoted remark on John's commune of London that his father would not have permitted it for a thousand thousands of silver marks. Henry, indeed, showed himself less liberal than his grandfather. While continuing and cautiously extending the elder Henry's policy of leasing the *firma burgi* to the burgesses, he never made or confirmed such a grant in fee, reserving in every case the power of revoking it at will. In most cases, too, these concessions were obviously prompted by the initial fines and the additions to the farms which were obtained from the burgesses as the price of the privilege.[1]

Both aspects of his policy are perhaps illustrated by his treatment of Lincoln. If Henry I's grant to its citizens had been in fee farm, it was superseded by a charter, which must belong to the early days of his grandson's reign, simply delivering the city to them at the farm it had paid in the time of the first Henry.[2] Accordingly at Michaelmas 1155 their reeve accounted at the exchequer for £140 (blanch) *de firma*, the exact amount for which the sheriff of Lincolnshire received allowance in his account.[3] But by the next account the amount of their farm had been raised to £180 by tale (£171 blanch) at which it remained.[4] Their uncertain tenure of it was emphasized when two years later it was transferred to the (new) sheriff, for no apparent reason, as it was not in arrears.[5] The new arrangement was perhaps not regarded as more than temporary, for although the £180 was lumped with the farm of the county, it is shown to have been looked upon as

---

[1] Henry usually avoided mediatizing boroughs, as that meant loss of revenue, but he granted Stamford to Richard de Humez, his constable for Normandy. *P.R.* 2 Hen. II, p. 24.

[2] Ballard, *British Borough Charters*, i. 221.

[3] *Red Book of Exchequer*, ii. 656-7.

[4] *P.R.* 2 Hen. II, p. 28.   [5] *Ibid.* 4 Hen. II, p. 136.

really separate (though in the same hands) by the heading
de nova firma Comitatus et de firma Civitatis Lincol' and by
the retention of the sheriff's old allowance of £140. This was
an awkward bit of book-keeping, and in 1162 his account for
the city was rendered separately.[1] Next year the farm was
restored to the citizens, for William de Paris and Ailwin Net,
who accounted at Michaelmas 1164,[2] were the reeves of the
city and not in this case likely to be farming it on their own
account.   The reeves continue to account to the end of the
reign, and their representative position is sufficiently proved
by the appearance of the citizens in their own name as accountants or rather as defaulters in 2 Richard I.[3] The sheriff
took the farm into his own hands until the citizens received
a fee farm by charter in 1194.

London could not expect from Henry even the modest
degree of favour that fell to Lincoln, for while that city had
never come into personal conflict with his mother, London
had ignominiously expelled her and ruined her cause.   Henry's
charter confirming that of his grandfather, granted apparently
in 1155, omitted its most prized concessions, the fee farm and
its low figure of £300 as well as the election of sheriff and
justices.[4] But as even Stephen, in part of his reign at any
rate, had ignored these concessions, their omission was not so
marked a rebuff as it would otherwise have been.   If election
of sheriffs had been resumed in Stephen's later years, it now
certainly ceased and throughout the reign of his successor
London had less control over its financial officers than
Shrewsbury or Bridgenorth.

This grievance would have been less galling, had it not been
accompanied by a return to the heavy farm in force before the
charter of Henry I. Owing to the unfortunate loss of the
Pipe Roll for the first year of Henry II, we cannot be sure
that Stephen was not responsible, in whole or part, for this
reversion, after the death of Geoffrey de Mandeville.   His
indebtedness to the Londoners may seem to render this unlikely, but on the other hand the full farm of his successor's
reign, which was already exacted in his second year, was a
composite figure, due apparently to a slight raising of a rounder
figure at some earlier date.

From Christmas 1155, the London accounts for the reign
are complete, except for the fifth year.   By disclosing the

---

[1] *P.R.* 8 Hen. II, p. 20.   [2] *Ibid.* 10 Hen II, p. 23.
[3] *Ibid.* 2 Ric. I, 76.   [4] Round, *Geoffrey de Mandeville*, 368.

amount of the farm and the details of the sheriff's payments for a long series of years they would seem to make possible an estimate of the equity or otherwise of a farm which during the greater part of the reign was more than two and a half times higher than that of Southampton, the wealthiest town after London. In the hope of some light on this point, I have made a detailed examination of the Pipe Roll figures. The results of such an examination cannot be explained clearly without a preliminary word or two on the form of the sheriff's account. As is well known, the amount of the farm, being well known to the officials of the exchequer, is not usually stated on the rolls, but is easily ascertained by adding the payments with which the sheriffs were credited to their debt on the year.[1] In point of fact, however, owing to a temporary change in the system of account between 1169 and 1173, the actual figure of the farm is for that period given upon the rolls. On two occasions, as will be seen later, that figure was slightly reduced for a particular year. Against it in the rolls the sheriffs are credited with (1) cash paid by them into the Treasury, (2) allowances for sums expended by them in the financial year on the king's behalf, by custom or by his writs or those of his deputies. Cash payments, however, were only made in seventeen of the thirty-two years of the reign for which we have complete accounts. The allowances, technically known as the issue (*exitus*), *i.e.* disbursements, of the farm, were the permanent item in the sheriffs' credits. In three years only did these credits exactly balance the farm or give the sheriffs a slight surplus.[2] For the rest, a larger or smaller debt was carried over from every Michaelmas audit.

The number of sheriffs was normally two, but once (in 1176–77) only one and for considerable periods three or four. As they were each personally responsible for an equal share of the arrears of the farm,[3] their multiplication facilitated the collection of outstanding debt. There is one apparent exception to this liability when the new sheriffs of 1162–63

---

[1] Though in the case of farms which were paid partly in the depreciated currency of the time and partly in a money of account that allowed for this depreciation ("blanched" money), the two elements cannot be isolated, unless they are kept apart in the account. The total must be calculated in one or other of the two modes of computation.

[2] 1162–63, 1164–65, 1176–77. In three other cases, new sheriffs entering office during the financial year had no debt at the end of their first quarter or half-year.

[3] The widow of one was charged with the balance of his arrears.

paid the arrears of their predecessors for the two preceding years, amounting to over £250.[1] This may have been by private arrangement.

The first extant account, that of Michaelmas 1156,[2] is only for nine months, but assuming that the farm was wholly payable in blanched money and reducing the allowances, which were always expressed by tale (*i.e.* in current coin), to blanch by the exchequer method of deducting a shilling in each pound, we discover that the sheriffs accounted for £390 13s. 6d. blanch or at the rate of £520 18s. per annum. Similar treatment of all the other farming accounts of the reign but two produces the same total.[3] County farms payable entirely in blanched money were rarely round sums and it is not until Michaelmas 1160 that we get the least hint that the farm of London and Middlesex was in part paid in current coin. In that account the sheriffs' debt, much the highest so far, is divided into £364 11s. 7d. blanch and £22 by tale.[4] The distinction is clearly connected with the simultaneous reduction of the farm for the following year, the last of these sheriffs, to £500 blanch,[5] for by the exchequer system £22 by tale was blanched to £20 18s. It seems a probable inference that at some earlier date, perhaps down to 1156, the farm had been exactly £500 blanch and that the £22 by tale was an increment. When the debt of 1160 was paid in the following year, only the larger blanch sum is described as " of the old farm," which suggests that the tale payment was regarded as an appendage to, rather than integral part of, the farm, an appendage which might, as in the present case, be dropped as a favour to overburdened sheriffs. No such favour was extended to the new sheriffs of 1161–62, but the fact that their cash payment was reckoned as £198 8s. 2d. blanch and £22 tale shows that the distinction between the two items of the farm was not a purely momentary one. Indeed a few years later, in 1166–67, the farm was again reduced to £500 blanch in favour of sheriffs whose debt was the next highest, though *longo intervallo* to that of 1160,[6] and while the full amount was exacted for the rest of the reign, the tale

---

[1] *P.R.* 9 Hen. II, pp. 71-2.   [2] *Ibid.* 2 Hen II, p. 13.
[3] In a few years, the sum does not come out exactly, the variations ranging from 3d. up to £2 17s. but these are evidently due to mistakes of the scribe or printer or to errors in my arithmetic.
[4] *P.R.* 6 Hen. II, p. 13.   [5] *Ibid.* 7 Hen II, p. 18.
[6] *Ibid.* 13 Hen. II, pp. 2-3.

payment is from time to time stated on the rolls as a distinct and separable item in the farm.[1]

If the motive which has been suggested for the reduction of the farm in 1160 and 1167 be the true one, the emergence of much heavier debts in the middle period of the reign may have made this very moderate relief too ludicrously inadequate to be resorted to again. The very sheriffs who obtained the relief in 1166–67 were charged the full amount in 1167–68, though they paid only a little over £3 of it in that year.[2]

It would be hasty to conclude from such debts that the amount of the farm was in itself too heavy to be borne. On several occasions, as already mentioned, the whole sum was paid off within the year and in nearly as many cases the debt fell well below £100. Practically the entire indebtedness of the sheriffs was also wiped out sooner or later, though only, no doubt, by multiplying them and changing them frequently, thus leaving each free to work off his debt. A considerable part of the farm must have been neither more nor less than a fine on the sheriffs. Yet this perhaps need not have been the case, had the farm been the only financial burden imposed upon the city. The oppressive *auxilia* and *dona* levied upon London as upon other boroughs,[3] at fairly frequent intervals,

---

[1] In his valuable paper on "The Sheriff's Farm," Mr. G. J. Turner correctly states the farm as £500 blanch and £22 by tale for all the years he examined but one (*Trans. Roy. Hist. Soc.*, N.S. xii (1898), 145). The farm in 13 Hen. II was £500 only. Perhaps there is a misprint for 15 Hen. II. Dr. Round, though he did not work out the accounts, gives the correct amount of the farm for the years 1169–74, where it is stated in or directly deducible from them, but, apparently misled by a tale payment in sheriffs' arrears, he speaks of the farm as £500 blanch " plus a varying sum of about £20 ' numero ' (*i.e.* tale)," and as being " between £520 and £530 " (*Commune of London*, 1899, pp. 229, 233). Mr. Page ignores the £22 altogether (*London*, p. 106). Dr. Round's conversion of the whole farm into £547 by tale (by adding a shilling in the pound on the £500 blanch) is useful for comparison with the accounts of the keepers of 1174–76, which were not blanched, but has helped to mislead Sir James Ramsay. Misunderstanding the remark that " the exact amount of the high farm is first recorded in 1169," Sir James refers to " the £547 to which the farm had been raised in 1169 from the £300 at which it had been previously held " (*Angevin Empire*, p. 317). Apart from the post-dating of the rise in the farm by many years, the figures compared are not expressed in the same mode of computation.

[2] *P.R.* 14 Hen. II, p. 2.

[3] See Carl Stephenson, " The Aids of the English Boroughs," *E.H.R.* xxxiv. 457-75. In his table (p. 469) Mr. Stephenson inserts among the London taxes a *donum* of 1000 marks in 7 Hen. II and an aid of the same amount in 8 Hen. II. That there was aid in the latter year is certain and it is quite likely to have been 1000 marks, but the membrane of the Pipe Roll is imperfect and shows no total. Has Mr. Stephenson identified it with the " old aid " of 1000 marks on the roll of the ninth year (p. 72) ? That is certainly the *donum* of 7 Hen. II (*P.R.* p. 18).

seem sometimes to coincide significantly with a crisis in the collection of the farm. Some light is perhaps thrown upon the incomplete account of 1159 and the large debt of the next year by the payment of a *donum* of £1043. It can hardly be mere coincidence either that 1168 when the farm practically remained unpaid was also the year in which £537 was collected from the city towards the *aide pur fille marier*. Nevertheless, it must be admitted that an aid of nearly £300 in 1165 and of £630 in 1177 do not seem to have interfered in the least with the raising of the farm.

When the two sheriffs of 1163–68 went out of office at Easter 1169, they were required to account for their large debt jointly with the half-year's farm, instead of separately as heretofore,[1] and the same arrangement was applied annually to their four successors, who held office until Christmas 1173. If it was hoped to secure any financial advantage thereby, the change of system was a disastrous failure, for the sheriffs paid nothing into the treasury after 1170 and accumulated a debt of nearly £950, about twice the average *per annum* for the period before 1168, and the Crown had to wait much longer for its money. The arrangement, however, was continued under new sheriffs for eighteen months until in June, 1174, two keepers (*custodes*) were appointed who, unlike the sheriffs, were not to answer for the farm, but only for its issue (*exitus*).[2] In other words, they accounted merely for the disbursements they made by the king's order, paying no cash into the treasury and making no heavy debts. The actual Crown receipts from them were not very greatly less than those from the sheriffs of recent years, for the sum of roughly £200 blanch which the keepers accounted for in their one complete financial year, 1174–75, after deducting their expenses,[3] did not fall much more than £30 below the total receipts of 1173 [4] or more than £66 below the average of those of 1171 and 1172. But the Crown of course lost a great deal more than this, something like £320 per annum in all, because it no longer collected the debts due from sheriff farmers as arrears of their farm.

There can be no doubt that Dr. Round is right in regarding

---

[1] *P.R.* 15 Hen. II, p. 169.   [2] *Ibid.* 20 Hen. II, p. 9.

[3] *Ibid.* 21 Hen. II, pp. 15-17.   The keepers accounted in current money, but it is here blanched to facilitate comparison with the payments of years in which the city was at farm.

[4] The outgoing sheriffs paid up most of their arrears by Michaelmas, but these were charged to them individually in equal shares (*ibid.* 19 Hen. II, pp. 187 ff.).

this sacrifice as a measure of relief to the citizens.[1]   June,
1174, was the critical point in the feudal revolt of 1173–74.
An invading force from Flanders had just landed on the east
coast.   The city was raising a *donum* of 1000 marks, supple-
mented by large contributions from three leading citizens,
one of whom was William fitz Isabel, the most prominent
sheriff of the reign.   It was manifestly in the king's interest to
show liberality at such a time.   At the end of two years, however, the keepers were dismissed and the farming system was
restored at the old high rate, but with some salutary improve-
ments in the system.   From Midsummer 1176 until Easter
1187, except for the year 1178, William fitz Isabel was sheriff,
with a colleague for the three years following that, but for
the greater part of the time alone.   This bold departure from
the policy of dividing the burden of the farm among as many
as four sheriffs, might seem risky, but on the whole it proved
successful.   Debt was kept down to more moderate figures
by greater and more continuous cash payments combined,
in the earlier years at least, with larger royal drafts under the
head of *exitus*.   Fitz Isabel's first year and a quarter were
entirely free from debt, despite a heavy aid, and until 1183 the
adverse balances never rose above £188.   As in the early
years of the reign, each debt account was kept separate and
closed in the year following that in which it was incurred.
And so, though fitz Isabel's payments were unusually low in
1184, for no apparent reason, and in 1186, his last full year,
probably because he had been amerced 1000 marks for accepting weak pledges, he went out of office six months later, owing
only £184 odd.[2]   His successors had only a slightly larger
debt at Henry II's last Michaelmas audit.

A review of the history of the London farm during the
reign suggests that it was extortionate, but not crushing.
It could be paid without great difficulty in two annual instal-
ments over periods of years, but it was always liable to be
disturbed by other burdens cast upon the city, and unless the
sheriffs obtained some assistance from their wealthy fellow
citizens, which is hardly likely, they must have paid a large
part of the farm out of their own pockets.   At the same
time, too much stress ought not perhaps to be laid upon the
debts of the sheriffs, owing to the peculiar form of their
account.   The only payments compulsory upon them in the
current year were the royal drafts.   These were normally

---

[1] *Commune of London*, p. 232.   [2] *P.R.* 33 Hen. II, p. 39.

for (1) fixed alms and wages, less than £50 in all, and (2) household and national expenses, which varied considerably according as the king was at home or abroad, at peace or at war and so on, though for the most part the range of variation was between about £200 and about £320. There is little evidence of attempts to correct these variations by cash payments, for it must often have been the sheriff's apparent interest to postpone as much of his indebtedness as possible to the next year. William fitz Isabel's steady cash payments in the later years of the reign showed sounder finance.

It was always in the power of the Crown to draw more heavily upon the sheriffs, if it was wished to obtain a larger portion of the farm in the current year or to close a sheriff's account. This was not infrequently done by " attorning " to the farm part of the king's debts to the financier William Cade in the early years of the reign and afterwards, but more rarely and in lesser amounts, to the Jews. The most striking case occurred in 1163 when the sheriff paid nothing in cash and a debt of £266 7s. 3d. was declared after the issue of the farm had been allowed for, but was immediately wiped out by an order to pay the whole sum to Cade.[1] Such heavy calls were, however, exceptional and as a rule the sheriffs were allowed what advantage there might be in payment extended over two years.

The farm of London and Middlesex included so slight a contribution from the county [2] that London really ranks with the boroughs which were farmed apart from their counties by the sheriffs or other royal officials, and it will be convenient to deal with these here, more briefly, before returning to the grant of farms to burgess communities from which we digressed after disposing of the early case of Lincoln. Of the nine [3] towns which fall in the category in question for the whole or part of the reign of Henry II, five, Southampton, Winchester, Northampton, Dover, and Colchester, had already been

---

[1] *P.R.* 9 Hen. II, p. 72. As the debt was in blanch money, it was converted to tale for the purpose of this payment, by the usual addition of a shilling in the pound, Cade receiving £279 13s. 8d.

[2] When London was again in the hands of keepers in 1189–90, the county was farmed by John Bucuinte for £37 9s. 6d. (*P.R.* 2 Ric. I, p. 156; 3 Ric. I, p. 135).

[3] Not including two cases on the first Pipe Rolls of the reign which were relics of Stephen's arrangements. Canterbury was held by William de Ypres down to Easter, 1157, the sheriff being allowed £129 blanch and £20 tale, Hertford was separately farmed for £12 by Stephen's last sheriff, Henry of Essex, down to Easter, 1155. The momentary instances at Yarmouth and Norwich are also not reckoned (see p. 172).

separately farmed in his grandfather's time; Orford, Grimsby, Scarborough, and Newbury were additions to the class.

Southampton affords a striking contrast to London in the inability or unwillingness of most of its farmers to meet their full liabilities even after the original farm of £300 blanch had been reduced by a third. One of its early farmers in this reign was the sheriff of the county (1156–57),[1] another, Emma, viscountess of Rouen (1158–63). When she resigned the farm, her debt amounted to no less than £1423 9s. 2d. blanch.[2] Two years later it was made payable in the king's chamber and the item disappears from the Pipe Rolls.[3] The three reeves of the town who succeeded her for nearly four years were little more successful, retiring with arrears of over £530. They declined responsibility for them, calling the king to warrant that they had not held the town at farm [4] and, however this may have been, the debt does not appear again on the rolls. Their contention, no doubt, was that they had acted as *custodes* or keepers only. Coupled with the absence of any record of the acquisition of the farm by the burgesses, this leaves no doubt that the reeves acted as officers of the king, not of the town.

With Richard de Limesey as reeve and farmer, the farm was reduced to £200 blanch.[5] Yet after a little more than five years' tenure, Limesey's arrears amounted to over £457 [6] and thirteen years later he still owed nearly £400.[7] Robert de St. Laurence, one of the three reeves who first took the farm, did better alone and so did his wife Cecily, first as his deputy and afterwards on her own account. But Gervase de Hampton, who succeeded her in 1181, owed over £456 at the end of the reign, which he was allowed to wipe off in 1190 by a payment of 200 marks.[8] It is significant that in the hands of keepers for the first nine months of this year, the town yielded a revenue to the Crown equivalent to not more than £130 per annum.[9]

---

[1] *P.R.* 3 Hen. II, p. 107.

[2] *Ibid.* 9 Hen. II, p. 56. For the viscountess, who also farmed Rouen, see Tout, *Chapters in Administrative History*, i. 106-7, 111-12. She answered for the debt on the farm of 1157–58 at Michaelmas 1159 as well as for the farm of 1158–59 (*P.R.* 5 Hen. II, p. 50), but William Trentegernuns is given as the farmer of the former year incurring the debt (*ibid.* 4 Hen. II, p. 178).

[3] *Ibid.* 11 Hen. II, p. 44.   [4] *Ibid.* 13 Hen. II, p. 194.

[5] *Ibid.* 14 Hen. II, p. 189.   [6] *Ibid.* 19 Hen. II, p. 53.

[7] *Ibid.* 32 Hen .II, p. 180. The debt then disappears from the rolls.

[8] *Ibid.* 2 Rich. I, p. 6.

[9] From 1191 it was farmed again, at the low figure of £106 13s. 4d., but this was afterwards raised once more to £200.

Winchester, which, unlike her neighbour, had been formerly in the *corpus* of the county, differed from her also in being farmed by the sheriff, except in 1155–57.[1] The sheriff's allowance in the county farm being £80 blanch and his farm of the city £142 12s. 4d. blanch, one motive at least for its separate farming is obvious. Richard fitz Turstin, who was removed from the sheriffwick in 1170, left in debt on the city farm to an amount between £100 and £200, but normally there were no heavy deficits.

Of Northampton nothing need be said here, as its burgesses received a grant of the farm before the end of the reign which is dealt with later. For a similar reason Grimsby is omitted here.

Dover affords a rather remarkable instance of the persistence of a farm fixed before 1086. It had been higher in Henry I's time, but from the beginning of his grandson's reign its amount was £54 as in Domesday Book and the shares of the king and the earl were still formally discriminated, the latter belonging to the escheated fief of Bishop Odo of Bayeux. The only difference was that the old king's share which in 1086 had been payable in pennies of twenty to the ounce was now required to be paid blanch. Down to 1161, the farmer was the financier William Cade, afterwards the sheriff, except for eighteen months in 1183–85 when the keep of the castle was being built at great expense and the reeves of the town, who were overseers and paymasters of the work, were appointed keepers of the borough issues.[2] Earlier in the reign, the account had been sometimes in arrears, Cade paying up for two and a half years in 1157 and nine years passing without account up to Michaelmas 1173.

Colchester was still farmed as in 1130 at £40 blanch, by Richard de Luci[3] to 1178, by the town reeves from that year.[4]

The farm of Orford first appears on the Pipe Rolls in 1164.[5] The town was farmed by the sheriff, except in 1173–75 when it was in the hands of two keepers, in 1175–76 when it was farmed by one of them with a merchant and two clerks, in 1179–80 when the farmer was a sheriff's son and in 1187–89 when he was an ex-sheriff. Beginning at £24 [by tale], the farm was raised to 40 marks in 1167–68 and to £40 in 1171–72,

---

[1] When it was farmed by Stigand, perhaps the reeve of the city.
[2] *P.R.* 30 Hen. II, p. 150 ; 31 Hen. II, p. 233.
[3] He was also sheriff in 1155–56.
[4] But see the appendix to this article, below, p. 188.
[5] *P.R.* 10 Hen. II, p. 35. Without allowance in county farm.

reduced to 40 marks again for three years (1175–78) and then restored to £40 at which it remained until it disappeared from the rolls in 1189–90. In the two years when it was in custody, it returned under £23. When the fee farm was granted in 1256,[1] it was fixed at £30 by tale. *Extra firmam* was a ship custom which sank from £64 in 1157 to nothing from 1186 onwards.

Scarborough, like Orford, was first farmed separately in 1163–64.[2] The farm, which was held by the sheriff, began at £20 (tale), was raised to £30 in 1168–69 and to £34 in 1173, at which it remained until the end of the reign. At Michaelmas 1189 the sheriff accounted for £33 by tale and an increment (amount unstated),[3] but the farm does not appear on the rolls of the three following years. Newbury, in Berkshire, is not mentioned in this connexion until 1180, when an addition to the roll records that Godfrey and Richard de Niweberia accounted for a full year's farm at Easter 1181, the amount being £49 (tale).[4] At Michaelmas 1181, therefore, they accounted for half a year only. Godfrey and Simon (with Richard from 1185) afterwards account until in 1187 the entry disappears. The borough seems to have been only temporarily in the hands of the Crown. It was on the fief of the count of Perche.

For a moment, at the beginning of the reign, Yarmouth and Norwich were separately farmed, Yarmouth in 1155–56 by the sheriff of Norfolk for £40,[5] and Norwich in 1157 by the sheriff of Norfolk and Suffolk for six months at the rate of £108 per annum.[6]

Apart from Lincoln, the first town allowed by Henry II to farm itself was Wallingford, which had been farmed independently of the county by Brian fitz Count in 1130. For their services to Henry in securing the crown its burgesses received a charter of liberties in 1155,[7] and during the next seven years they or persons who doubtless were their reeves

---

[1] Ballard and Tait, *British Borough Charters*, ii. 316.
[2] *P.R.* 10 Hen. II, p. 12. Without allowance in the county farm.
[3] It was an addition of the same amount in John's grant of the farm to the burgesses (1201) " quamdiu nobis bene servierint " (*B.B.C.* i. 226).
[4] *Ibid.* 27 Hen. II, p. 142.   [5] *Ibid.* 2 Hen. II, p. 8.
[6] *Ibid.* 3 Hen. II, p. 76. In these and similar cases above the sheriff received no corresponding allowance in the county farm. The separate borough farm was in effect an increment on that.
[7] Corrected from 1156, Ballard's date, given in the article as first printed. See appendix below, p. 189. For the charter, see Gross, *Gild Merchant*, ii. 244 f.

made fitful and very unsuccessful efforts to pay a farm of
£80 blanch increased in 1159 by £5 tale in lieu of a *paleum*.
For the year 1163–64, the king by writ reduced their farm to
£30 by tale.[1] Then for fourteen years the borough disappears
from the Pipe Rolls. Not until the exchequer audit at
Michaelmas 1178 is any explanation forthcoming. It appears
that Henry by a charter, which must have been granted in
1164, had reduced the original farm to £40 burnt and weighed
(*arsas et pensatas*), but the officials of the exchequer had pedan-
tically refused to allow them to account because this technical
expression for the assay (or deduction in lieu thereof) was no
longer in use,[2] and the term blanched (*blancas*) should have
been employed. They now accounted for arrears amounting
to £560 and paid off rather less than half. Next year, " in
the Treasury after the Exchequer audit," the deficit was
apparently wiped out by order of the king.[3] For some reason
unexplained no further account was rendered until 1183
when it closed with a debt of over £50 on the preceding three
and a half years.[4] This delay and the transference of the
town for the rest of the reign to the keeper of the honour of
Wallingford, who was never able to obtain more than about
£18 in any year, may suggest that there was something more
than the pedantry of the exchequer behind the earlier and
heavier arrears.

The burgesses of Grimsby had a much briefer tenure of
their farm. For four years down to 1160 the borough was
farmed by Ralph, son of Dreu, of Tetney, Holton, and Humber-
stone, for £111, but this was probably, as usual, excessive ;
he ran up a large debt [5] (more than half of which was wiped
off and the rest his sons paid in birds (*aves*) eight years later),
and in 1160–61 the men of Grimsby accounted for three months'
farm and paid off the greater part of it.[6] In the following year,
the farm reverted to the sheriff who retained it until John's
reign.[7] The burgesses got a fee farm grant in 1227, amended
in 1256.[8]

Gloucester was the next borough to secure control of its
own farm, but only for a decade. At Michaelmas 1165
Osmund the reeve accounted for half a year's farm at the rate

[1] *P.R.* 10 Hen. II, p. 43. See also the next reference.
[2] *Ibid.* 24 Hen. II, p. 99. [3] *Ibid.* 29 Hen. II, pp. 138-9.
[4] *Ibid.* [5] *Ibid.* 6 Hen. II, p. 45.
[6] *Ibid.* 7 Hen. II, p. 17. *Cf.* p. 15. [7] *Rot. Litt. Claus.* i. 358a.
[8] *B.B.C.* ii. 305, 315.

of £55 blanch per annum, an increment of £5 on the figure previously paid by the sheriff, as shown by the allowance made in the county farm.[1] Whether the concord arranged in the same year between the burgesses and Ailwin the Mercer, of whom we shall hear more, for which they had to pay 90 marks and he 10, had any connexion with this change is not stated,[2] but it may be noted that no fine for the privilege, other than the increment on the farm, appears on the roll. Osmund continued to account down to 1176 when the farm reverted to the sheriff,[3] who, however, accounted separately from 1178 for the £5 *de cremento burgi de Gloecr' dum fuit in manu burgensium.*[4]

It seems possible that the first steps towards the acquisition of their farms taken by the burgesses of Shrewsbury and Bridgenorth were connected with the Inquest of Sheriffs in 1170. Geoffrey de Vere, the sheriff of Shropshire, died before the Michaelmas audit and the two towns seem to have judged the occasion suitable for securing financial independence of the sheriff. The burgesses of Shrewsbury paid £12 to have their town at farm, " ut dicunt," whatever that may mean. Those of Bridgenorth paid £13 6s. 8d. for the same privilege and also undertook, through Hugh de Beauchamp, perhaps one of the commissioners who conducted the inquiry, to pay 2½ marks a year " beyond (praeter) the farm of the town which is in the farm of the county," which was £5.[5] Although the payment and the promise are separately entered, one would naturally connect them and suppose that the burgesses were to pay directly the whole farm so augmented. Instead of which, for six years (1171–6) they paid the increment to the exchequer but continued to render their old farm to the sheriff. It looks like a piece of sharp practice, perhaps engineered between the new sheriff, Guy Lestrange, and the exchequer. Shrewsbury, too, got nothing for her £12, though she escaped an increment. At last, in 1175, it was agreed

---

[1] *P.R.* 11 Hen. II, pp. 12, 14.
[2] For a conjecture that it was an agreement between the town and the merchant gild, see below, p. 177. [3] *P.R.* 23 Hen. II, p. 42.
[4] *Ibid.* 24 Hen. II, p. 56. Dr. Stephenson suggests that this remark is a slip, on the ground that so long a tenure of office by a single reeve would indicate that he was not elected (*Borough and Town*, p. 167, *n.* 5). It was certainly very unusual, but does not justify the rejection of so definite a statement. It will be noted that Dr. Stephenson here assumes that if the burgesses had really farmed the town, there would have been an elected reeve. This is contrary to his general thesis. See appendix II to this article. [5] *P.R.* 16 Hen. II, p. 133.

that both towns should pay their own farms, but Shrewsbury was to give 100 marks and four hunting dogs (*fugatores*) for the privilege, and Bridgenorth 30 marks and two dogs. Shrewsbury was also to render two dogs a year as an increment on the old farm of £20 by tale paid to the sheriff.[1] From the next year, therefore, the burgesses accounted separately at the exchequer at this rate, those of Bridgenorth for £6 13s. 4d. including the increment paid since 1170, and the sheriff was excused the amount of the old farm in each case.[2]

The last towns in this reign to obtain the right to farm themselves were Northampton and Cambridge who secured it in the same year, 1184–85. Cambridge had always been farmed by the sheriff of the county, but Northampton, as we have seen, was taken out of the farm of Northamptonshire and mediatized as early as the reign of Rufus. In the hands of the Crown in 1130, it had been restored by Stephen with the earldom to Simon de Senlis II.[3] Henry II resumed it and it was farmed apart from the county, though from 1170 the sheriff was the farmer.

The Pipe Roll of 1185 records a payment of 200 marks of silver by the burgesses of Northampton to have their town *in capite* of the king and of 300 marks of silver and one mark of gold by those of Cambridge to have their town at farm and be free from the interference of the sheriff therein.[4] That these expressions were equivalent is shown by the king's charter granting Cambridge to the burgesses to be held of him at farm *in capite*.[5] But the two newly privileged boroughs did not fare equally well. The Northampton burgesses had no difficulty in meeting their farm, which, having stood at £100 by tale since 1130 at least, was now raised to £120, and they paid off their fine in two years. Cambridge was a much poorer town and its fine was excessive, even allowing for the fact that nothing was added to the old farm of £60 blanch paid to the sheriffs. The burgesses still owed £70 of it at the end of the reign and had paid no farm at all. Richard I wound up the account at some sacrifice and took the town

---

[1] *P.R.* 21 Hen. II, p. 38. When in the next reign the whole farm was expressed in money, the dogs were reckoned at 5 marks apiece.

[2] *Ibid.* 22 Hen. II, p. 55.

[3] He addressed as earl a charter in favour of the priory of St. Andrew to Richard Grimbaud and G. de Blosseville and all his ministers of Northampton (Cott. MS. E. xvii. f. 5b). I owe this reference to Professor Stenton.

[4] *P.R.* 31 Hen. II, pp. 46, 60. For a farm *in capite* from a sheriff see *P.R.* 6 Ric. I, p. 120.

[5] Stubbs, *Select Charters*, ed. Davis, p. 196.

into his own hands again. The terms of the settlement are given in the Pipe Roll of 1189.[1] The burgesses paid £196 7s. 10d. by tale, the rest of the debt of £276 15s. by tale on their farm was met out of their payments on the fine (£133 6s. 8d.) and the surplus of these was set off against the outstanding amount of the fine, leaving only £19 13s. 10d. which was excused them. Thus the Crown recovered the whole of the farm for four and a half years and rather more than a fourth of the fine.

In the last year of the reign of Henry II, only five boroughs, Lincoln, Cambridge, Northampton, Shrewsbury, and Bridgenorth, were clearly being farmed by their burgesses, the first three by charter. Grimsby, Wallingford, and Gloucester had been in this position for longer or shorter periods, but occupied it no longer. Colchester and Southampton were being farmed by the town reeves, as Orford and Newbury had been for a time, but there is no hint[2] on the rolls that these officers were acting for the burgesses and in the case of Southampton there seems to be evidence to the contrary. The reeves, like the sheriffs of London, were primarily royal officers.

Henry II was not only sparing with the farming privilege ; he deliberately avoided granting it in perpetuity. In no case did a borough receive a grant in fee farm from him. His grandfather's cancelled charter to London remains the only certain grant of the *firma burgi* in fee yet made. Henry II's grants were experimental and the experience of Gloucester and Wallingford emphasized their revocability.

So modest a concession of self-government and so rarely bestowed did little to satisfy the more aspiring spirits, well acquainted with the status of the more advanced of the continental communes. Two attempts to secure wider privileges under the name of a commune have left traces, unluckily scanty, on the Pipe Rolls of the reign. That at Gloucester in 1169–70 is the more interesting of the two, because it makes clear that a royal grant of a town *in capite* to its burgesses for the purposes of the *firma burgi*, despite the apparent analogy with the *seigneurie collective populaire* of the Continent, did not realize the ambitions which were embodied in the demand for a commune. As we have seen above (p. 173), the burgesses of Gloucester received their town at farm from Easter 1165.

---

[1] P. 188. In the second line of this entry IIII is an error for III.
[2] See, however, appendix II below, p. 188.

Their concord with Ailwin the mercer may possibly have arranged the relations of town and gild merchant. Ailwin was perhaps alderman of the gild. He was certainly the most prominent citizen and when, five years later, the community incurred a fine of over £183 *pro communa*, Ailwin's share was considerably more than half.[1] It is unfortunate that no more detailed hint is given of the objects of the conspirators, one of whom fled and had his chattels seized. Despite their offence, the burgesses continued to farm the borough, through their reeve Osmund, until Michaelmas 1176 when it determined, perhaps by effluxion of time, perhaps in consequence of a new amercement of 60 marks incurred by them. The change may have been provisional at first, for it was not until the second year afterwards that the sheriff was charged with the increment of £5 upon the original farm which the burgesses had paid for over ten years.[2] The king took care not to lose anything by the reversion to farming by the sheriff. Obscure as the story of the Gloucester commune is and must remain, it leaves no doubt that a good deal more than financial independence of the sheriff was aimed at.

The year which saw the end of burgess farming at Gloucester for the present, was marked by another futile attempt to set up a commune, this time at York, where Thomas of Beyond-Ouse was fined 20 marks " for the commune which he wished to make."[3] York had more reason for discontent with its status than Gloucester had six years before. The city still paid its farm through the sheriff and continued to do so, with one brief interval in the next reign, until its acquisition of a fee farm in 1212.[4]

(5) The First Fee Farms and the Commune of London, 1189–91

Richard I's urgent need of money for his crusade put an end at once to his father's cautious policy towards the aspirations of the growing boroughs. It is true that one of the first steps of the new king, the restoration of the farm of Cambridge to the sheriff, was reactionary, but the burgesses had conspicuously failed as farmers and were ready to lay down a large sum to close the account.[5] On the same principle of

---

[1] *P.R.* 16 Hen. II, p. 79. [2] *Ibid.* 24 Hen. II, p. 56.
[3] *Ibid.* 22 Hen. II, p. 106 ; Farrer, *Early Yorkshire Charters*, i. nos. 118, 333.
[4] *B.B.C.* i. 230. [5] See above, p. 175.

taking what he could get, Richard accepted from the farmer
of Southampton about a third of his arrears in full payment and
placed the town in the hands of keepers.   In this case, however,
the farmer does not seem to have been the elected representative of the burgesses and in neither perhaps was the failure
without excuse.   Too high a price had been exacted for the
privilege from Cambridge, and the resumption of farming at
Southampton a year later at little more than half the former
rate may have been a confession that, for the time being
at any rate, it was excessive.[1]

It was not, of course, any sympathy with municipal liberties[2] which led Richard in the first weeks of his reign to grant
the *firma burgi* during pleasure to yet another borough, to
confirm it to one which had long possessed it on those terms,
and to extend the privilege permanently to five others, only
one of which had enjoyed the temporary right.   Nottingham
received the lesser privilege just before the town was granted
to John, and disappeared for a while from the Pipe Rolls.[3]
Shrewsbury for 40 marks, the amount of one year's farm,
was confirmed in her revocable tenure of it.[4]   The richer
Northampton by a fine of £100 obtained a regrant of its
farm in perpetuity with other liberties.[5]   Four towns, hitherto
farmed as part of their counties or (in one case) by special
farmers, Bedford,[6] Hereford,[7] Worcester,[8] and Colchester,[9]
were granted the privilege of self-farming in the same form
as Northampton, in fee farm.   All but Worcester received
grants of other liberties as well.   In view of this, of the concession in hereditary succession and the absence of any
increments on the farms previously paid to the sheriffs
or other farmers, the fines taken compared very favourably

---

[1] *P.R.* 3 Ric. I, p. 92.

[2] Richard's need of new sources of revenue was made acute by his
alienation of six counties and the honours of Lancaster and Wallingford,
etc., to his brother John, a loss on the former alone of over £4000 a year
(Norgate, *John Lackland*, pp. 26-8).   By these grants, many royal boroughs
were mediatized for five years.

[3] *B.B.C.* i. 244, 247.

[4] *Ibid.* p. 233 ;   *P.R.* 2 Ric. I, p. 124.   [5] *B.B.C.* i. 222.

[6] *P.R.* 2 Ric. I, p. 138 ; 3 Ric. I, p. 109.   For the amount of the farm
in this and the following cases, see the appendix, p. 184.

[7] *Ibid.* 2 Ric. I, p. 46 ;   *B.B.C.* p. 222.   It was a condition of the grant
that the citizens should help in fortifying the city.

[8] *P.R.* 2 Ric. I, pp. 22, 24 ;   *B.B.C.* p. 222.

[9] *P.R.* 2 Ric. I, p. 111 ; 4 Ric. I, p. 174 ; *B.B.C.* p. 244.   The charter
does not contain a definite grant of fee farm, but the absence of any later
grant and the formal recognition of elective reeves seem decisive.

with those exacted by Henry II for lesser liberties.[1] How far this moderation was due to a realization that excessive demands ultimately defeated their own end, how far to an immediate policy of making the concession as attractive as possible in the hope of raising the money quickly, it is difficult to decide.   The latter suggestion seems to find support in the sudden introduction of the perpetual grant of the *firma burgi*, for up till now the only grant of the kind which can be proved to have been made was that of Henry I to London which had been revoked very shortly afterwards.   But, however temporary the motive of this innovation may have been, it was one which, once made, could not be undone.   Grants during pleasure continued to be issued, but even in the reigns of Richard and John they were far outnumbered by those in fee farm.   Apart from those of 1189, eighteen such grants by charter before 1216 are known and nearly a dozen more were made by the end of the thirteenth century.   It would be easy of course to overstress the accidental initial aspect of a change which must have played no inconsiderable part in the decline of the power of the sheriff and in the evolution of that nice balance of attraction and repulsion between county and borough which resulted in the House of Commons. Henry I had laid the train, and Henry II's restrictive policy could not have been permanently maintained.

So far as the new policy was an immediate financial expedient, it was hardly a success.   Worcester and Northampton alone paid their fines promptly.   The others did not even pay their farms at Michaelmas 1190, and it was two years after that before Colchester paid up three years' farm and part of its fine.   Nevertheless, William de Longchamp, Richard's chancellor and viceroy, apparently continued the policy, for the citizens of York began to farm the city at Easter 1190 at the rate of £100 blanch per annum.[2]   It may be, however, that this was a deferred enjoyment of one of the liberties for which they had promised a fine of 200 marks.[3] They paid nothing of either and the privilege was withdrawn after six months.   A year later they paid the farm for that period with an increment of £10 by tale, of which there had been no mention in the roll of 1190.

That Longchamp's policy was opportunist is shown by the fact that the grant of their farm to the citizens of York was

---

[1] Hereford 40 marks, Worcester and Colchester 60 each, Bedford 80.
[2] *P.R.* 2 Ric. I, p. 39.   [3] *Ibid.*, p. 68.

coincident with the withdrawal of the same privilege from those of Lincoln, who, with one short interval, had probably enjoyed it since the later years of Henry I's reign. The city was handed over to a royal official, Hugh Bardolf, for the rest of the year and the first half of the next, after which it was farmed by the sheriff. There are indications that this was a punishment for some action of the citizens. The keepers of escheats in Lincolnshire account in this year for a small sum " *de terra civium Lincol' de misericordia sua dum fuit in manu Regis*." [1] This is perhaps to be connected with the amercement of some ninety-five men of Lincoln, in sums ranging from half a mark to forty marks, for an assault on the Jews, which appears on the rolls of 1191 and 1192.[2]

Longchamp's rivalry with Bishop Hugh of Durham and (in 1191) with the king's brother John would be likely to make him conciliate the city of London, and there seems evidence that he did. At Michaelmas 1189 Richard had transferred the city from the sheriff to three keepers.[3] Mr. Page suggests that this was done with the object of extracting more money from the city, and finds confirmation in the sub-farming of the tron and the customs of the markets, etc., and in the exaction of very large sums from the Jews.[4] But to suppose that Richard and Longchamp expected to get more than the amount of the farm, £520 18s. blanch, from the keepers is to believe them guilty of an incredible miscalculation. The sums wrung from the Jews must be left out of account. They were no concern of the keepers. The sum they actually accounted for, after the fees of clerks and serjeants were paid, was just short of £272 blanch, and of this nearly £45 due from the sub-farmers was not paid until Michaelmas 1191. It is true that a debt of nearly £200 on the farm of 1188–89 was carried forward to the next account, but it was not a bad debt and the actual revenue drawn from London within the financial year 1188–89 was more than £100 greater than that of 1189–90. Moreover, the sources from which it was derived were as to a considerable part fixed and the rest could be estimated within not very wide limits. Nor can the Crown officials have been unaware of the even lower receipts obtained from the keepers

---

[1] *P.R.* 2 Ric. I, p. 7. The citizens recovered the farm at Easter 1194 (*ibid.* 6 Ric. I, p. 103).
[2] *Ibid.* 3-4 Ric. I, pp. 15, 242. For some leading citizens among the offenders, see *The Earliest Lincolnshire Assize Rolls 1202–09* (Linc. Rec. Soc. 22), p. 261.
[3] *Ibid.* 2 Ric. I, p. 156.   [4] Page, *London*, p. 106.

of fifteen years before.[1] It is likely, indeed, that the motive for the institution of keepers was now as then the opposite of that suggested by Mr. Page, a desire to give temporary relief from an oppressive farm and to conciliate the powerful city interests. The two sheriffs of 1188–89 had been left with a debt of nearly £200 apiece, and only one of them had been able to pay it off at once.[2] It is not impossible, indeed, that the appointment of keepers had been deliberately intended to pave the way for the much more notable concession which was made at Michaelmas 1190, when the farm of the city was restored to the citizens at the traditional rate of £300 fixed in the charter of Henry I, and with it of course the right to elect their own sheriffs.[3] It may be that keepers had been set up for twelve months to make sure that the actual receipts from the various sources of Crown revenue in London did not exceed £300, and that the concession could be made without actual loss. If so, Longchamp would be deprived of the sole credit for this most important step, which otherwise must be his, though only as an astute move in the contest with his powerful enemies.

Thus after the lapse of nearly sixty years, the financial privilege which Henry I had given and his nephew and grandson had taken away was restored to the Londoners, but there is no evidence that as yet it was given back in perpetuity. That would require the assent of the king, and there is nothing to show that it had been obtained.

By a slip very rare with so accurate a scholar, Dr. Round has associated this reduction of the farm with Count John's grant of the commune on 8th October, 1191. Finding the citizens accounting for the farm of £300 at the Michaelmas audit in that year, he jumped to the conclusion that the two concessions were made simultaneously, forgetting that the account being rendered for the preceding twelve months, there must have been that interval between them.[4] The audit was over more than a week before John reached London.

---

[1] See above, p. 167.   [2] *P.R.* 1 Ric. I, p. 225.

[3] *Ibid.* 2 Ric. I, p. 135: "Cives Lond' Willelmus de Hauerhell et Johannes Bucuinte pro eis reddunt compotum de ccc li. bl. hoc anno."

[4] *Commune of London*, pp. 233-5. He speaks of John's charter of 1199, after he became king, as confirming "the reduction (of the farm) which they had won at the crisis of 1191." In *Ancient Charters*, pp. 99-100, he postdates a document by a year, but this was due to forgetfulness that under Richard I the Michaelmas audit fell at the beginning of the regnal year, not at its end.

Dr. Round has here misled Sir James Ramsay.[1] Mr. Page, on the other hand, dates the reduction of the farm and its grant to the citizens correctly at Michaelmas 1190 (though without calling attention to Dr. Round's error), and points out that the privilege would naturally carry with it the right of electing the sheriffs.[2]

Longchamp's successor, Walter of Coutances, was more cautious as regarded the farm until the king's wishes could be known. He did not venture to restore the old high rate, but for the next three years the sheriffs accounted personally, not 'pro civibus,' for the £300. Richard on his return in the spring of 1194 was offered a large *donum* by the citizens 'pro beneuolentia regis et pro libertatibus suis conservandis.'[3] This no doubt was primarily for the confirmation of his father's charter which he granted in April of this year, but his benevolence went beyond this, for at Michaelmas the citizens began again to account for the farm.[4]

In the struggle between Longchamp and Count John in 1191, Henry of Cornhill took the side of the chancellor and Richard fitz Reiner that of John.[5] Mr. Page represents them as leaders of rival civic parties, Cornhill heading the aristocratic party and fitz Reiner the opposition. There is not much evidence of this, and it is difficult to know what to make of the statement that Cornhill and his friends were opposed to the farming of the city by the citizens.[6] If this opposition preceded their acquisition of the farm at Michaelmas 1190, it had no relation to the strife between John and Longchamp, for John was not yet in England. Longchamp, moreover, must have overruled any such objections of his partisans. If it is placed in 1191, it is perhaps only an inference from the temporary loss of the farm which cannot have been due to them. If there was any party in the city opposed to further demands, it was reduced to silence by the chancellor's flight to London before John, and the whole community joined in his supersession in favour of Walter de Coutances and received the oaths of John and the barons to the coveted " commune " of London.

---

[1] *Angevin Empire*, p. 317.　　　　[2] *London*, pp. 106-7.
[3] *P.R.* 6 Ric. I, p. 182.
[4] *Ibid.* 7 Ric. I, p. 113. Page (*London*, p. 116) has created confusion by post-dating this event by a year. But further study of the Pipe rolls has convinced me that the suggestion in my article as first printed, that the citizens were the real farmers between 1191 and 1194, cannot be sustained.
[5] Giraldus Cambrensis, *Opera* (Rolls Series), iv. 404.
[6] *Op. cit.* p. 108.

Into the disputed nature and duration of the commune as revealed by the documents preserved in " A London municipal collection of the reign of John " [1] I do not here propose to enter. We have reached a point where a halt may legitimately be called. The event of 8th October, 1191, is the high-water mark of the pioneer period of English municipal progress. If the Pipe Rolls have disclosed nothing positive as to the aims of English communalism, they have at least established the negative conclusion that farming by the burgesses, even the fee farm, though doubtless a necessary preliminary or concomitant, formed no part of the conception of the " commune." Two of the three boroughs which are known to have openly aimed at a commune, London and Gloucester, had already possessed the farm. That distinction is what might be expected. The right of farming the royal revenue from the borough merely eliminated the sheriff middleman. The idea of the " commune " embodied the aspiration of the more advanced towns to full self-government. The aspiration was a natural and inevitable one and, freed from the more questionable features of its foreign model, was realized in the modified form most appropriate to the needs of a compact and strongly governed kingdom.

APPENDIX I

Table of Borough Farms, etc.

THE following list of boroughs includes only towns (except Bridgenorth, Grimsby, and Newbury) which were in the hands of Edward the Confessor or of Queen Edith in 1066, and some of these are omitted because their renders are not fully given or are involved in those of rural manors or *firma noctis* groups. Those which are definitely stated in Domesday Book to have been farmed in 1066 or 1086 are marked with a dagger, but Domesday " values " are only distinguished from farms or " renders " (which may often be farms) when they are contrasted in the survey. The figures include both the king's and the earl's share. Smaller payments in kind or money to which certain boroughs were liable at this date are omitted, but such boroughs are marked with an asterisk. Revenue

---

[1] *E.H.R.* xvii, 480 f., 707 f.   See below, pp. 251 ff., 266 ff.

	1066	1086	Henry I	Henry II	Richard I
Arundel	£4	£12 (£13 v)			
Barnstaple		£2 w + £1 t			
Bedford		£5		[£40 bl]	£40 bl
Bridgenorth				£5 to £6 13s. 4d.t	£6 13s. 4d. t
Buckingham	£10 t	£16 ws			
Cambridge		£14 2s. 10d.		£60 bl	£60 bl
Canterbury	£51	£30 bw + £24 t† (£50 v)		£29 bl + £20 t (1156–57)	
Chester	£45†*	£70 + 1 gold mark			
Chichester	£15	£35 (£25 v)			[?£38 10s.] [1]
Colchester	£15 5s. 3d.	£80*	£40 bl	£40 bl	£40 bl
Derby	£24	£30			[£60] [2]
Dover	£18	£24 xx + £30 t	£90 19s. 9d. bl	£24 bl + £30 t	£24 bl
Droitwich	£74†	£65 w*			
Dunwich	£10	£50 + 60,000 herrings*		[£120 + 24,000 herrings]*	£120 + 24,000 herrings*
Exeter		£12 t + £6 bw			£12 19s. [3]
Gloucester	£36 t*	£60 xx		£50 to £55 bl	£55 bl
Grimsby				£111	[£111 t] [4]
Guildford	£18 0s. 3d.	£32 (£30 v)			
Hereford	£18	£60 t, ws		[£40 bl]	£40 bl
Hertford	£7 10s. t	£20 bw		£24 (1154–55)	
Huntingdon	£45	£45		£20 bl (1173–74)	[?£35 bl + £10t] [5]
Ilchester		£12		£30 ws [6]	£30 ws
Ipswich	£15*	£37*			£35 bl + £5 [7]
Leicester	£30 t xx			£75 3s. 4d.	
Lewes	£26	£34			
Lidford		£3 w			£4 4s.
Lincoln	£30	£100 t	[£140 bl]	£180 t (from 1155)	£180 t
London		[£300]	£525 0s. 10½d. bl	£500 bl + £22 t (£500 bl 1160–61, 1166–67)	£300 bl (from 1190)
Maldon	£13 2s.	£16 w			
Malmesbury [8]	£14† (with two hundreds)	£14†	£20		
Newbury				£49 t	
Northampton		£30 10s.	£100 t	£100 t to £120 t (from 1184)	£120 t
Nottingham	£18	£30			[?£52 bl] [9]
Norwich	£30*	£70 w + 20 bl*		£108 (1157)	£108 bl [10]
Orford				£24 t to £40 t	
Oxford	£30*	£60 t xx			
Reading		£5† (£4 3s. v)			
Rochester	£5	£40† (£20 v)			£25
Scarborough				£20 t to £34 t	£33 t (with increment)
Shaftesbury		£3 5s. (Abbey)			
Shrewsbury	£30	£40		£20 to £26 13s. 4d. t	£26 13s. 4d. t
Southampton	£7 (?)	£7 (?) + £4 0s. 6d.		£300 bl to £200 bl	£106 13s. 4d. [11]
Southwark		£16			
Stafford	£9	£7			
Stamford	£15	£50†			
Sudbury	£18	£28 t			
Thetford	£30 t*	£50 w + £20 bl + £6 t			
Torksey	£18	£30			
Wallingford	£30	£80 t† (£60 v)	£53 6s. 2d. bl	£80 bl + £5 t to £40 bl	£80 bl
Wilton		£50			
Winchcombe	£6†	£28 xx (with three hundreds)			
Winchester			[?£80 bl]	£142 12s. 4d. bl	£142 12s. 4d. bl
Worcester [12]	£24	£31 5s. w		[£24 bl]	£24 bl
Yarmouth	£27 (with three hundreds)	£27 16s. 4d. bl*		£40 [1156]	
York	£52 (King)	£100 w (King)			£100 bl (1190)

[1] Madox, *Firma Burgi*, p. 13, *n. t.*
[2] *Cal. Charter Rolls*, i. 96.

[For footnotes 3 to 12 see opposite page.

from mints, mills and fisheries, if separately stated, are not given. The forms in which the borough farms, etc., were paid, when ascertainable, are indicated by the following abbreviations : bl = blanch ; bw = burnt and weighed ; t = by tale or numero ; w = weighed ; ws = white silver ; xx = 20d. to the ounce. Figures in square brackets are based on evidence later than the date to which they are referred in the table.

APPENDIX II

The Firma Burgi and Election of Reeves (Bailiffs)

In 1913 Ballard thought it " not unreasonable to believe that the grant of the *firma burgi* (to royal boroughs) always carried with it the right to appoint the reeves, whether this right had been mentioned in the charter or no." [1] He grounded this belief on the association of the two privileges in a number of charters, especially closely in those of London (1131, 1199) and Dublin (1215), and on the necessity of burgess control over the official who collects the dues, if they are to be answerable for them or a sum paid out of them. His conclusion is, for the first time, contested by Dr. Carl Stephenson, who extends the inquiry to those farming leases of which the only surviving evidence is on the Pipe Rolls.[2] He claims to have shown that Ballard's view is inconsistent with what is known or may be conjectured with probability about the farms of boroughs before these leases and with the recorded history of the leases themselves.

(1) These leases first made burgesses directly responsible at the exchequer for the farm of their town in place of the

[1] *B.B.C.* I. lxxxvi.
[2] *Borough and Town*, pp. 166-70. He does once, unconsciously, make Ballard's assumption himself. See above, p. 174, *n.* 4.

---

[3] Madox, *op. cit.* pp. 267-8 *n.* ; *cf.* Ballard and Tait, *British Borough Charters*, ii. 316.
[4] *Ibid.* p. 305.
[5] Madox, *op. cit.* p. 8, *n.* y from *P.R.* 2 Hen. III, rot. 8a .
[6] *B.B.C.* i. 229 ; *Book of Fees*, i. 79 f. ; *E.H.R.* v. 638, *n.*   From 1204, at latest, it was reduced by allowances for grants to £19 10s.
[7] Madox, p. 122, from *P.R.* 9 Ric. I, rot. 16, m 1a, reads £25 incorrectly.
[8] See above, p. 151.
[9] *P.R.* 2 John, p. 9.
[10] *P.R.* 6 Ric. I, p. 47.
[11] With Portsmouth in 1200 (*P.R.* 2 John, p. 193) £200.
[12] See above, p. 143, *n.* 1.

sheriff or other royal nominee, but they were not the beginning of burgess farming. Already in 1086 the burgesses of
Northampton were farming their town from the sheriff and,
though this is the only record of the kind, we may, Dr.
Stephenson suggests, feel pretty sure that such sub-farming
was not uncommon in the twelfth century. Farming of this
kind, of course, would not entail election of the royal town
reeves, even where they and not the sheriffs were the Crown
farmers. It seems to be further suggested that when burgesses
became Crown farmers themselves, on receiving a grant of
their borough *in capite* of the king or *in manu sua*, there
would be no need of any change in this respect. This, however, seems very doubtful. The burgesses in their court
might have arranged a sub-farm with the sheriff or other
farmer, but as Crown farmers they must be represented at
the exchequer of account by responsible persons. The reeve
or reeves, as the king's financial representatives in the town,
were the natural persons, but their position had been changed
by the grant to the burgesses. They were now subordinate
in finance to the farming burgesses. The grant to Dublin
expressed this change with all clearness when it enfeoffed the
citizens with the office of reeve (*prepositura*).[1] They needed
no separate grant for election of their bailiffs, as it was then
becoming the practice to call the old reeves, nor did they ever
get one. Election was a natural consequence of the transference of the farm to the citizens. No other explanation of
its introduction is offered by Dr. Stephenson.

(2) It is, however, not so much upon general considerations as upon the evidence of charters and Pipe Rolls that he
rejects the idea of any necessary connexion between farming
by the burgesses and the election of their reeves. There is
no proof, it is claimed, of such connexion. Neither of the
two extant charters of Henry II [2] conferring farming leases
on burgesses gives the right of election, nor is election mentioned in the case of any of the leases which are only known
from the Pipe Rolls. Formal grants of election first appear in
1189 when perpetual leases of farms, fee farms, begin, charters
are freely granted and are carefully preserved. Yet even now
less than half of the fee farms granted down to 1216 are accompanied by an election clause, and the proportion falls even

---

[1] *B.B.C.* i. 231.
[2] To Lincoln and Cambridge (*ibid.* i. 221). That similar charters to
other boroughs have been lost appears from *P.R.* 24 Hen. II, p. 99.

lower in the rest of the thirteenth century. It is not contended that election of reeves did not exist where it is not recorded, but merely that its existence was independent of farming. Evidence of such election, even under Henry II, is recognized in the frequent changes of the reeves whose names are recorded on their accounting at certain periods for the farms of boroughs, Lincoln and Northampton for instance, though the commoner practice was to record the *cives, burgenses* or *homines* themselves as the accountants. It is claimed, however, that in individual cases election is found before the grant of the farm and that in others the right is not obtained for some time after the date of the lease. The choice of Northampton as an example of the former kind seems due to overlooking a Pipe Roll record. Dr. Stephenson points out that from 1185 the farm of that town was being accounted for by men who were evidently elected reeves, whereas the borough's first charter for both farm and election was granted by Richard I in 1189. But, though no earlier charter survives, the Pipe Roll of 1185 shows that the burgesses had bought the farm, doubtless a revocable one, for 200 marks and that the elected reeves began at once to account at the exchequer.[1] So far as it goes, the case favours Ballard's view rather than Professor Stephenson's. Richard's charter made the revocable farm perpetual and it was surely natural to include a formal authorization of the liberty to elect their reeves which had been exercised for four years on a less permanent basis. Dr. Stephenson, indeed, does not always keep in mind the vital difference between farms granted to burgesses during good behaviour (*quamdiu bene servierint*) and fee farms such as Northampton obtained in 1189. He describes Richard's confirmation (1189) of the revocable farm which Shrewsbury had bought from Henry II as a grant of fee farm (p. 168), though that was first obtained in 1205.

The Shrewsbury case has an important bearing on the question before us. Richard merely confirmed the terminable farm in a single clause, but John in 1200 added to a brief general confirmation of the Shrewsbury liberties the clause allowing election of reeves which he was including in a number of other charters during this year. The repetition of this clause in his long charter of 1205 seems a warning that the clause of 1200 may also be a confirmation by regrant

---

[1] *P.R.* 31 Hen. II, p. 46.

—the customary method then—of an existing privilege, though no previous charter is extant.

The Colchester case adduced by Dr. Stephenson is more difficult. Richard in a long charter (1189) gave the burgesses the right to elect the reeves, and in my article (above, p. 171) I used this as one argument for regarding the reeves who accounted for the farm from 1178 to 1189 as still royal nominees. Dr. Stephenson rightly describes the argument as inconclusive, and the frequent change of the names of the reeves is usually considered a sign of election. On the other hand, the Pipe Roll of 1178–79 contains no evidence that the burgesses had bought the farm on the retirement of the justiciar Richard de Lucy, who had farmed the town for many years. It seems also significant that on the accession of Richard the burgesses having offered 60 marks for their liberties and no account having been rendered until in 1192 they were able to pay the larger part of their proffer and the arrears of the farm, John and Osbert *burgenses* appear as accountants and continue for two years. After an interval during which the farm was perhaps held by a royal nominee, the burgesses in 1198–99 paid 20 marks to have their town at farm and at the first exchequer audit of John's reign " cives de Colecestr' " account for the farm.[1] If they had really been farming the borough, with the possible exception named, since 1178, the argument in favour of Ballard's view is strengthened instead of weakened. We have, in that case, two instances, at Northampton and at Colchester, in which the appearance of elected reeves is coincident with the grant of the farm to the burgesses. That is not, of course, absolute proof that the one was the result of the other, but, in the absence of any clear evidence of election before farming, it establishes a *prima facie* probability. Dr. Stephenson, however, overlooking the Northampton purchase of its farm, insists that there is no proof here or at Colchester, as there is at Lincoln, of a formal farming lease by Henry II, which might include tacit permission to elect their reeves, that *both* privileges were conferred by Richard [2]

---

[1] It seems clear that so far they had only a revocable farm, not a fee farm. The most puzzling feature is that Richard's charter had given them neither the one nor the other. Professor Stephenson assumes that it did (*Borough and Town*, p. 169 and *n.* 1), but the confirmation to the burgesses of river tolls towards the king's farm (*B.B.C.* i. 225) no more proves that the burgesses were farmers of either kind in 1189 than in the reign of Henry I to which it traces the practice.

[2] But see *n.* 1 as to Colchester.

and that it is therefore permissible to suppose that they were granted separately by Henry II with or without formal documents not now on record. In other words, Colchester may have had elective reeves before 1178, Northampton before 1185. All this is very conjectural and even if the grants of farm and election were not, as we shall see they were, brought into the closest relation in some charters, the duality seems too slight a ground to bear the inference proposed. Moreover, this inference raises a new and serious difficulty. What possible motive can have actuated the Crown in relinquishing its appointment of the town reeves, if they, personally or under the sheriffs, were still to be solely responsible for the royal revenue ?

In proof of the distinctness of the two privileges, Dr. Stephenson not only adduces cases in which election is claimed to have preceded farming, but at least one in which the reverse order is said to be observable. He states, correctly, that Henry II's charter to Wallingford " does not mention the *firma burgi* and clearly contemplates a royal reeve." " Yet," he adds, " the men of Wallingford at that very time are recorded as rendering account of the farm." Here he has been misled by the current misdating of the charter by a year. Its real date, January, 1155,[1] left twenty months before the burgesses began farming at Michaelmas 1156, and that allowed plenty of time for an arrangement by which the burgesses took over the farm and were allowed to elect their reeves. Dr. Stephenson is strangely reluctant to accept the changing reeves of Wallingford as elected, though he has no doubts about those of Colchester or Lincoln, and concludes that, even if they were, " there is no reason why their election should be thought to be necessitated by the holding of the farm." Here again the meagreness of the record precludes certainty, but the facts we have, which do not include any clear case of an elective reeve before a burgesses' farm or of a nominated one during it, justify, at least as a working theory, the connexion which he denies.

The formal grant of election in later charters conceding fee farms to boroughs which had had only short leases is, we have seen, explicable as the contemporary form of confirmation by simple regrant and cannot be taken to imply its non-existence during the terminable leases of Henry II.

[1] R. W. Eyton, *Itinerary of Henry II*, p. 2. Both I and Professor Stephenson followed Ballard in dating it 1156.

There is one case, however, in Richard's reign which may seem to support Dr. Stephenson's view. In 1194 the men of Ipswich paid 60 marks to have their town in hand and for a confirmation of their liberties. They at once appear on the Pipe Roll as responsible for the farm [1] but did not get the charter, whereas Norwich simultaneously for 200 marks got both and their charter included *fee* farm and election of reeves. It was not until John's first year that Ipswich, on payment of a further 60 marks, obtained a similar charter and, according to the unique record in their Little Domesday Book, proceeded to measures of re-organization which included the election of two reeves.[2] This, says Dr. Stephenson, was obviously their first choice of their own magistrates. But, if this were so, how is it to be reconciled with the case of Northampton which was farming through elected reeves for four years before it obtained in 1189 a charter on the same lines as those of Norwich and Ipswich. As to these Professor Stephenson is really arguing, with unconscious inconsistency, that election came with the acquisition of fee farm and not earlier. The attainment of perpetual farms, with the consequent security from the ordinary intervention of the sheriff, was indeed a marked advance in municipal progress. We are asked to believe that it had no political importance, but it was no accident that it coincided with the appearance in many boroughs of a new officer, the Mayor, from the first elected by the burgesses and of elective and sworn Councils. It is not surprising that on securing permanent emancipation from the sheriff's financial control, the burgesses should, as at Ipswich, have had to carry out some re-organization and in particular to provide a standing method of choosing the reeves, now established as officers of the community. But this is quite consistent at Ipswich with their having used some less formal method of appointment during the years when they were already accounting for the farm, but had not yet received security in a charter for its permanence.

Nor are we entirely without positive evidence that election of reeves was a necessary corollary of farming of either kind by the burgesses. The Dublin charter of 1215, as we have seen, treats the reeveship as granted with the farm. This

---

[1] *P.R.* 6 Ric. I, p. 47. They did not, however, render an account until 1197 (*ibid.* 9 Ric. I. p. 224).
[2] See below, p. 271.

was a fee farm, but Richard's grant to Nottingham in 1189 of a revocable farm, of the type universal under Henry II, gives the burgesses annual choice from their own number of a reeve " to answer for the king's farm and to pay it directly into the exchequer." [1] What is even more significant is that the charter contains no separate grant of the farm which therefore only comes in by a side-wind, as it were, as the essential business of the elective reeve. If we are told that we must not assume the same close connexion where charters grant fee farm without an election clause, we may point out that Oxford was choosing its own bailiffs, c. 1257,[2] though it had no charter authority therefor, unless the grant of a fee farm in 1199 authorized it.

It is true that mesne towns, which were rarely farmed by the burgesses, sometimes received by charter the right of electing their reeves. But they were in a different position than the royal towns. Their lords were usually close at hand and there was no middleman sheriff between them and their burgesses. Election of the reeve probably made easier the collection of the lord's rents and dues. Yet at Leicester, probably the largest of mesne towns, there is only a single case of elective reeves before the belated grant of a (revocable) farm by charter in 1375, and the election of 1276–77 was most likely the result of a temporary unchartered farm.[3] Edmund of Lancaster, who was then lord of the borough, is known to have farmed it out to individuals,[4] and he may have tried the experiment of burgess farming.

Dr. Stephenson's *prima facie* conclusion from the absence of the election clause from some 50 per cent. of the charters in which Richard and John granted borough farms, that there was no necessary connexion between the two privileges, not only contradicts the evidence of the Dublin and Nottingham charters and of Oxford usage, but asks us to believe that where the clause does not appear, it is because the borough either had the right already or continued under reeves nominated by the king. The first assumption is, we think, rash unless the burgesses had already been farming, the second is confronted with known facts in some cases and with general

---

[1] *B.B.C.* i. 244, 247. Cf. *Rot. Litt. Claus.* i. 359a.

[2] *Cal. Inq. Misc.* i. no. 238. The "lesser commune" complained that the fifteen Jurats alone chose the bailiffs.

[3] M. Bateson, *Records of Leicester*, i. xliv. 174; ii. xxvii. *n.* The text does not justify the statement that the Mayor nominated the electors.

[4] *Ibid.* ii. 89.

probability elsewhere. The erratic appearance of the clause
ceases to be a difficulty if the circumstances, in which these
charters were granted, are understood. Charters varied widely
in the number of liberties they included. It was not every
borough that could afford to pay sums up to 200 or 300 marks
for a full enumeration of their franchises, and it is perhaps
significant that under Richard and John the charters which
grant fee farm, but not election of reeves, are comparatively
short, containing, with two exceptions, not more than six
clauses and in four cases only the fee farm grant itself,[1] while
those which include election comprise from thirteen to twenty
clauses. In view of the close connexion between the two
privileges shown by the Dublin and Nottingham grants, may
we not feel pretty sure that where money was scarce the
burgesses were content to rest the right of election upon the
grant of fee farm?

The general extension of election of reeves under the
fee farm system sufficiently explains the still larger proportion
of grants of the farm without the election clause in the charters
of Henry III and Edward I. Here again, in the election clause
of one charter, that of Bridport (1253), as in that of
Nottingham earlier, the first duty of the bailiffs is emphati-
cally stated to be to account for the farm at the exchequer.[2]
Indeed, it is hard to see how the burgesses could have been
in any real sense responsible to the Crown for it, unless they
chose the officers who represented them there. In case of
default these, as their agents, were first held responsible,
but failing them, the burgesses were individually liable for
their share of all arrears.

This intimate relation between farming by the burgesses
and election of their reeves or bailiffs seems further confirmed
by events at Liverpool out of which arose the complaint of
the burgesses in 1292 mentioned below in another connexion.
In answer to a writ of *Quo Warranto* addressed to " the
bailiffs and community of Liverpool," they explained that at
present they had no bailiff of their own (*de se*), Earl Edmund
of Lancaster, their lord since 1266, having put in bailiffs of
his own appointment and prevented them from having a
free borough.[3] His action had a further effect which they do
not mention as it was not immediately relevant. With the

---

[1] Worcester, Southampton, Oxford, York.
[2] *B.B.C.* ii. 353.   [3] See below, p. 196, *n*. 2.

appointment of bailiffs by the earl, the succession of terminable leases of the farm which they had had since 1229 came to an end and the whole revenue was collected for the earl's use, more than doubling the amount he would have received, had he renewed the farming lease.[1]

[1] Ramsay Muir, *Hist. of Liverpool*, p. 27.   He is mistaken, of course, in calling the lease a fee farm.

VIII

LIBER BURGUS [1]

THE formulæ used by the royal chancery and by feudal lords in early town charters in this country have never been throughly studied, and there is good reason to believe that much needed light upon certain obscure problems of the borough has thereby been missed. A case in point seems to be afforded by the well-known clause which granted the status of " free borough " (*liber burgus, liberum burgum*). Its sudden appearance in charters at the very end of the twelfth century, though the term is known to have been already well understood and applied to many boroughs which never received the formal grant,[2] has not been satisfactorily explained. The difficulty would be less pressing had the grant been made to new boroughs only, but this was not the case.

The absence of any early definition of the term, save in one obscure seignorial charter, and its application to every degree of chartered town from manorial boroughs like Altrincham and Salford to the greatest cities of the realm, have led to some bad guessing on the one hand, and on the other to difference of opinion and misunderstandings among those who have seriously searched the evidence for a definition. Lawyers, with their too common indifference to historical facts, used to explain a grant of free borough as conferring " a freedom to buy and sell, without disturbance, exempt from toll, etc." [3] It is more surprising to find so well equipped

---

[1] Reprinted from *Essays in Medieval History presented to Thomas Frederick Tout*, ed. A. G. Little and F. M. Powicke (Manchester, 1925), pp. 79-97.
[2] See the frequent references to *liberi burgi nostri* in the Ipswich charter of 1200 (Gross, *Gild Merchant*, ii. 116). At Michaelmas 1199 the burgesses of Canterbury apparently offered 250 marks to have their town at farm and with such liberties as " *liberi et dominici burgi* domini regis habent qui libertates habent " (*Pipe Roll* 1 John (P.R.S. no. 10), 160. *Cf. Book of Fees*, i. 87 (a. 1212)). For a very questionable earlier reference, see below, p. 213.
[3] Jacob, *Law Dictionary*, ed. 1782, s. " Borough."

a scholar as Mr. E. A. Lewis identifying as the essential attributes of the *liber burgus* " the non-intromittat clause exempting them from the sheriff's control as well perhaps as the grant of the *gilda mercatoria*." [1]

Even Maitland's well-known interpretation has led to some misapprehension, because it has not been kept in mind that he was dealing only with new boroughs, to whose charters the free borough clause is mostly confined, and in particular with that relatively simple type of new borough which was created by a mesne lord. What happened, Maitland asked himself, when a manorial vill was converted into a borough with a grant of *liber burgus?* His answer was that a free borough of that type was one whose lord had abolished villein services, heriot, and merchet, and instead thereof took money rents.[2] In other words, burgage tenure of land was the essential feature of the *liber burgus* of this kind. Ballard agreed that it was essential, but considered that a court for the borough was also a fundamental requisite. These two features, and these only, were, he considered, common to all boroughs, and he could find no difference between a borough and a free borough,[3] the adjective merely emphasizing the freedom of the borough as contrasted with the manorial world outside. His definition of *liber burgus* is therefore a complete one, applicable to the older and larger boroughs as well as to the new creations of the feudal period to which Maitland's *obiter dictum* was confined. But Maitland himself has incidentally made it clear that he regarded burgage tenure as at least the most fundamental, though not an original, feature of the older and more complex boroughs, and (along with French *bourgs*) providing precedents for this tenure in the newer boroughs.[4]

On Ballard's view, a grant that a place should be a free borough, with or without the addition, " with the liberties and free customs pertaining to a free borough," conveyed no more in any case than burgage tenure and a special court with the liberties and customary law that had become appurtenant to them in existing boroughs. It did not include any of those further rights and exemptions which were being

---

[1] *Mediæval Boroughs of Snowdonia*, p. 39.

[2] *Hist. of English Law*, i. 640 (2nd ed.). Heriot was by no means always forgone (*British Borough Charters*, i. 76, ii. 95).

[3] *The English Borough in the Twelfth Century*, p. 76. A grant of free borough by the Crown would imply a hundredal court, a grant by a mesne lord, a manorial one.

[4] *Op. cit.* i. 639 ; *Domesday Book and Beyond*, p. 217.

steadily accumulated by charter either from the Crown or in a less degree from mesne lords, such as the gild merchant and exemption from tolls without the borough. Here, though without naming him, Ballard is challenging the extreme opposite view developed by Gross in his *Gild Merchant*. In the notion of free borough, according to Gross, was comprehended every privilege that was conferred on boroughs up to and including the *firma burgi* and the return of writs which' together secured the almost complete emancipation of the borough from the shire organization. But as these privileges did not come into existence all at once, and were granted in very varying measure to boroughs that differed widely in size and importance, *liber burgus* was necessarily " a variable generic conception." [1] Burgage tenure is regarded in this view as a very minor ingredient of the conception and relegated to a footnote, because it does not appear in the charters of the greater boroughs ; in their case it is taken for granted. Things that are taken for granted are apt to be among the most fundamental, and a variable conception offends the logical mind, but it would certainly be strange if the extensive privileges won by the great towns in the twelfth and thirteenth centuries formed no part of the contemporary conception of a borough. We say borough simply because, as will be seen later, Ballard was right in denying that " free borough " implied any class distinction between boroughs. [2] All boroughs were free, though their share of privilege varied within very wide limits. A decision between the opposing views propounded by Ballard and Gross can only be reached by a close

[1] *Gild Merchant*, i. 5. His view is accepted in the latest discussion of the term by Mr. T. Bruce Dilks in *Proc. Somerset Archæol. and Nat. Hist. Soc.* lxiii. (1917), 34 ff. Mr. Dilks was, however, misled by my insufficiently qualified reproduction of Maitland's *dictum* in *Mediæval Manchester* (p. 62) into regarding it as intended as a general definition.

[2] Such a distinction might be thought to be implied in the answer to a *Quo warranto* writ of 1292, addressed to " the bailiffs and community " of Liverpool, that they had now no bailiff of their own, Edmund de Lancaster, lord of the town, having refused to renew the lease of their farm and to allow them to have a free borough, *Placita de Quo Warranto*, p. 381 ; Muir and Platt, *Hist. of Municipal Government in Liverpool*, pp. 397-8. But, though financial autonomy was not enjoyed by every borough, it was no essential ingredient in the concept of free borough. Liverpool itself ranked as a free borough for nearly a quarter of a century before receiving its first lease of its farm in 1229. The burgesses in 1292 were probably only insisting that free borough *in their case* had included financial autonomy. This would support Gross's view of the extensibility of the idea.

It is worth noting that the burgesses still claimed as their own several liberties which did not contribute to the farm.

scrutiny of the charters of the thirteenth century, and to this
we now proceed.

I

The free borough clause is first found in extant royal
charters at the beginning of the reign of King John. A
month after his accession in 1199, John granted to the burgesses of Dunwich : " quod burgum de Dunwichge sit liberum
burgum nostrum," [1] and in 1200 to William Briwerr, lord of
Bridgewater, that that town should be a " liberum burgum."
In the next eight years the same clause was granted in the
case of six other towns.[2] Of three of these, Helston (1201),
Stafford (1206), and Great Yarmouth (1208), the king was
lord; three, Wells (1201), Lynn (1204), and Chesterfield
(1204), belonged to mesne lords. Lynn, Stafford, and
Yarmouth received the grant *inperpetuum*. Dunwich,
Stafford, Great Yarmouth, Wells, and possibly Helston were
old boroughs, the rest new creations. The Bridgewater and
Wells charters not only conceded that the borough should
be free, but that the burgesses should be free too (*sint liberi
burgenses*).[3]

The most instructive of these cases, because the best
documented, are those of Lynn (now King's Lynn) and Wells.
Lynn's promotion to burghal rank required, or at least produced, three charters, two from the king and one from its
lord, the bishop of Norwich. They enable us to retrace every
step in the transaction. The bishop first asked that the vill
should be a free borough. John acceded to his request in
a charter of a single clause, recited in the *Quare volumus*
with the addition : " and shall have all liberties and free
customs which our free boroughs have in all things well and
in peace," etc.[4] This was less vague than it seems, for the
bishop tells us, in the charter he proceeded to grant to the
vill, that it gave him the option of choosing any borough in

---

[1] *Rot. Chart.* 51b. The passage is incorrectly given in Ballard, *British
Borough Charters*, i. 3.

[2] Seven, if Totnes should be included, but its charter is spurious as
it stands, though Ballard believed it to be based on a genuine grant (*ibid.*
I. xxxviii.).

[3] *B.B.C.* i. 101. This clause was used alone in John's charter to
Hartlepool (1201) in place of the *liber burgus* one.

[4] *Ibid.* p. 31.

England as a model for his own.[1]　He chose Oxford, and his charter is a grant that Lynn should be a free borough with the liberties of Oxford.[2]　As authorized by the king's charter, he reserved his own rights in the vill of Lynn.　The final step was a second charter from John, in which he repeated, to the burgesses and their heirs this time, the grant of a free borough and appended a number of specific franchises, some of which (including a merchant gild), but not all, are found in Henry II's charter to Oxford.　As Oxford enjoyed the liberties of London, the fullest record of her privileges would be found in the charters of London.　The Lynn clauses relating to Crown pleas and to land suits specially prescribe the law and custom of Oxford, and there is general provision for reference to the mother town in case of doubt or contention as to any judgement (*de aliquo judicio*).

The free borough clause no doubt authorized those fundamental changes of personal status and land tenure on which Maitland and Ballard lay such stress, and here at least the burgess court which the latter regards as equally fundamental, but, if Gross be right, it was meant to authorize a great deal more.　It remained indeterminate until it was individualized by the grant of the status of an existing free borough, the choice of which was left to the mesne lord.　The gild merchant and general exemption from toll, which the king conferred, *inter alia*, on the new borough as Oxford privileges, were as much part of the conception of free borough as burgage tenure and borough court.

Why did John grant the privileges of Oxford in detail immediately after the bishop, with his licence, had granted them in general terms ?　As the king granted the liberties of Nottingham to William Briwerr for his new borough at Chesterfield [3] without a further charter, the reason probably was that the burgesses of Lynn secured the great advantage of a direct grant to themselves and their heirs from the ultimate authority and in the fullest terms.

Wells in Somerset belonged, like Lynn, to episcopal lords, but it had been a borough by their grace for some time.　Bishop Robert (1136–66) had granted that it should be a borough (not called free) for ever.　Bishop Reginald had confirmed his

---

[1] Stafford received the same right of selection in the less ambiguous form : " All liberties, etc., which any free borough in England possesses," which in the case of Liverpool (1207) was restricted to maritime boroughs.

[2] *B.B.C.* i. 32.　　　　　　　　　　[3] *Ibid*. p. 33.

charter with slight additions, and a second confirmation was issued by Reginald's successor Savaric in or before 1201. He states that his predecessors had conceded the liberties and free customs " of burgesses and boroughs enjoying full liberties," and ordains that the whole territory of Wells shall be a free borough and enjoy these liberties.[1] There is nothing to show that either Reginald or Savaric added anything vital to Robert's creation. Savaric's " free borough " seems to have been Robert's " borough " and no more. No royal licence for a grant of borough privileges is so far mentioned, but a charter was obtained from John in 1201 which granted that Wells should be a free borough and the men of the vill free burgesses, and confirmed its market and fairs, but, save for a fifth fair, made no express addition to its liberties. The *Quare volumus* clause runs : " that they and their heirs shall have all the liberties and free customs of a free borough (*liberi burgi*) and of free burgesses, and (those) pertaining to such a market and fairs." [2] The first part of this clause, like the second, may only have been a royal confirmation of existing privileges, but the almost identical formula which closes the very similar charter to William Briwerr for Bridgewater (1200) : " with all other liberties and customs pertaining (*pertinentibus*) to a free borough (*ad liberum burgum*) and to a market and fair," was used to confer liberties, etc., on a new borough,[3] What liberties, we ask, for we know that there was no fixed set of privileges which every free borough enjoyed. The subsequent history of the Bridgewater formula " liberties and free customs pertaining to a (free) borough," which came to be almost regularly associated with grants of (free) borough in the thirteenth century,[4] shows that its effect was to give the grantee the right of choosing the borough which was to serve as a model, just as a grant of the liberties of all free boroughs or of any free borough to Lynn and Stafford respectively had conceded that right.[5] Thus Richard or John's charter to the abbot of Burton empowering him to make a borough at Burton-on-Trent with all liberties, etc., pertaining

---

[1] *B.B.C.* i. 2.   [2] *Ibid.* p. 31.   [3] *Ibid.* p. 176.

[4] In the shortened form " liberties pertaining to a free borough " it occurs incidentally before the appearance of the *liber burgus* clause in a Launceston charter earlier than 1167 (*B.B.C.* ii. 379-80). But it is not certain that we have the original text of the charter in its integrity. See below, p. 213.

[5] In the case of Lynn it was definitely *royal* free boroughs, but as it was merely " any free borough " in the Stafford charter, it would be unsafe to infer that the Bridgewater formula imposed any restriction of choice.

to a borough was used by him to grant to his burgesses all
the liberties, etc., which it was in his power to give, " like the
free burgesses of any neighbouring borough," [1] and a similar
grant by Henry III to a later abbot for a borough at Abbots
Bromley (1222) was his authority for his gift of the liberties
of Lichfield to that borough.[2]   Abbot William, in his charter
to the men of Burton, did not, like the bishop of Norwich at
Lynn, begin with the *liber burgus* clause, but with one assuring
free tenure to those who took up burgages and to their heirs.
As we descend in the scale of boroughs, the primary feature
of free tenure naturally receives greater emphasis.

John's charter, or rather writ, to those who were willing
to take up burgages at Liverpool, granting them the liberties
and free customs of any free borough by the sea [3] is likewise
without the *liber burgus* formula.   Liverpool's second charter
(1229) containing that formula with specified privileges has
been hitherto regarded as raising the status of the borough,
but a town which was given the liberties of the most highly
privileged maritime borough (for such was the effect of the
grant of 1207) was already a free borough.   It would seem
therefore that Henry III's grant was merely one of those con-
firmations by regrant which were common in the years which
followed the close of his minority.

The appearance of the free borough clause in charters
granted to existing boroughs, some of which are registered
as such in Domesday Book, whether mesne or royal, presents
a difficulty on any interpretation of the formula, but it is
perhaps less serious if we adopt Gross's view than if the
meaning of the term is definitely restricted to the fundamental
requisites of a borough.   One may suspect some connexion
with the contemporary refusal of the royal courts to admit
the claim of burgesses to the " liberty " of having all
cases, other than pleas of the Crown, arising in the borough,
tried in their own court, unless a charter was produced.[4]
None of the royal boroughs which got the clause had any earlier
charter, so far as is known.   A formal recognition of their
position as royal free boroughs of the highly privileged type
was, in their case therefore, essential.

Objection may be taken to Gross's view of the comprehensive implications of " free borough " on the ground that
the Wells and Bridgewater charters agree in granting the

---

[1] *B.B.C.* i. 21 (*cf.* p. 42).   [2] *Ibid.* ii. 18, 45.
[3] *Ibid.* i. 32.   [4] *Curia Regis Rolls,* iii. 153, 252 ; v. 28, 327.

liberties pertaining to market and fairs separately from those of a free borough. It will be best to deal with this difficulty in the next section, when the evidence becomes fuller.

2

Under Henry III and Edward I grants of *liber burgus* status became much more common. They were made to twenty-four royal boroughs and to a slightly larger number of mesne boroughs.[1] Most of these were new foundations, Edward I's new boroughs in Wales and elsewhere figuring largely in the list. The old boroughs which received the grant were Liverpool (1229), Bridport (1253), Berwick (1302), possibly Windsor (1277), and in Ireland the two Droghedas, the only instances of the use of the *liber burgus* clause at all in that country. The " free burgess " clause was now much more frequently associated with that of " free borough." [2]

Grants by mesne lords sometimes refer to a royal or other licence, as at Abbots Bromley (1222), Stockport, *c.* 1260 (earl of Chester), Ormskirk (1286), and Kirkham (1296), but more usually there is no record of licence or early confirmation.

In the case of Abbots Bromley the licence was for a borough simply, but as the abbot was able to bestow upon it the liberties, etc., of Lichfield, we have here clear evidence, if that were still needed, that the epithet was descriptive, not restrictive. The charter of Weymouth (1252) affords corroboration by referring in the common tallage clause to the king's *free* boroughs where the adjective is rare in this context.[3]

In the case of three new boroughs, Lydham and Clifton (1270), and Skynburgh (1301), we have only the royal charter to the lord granting free borough, etc., and no evidence that the latter issued one of his own. In the Agardsley (Newborough) charter (1263) there is no express grant of free borough, but the new foundation is incidentally so described in the first clause of its charter.[4] The experimental character of the formulæ used in John's reign for the conveyance of

---

[1] *B.B.C.* ii. 2-7. Altrincham has been accidentally omitted.

[2] *Ibid.* p. 132.

[3] *Ibid.* p. 117. The adjective does not appear to be used in any but municipal documents.

[4] *Ibid.* p. 47. This long extinct borough was of a very simple type. Its humble privileges were recited in full and confirmed " with all liberties and free commons and easements pertaining to the aforesaid burgages " (*E.H.R.* xvi. 334). The only reference to other boroughs was a grant of all " assizes " which the burgesses of Stafford had.

" liberties and free customs," where no borough was prescribed as a model, is somewhat mitigated in this period.
Grantees are no longer referred to the privileges of " any free
borough " or those of " a free borough," and only in a single
case (Windsor) to those " used by the burgesses of our other
boroughs in our realm." [1] The formula now in general use
is that employed in John's Bridgewater charter : " libertates
et liberae consuetudines ad (liberum) burgum pertinentes
(spectantes)." [2] Sometimes a mesne lord would bestow the
liberties, etc., " quas debet (decet) liber burgus (burgenses)
habere," [3] and this might be qualified by an " et quas mihi
licet conferre," [4] such lords having no power to give certain
privileges for which they had not a royal grant. The Abbots
Bromley charter shows that one way at least, perhaps the
usual way, of using a grant expressed in these terms was to
copy the liberties and customs of a neighbouring borough.

It is by examination of cases in which this formula is
employed or implied that the validity of Gross's " variable
generic conception " must be tested. The crucial instances
are found in the case of three royal foundations towards the
close of the century. They have their difficulties, it will be
seen, but cumulatively they seem to establish the main point
on which Gross insists.

When Edward I, in 1284, wished to found a borough at
Lyme (Regis) in Dorset, which should have a gild merchant
along with the liberties of Melcombe in the same county,
which did not include the gild, he used the free borough and
free burgess clauses followed by these words :

" Ita quod Gildam habeant Mercatoriam cum omnibus ad
hujusmodi Gildam spectantibus in burgo predicto et alias
Libertates et liberas Consuetudines per totam Angliam et
Potestatem nostram quas Burgensibus de Melecumbe . . .
nuper concessimus." [5]

Although the liberties of a free borough are not directly
mentioned, the wording of the charter certainly seems to imply
that a gild merchant and the liberties of Melcombe were not
a mere addition to, but part and parcel of the free borough
then created.

More decisive, though not without its difficulties, is the

---

[1] *B.B.C.* ii. 24.   [2] Above, p. 199.
[3] *B.B.C.* ii. 16 (Carlow), 22 (Yarmouth (I.W.)).
[4] At Carlow. *Cf.* the Burton charter above, p. 200.
[5] Gross, *Gild Merchant*, i. 14 *n.* Melcombe had received in 1280 the
liberties of London as contained in the charter of 1268 (*B.B.C.* ii. 24).

charter which Edward gave to the new borough of Caerwys in
Flintshire in 1290.[1] In its brevity and the disposition of its
parts, it closely resembles that of Lyme, falling into three
divisions : (1) free borough and free burgess clauses ; (2)
grant of a gild merchant (but introduced by " et quod ") ; (3)
grant of the liberties of a specified borough (two, Conway and
Rhuddlan are mentioned but their charters (1284) were identical). Here, as in the case of Lyme, much parchment and
labour were saved by a general reference to the privileges of
boroughs which had recently received comprehensive charters.
But it is the differences rather than the likenesses of the
Lyme and Caerwys charters which concern us here. In the
latter the liberties granted are definitely described as " liberties
and free customs pertaining to a free borough such as (*quales*),
namely, our free burgesses of Conway and Rhuddlan have
in their boroughs." [2] Thus the many privileges granted in
identical charters in 1284 to these and five other new castle
boroughs in North Wales, including gild merchant, general
exemption from tolls, a free borough prison, and a number of
liberties which had only been given to boroughs in comparatively recent times, are clearly labelled as privileges
belonging to a free borough. There was nothing novel, as
we have seen, in giving a new borough the liberties of an older
one by the grant of the privileges pertaining to a free borough,
but in the case of Bridgewater and Abbots Bromley the choice
of the model was left to the grantee, here it is practically
prescribed, and we are thus enabled to identify a definite set
of fairly advanced liberties as comprised in the conception of
free borough.

The separate grant of gild merchant to Caerwys despite
its inclusion among the liberties of Conway and Rhuddlan is
hard to understand, and runs directly counter to the inference
one seemed entitled to draw from the Lyme charter. But
the difficult question of the relation of gild to borough must
be reserved for the moment.

Further light is thrown upon the conception of free borough
by the documents relating to Edward I's foundation of the
borough of Hull (Kingston-on-Hull), and this was the case on

---

[1] Gross, *op. cit.* ii. 356. Newborough in Anglesey received a charter
in almost exactly the same form in 1303 (Lewis, *Mediæval Boroughs of
Snowdonia*, p. 283). Rhuddlan only is set as its model.

[2] The addition of " or our other burgesses in Wales (have) " clearly
involved no real alternative. For the general affiliation of Welsh boroughs
to Hereford, see Lewis, *op. cit.* p. 17 and Gross, *op. cit.* ii. 257.

which Gross mainly relied. The actual charter (1299) might indeed seem incompatible with his view. It opens with the *liber burgus* clause to which is attached the grant of the liberties pertaining " ad liberum burgum " usually reserved for the *Volumus* clause, with a proviso (*ita tamen quod*) that the borough should be kept by a warden appointed by the king, *i.e.* not by an elective mayor. Eight liberties and customs are then separately granted : the right of devise, return of writs, freedom from external pleading, an elective coroner, a royal prison and gallows (for judgement of infangenethief and utfangenethief), freedom from tolls throughout the king's dominions, lot and scot in tallages by all enjoying the liberties, and two markets and a fair. The free borough and liberties clause and each of these grants are individually recited in the *Volumus* section.[1] On the face of it, there seems to be a distinction made between the liberties pertaining to a free borough and those which are specified. Fortunately, there has been preserved and printed by Madox [2] the petition from the men of Kingston on which the charter was granted, and this contains the substance of its clauses in practically the same order. The inclusion of the proviso about the warden, and the petition and charter of the men of Ravenserod, identical except in the market and fair clause, seem to show that the petition was not uninfluenced from above,[3] but it may well be that the anxiety of the applicants to have their most important privileges set out in full accounts for their separate position in the charter. At any rate, we have a definite statement in the report of an *ad quod damnum* inquiry before the royal council (which has preserved the petition), that these were free borough privileges. The petitioners, it is stated, asked to be allowed to use and enjoy "quibusdam Libertatibus ad Liberum Burgum in Regno vestro pertinentibus." For any liberties and customs not specified but authorized by the general clause of their charter the new burgesses perhaps used Scarborough as their model, since they asked for exemption from toll as enjoyed by the burgesses of that town.

---

[1] Madox, *Firma Burgi* (1726), pp. 272-3.

[2] *History of the Exchequer*, i. 423.

[3] The town had been governed by royal wardens since Edward I acquired it from the abbot of Meaux in. 1293. The townsmen had held by rent from the abbey and under the king the vill is occasionally called a borough before 1299 (J. Bilson, *Wyke-upon-Hull in 1293* (Hull, 1928), pp. 61 ff., 71, 104). It will be noted that the warden proviso implies that an elective head was a normal liberty of a free borough.

Still further confirmation of Gross's interpretation of *liber burgus* comes from a charter of Edward which does not found a new borough, but enlarges an old one. In 1298 he annexed the lands of Pandon to the borough of Newcastle-on-Tyne and ordained that they should be one vill and one borough.[1] The charter goes on to grant that the burgesses of Newcastle should have in the lands and tenements of Pandon " liberum burgum sicut habent in predicta villa Novi Castri cum omnibus libertatibus et liberis consuetudinibus ad liberum burgum pertinentibus." [2] Here *liber burgus* must certainly carry more than the mere conversion of the Pandon lands and tenements into Newcastle burgages, for that is the subject of a special clause.[3]

Lastly, at Liverpool, where there was no question of new foundation or extension, we find the burgesses in 1292 identifying free borough with their lease of the farm of the town.[4] Their case was weak, for they had no perpetual lease, but the claim confirms Gross's view.

This Liverpool identification of *liber burgus* with financial autonomy perhaps reveals a tendency of the term at the end of the thirteenth century to take on a narrower and more technical meaning. For the number of *liberi burgi* was certainly decreasing. This was the inevitable result of the extension of higher franchises to the more advanced boroughs and the differentiation produced by the reorganization of the police system culminating in the Statute of Winchester (1285) and by the introduction of a higher borough rate in national taxation. The smaller mesne boroughs whose privileges did not extend much beyond burgage tenure were losing burghal status and descending into the new category of *villae mercatoriae*. The process was somewhat slow, and was not complete until the fourteenth century was well advanced, but its causes lay far back. Among the boroughs which suffered this fate was Manchester. Recognized as a borough in royal inquisitions as late as 1322, and having a charter of 1301 closely following that of Salford (a *liber burgus*), it was judicially declared in 1359 not to be held by its lords as a borough but as a *villa mercatoria*,[5] a

---

[1] *B.B.C.* ii. 41. [2] *Ibid.* p. 6. [3] *Ibid.* p. 52.
[4] See above, p. 196, *n.* 2. The Liverpool historians describe the lease as a fee farm, but a fee farm was a lease in perpetuity and the Liverpool grants were only for terms of years.
[5] Harland, *Mamecestre*, iii. 449. Yet in the sense of " merchants-town " the term could be applied even to Norwich (Hudson, *Rec.* i. 63) ; *cf. Law Merchant* (Selden Soc.), ii. 104 ; Madox, *Firma Burgi*, 250, *i*, and *B.B.C.* II. lii. ff.

P

"market town." No reasons are given, but it is evident that by that date mere burgage tenure and portmoot or borough court was not considered a sufficient qualification for borough rank.

The earlier and more comprehensive application of the term "(free) borough" is well illustrated by another judicial decision. In 1270 Penryn in Cornwall was decided to be a free borough, though its charter from a bishop of Exeter (1236) did not use the term, and gave it only free tenure and a low judicial amercement.[1] At Higham Ferrers the conversion of some eighty villein tenements into burgages was sufficient to constitute a free borough (1251).[2] This limited conception of *liber burgus* is seen also in the only really contemporary definition of the term before the fourteenth century with which we have met. In granting that status to Welshpool, between 1241 and 1286, Gruffydd ab Gwenwynwyn explains : "so that the aforesaid burgesses and their heirs shall be free of all customs and services pertaining to me and my heirs in all my lands, wherever they may be."[3] This case is the more notable that, Welshpool being in the March of Wales, Gruffydd was able to give his new borough such unusual privileges for a mesne borough as the right to imprison and try homicides as well as thieves, and the old year and day clause for villeins settling in the borough, in addition to a gild merchant and the law of Breteuil as enjoyed by Hereford. Here it is the fundamental liberty of burgesses as contrasted with the manorial population without that is referred to the grant of *liber burgus* and not the whole body of liberties and customs granted, as in the royal charters we have examined.

It was natural that in seignorial boroughs of a simple type emancipation from manorialism, more or less complete, and the new burgage tenure should overshadow everything else, while in the great boroughs of immemorial origin and high franchises, in important mesne boroughs like Lynn, whose lords obtained similar franchises for them from the Crown, and in royal castle boroughs in Wales which were English garrisons in a newly conquered country, burgage tenure, though vital, was subordinated to the extensive liberties enjoyed by them. The ordinary feudal lord who founded a borough without a special royal charter could indeed add little to the initial boon

---

[1] *B.B.C.* ii. 46, 216.　　　　[2] *Ibid.* pp. 47, 142. *Cf.* p. 354, *n.* 3.
[3] *Ibid.* p. 6. *Cf.* the *liberi custumarii* of Chester, c. 1178 (above, p. 134, *n.* 3).

of free borough tenure. Unless in his manor which in whole or part became a borough he already possessed by grant or prescription, as was perhaps often the case, such franchises as market and fairs, the right of trying thieves and the enforcement of the assize of bread and ale, these had to be sought from the king or palatine lord.[1] It must be kept in mind, however, that burgage tenure in itself involved a very considerable body of legal custom, much of it peculiar to the boroughs, the scope and importance of which has been fully revealed in Miss Bateson's volumes on *Borough Customs*.[2] Thus, when Bishop Poore of Salisbury created new burgages at Sherborne in 1227–28, he granted them " with all liberties and free customs pertaining to burgages of this kind." [3] A comparison of the phrasing here with that of Edward I's charter annexing Pandon to Newcastle-on-Tyne [4] is instructive, because chartered liberties unconnected with tenure had to be included in the latter case.

As the lord had often a manorial market and fairs available for his new borough, so he had always a manorial court, with or without franchises, which could be used as it stood or divided according as the whole manor or only a part of it was included in the borough. It may sometimes have remained undivided even in the latter case. The extent to which this court became a really independent borough court depended on the will of the lord.[5] As a definite grant of a borough court by charter was excessively rare,[6] and some charters of creation contain no reference even to the lord's court, we must infer that this requisite of a borough was either taken for granted as already there or implied in the grant of burgage tenure. It seems clear, in any case, that if we look only at the humbler boroughs, which had but partially escaped from manorial fetters, their court was less distinctive and less fully developed a burghal feature than was burgage tenure.

As regards a large class of mesne boroughs, then, Maitland's explanation of the effect of a *liber burgus* clause would appear

---

[1] The monks of Durham founded a little borough at Elvet between 1188 and 1195, while still uncertain whether the bishop would grant them a licence for a market and fairs (*B.B.C.* i. 171 ; *C.Ch.R.* iv. 323).

[2] Selden Society.

[3] *B.B.C.* ii. 45 ; *cf.* Agardsley above, p. 201.   [4] Above, p. 205.

[5] The burgesses of Warrington renounced their free borough court in 1300 on the demand of the lord (*B.B.C.* II. lxxxv. 182, 386) and accepted the legal status of " free tenants."   [6] *B.B.C.* ii. 146.

to be sufficiently confirmed. It does not profess to be a general definition of the term. Ballard's interpretation, on the other hand, which does make that profession, overstresses the jurisdictional aspect of the humbler borough, though admitting that its court was inferior to the hundredal court of the greater towns, and ignores some of the higher non-tenurial liberties of the latter.

There is one class of mesne boroughs which we have reserved for separate consideration. It comprises those that were either founded by royal licence and seignorial charter or by royal charter to the lord, which apparently dispensed with the necessity of a charter from him. In some instances of the former kind, e.g. Ormskirk and Kirkham, there are indications that the licence must have specified the particular privileges to be conferred.[1] Among those contained in the Kirkham charter (1296) are two which are specially referred to the conception of the free borough : " prison, pillory, ducking stool and other judicial instruments *pertaining to a free borough* by which malefactors and transgressors against the liberties of the said borough may be kept in custody and punished," [2] and " assize of bread and ale *as pertains to a free borough*." [3]

More commonly in both kinds of royal charter brevity was secured by coupling the grant of (free) borough with a general grant of liberties in the formula now familiar to us in connexion with greater boroughs : " liberties and free customs pertaining to a (free) borough." The case of Abbots Bromley shows that this was a licence to copy the institutions of some neighbouring borough.[4] Unfortunately, we do not know under what conditions, not expressed in the licence, such permission was given. It is improbable, of course, that the grantee was empowered to invest his borough with all the liberties enjoyed by a highly privileged royal borough that were relevant to its mesne status. Even in the case of royal boroughs, we have seen the vague general formula elucidated either by specification of the higher franchises as at Hull or by mention of the borough to be copied as at Caerwys. Possibly, the feudal lord who got a licence for a borough in this form had to submit his choice for approval This hypothesis would hardly be so necessary if the formula

---

[1] *B.B.C.* ii. 5, 283. *Cf.* the procedure in John's reign, above, pp. 197 ff.
[2] *Ibid.* p. 170.
[3] *Ibid.* p. 223. The burgesses of Agardsley (above p. 201) had this liberty, but the lord of the borough reserved one-third of the amercements (*E.H.R.* xvi. 335).
[4] See above, p. 200.

when unqualified gave no title to certain important franchises.
For this there is some evidence. That markets and fairs were
excluded may be asserted with a certain measure of confidence.
It will be remembered that in two of John's charters, a market
and fairs were granted separately from the liberties pertaining
to a free borough. Now, this distinction recurs in the charter
of Richard, king of the Romans, to Camelford, confirmed by
Henry III in 1260,[1] and in that of Edward I to the abbot of
Holme Cultram for Skynburgh (1301).[2] Moreover, Henry III's
licence to the abbot of Burton for a borough at Abbots Bromley
(1222) grants a fair (there was doubtless a market already)
separately from the liberties.[3] The lucrative right of authorizing markets and fairs, which in England were not confined
to boroughs as they were in Scotland, was a jealously guarded
prerogative of the Crown and the possessors of palatine powers.
In many cases the founder of a borough had a market or fair
or both, by their grant, in his manor long before he thought of
making a borough there. Where this was not the case, a bare
general grant of borough liberties would not, it appears, include
this franchise. But, when once granted, it could be described
as one of the liberties pertaining to a free borough in the
particular case. Thus the borough of (High) Wycombe was
granted in fee farm to the burgesses by its lord in 1226, " with
rents, markets and fairs and all other things pertaining to a
free borough," [4] and at Hull in 1299 the market and fairs,
though granted separately in the charter, are included, as we
have seen, in another document among liberties pertaining to
a free borough.

Another privilege which can hardly have been conveyed
by a general formula, but must surely have required a specific
grant, is that most valuable one of exemption from tolls
throughout the kingdom and the other dominions of the king.
It is inconceivable that a petty borough such as Abbots
Bromley should have been able to acquire this great liberty
by *verba generalia*.[5]

The wording of some charters seems almost to suggest
that a general grant of liberties did not entitle the grantee to

---

[1] *B.B.C.* ii. 4.   [2] *Ibid.* pp. 28, 247, 249.
[3] *Ibid.* p. 45.   [4] *Ibid.* p. 303.
[5] We may quote here, though no royal licence for it is on record,
Baldwin de Redvers' charter to Yarmouth (I.W.) between 1240 and 1262 :
" de omnibus libertatibus, etc. quas liber burgus habere debet, *necnon* de
libertate et quietancia de teolonio," etc. (*ibid.* ii. 22). The exemption was
only for his own lands.

set up a gild merchant. Edward I's charter to Caerwys (1290), already referred to,[1] granted " a gild merchant with hanse and all liberties and free customs pertaining to a free borough," though the constitution of Conway and Rhuddlan, which was named as a model for the new borough, included the gild. In the Kirkham charter, six years later, a free gild was granted " with the liberties which pertain to a free borough and to a free gild." [2] Gross remarked long ago that in charters gild and borough are often treated as distinct conceptions, which indeed they were. Though peculiar to boroughs and *quasi*-boroughs,[3] the gild was absent in many of them, including some of the greatest ; where it existed it sometimes came into conflict with the purely burghal organism, successful conflict in certain cases, and it often comprised non-burgesses as well as burgesses. On the other hand, the wording of the Lyme Regis charter (p. 202) seems to imply that the gild was granted as a liberty of free borough in that case. It is true also that mesne lords could apparently grant the gild without any licence, and it may therefore seem unlikely that they were debarred from doing so under a general licence. Stress has also been laid upon the fact that the gild at Bridgewater has no known creation unless it was authorized by John's general grant of the liberties pertaining to a free borough.[4] One is prepared, too, for the suggestion that in the Caerwys charter the gild is only singled out as the most important of the borough liberties, just as it is occasionally specially mentioned among the liberties and customs of existing boroughs. But with the exception of the Lyme Regis case, none of these arguments seems strong. A mesne lord might have the power to allow the gild, but not as a burghal liberty in the strict sense. The lords of Bridgewater may have used their power to set up a gild independently of John's grant and even without a charter. If the gild in the Caerwys charter were included among the liberties mentioned in close association with it, we should have expected the sentence to read : " with hanse, and with all *other* liberties," etc. The singling out of the gild among the liberties and customs of established boroughs is capable of interpretation in just the opposite sense. However liberties were classified in grants to new boroughs, whether as strictly

---

[1] Above, p. 203.   *Cf. R.L.C.* i. 345 *b* (ann. 1217).   [2] *B.B.C.* ii. 283.
[3] *E.g.*, Kingston-on-Thames, which, though it had burghal features, was never called a borough, and was taxed as part of the royal demesne.
[4] Dilks in *Proc. Somerset Archæological and Natural History Society*, lxiii. (1917), 44.

burghal or otherwise, they were all privileges of the free borough which had received them, and if one of them was given special mention, the inference is perhaps rather that it was felt to be different in kind from the rest than that it was presented merely *exempli gratia*.

If this line of reasoning be sound, and if I was correct in my suggestion (p. 204) that the men of Kingston-on-Hull copied Scarborough for the liberties which were not granted to them specifically (which did not include the gild), it might explain why there was no merchant gild at Hull, though Scarborough had one. However this may be, we shall see in the next section that in the first half of the twelfth century a clear distinction between gild and borough liberties was made in an important charter of creation (p. 214).

There are more " ifs and ans " here than one could wish, but it may be hoped that detailed investigation of the municipal history of particular boroughs will some day show exactly what was obtained under these general powers.

We are now in a position to summarize the main conclusions to which our inquiry, so far as it has gone, appears to have led : (1) In the thirteenth century as in the twelfth any place, large or small, old or new, royal or mesne, which had the specific burgage tenure could be described as a borough, or free borough, for the epithet merely emphasized the contrast with manorial unfreedom, but beyond this there were wide differences in the privileges enjoyed by them. (2) A simple grant that a place should be a (free) borough and its inhabitants free burgesses involved liberties and free customs appurtenant to burgage tenure, but new creations usually contained also an express grant of such liberties and customs either (*a*) by specification, or (*b*) by gift of the liberties, etc., of some borough which was named in the charter, or (*c*) by a general grant of the liberties pertaining to a free borough, with or without partial specification. (3) As there was no single standard of borough liberties, the effect of (*c*) certainly, and of (*a*) probably, was to allow some freedom of choice in regard to the borough whose institutions were to be followed. (4) The limitations under which this freedom of choice was exercised in the case of mesne boroughs remain at present uncertain, but there is good reason to believe that markets and fairs, if not already possessed by the manorial lord, and general exemption from toll required a special grant. (5) In the case of royal creations and of established boroughs generally the

" liberties, etc., pertaining to a free borough " included these and any other privileges enjoyed by the individual borough, irrespective of their nature and origin, though such distinctions may be still occasionally recognized in a formal way. Thus the connotation of " free borough " varied from the privileges of London or Winchester to the mere burgage tenure of the humblest seignorial borough. (6) By the close of the thirteenth century the administrative and financial policy of the Crown was drawing a line which ended in the denial of burghal status to a large number, perhaps the majority, of mesne boroughs.

Clumsy as this variable conception of free borough and its liberties may appear to be, especially in its application to the creation of new boroughs, it represents a real attempt on the part of the royal chancery to introduce some form and order into a very intractable set of facts due to earlier want of system and to the great outburst of feudal borough making, which was only partly under the control of the Crown. This will become clearer in the next section, where we trace the antecedents of the *liber burgus* formula in the twelfth century.

So far we have been testing the modern interpretations of that formula by the light of charter evidence, some of which has not hitherto been taken into consideration. The result seems to show that Gross was right in asserting that *liber burgus* was a variable conception, but did not observe, or failed to make clear, that in a general grant of that status to a mesne borough the term seems to exclude those privileges which only royal power could grant and to be more or less limited to liberties involved in the primary fact of burgage tenure, even when some of these higher privileges were conceded. Maitland and Ballard, on the other hand, by concentrating their attention too exclusively on this simpler type of borough, missed the fuller conception of *liber burgus* in the case of the greater towns where the higher privileges overshadowed burgage tenure. Maitland did not attempt a general definition, and is substantially correct so far as he goes. Ballard's definition is scientific in its elimination of every feature which was not common to all boroughs, from the greatest to the least. But contemporaries were less concerned with scientific definition than with a terminology which would represent actual facts. If we give a rather wider interpretation to " burgage tenure " than Ballard seems to do,[1] there had doubtless been a time

---

[1] See below, p. 213.

when his definition was approximately true of all boroughs, and traces of the old restricted meaning of " borough " are, as we have seen, clearly visible in the charters of the lesser boroughs of the thirteenth century. What he failed to notice was that the conception was an elastic one, and was expanded in that century to include the great franchises of the more important towns.[1]

None of these writers seems to have observed the device which enabled a brief general grant of borough liberties to be made, despite the absence of a common standard among boroughs. In the next section, too, it is hoped to show, what has not been yet noticed, that the *liber burgus* formula was not an absolutely new conception of John's chancery, but merely an adaptation of an older and less convenient formula.

3.

If we could trust the text of a charter which Reginald, earl of Cornwall, granted to the canons of Launceston between 1141 and 1167,[2] we should have to admit that *liber burgus* and " liberties pertaining to *liber burgus* " were terms already in use about the middle of the twelfth century and perhaps much earlier. But their absence from all other known charters before 1199 and the use of less advanced formulæ down to that date throw grave doubt on this feature of Reginald's charter. Proof of the second objection will now be adduced.

New boroughs were rare in the twelfth century as compared with the thirteenth and were created by the concession of the liberties and free customs of some one town or by a grant of specified liberties and customs. Bishop Hugh de Puiset prefaces his grant of the liberties of Newcastle-on-Tyne to his borough of Durham with a single clause which rather closely anticipates Maitland's description of the effect of a later grant of *liber burgus* in the case of a mesne borough : " Quod sint liberi et quieti a consuetudine quod dicitur intoll et uttoll et de merchetis et herietis." [3] Intoll and uttoll were dues on the

---

[1] The cancellation of the Wells charter of 1341, granting high burghal privileges, because it had not been preceded by an inquisition *ad quod damnum* is no proof, as Ballard thought (*English Borough in the Twelfth Century*, pp. 77 ff.), that Gross's view is untenable. An early grant of *liber burgus*, such as Wells had (1201), could not carry privileges which were not then conveyed by it or which were of later institution, but after they had been legally conferred they might be described as liberties of *liber burgus*.

[2] *B.B.C.* ii. 379-80.

[3] *Ibid.* i. 192. The clause is out of place here.

transfer of tenements. For our present purpose, however, it is the formulæ of the royal chancery that we are seeking. The most instructive of these appears in the very interesting charters by which the borough of Beverley was founded. About the year 1125 probably, Thurstan, archbishop of York, with leave from Henry I, granted to the men there the liber-ties (later described as free customs) of York with hanshus or gildhall, farm of the town tolls, free entrances and exits and exemption from toll throughout Yorkshire.[1] The king's confirmation took the form of a grant to them of " *liberum bur-gagium* secundum liberas leges et consuetudines burgensium de Eboraco," with their gild, toll, and all their free customs and liberties as bestowed by Thurstan.[2] An interesting varia-tion of the royal formula appears in the confirmation issued twenty years later by Archbishop William, where it reads : " liberale burgagium juxta formam liberalis burgagii Eboraci." [3] The points of importance for us here are : (1) That in the twelfth century as in the thirteenth an ordinary vill could be raised to borough rank by the gift of the liberties, etc., of some existing borough without an express formula of creation. (2) That the royal chancery has found a formula which remedies this omission by the introduction of the ab-stract notion of *liberum burgagium*, which is applicable to all creations but is individualized by reference to the liberties and customs of a particular town. In Archbishop William's charter the abstract idea takes on a concrete shape. The laws and customs of York are the *liberale burgagium* of that city. (3) That certain liberties, those of gild merchant and of toll, are made the subject of specific grant, though enjoyed by the city which served as model. (4) That a sharp distinction between liberties and free customs is not preserved, in Thurstan's charter at least, and that " laws " might be used to cover both.

In the use made of *liberum (liberale) burgagium* in two of the three Beverley charters, and especially in that of Arch-bishop William, we have a clear anticipation of the *liber burgus* formula which expressed the same idea in another form. It is usual to translate *burgagium* in this sense by " burgage tenure," but " borough tenure " would be preferable

---

[1] *B.B.C.* i. p. 23 ; Farrer, *Early Yorkshire Charters*, i. 90.
[2] *Ibid.* 92 ; *B.B.C.* i. 23.
[3] *Ibid.* p. 24 ; Farrer, p. 100. *Cf.* the " juxta formam legum burgen-sium de Eboraco " in Thurstan's description of the king's original licence.

as avoiding confusion with the derivative use of *burgagium* for the individual burghal tenement and leaving room for a good deal of " liberty " or " law " or " custom " which was not all tenurial, though the free tenement at a money rent was the most fundamental element in the borough.[1] It was not merely the individual tenement which was held in free burgage, but the town as a whole with all its liberties, etc. An instructive case is that of Drogheda in Meath, which vill with its newly created burgages and the law of Breteuil was granted to the burgesses in 1194 by Walter de Lacy *in libero burgagio*.[2]

" Free burgage," like the later " free borough," was a " variable generic conception." The gild merchant and exemption from toll, however, were not, apparently, regarded as included in this conception, but as supplementary to it. This is important in view of some evidence already discussed that these privileges may not have been included in general grants of the liberties of a free borough.[3]

There is ample proof that the formula of " free burgage," though rarer than the later " free borough," continued to be used in the foundation of new boroughs during the reign of Henry II. Henry himself between 1167 and 1170 made a grant of *liberum burgagium* in Hedon (Holderness) to William, earl of Albemarle, and his heirs, in fee and inheritance, " so that his burgesses of Hedon may hold freely and quietly in free burgage as my burgesses of York and Lincoln best and most freely and quietly hold those [? their] customs and liberties." [4] Reginald, earl of Cornwall, gave to his burgesses of Bradninch their burgary and their tenements (*placeas*) before 1175,[5] and somewhat later Abbot Richard granted Whitby for ever *in liberam burgagiam* (sic), and to the burgesses dwelling there " liberty of burgage and free laws and free rights." [6] As late as 1194 Roger de Lacy founded a borough

---

[1] The wider meaning is well illustrated in one of the conditions imposed upon a tenant of Bridlington Priory in Scarborough between 1185 and 1195. He was not to give, sell or mortgage his toft and land ; et nec per burgagium de Scardeburg' nec per aliam advocationem se defendet ut minus justiciabilis sit nobis in curia nostra de omni re ad nos pertinente (Farrer, *Early Yorkshire Charters*, i. no. 369). As late as the fourteenth century admission to the franchise of Colchester was " entering the burgage " (*Colchester Court Rolls*, ed. Gurney Benham, i. 41, 65 *et passim*). In this sense of the term we find instances of messuages (*mansurae*), in York itself, about the middle of the twelfth century, described as held *in libero burgagio* (*Early Yorkshire Charters*, nos. 236, 333, etc.).

[2] *B.B.C.* i. 48.   [3] Above, pp. 208 ff.
[4] *B.B.C.* i. 38.   [5] *Ibid.*   [6] *Ibid.* p. 39.

at Pontefract by the gift to his burgesses of " liberty and free burgage and their tofts to be held of me and my heirs in fee and inheritance." [1]

If more direct proof of the equivalence of this formula with the later one of " free borough " be needed, it is not wanting. Dunwich, for instance, which was the first town to receive the *liber burgus* clause, had a later charter from John in 1215, in which that clause did not appear and was replaced by a grant of free burgage.[2] Much later still, in the parallel statements of their baronial privileges made by two Cheshire magnates, Henry of Lancaster claims to hold Halton and Congleton as free boroughs and to have there free burgesses,[3] but Hamon de Massey claims to hold the vill of Altrincham *libero burgagio* and to have free burgesses there.[4] As Massey's charter (*c.* 1290) had made Altrincham a free borough, the two phrases are clearly identical in meaning even at the end of the thirteenth century.

The Beverley town charters show that the privileged status of a great and ancient town like York could be summed up in the same term " free burgage " as was applied to new mesne boroughs, though in the first case no grant to that effect was producible. Madox has adduced clear evidence that in the fourteenth century royal towns, including York and London, were accounted as held of the Crown by free burgage (*in liberum burgagium*).[5] He restricts this status to those boroughs which had grants of fee farm and so paid their rents, etc., in a fixed sum to the Exchequer. But the validity of this limitation may perhaps be questionable. We have already seen the burgesses of a mesne borough, Drogheda in Meath, enfeoffed for themselves and their heirs with that vill as well as their individual burgages and the customs of Breteuil *in libero burgagio*, though here the money service was a render from each burgage, not a lump sum from the town. If we may argue from this case and from general probabilities, any grant to the burgesses of a new borough in fee and inheritance, with reservation of a money rent only, must have been in free burgage.

The motive which dictated the substitution of *liber burgus* for *liberum burgagium* in charters of creation from John's reign

---

[1] *B.B.C.* i. 41. [2] *Ibid.* p. 45.
[3] Ormerod, *Hist. of Cheshire*, i. 703. [4] *Ibid.* p. 526.
[5] *Firma Burgi*, pp. 21-3. For an earlier London formula, see above, p. 107, and below, p. 218.

onwards is sufficiently obvious.   The same idea was expressed in a more concise and concrete form and the grant of borough liberties by a general formula, which did not tie the grantee to a particular model, was made possible.   We ought perhaps to note that Ballard had already suggested that " the term (*liber burgus*) was introduced by the lawyers of John's reign to shorten the verbiage of charters," but verbiage is too strong a word in this connexion, and he did not realize that the term had a definite predecessor not much longer, though less convenient for practical use.   Both devices had the advantage of enabling a small borough, which could not face the cost of a long enumeration of liberties, to obtain a short and comparatively inexpensive charter.   Such brevity had indeed its dangers, as the burgesses of Huntingdon were to discover. Their first charter, in 1205, though it did not contain the *liber burgus* clause, granted them the liberties and free customs of the other royal free boroughs and free burgesses of England and nothing else but the fee farm of their borough and a clause excluding the sheriff.[1]   In 1348 it was found necessary to get a charter specifying their liberties, their right to them under the general terms of the earlier charter being disputed.[2]

ADDITIONAL NOTE

In *Borough and Town* (pp. 138 ff.) Dr. Stephenson criticizes my conclusions on *Liber Burgus* in the light of his view that, for the most part, " free burgage " and the " free borough "

[1] *B.B.C.*, pp. 15, 122, 230.   There is one of John's charters, that to Ipswich in 1200 (Gross, *Gild Merchant*, ii. 115), which, after reciting a detailed list of liberties and free customs, describes them as having been or being enjoyed by the other (*ceteri*) burgesses of the royal free boroughs of England. With the exception of a merchant gild and the protection of their general freedom from toll throughout the king's land and its seaports by a fine instead of the right of distress, these were London liberties, occurring with little verbal difference in the charter of 1155 to that city and described as such in charters rather similar to that of Ipswich granted by Richard I to Northampton, Lincoln, and Norwich.   The divergences mentioned above doubtless suggested the use of the new general formula.   In spite of appearances, it clearly did not mean that every royal free borough had all the liberties confirmed to Ipswich, for not all had a merchant gild or the same custom with regard to illegal tolls.   The formula could mean no more than that all were liberties possessed by some royal boroughs.   In his Huntingdon charter then, John was not granting a foreknown set of liberties and still less all the liberties enjoyed by such boroughs.   Less ambiguous is his Stafford charter of 1206 (*B.B.C.* i. 15) creating the town a free borough with the liberties, etc., of any free borough of England.
[2] *Cal. Chart. Rolls*, v. 94-5.

were results of French mercantile settlement after the Norman Conquest. Gross's interpretation of free borough as a " variable generic conception " is inacceptable as minimizing the fundamental importance of the burgage tenure of land and obscuring its origin as a Norman innovation. As a matter of fact, Gross did include it in the conception of free borough, but regarded it as so ancient and fundamental a feature of the old English boroughs that it was seldom mentioned in their charters, while it was naturally prominent in new foundations. The question which is really at issue, therefore, is whether burgage tenure in the older boroughs existed, though not under that name, before the Conquest. Mr. Stephenson himself in other chapters of his book, but not here, admits, rather grudgingly, that to some extent it did so exist. But we may go further than that. Evidence has been adduced above which, to my mind, shows that the Conquest involved no essential change in burghal land tenure in the ancient boroughs. Not only is there no trace of conversion, but its possibility is excluded by the survival of Anglo-Saxon nomenclature alongside the new Norman one. The burgesses of London for two and half centuries after the Conquest held their tenements in socage,[1] and it was not until the fourteenth century that the name of their tenure was changed to free burgage. Nor was this peculiar to London. The same term was used at Worcester,[2] occasionally at Bristol[3] and probably in other boroughs. This usage throws a useful light upon the legal conception of burgage tenure as being a form of socage. Socage, too, was the tenure in those towns on the privileged ancient demesne of the Crown, such as Basingstoke, Godmanchester, and Kingston-on-Thames, which, without being formally considered as boroughs, had burghal liberties and were ultimately incorporated.

Dr. Stephenson's insistence on the novelty of burgage tenure causes him to attach excessive importance to Maitland's *obiter dictum* on *liber burgus*. It only applied to new boroughs of the simplest kind, created by the enfranchisement of manors, and he suggested that " the free tenure of houses at fixed and light rents which was to be found in the old shire towns "

---

[1] See above, p. 107.

[2] Cartulary of Worcester Priory, no. 395. Simon Poer acquits land of a tenant against the king's reeve of $4\frac{1}{2}d$. " qui sunt de socagio domini regis." I owe this reference to Mr. R. R. Darlington.

[3] E. W. W. Veale, *The Great Red Book of Bristol*, Introd., Part I, p. 167. (Bristol Record Society, vol. II, 1931.)

formed at least one of its models. Mere enfranchisement was
at any rate an absolute minimum and must have been sterile
without further liberties. Indeed Dr. Stephenson has to
admit that the " free burgage " conferred on various new
boroughs in the twelfth century, from Beverley onwards, was
not merely burgage tenure of land, but the sum total of the
liberties that made them boroughs.[1] This abstract conception
had no direct reference to the free burghal tenement, for
burgage in the concrete sense of such a tenement was derived
from the word in its wider sense of " borough status,"
" borough liberties," and it was rarely used in the older and
larger boroughs. In seignorial charters the distinction is
sometimes quite clearly expressed, as, for instance, in that of
Pontefract (1194) which grants to the burgesses " libertatem
et liberum burgagium et toftos suos tenendos de me et her-
edibus meis in feodo et hereditate . . . reddendo annuatim
. . . xii denarios pro quolibet tofto." [2]

As all boroughs had not the same liberties, free burgage
meaning, " the sum total of the liberties which made a place
a borough " sounds so like a " variable generic conception "
that Dr. Stephenson hastens to add to his recognition of the
fact that we are not thereby driven to accept Gross's dictum.
" The concept of the free borough or of free burgage in
the twelfth century . . . was," he says, " not variable, but
stable." The period is limited in order to exclude the possibility—doubt is thrown on probability—that the evidence
of late thirteenth-century date adduced in support of Gross's
theory of the extensibility of " free borough " to include
successive new liberties may prove well-founded. But was
the " free burgage " of the previous century really stable and
non-extensible ? Evidence is much scantier, but if York,
for instance, had secured a new liberty after the grant of its
old ones to Beverley, a subsequent grant of its " free burgage "
to some other new borough would surely have included this
addition ? It was this instability, this variation of content
which made it necessary when " free burgage " was granted
to a new borough to define it by reference to some existing
borough or boroughs. Affiliation of this kind and that produced by the gift of the higher liberties of some old boroughs
to others less highly privileged tended no doubt towards a
fixed conception, but it was only a tendency and was always

[1] *Op. cit.*, pp. 142-3.   [2] *B.B.C.* i. 41, 48.

liable to counteraction by the aspiration of the wealthier boroughs to still higher liberties. Free burgage then, with its later equivalent free borough, was a variable conception. The more concrete term is accurately glossed by anticipation in Glanvill's *villa privilegiata*, a town that has privileges, liberties, and such privileges varied more or less from borough to borough.

IX

THE BOROUGH COMMUNITY FROM THE TWELFTH CENTURY [1]

In Latin documents of the twelfth century in England the terms *commune, communa, communia* or, as yet more rarely, *communitas* in ordinary usage were still so far from implying incorporation in the later legal sense as to be applied indifferently to any permanent association of men, however loosely organized. Hence the " comune Iudeorum " of the Pipe Rolls (1177) and the " communa liberorum hominum " of the Assize of Arms (1181). The rural vill was just as much a commune as the vill which was also a borough. Abroad, however, the word had acquired a specialized meaning, that of sworn urban association. It was this independent commune that Henry II and Richard I, according to Richard of Devizes, did not want to see in England.[2] It made but a passing appearance at London during the anarchy of Stephen's reign and was stifled at birth by Henry at Gloucester and York,[3] nor did it get a real footing until Count John allowed it at London while his brother was absent on crusade.[4]

From John's reign the sworn commune was tacitly recognized in a form suited to English conditions, but neither he nor any of his successors before Edward III ever formally authorized a *commune* or *communitas*.[5] Charters were granted to the burgesses and their heirs or the like, not to the commune or community. Even in less formal documents these terms were rarely used in the thirteenth century. It is significant that, familiar as the English chancery was with the address

---

[1] Reprinted with alterations from *E.H.R.* xlv. (1930), 529-51.
[2] Stubbs, *Select Charters*, ed. Davis, p. 245.
[3] See above, p. 162.
[4] See above, p. 182, and below, p. 251.
[5] For the creation of a *communitas* at Coventry in 1345, see Gross, *Gild Merchant*, i. 93 *n*. The burgesses of Hedon in Holderness obtained a similar grant in 1348 (*C.Ch.R.* v. 87 ff.).

" to the mayor and commune " in their letters to foreign communities, it was hardly ever used at this date, or for long after, in royal letters to English towns.[1]

The little that is known of the English borough community in the earlier sense of the word during the greater part of the twelfth century can only be profitably discussed in connexion with the remarkable institution on which a flood of light was thrown half a century ago by the late Dr. Charles Gross in his elaborate monograph, *The Gild Merchant*. Some modification of the picture which he presents of the gild in its earliest stage is now made necessary by new evidence and a rather different interpretation of part of that which he had before him.

1. The Borough Community and the Gild Merchant before the Age of Mayors and Fee Farms

Gross had an easy task in refuting the view of some of his predecessors that the gild merchant in English towns was merely a private trading society, with no public administrative functions, but he found the opposite contention, that it was the source and vital principle of municipal government, much more difficult to deal with, because it was an exaggeration of that intimate relation between community and gild which is plain upon the face of the evidence. Stated briefly, nearly in his own words, Gross's conclusion was that there were two distinct threads in the woof of municipal government, the original community of burgage-holders and the superadded gild of traders, not always quite identical bodies, and with different officers, reeves, bailiffs, and mayors in the one case, aldermen, stewards, etc., in the other, meeting the one in portmoot, the other in morning-speech or gild-meeting, yet so much merely different aspects of one body as, after a while, to tend constantly towards, and ultimately in many cases end, in amalgamation. As a rough general description of a relationship which varied locally from a dominant gild organization to no separate organization at all, or only for occasional feasting and admission of burgesses, this may serve, but the very firmness with which Gross held to the original

---

[1] An exception is a notification by King John to the mayor and commune of London on 5th April, 1200 (*Rot. Chart.*, p. 60b). *Cf.* references to the mayor and commune in royal orders of 1221 and 1225 (*Rot. Litt. Claus.* i. 445b, ii. 45b). The former also mentions the mayor and commune of Winchester.

duality of community and gild blinded him to some indications of their intimate connexion already in the twelfth century and made him too prone to explain away other evidence
tending in the same direction. It was natural, indeed, that
he should reject the *prima facie* meaning of " in eorum communam scilicet gildam " in the well-known clause of Glanvill
dealing with the enfranchisement of villeins by settlement in
towns,[1] for it was " the only plausible argument " for the
identity of community and gild ; and he may be right in this
instance, but he is driven into strange shifts to maintain his
position. He suggests alternatively that (1) the whole sentence from *ita quod* to *fuerit* is a later interpolation ; (2) *communa* is not *the* (borough) community, but *a* community
within it, *viz.*, the gild (merchant) ; (3) " communam scilicet
gildam " means " common charge, that is geld," *i.e.* scot and
lot.[2] As to the first suggestion, Dr. G. E. Woodbine of Yale
University, who is preparing an edition of Glanvill, informs
me that " no sentence in the whole of the treatise is more
firmly supported by manuscript authority." [3] The third,
though preferred by Gross, gives a very strained sense to
communa [4] and is otherwise refuted by the " in *prefata* gilda "
of the enfranchisement clause of many boroughs in the west
of England and in Wales, referring to the gild merchant
granted in a previous clause.[5] With the second and more
reasonable suggestion there may be considered the rival interpretation offered by Karl Hegel.[6] Unlike Gross, he takes
communa to be the borough community, but argues that if
that and the gild had been identical, there would have been
no need for " scilicet gildam " which he explains as meaning

[1] " Item si quis nativus quiete per unum annum et unum diem in aliqua
villa privilegiata manserit, ita quod in eorum communam scilicet gildam
tanquam civis receptus fuerit, eo ipso a vilenagio liberabitur " (*De Legibus
Anglie*, lib. V, c. 5).

[2] Gross, *Gild Merchant*, i. 102-3. Gneist had earlier stigmatized
" scilicet gildam " as a later gloss (*Gesch. der Communalverfassung*, 2nd ed.,
p. 110).

[3] Dr. Woodbine kindly supplied me with the correct text of the whole
clause as given in *n.* 1 *supra*. The reading *communem* for *communam* in
some manuscripts is therefore condemned, and where they read s. not sc.,
scilicet not *seu* is meant. Dr. Woodbine's edition has since been published.

[4] Gross (i. 103) even explains the (*de*) *communitate* of the Huntingdon
writ of Henry I as such a charge !

[5] Ballard and Tait, *British Borough Charters*, i. 105 ; ii. 136. They
begin with the Hereford and Dunwich charters of 1215. Overlooking
prefata, Gross explains " in gilda et hansa et lot et scot " as " a tautological
expression " for " in scot and lot " (*op. cit.* i. 59).

[6] *Städte und Gilden der germanischen Völker*, i. 66-8.

that villeins were admitted into the commune by admission into the gild or, he adds less happily, into a gild.[1] This interpretation would be more convincing if the text read " *in* gildam," but to translate with Gross " in a commune of theirs " is more awkward, and he himself clearly had little or no confidence in his suggestion. It is not obvious why Glanvill should have introduced the gild by a term of double meaning when gild alone was deemed sufficient in the clause of the Hereford type of charter referred to above. *Communa* was certainly not understood in the narrower sense in a London version of Glanvill's sentence, inserted in a copy of the *Exposiciones Vocabulorum*,[2] which omits " scilicet gildam," because there was no gild merchant there. Hegel's explanation of *communa* seems, therefore, preferable to that ventured by Gross,[3] and if his interpretation of the whole passage be right, it would appear to have become ambiguous and incomplete [4] by over-conciseness.

It would probably be rash to suggest, as an alternative, that Glanvill may have been more concerned to disclaim for *communa* any association with the foreign " commune " than to distinguish nicely between two aspects of the burgess body. It may be said, however, on the strength of evidence unknown to or misunderstood by Gross, that the gild played a much more prominent part in the twelfth-century borough than either he or Hegel supposed, and that some confusion between the two aspects is already not inconceivable.

In his discussion of the relation of borough community to gild, Gross took little or no account of the great development which the community underwent when the repressive hand of Henry II was withdrawn.[5] He seems to assume that the powers of the community were much the same before as after that event, that, for instance, the reeves were elected as its chief officers precisely as mayors and bailiffs were later. As a matter of fact, however, the borough community *qua* community had, generally speaking, very little more independence

---

[1] To meet the case of towns like London with no gild merchant. But admission through craft gilds did not come until the fourteenth century.

[2] *Hist. MSS. Comm., Rept. IX*, App., pt. i, p. 60 ; *Red Book of Exchequer*, iii. 1038. See below, p. 232, *n.* 8.

[3] It is doubtful whether the gild was ever spoken of as a commune, except where it had a strong separate organization, as at Leicester and Southampton.

[4] Incomplete because, despite Hegel's suggestion, it does not cover the case of boroughs, like London and Norwich, which had no gild merchant.

[5] Above, pp. 177 ff.

of action before 1189 than its rural cousin. The privileges of the *villa privilegiata* were mostly of a passive order, fixed rents for all service, a special court, the portmoot, for their own cases and so forth. Its reeve or reeves in royal towns seem usually to have been named by the king or the sheriff and were Crown officials, whose main duty was the collection of rents, tolls, and court amercements which made up the farm due to the king. In a very few cases they paid it directly to him, but generally to the sheriff or other royal farmer.[1] They presided in the portmoot, which was primarily a court of justice.[2] The community could hold land, but had no common seal with which to authenticate grants of it. It is doubtful whether it could tax itself for any but the most obvious practical needs,[3] and its annual revenue (apart from that earmarked for the farm) must in most cases have been almost negligible. Any sworn combination of the burgesses for communal action was severely punished.[4] There was a natural antagonism between the king's interest in the borough, the provostry (*prepositura, provostria* from *prepositus*, " reeve "), and the communal interest of the burgesses. This antagonism lasted on in a milder form long after they had won the right to elect the reeves. A clause in a Northampton custumal of *c.* 1260 forbade the making of any *communa* whereby the provostry should lose its rights.[5]

The borough community would have been sorely handicapped in its aspirations to greater freedom of action if it had not very generally secured at an early date, by grants of gild merchant, a larger measure of independence than it could exercise in portmoot. It is true that such gilds were licensed purely for trading purposes, but they were readily adaptable to other ends. The right to exact entrance fees, which was expressly granted, laid the foundation of a substantial revenue available for communal objects. Only in mesne boroughs like Leicester do we hear of the gild being subject to payments to the lord of the town.[6] Even more important was the right,

---

[1] Above, pp. 149, 176.

[2] Yet we have seen that as far back as 1018 the borough magnates could be dealt with, in some matters, directly, not through the reeve (above, 42).

[3] Even at the end of the century, the citizens of Lincoln were only *claiming* the right to levy rates for civic purposes (*Curia Regis Rolls*, i. 418-19 ; *E.H.R.* xxxix. 271). [4] Above, p. 176.

[5] Bodl. MS. Douce 98, fo. 161. I owe this reference to Miss Cam. For a later English version, see Markham and Cox, *Records of Northampton*, i. 228.

[6] Stenton, *Danelaw Charters* (Brit. Acad.), pp. 259, 293. *Cf.* Trenholme, *The English Monastic Boroughs* (Univ. of Missouri Studies, 1927), p. 22.

inherent in a gild, to elect its own officers headed by an alderman and to hold meetings over which he presided. As the membership of the community and of the gild did not greatly differ, even where it was not identical, and the ruling class was the same in both, the practical effect of the privilege was to invest the community with wider powers which it might either exercise in separate meeting or in portmoot, where the reeve's domination was proportionately abated.

Borough evidences are deplorably scanty for the' twelfth century ; but a few monastic charters throw a little light upon the way in which the burgesses turned their possession of the gild privilege to municipal advantage. In 1147 the citizens of Oxford of the commune of the city and of the gild of merchants (*de communi civitatis et de gilda mercatorum*), by common consent in portmanmot, made a grant to the canons of Osney of their " island " of Medley, in perpetual alms, subject to an annual rent of half a mark to be paid where the citizens should direct. The grant concludes: " et hanc eandem fecimus in capitulo coram canonicis eiusdem loci et in presentia Willelmi de Cheneto, aldermanni nostri, et per eum, et postea cum ipso supra altare cum textu obtulimus." [1] The words " per eum " seem to refer to a grant of the island in his own name by Chesney, calling himself alderman of the gild of merchants of Oxford, made in the chapterhouse on that occasion " prout concessum a civibus fuerat in portmanmot." [2] Chesney's statement that the citizens had enfeoffed *him* with Medley, and his direction that the rent should be set off against the tithes due to the canons from his mills near Oxford castle may look like the buying out of an existing interest, but it is more likely that he was formally enfeoffed to act for the citizens, and that the words " de qua eos (*i.e.* the canons) omni anno acquietabo," which precede the mention of the exchange for tithes, mean that he would pay the half mark to the citizens. It was as their gift, not Chesney's, that the grant was confirmed by the bishop of Lincoln and Henry II.[3] The complicated

[1] *Cart. Oseney* (Oxf. Hist. Soc.), iv, no. 62 ; *English Register of Osney Abbey* (E.E.T.S., Orig. Ser. 133), i. 69. I had to thank the Rev. H. E. Salter for copies of this and other then unprinted charters in the Osney cartularies.

[2] *Cart. Oseney*, iv. 62A, from B.M. Cott. MS. Vitell. E. XV, B. 89. This is the earlier of the two Latin cartularies, begun, Mr. Salter believes, in 1198. The Christ Church cartulary was made in 1284. It does not contain Chesney's charter, which was doubtless omitted as being no longer of importance as a title-deed.

[3] *Early Oxford Charters*, ed. Salter, no. 79 ; *English Register of Osney Abbey*, i. 71. See Addenda, above.

procedure followed in this transaction brings out very clearly the lack of legal corporateness in the borough community at this date and the value of the municipal officer whom it owed to its possession of gild powers. It will be observed that the citizens, though their double capacity as members of the commune and of the gild is clearly defined, speak of this officer simply as " our alderman " and with his help transact town business which has nothing to do with trade. They act, in fact, as one body with two aspects, not as two which were merely in large part composed of the same persons. If Oxford had ever had a separate gild organization, it had gone far towards its amalgamation with that of the community by 1147. Chesney was not, indeed, quite a normal alderman,[1] but there is ample evidence that the alderman (or aldermen, for there were often two) was the chief officer of the town during the next half century.[2]

With the Oxford procedure in the land grant of 1147 we may compare a grant of land for an aqueduct to the priory of St. Nicholas, Exeter, by " omnes cives Exonie," of nearly contemporary date, which ends with an intimation that seisin was delivered " manu nostra " by Theobald fitz Reiner, " ut dapifer noster," who may be the predecessor of the seneschals of the " gilda mercanda " of the city, who make one or two appearances towards the close of the century.[3] It is noticeable that the reeves of Oxford are not named as taking any part in the gift to Osney, unless they were among the witnesses omitted in the cartulary. They may even have been opposed to it. When Henry II, nine years later, rewarded the services of the burgesses of Wallingford in the recovery of his hereditary right in England with a charter of unusual length,[4] and as the first of their privileges confirmed their gild merchant, " cum omnibus consuetudinibus et legibus suis," he forbade his reeve there, or any of his justices, to meddle with the gild,

[1] He was not a merchant, but Stephen's redoubtable commandant in Oxford, the " praeses Oxenefordensis " of the *Gesta Stephani* (Rolls Ser. iii. 115), and a considerable landowner in the neighbourhood, whose brother Robert soon after became bishop of Lincoln. No such magnate is known to have held civic office in Oxford during the rest of the Middle Ages. The gift of the citizens to Osney Abbey may not have been so voluntary as it is represented in the documents.

[2] *Early Oxford Charters*, nos. 86-90, and below, p. 231.

[3] Cart. S. Nich. Exon., fo. 136 (old 66d-67) ; Exeter Misc. Books 55, fo. 80 ; *Hist. MSS. Com. Var. Coll.* iv. 16. I owe these references to Miss Ruth Easterling. It is significant that the reeve of Exeter is only mentioned in the dating clause of the grant to the priory.

[4] Gross, *op. cit.* ii. 244-5.

but only their own alderman and minister. By other clauses his officers were forbidden to accuse the burgesses in any court but their portmoot, and if the reeve impleaded them without a prosecutor they need not answer. He was also prohibited, under heavy penalty, from oppressing them with burdensome exactions, old or new. There are two points of interest here. First, the reeve is not the elected head of the community of burgesses, but a royal officer against whom they have to be protected. Secondly, it is only as members of the gild that they are dealt with in a corporate capacity and have an officer of their own. Their other privileges are merely guaranteed to them jointly and severally.

It would be going much too far to suppose that the royal reeves in the boroughs were always on unfriendly terms with the burgesses. They were burgesses themselves, and at Oxford, at least in the second half of the twelfth century, they are found holding the office of alderman after they had been reeves. Nevertheless, their first duty was to the king, and the enforcement of his financial claims, often excessive, was bound to cause friction from time to time. It is true that in some eight cases, at one time or another during his reign, even Henry II allowed the burgesses themselves to farm their town and thus not only relieved them of the direct control of the sheriff over their finances, but gave them more hold over their reeves. These arrangements, however, were always terminable at the king's will, and sometimes of short duration.[1]

The antagonism of reeve and burgesses at Wallingford strongly reminds us of the state of things in the many mesne boroughs where the courts were under the control of bailiffs chosen by the lords, in the case of which Gross admitted that as early as the thirteenth century the gild became " the real axis of the burghal polity—the only civic centre round which they could rally their forces in struggling . . . for an extension of their franchises or in battling for any other cause." [2] Except that the king was more remote and they themselves stronger, this exactly describes the position of the burgesses of royal towns during the greater part of the twelfth century. An exchange of land between the abbey of Malmesbury and " the burgesses who are in the merchant gild of Malmesbury," apparently of thirteenth-century date, in which the alderman of the gild with seventeen other named persons " et tota communitas intrinseca eiusdem ville et gilde mercatorie "

---

[1] Above, p. 176.   [2] Gross, *op. cit.* i. 90-1.

quitclaimed part of Portmanshethe to the abbey, has some features which recall the proceedings at Oxford in 1147, though here community and gild are more inextricably intermixed.[1]

The short style above, applied to the burgesses in the abbey deed, may throw some light upon the same formula as used in certain twelfth-century charters to Winchester and charters to other boroughs copied from them, which formed the main argument of the advocates of the complete identity of borough community and gild, but which Gross maintained to be only employed when the privileges conferred specially concerned merchants. An early charter of Henry II, granting freedom from toll alone to " cives mei Wintonienses de gilda mercatorum," complies with this interpretation,[2] but it will not explain the general charter of Richard I in 1190, which begins with a grant to the same of the usual privilege of exemption from outside courts, and grants each further privilege (including exemption from trial by battle) to them (eis).[3] It is true that King John's regrant and expansion of this charter (1215) is made generally to the citizens and their heirs, but it still retains the concession of the right of trial in their own courts to the citizens who are in the gild merchant.[4] Now, this was not, as Gross claims, a special concern of the merchant, but perhaps the most vital security of every burgess. For what was meant was not, as Gross seems to have thought, freedom from trial in towns to which business took them, but from all external jurisdiction in cases arising within the town itself. It was a privilege widely conferred upon boroughs without qualification. Why should it have been limited to a special class in the second city of the realm ? The only reasonable conclusion from the facts before us would seem to be that at Winchester in 1190, as at Malmesbury in the next century, the borough community and the gild were only two aspects of the same body, and the gild with its right of combination under an alderman was still the dominant aspect.[5]

---

[1] Gross, op. cit. ii. 172.

[2] B.B.C. i. 181. The privilege was sometimes granted to the burgesses of other towns " as the burgesses of Winchester who are of the gild merchant are quit," but without mention of the gild of the recipients (ibid. p. 185).

[3] Stubbs, Select Charters, ed. Davis, pp. 260-1.

[4] Gross, op. cit. ii. 253.

[5] When Hawise, countess of Gloucester, between 1183 and 1197, granted to all her burgesses who had built or should build in Petersfield " all the liberties and free customs which the citizens of Winchester have in their city who are in gild merchant " (ibid. ii. 387), we may suspect that

By the date of John's charter the borough community had secured an elective head of its own, a mayor, and the gild organization fell into the background.

An interesting confirmation of the interpretation, here offered of the formula in dispute, comes from Gloucester. In 1200 King John gave his burgesses there control of the provostry in fee farm, empowering them to elect the reeves.[1] The borough community thus attained a certain corporate status and provided itself with a communal seal. But as John had included in his charter the privileges of Winchester copied from its charter of 1190, the burgesses inscribed on the seal, which with slight variations remained in use until 1660, the legend : SIGILLVM BVRGENSIVM DE GILDA MERCA-TORVM GLOVCESTRIE.[2]

The same conclusion can be reached from another side. There is some evidence that, where the gild merchant did not include all the burgesses, the privilege of general exemption from tolls was not confined to the gildsmen. At Southampton, at any rate, where there was a class of franchised men who were outside the gild, this privilege belonged to " the men of Southampton," without mention of the gild.[3] As in the great majority of boroughs this privilege was granted to " all the burgesses," and, as it was enjoyed prescriptively by all tenants on ancient demesne, it would have been strange had it been limited to a section of the burgesses in one small group of towns.

So far, a certain amount of evidence has been brought together which seems to reveal the organization of the burgesses in gild merchant as the active communal principle in the English borough until the end of the twelfth century. An association originally allowed merely for trading purposes

it is not merely trading privileges that she is bestowing. For admission to the gild at Winchester from the thirteenth century onwards as the one and only means of being admitted to the franchise of the city, though its constitution was not framed on gild lines, see Furley, *City Government of Winchester* (1923), p. 73.

[1] Gross, *op. cit.* ii. 373.

[2] G. S. Blakeway, *The City of Gloucester*, 1924, p. 38. Gross mentions this seal (*op. cit.* ii. 374), but does not attempt to explain the legend. One would have expected the same inscription on the thirteenth-century seal of Winchester, but according to Mr. Furley (*The Ancient Usages of Winchester*, 1927, p. 56) it was SIGILL. CIVIVM WINTONIENSIVM, though no trace of it is visible in his photograph.

[3] Gross, *op. cit.* ii. 174. The wording is the more significant because the writ prescribes reciprocal freedom from toll with " homines nostri de Marleberg' *qui sunt in Gilda Mercanda de Marleberg'*."

acquired importance in civic affairs owing to the weak, dependent organization of the borough community in its portmoot. The burgesses, in their gild capacity might act through a separate organization as at Southampton and Leicester, or more commonly, as appears to have been the case at Winchester [1] and at Oxford,[2] through the portmoot itself. In either event, the gild alderman became the recognized head of the community. It is not surprising that this should have led to some ambiguity in nomenclature.

It may, perhaps, be objected, however, that the evidence we have adduced for assuming this gild prominence is too largely of a diplomatic kind, interpretation of phrases in charters and the like, that the only actual instance given, that of Oxford, comes from the anarchy in Stephen's reign, and that Chesney was no normal gild alderman. When, in the thirteenth-century custumal of Southampton, the alderman is described as " head of the town and the gild," this is said by Gross to be a clear mark of a later stage of development.[3] But evidence, that has come to light since Gross wrote, shows that this was an overhasty judgement. Chesney's position at Oxford in 1147, though exceptional in his personality, was normal in other respects. Down to the end of the century at least, the alderman (or aldermen) was the head of the town administration, frequently heads the list of witnesses to deeds executed in portmoot or elsewhere, and occasionally confirms such a deed by his (private) seal,[4] which was used in 1191 to authenticate an agreement [5] between the canons of St. Frideswide's and the citizens. About 1200 he attests a land grant as " alderman of Oxford." [6] The mention of the alderman and reeves of Lincoln in this same year is not quite so clear, because the action for which they were called to

---

[1] There is no trace later at Winchester of any trade legislation elsewhere than in the boroughmoot, the gild meetings being devoted to conviviality and the collection of funds from the citizens for the city treasury (Furley, *City Govt. of Winchester*, pp. 71 ff.).

[2] See above, p. 226. It is significant that in a deed of 1183 or 1184 the town court (*placita regis*) is said to be called Moregespeche, " morning speech," a term usually confined to gild assemblies (*Oseney Cartulary*, ed. Salter (Oxf. Hist. Soc.), i. 71) ; Gross, *op. cit.* i. 32 *n.* Gross rashly infers that its gild use was derivative. The meeting of the pre-Conquest thegns' Gild at Cambridge was a *morgenspæc* (Thorpe, *Diplomatarium*, p. 610).

[3] Gross, *op. cit.* i. 62 *n.*

[4] Salter, *Early Oxford Charters*, nos. 86-90.

[5] *Cartulary of St. Frideswide's* (Oxf. Hist. Soc.), i. 36, 38 ; *Cartulary of Oseney*, iv. no. 63B. See below, p. 235.

[6] *Cartulary of Eynsham Abbey* (Oxf. Hist. Soc.), ii. 228.

account had a gild aspect,[1] but the title conforms to the Oxford use. It is almost certain, too, that the alderman of the gild merchant of Leicester, who about 1226 is called " alderman of Leicester," [2] held the same position as chief officer of the town until his title was changed to that of mayor ; and the same may be said of the alderman of the Southampton gild, which succeeded in suppressing the mayoralty when one was created, and finally invested the alderman with the rival title.[3] There was a tradition or belief also at Chester [4] and at Lynn [5] that, before they had a mayor, the warden or alderman of the gild merchant was their civic head. Gross passes this over in silence, and the existence in the later middle ages of some eight boroughs whose principal officer was an alderman only suggested to him an untenable theory of descent from an Anglo-Saxon town officer, who, as a matter of fact, never bore that title.[6]

The evidence advanced above, and especially the last part of it, may seem to be undermining Gross's main contention and reviving the view, which he is supposed to have refuted, that the medieval town constitution was merely an enlargement of the gild merchant. For he singled out as a typical expression of this view " the words of Thompson, the historian of Leicester," that " the whole area of municipal government was occupied by the Gild Merchant, the head of the borough and that of the Gild being identical and ' burgess ' tantamount to ' gildsman '." [7] It is possible, however, to hold that both these statements are roughly true of some, perhaps many, twelfth-century boroughs, without conceding the whole position to the advocates of the gild theory. The municipal history of London, Norwich, and Colchester, none of which had a gild merchant,[8] sufficiently shows that the gild was not the

---

[1] They had seized the cloths of the dyers and fullers ; the fullers' cloth was seized, however, because " non habent legem vel comunam cum liberis civibus " (*Curia Regis Rolls*, i. 259-60). The dyers had dyed their own cloth, a definitely gild offence. A rather cryptic writ to the bailiffs of Lincoln on 3rd November, 1217, ordered them to give such seisin of the aldermanry of Lincoln and its appurtenances to John de Holm as his uncle Adam had *die quo se dimisit de majoritate* (*Rot. Litt. Claus.* i. 340b). The mayor of Lincoln appears as early as 1206 (below, p. 291, *n.* 4).

[2] Bateson, *Records of Leicester*, i. 27.   [3] *B.B.C.* ii. lvii. 386.

[4] Gross, *op. cit.* ii. 41-2.   [5] *Ibid.* pp. 168-9.   *Cf. B.B.C.* ii. 362-3.

[6] Gross, *op. cit.* i. 79. His reference in the Anglo-Saxon Chron. a. 886 relates to Ethelred, alderman of Mercia !   [7] *Ibid.* i. 61.

[8] It is a curious testimony to the widespread use of the gild as a doorway to citizenship in the thirteenth century that a royal charter of 1252, conferring all the rights of London citizens upon a Florentine merchant and his heirs, invents a London gild merchant to which to admit them (*E.H.R.* xviii. 315).

indispensable nucleus round which everything else gathered, and even in twelfth-century Oxford, where, as we have seen, there seems to have been little or no practical distinction between burgess and gildsman, and the gild alderman was undoubtedly head of the borough, the formal distinction between the two aspects of citizenship is preserved. Gross's reluctance to accept an interpretation of the early evidence, so far as it was known to him, which seemed to threaten his main point that the later municipal constitutions originated in the portmoot and its officers, not in the gild, might have disappeared, had he grasped the true course of municipal development in the twelfth century. He was unaware of the feebly developed status of the community in portmoot in that period and consequently did not realize the importance of the gild organization to the burgesses or the diminution of that importance in most boroughs when in the reigns of Richard I and John the borough community began to obtain, in its own right, a real corporate existence with an elected mayor or reeves (bailiffs) and to be freed from the local control of royal sheriffs and reeves by the acquisition of the fee farm. In a few towns where the gild had a strong separate organization —Andover, Leicester, and Southampton are the best known instances—it retained its hold upon the civic administration, though it was not without a struggle at Southampton, and the later substitution of the title of mayor for that of alderman there and at Leicester brought these two towns formally into line with the general type of borough government.[1] Andover, however, continued to be governed by its gild down to the sixteenth century.[2]

Thus while, with Gross, we must still claim for the borough community in portmoot and its officers their rightful significance in the evolution of municipal constitutions, we need not follow him in depreciating the part that the gild played in the earliest struggles for communal liberty, when other forms of unfettered combination were forbidden. If the gild was not, as the older school of municipal historians contended, the sole nucleus of borough institutions, it may claim a place as the most effective outlet for burgensic energy and aspirations until the last decade of the twelfth century. The gild

---

[1] *Oak Book of Southampton*, i. xix f. ; Bateson, *Records of Leicester*, i. Introd., p. xliii.

[2] Gross, *op. cit.* ii. 346-7 ; Furley, *City Government of Winchester*, p. 72.

alderman anticipated the elected mayor or bailiffs, the gild organization the borough assembly and town council, and the gild purse the borough treasury (*camera* [1]). It is, perhaps, not wholly fanciful to see in the absence of this early and stimulating association at Norwich and Colchester the explanation of their being among the latest of the larger English towns to set up a mayor.

2. THE BEGINNING OF MUNICIPAL INCORPORATION

Valuable as the gild merchant was in providing the twelfth-century borough with an elected head and an organization more independent of the king or other lord than the portmoot, this was a passing phase in almost all boroughs, except those mesne towns whose lords clung to their control of the burgess court. In many royal boroughs, the needs of the Crown forced it to grant the comparative freedom of action, hitherto confined to the gild, to the burgesses as members of the community whose organ was the borough court.[2] Their acceptance as farmers in perpetuity of the royal provostry, the collection and payment into the exchequer of the king's revenue from the borough with the consequent right to elect the reeves (*prepositi*) or bailiffs, as they came to be called, not only relieved them of the direct financial control of the sheriff, but gave them for the first time a basis of real municipal unity under officers of their own choice. No longer presided over by royal nominees, the portmoot acquired a new freedom of action. It is true that the bailiffs had a divided duty to king and town, but a simultaneous movement of entirely different origin was correcting this defect. Under the influence of the foreign " commune " the burgesses were organizing themselves as sworn associations and in the more advanced towns were symbolizing their new unity of administration by setting up an entirely new officer, the mayor, with a council of twelve or twenty-four to act with him on behalf of the community.[3]

[1] It is as gild officers that chamberlains are first heard of at Leicester (Bateson, *op. cit.* i. 25).

[2] The influence of the gild association on the formation of a corporate borough community is recognized in a general way by Maitland (*Hist. of Eng. Law*, i. 670 f.). He points out that by the system of formal admission to the franchise and payment of entrance fees, replacing the original burgage qualification, the borough community was becoming a voluntary association like the gild. Mr. A. H. Thomas has shown that this stage was reached at London by 1230 (*Plea and Mem. Rolls*, ii. xxx, xlix.)

[3] Below, pp. 251, 291.

Such councils were established even where no mayor was set up. This corporate development, which went on rapidly during the last decade of the twelfth century and the first two of the thirteenth, was marked by the appearance of municipal seals. The earliest on record, those of Oxford and York, occur only three or four years after Henry II's denial even of fee farm grants to his dominical boroughs, had been relaxed to help to pay for Richard's crusade. In July, 1191, the citizens of Oxford and the canons of St. Frideswide's were parties to a final concord before the king's justices at Oxford, by which the citizens, in return for some market stalls belonging to the priory, agreed to pay *de communa sua* to the canons a yearly rent of 8*s*.[1] for that " island " of Medley which, as we have seen, they had granted in 1147 to Osney Abbey at a rent of half a mark. The formal undertaking entered into by the *universitas civium* was authenticated by their common seal (*sigillo nostro communi*).[2] About the same time they confirmed the old grant to Osney at the increased rent of a mark, in return for their express warrant against all claims, such as St. Frideswide's had raised, and this document too was given under " communali sigillo nostro."[3] Neither deed is dated, but their contents would naturally suggest dates shortly before the final concord. There are difficulties, however, in accepting this suggestion. The final concord states quite definitely that the citizens made their deed under the seal of the alderman of their gild,[4] and it seems impossible that this could have been described as a common seal of the citizens. If, however, the common seal was something new, there is nothing to account for its first appearing in the summer of 1191. It is rash, perhaps, but tempting, to suggest that the citizens, who were privileged to enjoy all the customs of London, seized the occasion of the grant of a commune to their mother city in October, 1191, to assert legal personality for their own community by the adoption of a municipal seal, seven or eight years before they obtained a grant of fee farm.[5] Such an important change might very well lead to the substitution of documents under the new seal for those executed a few months before under the alderman's seal only.

---

[1] *Cart. St. Fridesw.* (Oxf. Hist. Soc.), i. 38 ; *Cart. Oseney*, iv. 63B.
[2] *Cart. St. Fridesw.* i. 36.   [3] *Cart. Oseney*, iv. no. 63.
[4] Through whom the rent was to be paid.
[5] In 1199 (Ballard, *B.B.C.* i. 225). The fact that the Oxford aldermen remained the chief officers of the town for some time after 1191 (*Cart. Eynsham* (Oxf. Hist. Soc.), ii. 228) may have some bearing on the disputed question as to what happened in London in that year (*cf.* below, p. 267).

Of the York seal we have fortunately a perfect impression attached to a deed now in the British Museum, a report by the citizens to Archbishop Geoffrey (1191–1206) on the ownership of a city church, perhaps at the beginning of Geoffrey's time, as they had in 1190 taken the city at farm, though they almost immediately lost the privilege.[1]   The seal is a remarkable one because on the obverse, round a triple-towered castle, the legend : SIGILLVM CIVIVM EBORAC. is followed by the words FIDELES REGIS, and still more because the seal of the cathedral church is used as a counterseal.[2] It is noteworthy, too, that the citizens call themselves neither *universitas* nor *communa*. The use of such seals is very fully expressed by the burgesses of Ipswich who had one made in 1200 :

" ad serviendum in grossis negociis tangentibus communitatem dicti burgi et eciam ad litteras inde consignandas de veritate testificandas pro omnibus et singulis burgensibus eiusdem burgi et ad omnia alia facienda que fieri debent ad communem honorem et utilitatem ville predicte." [3]

The seal of the community of Barnstaple is affixed to an original deed not later than 1210, which is preserved in the Archives Nationales at Paris.[4] Barnstaple had already a mayor : so too had Exeter, when its seal is first mentioned as attached to a city grant which was apparently made in 1208.[5] The Gloucester seal, to which reference occurs above,[6] probably belongs to the first years of this century. It may seem surprising that the common seal of London is not mentioned until 1219,[7] but evidence is scanty for this period and we need not doubt that it had possessed one since the end of the twelfth century.

When, at a much later date, grants of formal legal incorporation became customary, the use of a common seal was one of the marks of such incorporation and was often specified in the grant. Even before the earliest and least elaborate of such grants, the citizens of New Salisbury, when renouncing their mayoralty and other civic liberties in 1304, to avoid

---

[1] Above, p. 179.

[2] Drake, *Eboracum*, p. 313, App. ci. ; Farrer, *Early Yorkshire Charters*, i. 230-1 ; *Brit. Mus. Catalogue of Seals*, ii. 218, where the legends are assigned to the wrong sides. *Cf.* church on reverse of Ipswich seal (Wodderspoon, p. 75).   [3] Gross, *Gild Merchant*, ii. 119.

[4] Round, *Calendar of Documents in France*, p. 462.

[5] Exeter Misc. Book 55, fo. 38d.   I owe this reference to the kindness of Miss R. C. Easterling.   [6] Above, p. 230.

[7] As appended to letters of the mayor and *universitas* to the mayor and *universitas* of Bordeaux and of La Rochelle (*Pat. R.* 1216-25, p. 211).

tallage, were required to surrender their common seal,[1] and the enforced resignation by the burgesses of St. Albans in 1332 of the liberties they had extorted from the abbot and convent involved the surrender and destruction of their common seal as well as of their charter.[2]

Gross claimed for the English borough " a natural corporate existence " long before the juridical conception of an artificial civic body came into existence, and instances the possession of a common seal among the evidences of such incorporation.[3] He knew, however, of no earlier borough seal than that of Ipswich and did not inquire into the circumstances in which such seals were adopted. The evidence adduced above, especially from Oxford, points to the reign of Richard I as the time of the first introduction of municipal seals. Until then, though there was a borough community which " held property in succession " and could enfeoff an individual or a religious body with it, though it could hold funds and grant them away in perpetuity, this community was unable to give effect to acts of this kind without the aid of the deed or seal of its alderman or other chief gild officer. Legally it was no corporation, and even " naturally " it was only emerging from the " co-ownership " of the rural community. Suddenly, from 1191, its legal status is raised, not universally but gradually in individual cases ; the community or commune executes acts of various kinds under its own common seal.[4] How is this far-reaching change to be explained ? It might seem obvious to suggest that it was the result of the new policy of Richard and John in granting towns to their burgesses in fee farm, and at Ipswich, where alone a full account of what happened has survived, it was certainly made possible by a royal grant of fee farm and elective officers. But this cannot be the whole explanation. Oxford, as we have seen, had its communal seal eight years or so before it secured the fee farm. Winchester and Exeter for long had only grants of the farm during pleasure, and in this respect were no better off than certain boroughs in the repressive days of Henry II. Some other cause must have been at work, and this, it would seem, was the influence of the

---

[1] *Rot. Parl.* i. 176. They renounced their renunciation in 1306.
[2] *Gesta Abbatum*, ii. 260 ; Trenholme, *The English Monastic Boroughs*, p. 37. [3] *Op. cit.* i. 95.
[4] *Cf.* the somewhat qualified remarks of Maitland who hardly realized the force of the communal movement inspired from abroad (*Hist. of English Law*, i. 683 f.).

R

foreign " commune " either directly or through London. At
Exeter and Winchester civic heads with the foreign title of
mayor appear before the limited grant of their farms. Even
at Ipswich, which did not set up a mayor, the oaths of loyalty
to the estate and honour of the town which were required from
councillors and burgesses reveal the influence of the communal
ideal. It is, perhaps, significant that, until the new organization was complete and provided with a common seal, the
Ipswich assembly is only referred to in the record as " tota
villata," and it first appears as " communitas " when gathered
together to approve the constitutional ordinances made by
the council, in whose election they had had only an indirect
voice.[1] Apparently the community thus established is something different from that which the " villata," like other
urban and rural communities, had formed in the twelfth
century. Such a conclusion seems confirmed by the later
history of the term. In 1302 royal justices decided that the
burgesses of Bury St. Edmunds " having no union of a community (*unionem communitatis*) are not capable of freedom or
lordship like a community, since they have no captain of their
own number, but only the abbot, their lord." [2] After a
further rising in 1327, when they wrote to the mayor, aldermen, and community of London for advice and support,[3] as
one community to another, they were forced to disclaim for
themselves and their heirs any right to a *communitas*.[4] The
judges of 1302 laid stress upon their lack of an elected head of
their own, and though the first formal grant of incorporation,
that of Coventry in 1345, puts greater emphasis on the " unio
communitatis," " quod ipsi et eorum heredes et successores
Communitatem inter se habeant," it immediately adds :
" et Maiorem et Ballivos idoneos de seipsis eligere possint
annuatim." [5]

The phrases employed to describe the use of the Ipswich
seal, " pro omnibus et singulis burgensibus " and " pro
communi honore et utilitate ville seu burgensium ville," still
betray some juridical uncertainty, but leave no doubt that
essentially a corporate body is in existence.

With this still imperfect expression of corporateness the
inscriptions on early borough seals are in accord. These

---

[1] *Cf.* Gross, *op. cit.* ii. 116-18, with pp. 119-21.
[2] Gross, *op. cit.* i. 94, ii. 35 ; Trenholme, *op. cit.* p. 25.
[3] *Calendar of Plea and Memoranda Rolls of London*, ed. Thomas, i. 35.
[4] *Memorials of St. Edmunds Abbey* (Rolls Ser.), iii. 41-6 ; Trenholme,
op. cit. p. 40.   [5] Gross, *op. cit.* i. 93.

instruments usually describe themselves as being the seal or common seal of the citizens or burgesses or barons of the particular city or borough.[1] With the very doubtful exception of Barnstaple [2] and the more probable one of Leicester,[3] the legend, " seal of the community of X," is not known to have been used in the early part of the thirteenth century, and never became common.

The continued distinction of the *prepositura*, or department of the king's farm from the communal finances, is marked by the separate seal of the bailiffs (or of the provostry) [4] even where, in the absence of a mayor, they were the chief elective officers of the community.[5] An early and interesting case of this latter usage occurs at Northampton. In October, 1199, the liberties of that borough were granted to Lancaster by King John, and not long after, in response to an inquiry from Lancaster as to what these liberties were, the bailiffs of Northampton sent a letter, still preserved by the northern borough, congratulating them on their new liberties, enclosing a copy of their own new charter (17th April, 1200),[6] and authenticating their message, they state, with " the common seal of the provostry (*prepositorie*)." The seal, which survives, has the legend : + SIGILL. PREPOSITOR. DE NORHAMTON.[7]

Incorporation in the full sense in which it was elaborated by the royal chancery from 1440 [8] onwards was certainly not in the minds of the kings who first recognized, expressly or tacitly, the new status of their demesne boroughs. They

---

[1] " Common seal of all the citizens of Oxford " (Salter, *Early Oxford Charters*, no. 91 *n.*), " Seal of the citizens of Winchester," " Seal of the barons of London," etc.

[2] Above, p. 236. Round describes it as " the seal of the commonalty of B," but the British Museum Catalogue attributes to the thirteenth century a seal with the legend : SIG. COMMVNE BVRGI BARNSTAPOLAE.

[3] The spelling Leyrcestria on the earliest extant impression (fourteenth century) was going out of use in the early years of the thirteenth century (Bateson, *Records of Leicester*, i. xliii. 7 ; ii. 57). Unless there was a later change, the Ipswich seal of 1200 was also of this type.

[4] See that of Conway in the British Museum Catalogue.

[5] For an example of the use of a reeve's *private* seal to authenticate a document before 1181, see Salter, *op. cit.* no. 88. The raven seal of Colchester with the legend : SIGILL. CVSTOD. PORT. COLECESTR. (Benham, *Oath Book of Colchester*, p. 226), locally described as " the seal of the Portreeve used . . . before 1189," is more likely that of an officer similar to the warden of the Cinque Ports.

[6] Confirming *inter alia* Richard I's grant of fee farm.

[7] Brownbill and Nuttall, *Calendar of the Charters, etc., of the Corporation of Lancaster* (1929), p. 4. It is singular that no notice was taken of the limitation of John's Lancaster grant to the liberties of Northampton " as they stood at the death of Henry II."

[8] The date of the incorporation of Hull (*Cal. Chart. Rolls*, vi. 8 ff.).

never admitted the borough community to be so completely (in later language) a " body politic and corporate " as, for instance, to deprive the Crown of the power to enforce payment of the debts which the borough owed to it upon individual citizens, if their rulers defaulted.[1]

Nevertheless, the evidence collected above leaves no doubt that the reigns of Henry II's sons, whatever their personal attitude to town liberties may have been, saw a vital change in the status of the leading English boroughs, a change both legal and practical, which, however limited the new status and subject to frequent interference and even temporary withdrawal by the Crown, can only be reasonably described as a form of incorporation. The last decade of the twelfth century is marked off from the preceding period by the appearance of permanent farms and elective bailiffs, mayors, and councils and common seals, all the institutions which, with changes introduced by lapse of time, lasted down to 1835.

This sudden and remarkable development was, as we have seen, favoured by the needs and weakness of Richard and John, but shows unmistakable signs of the influence of the communal movement abroad, an influence, however, which on the whole was general rather than particular. Though sudden, it was not unprepared for. Only the heavy hand of Henry II had held the movement in check until the eve of the thirteenth century.

3. The Borough Community

" Quod ipsi (homines) . . . communitatem inter se decetero habeant." These words of incorporation in the Coventry charter of 1345, already quoted, may serve as starting-point for a brief inquiry into the burghal meaning or meanings of the hard-worked term *communitas* (and its vernacular equivalents), which could be applied to almost any association of men from the village up to the nation. We shall find that it was not used so vaguely as Stubbs and others have thought. The formal employment of the term in the first half of the fourteenth century, first in judicial decisions and finally in royal charters, for the corporate body of citizens or burgesses only set the seal on a development which, as we have seen, went back to the reign of Richard I. It was as *communitas* that the burgesses of a borough held property,

---

[1] Madox, *Firma Burgi* (1726), pp. 154 ff.

received and made payments, and entered into engagements with other corporations or persons. Except at the foundation of a new borough, this *communitas burgensium* [1] can rarely, if ever, have included all householders. There were officials and professional men who were excluded if a gild merchant really confined to traders and master craftsmen was the entrance gate to the freedom ; there were small tradesmen and craftsmen who were kept out by entrance fees and property qualifications. This non-burgess population was not, however, unless very poor, exempt from national and municipal taxes. There is some reason to think that the borough community which was required to send representatives to Parliament with full power to act on its behalf was, in theory at all events, this wider community of tax-payers. In the early writs for the collection of parliamentary taxes, these are said to have been granted by " the citizens, burgesses, *et alii probi homines* of the cities and boroughs, of whatsoever tenures and liberties they were." [2] The same conception of the community seems to be implied in the slightly later form in which the grant is stated to have been made by " the citizens, burgesses, and communities of the cities and boroughs," where citizens and burgesses are distinguished as the higher element of the borough community, just as the magnates, knights, and free-holders are distinguished in the same writ as the outstanding classes of the shire community. [3] It was only a theory, however, for, as a matter of fact, the borough representatives seem to have been everywhere elected by the burgess assembly, [4] and continued to be elected by it even when it had shrunk up into a narrow corporation from which most of the freemen were excluded. The Statute of 1445, which forbade their illegal election by the sheriff, distinctly states that they " have always been chosen by citizens and burgesses and no other." [5] It was not until the political struggles of the middle years of the seventeenth century that

---

[1] Bateson, *Records of Leicester*, i. 50 (1256).
[2] Stubbs, *Select Charters*, ed. Davis, pp. 430-1, 434.
[3] *Ibid.* p. 438. We may compare the use of *commune* in the accounts of twelfth-century aids and tallages. A lump sum proffered by a borough or vill and accepted could be described as given by the commune (*P.R.* 1 Joh., p. 148), but if the richer few were individually assessed by royal officers and a lump sum proffered for the rest, this sum was also " de communi ejusdem ville " (*ibid.*, 15 Hen. II, p. 90).
[4] Or, rarely, by a committee of it, as at Lynn (*Hist. MSS. Comm., Rept.* XI, App. III, 146 ff.), and at Cambridge (Stubbs, *Const. Hist.* iii. § 422).   [5] *Statutes of the Realm*, ii. 340.

the House of Commons in the exercise of its right of deciding upon election petitions, besides occasionally restoring the parliamentary franchise to the freemen at large,[1] sometimes gave the vote to all inhabitants.[2]

The existence of a wider town community than that which formed the borough assembly, even at its fullest, need not force us to accept the theory of the late Mrs. J. R. Green that it is the community of the style " maior, burgenses, et communitas " which occurs from an early date in charters and other documents. Mrs. Green contended that the corporate body (*burgenses*) is here distinguished from the immemorial vill community which underlay it.[3] The theory, however, crumbles as soon as it is confronted with the facts. As early as the middle of the thirteenth century the grant of a house to the " mayor, burgesses, and commune " of Leicester ends with a statement that the " mayor and burgesses " have given the grantor $6\frac{1}{2}$ marks, and in another deed his sister-in-law releases her rights in the messuage, to the same, without mention of the community.[4] It is clear that the style is only a variant of *communitas burgensium*. Maitland correctly divined its meaning : " it aims at showing that the mayor and burgesses are not to be taken *ut singuli*, but are, as we should say " acting in their corporate capacity '."[5] The wording is awkward, but if it is remembered that " burgesses " (or " citizens ") simply was the style consecrated by usage, it will not seem surprising that the need was often felt of expressing the new communal aspect of the burgess body by some such addition. When the burgesses of Bridgwater formed themselves into a gild merchant under Henry III and began to use a communal seal, they described themselves as " universi burgenses et communitas burgi de Brugewater."[6] There is no real ambiguity here, but, generally speaking, it must be confessed that " maior et burgenses de communi-

---

[1] *Hist. MSS. Comm., Rept. XI*, App. III, 150-2 (Lynn Regis).
[2] For examples, see Clemesha, *History of Preston in Amounderness* (1912), pp. 169, 201-8, and Markham and Cox, *Records of Northampton* (1898), ii. 498 ff.   Cf. *E.H.R.* xlv. 244 f.
[3] *Town Life in the Fifteenth Century* (1894), ii. 230-5, 334-6.
[4] Bateson, *op. cit.* i. 51-3.
[5] *History of English Law* (1898), i. 678 n.
[6] T. B. Dilks in *Proc. Somerset Archæol. Soc.* lxiii. (1917), 55. The document is there dated early in the reign of Edward I, but Mr. Dilks now sees reason to believe that it is somewhat older (*Bridgwater Borough Archives, 1200-1377* (Somerset Rec. Soc., vol. 48, 1933), no. 10 and Introd., p. xiv.

tate," of which I have only noted a single occurrence,[1] would have met the case better.

A totally different interpretation of the somewhat ambiguous formula in question sees in it a distinction between the ruling class (*maiores burgenses, potentiores*) or its organ, the council of twelve or twenty-four, and the mass of the burgesses (*minores burgenses, minor communa*).[2] This is far more plausible than Mrs. Green's view, because sooner or later *burgenses* and *communitas* undoubtedly took on the secondary and narrowed meaning which is suggested, but the distinction between the greater and lesser burgesses could hardly have been expressed in these terms before the end of the fourteenth century. Even then the contrast is not so acute as it seems, for *burgenses* in this sense was in some cases, perhaps in all, merely an abbreviation of *comburgenses* as applied to the mayor's council, a term which did not exclude the existence of other burgesses.[3] The narrower sense of *communitas*, " commonalty," arose earlier and more naturally. In the long run, it almost emptied " commonalty " of its comprehensive significance, but in origin it was harmless enough, merely distinguishing the unofficial many from the official few. There could, for instance, have been no suggestion of contempt or of essentially inferior status in the first application of the terms " commonalty " and " commoners " (*communarii*)[4] to all London citizens who were not aldermen, for the rich families from whom the aldermen were taken were equally commoners with the poorest citizens. It was the aggressiveness of the lower orders among the commoners from

---

[1] Bateson, *op. cit.* i. 57.

[2] W. Hudson, *Records of Norwich*, I, xxxvi-xxxviii, lxvi-lxvii. Mr. Hudson thinks that in the fifteenth century *cives* in the formula often meant the aldermen only (*ibid.* p. lxxii). For *maiores* and *minores burgenses*, see Round, *Commune of London*, pp. 252-3 ; for *minor communa*, *Cal. Inq. Misc.* (P.R.O.), i. no. 238. M. Petit-Dutaillis's recently expressed view that *communitas* in urban charters " often seems to mean the ancient free urban community prior to the oligarchical municipal government" (*Studies Supplementary to Stubbs' Const. Hist.* iii. 448 *n.*) is not altogether clear. He appears, however, to take *cives* (*burgenses*) in Mr. Hudson's sense and *communitas* in Maitland's. If so, he overlooks the strong evidence that the two terms in the charter formula covered the same body, but expressed different aspects of it.

[3] Mr. V. H. Galbraith has called my attention to an inquest of 1413 in which the burgesses of Nottingham are defined as those who had filled the office of mayor or bailiff. They were then at least forty-nine in number and claimed to have always elected the mayor and bailiffs (P.R.O. Inq. Misc. Chanc. C. 145/292/25).

[4] *Munim. Gildh. London*, i. (Liber Albus), 20, 143, no. 162.

the stormy times of the Barons' Wars onwards which gave a democratic stamp to the terms we are discussing. In London, while Simon de Montfort was triumphant, they advanced an exclusive claim to be the commune of the city, "excipientes aldermannos et alios discretos civitatis,"[1] and they took advantage of the struggle between Edward II and the Lords Ordainers to grasp some control of the executive for the commonalty.[2] Later still, when they claimed the sole right of nominating and electing the mayor, the aldermen objected, almost plaintively, that they too were citizens and of the community of the city, and the commoners were restricted to the nomination of two ex-sheriffs, from whom the mayor and aldermen chose one.[3]

It is more than questionable, however, despite Stubbs' opinion,[4] whether *communitas* in the style "maior, aldermanni, et (tota) communitas," as used in royal letters or in formal city documents, ever had this narrowed meaning. In the almost equally common "maior (et vicecomites) et communitas" it was certainly employed in its comprehensive sense and, awkward as it is, the fuller style no more implied that *communitas* did not include the mayor and aldermen than the modern "mayor, aldermen, and burgesses" implies that they are not burgesses. The apparent ambiguity is the result of combining the particular and the general in one brief formula.[5]

Another burghal term which acquired a secondary and narrower signification was *prudhommes* (*probi homines*). Long used by the royal chancery as equivalent to *burgenses*,[6] it had become restricted on local lips to the governing body. When, therefore, in 1312 the burgesses of Bristol refused to receive a royal mandate to the "maior, ballivi, et probi homines" of the town until *communitas* was added,[7] it is unnecessary to suppose that the chancery had been taking sides with the minority in the local strife.

Reverting to the formula *burgenses et communitas*, the

---

[1] *Liber de Antiquis Legibus*, pp. 55, 80, 86, 149.
[2] *Munim. Gildh. London*, i. 141-4.   [3] *Ibid.* p. 20.
[4] *Const. Hist.* ii. § 185, p. 168 (2nd ed.).
[5] As *communitas*, however, was used in ordinary parlance, especially in the towns themselves, in a narrow as well as a wide sense, it will be well to translate it by "community" when it is employed with this wide meaning, and not by "commonalty" which became as ambiguous as the Latin word. *Comunete, comounte, co(m)munite*, being more rarely used, almost escaped this double meaning. See *N.E.D.*
[6] Below, p. 286 *n.* 5.   [7] *Rot. Parl.* i. 359.

disjunctive interpretation finds no support even in the town
charters of the fifteenth century, in which both terms are
invariably used in their original and wider sense.[1] Interesting confirmation of the equivalence of *burgenses* (or *cives*)
and *communitas* in official language is found in the exception
made for the towns in the acts of resumption of 1464 and 1485.[2]
For their safety, the actual titles under which they acted and
were addressed are enumerated to the length of nearly a folio
column, seeming to include almost every possible variation
on mayor, bailiffs, aldermen, citizens (burgesses), and community, but lest the list should not be absolutely complete,
more general provisos were added at the end, one of which is
highly significant for our present point : " nor (shall the act
extend) to the citizens or commonaltie of any cite nor to the
burgeises or commonaltie of any borough." Formulas of
address were sometimes expanded to meet possible legal objections to the validity of grants enjoyed under varying titles.
Thus a reduction of fee farm was made in 1462 to " the mayor
and bailiffs, burgesses, men and community of our town of
Northampton, and their heirs and successors, by whatsoever
name they are incorporated, called or known." [3] Here burgesses, men, and community are clearly equivalents recited *ex
abundantia cautelae*.

When, therefore, Henry IV in 1404, instead of granting
his second charter to the citizens of Norwich simply, as all
previous kings had done, made his grant to " the citizens and
community," I do not believe with Mr. Hudson [4] that the
king's chancery clerks were distinguishing between the ruling
class and the body of the citizens or, indeed, thought they
were making any real change whatever. They were merely,
somewhat belatedly, adapting an old loose style to the more
modern ideas which required an expression of corporateness.
It is true that in their party conflicts the twenty-four prudhommes with the ex-mayors and sheriffs and other " sufficient
persons," the *gens d'estat* of the city, took the view, in 1414,
that they alone were the citizens, and that *communitas* in
the charter had encouraged the " commonalty " to assert
that every person of the lowest reputation had as much
authority and power in the affairs of the city as the most
sufficient ; and accordingly they recommended that it should

[1] *Cal. Charter Rolls*, vi. *passim.* [2] *Rot. Parl.* v. 515 ; vi. 338.
[3] Markham and Cox, *Records of Northampton*, i. 91.
[4] *Records of Norwich* (1906), i, lxvi.

be expunged.[1] Even some of the judges seem to have taken the same view when they were asked in 1481 to decide whether a clause of the charter of 1404, in which the re-grant to *cives* simply of a former grant had accidentally been left standing, was of the same effect as the rest of the charter, though two thought it was.[2] On the other hand, the " commonalty " in 1414 did not acknowledge any such distinction, but claimed to be " maior pars civium et communitatis Norwici," and reminded the arbitrator that it was the " community " which received the city revenues, and which had built the Worsted Seld.[3] It is quite evident from the composition of 1415 [4] and Henry V's charter of 1417 [5] that *cives* still had a much wider signification than the governing class had been endeavouring to put upon it, and even in the indenture of 1424 between the mayor, sheriffs, and aldermen the distinction drawn is not between *cives* and *communitas*, but between mayor, sheriffs, and aldermen and " *residuum* nostre communitatis." [6]

The class antagonism which gave a double meaning to *communitas* as (1) the whole body of citizens in their corporate capacity ; (2) that large proportion of them who were allowed no active part in the work of government, was still stronger on the other side of the Channel, where the town councils were more aristocratic than in England, with similar results in nomenclature. Here again, however, modern writers have been inclined to exaggerate the range of the narrower use of *communitas*. Arthur Giry, for instance, in his admirable *Histoire de la Ville de St. Omer*,[7] while admitting that in the early years of the thirteenth-century *communitas* (then just replacing the older *communio*) in the formula " maior, scabini, et (tota) communitas " still meant the " commune," the whole sworn body of citizens, maintains that by the end of the century it had come to mean the unprivileged citizens as contrasted with the échevinage. The class war was certainly more bitter than it usually was in English towns except during the Barons' Wars, and the people, accepting and turning to honour a term used in depreciation by their masters, claimed, as the Londoners did in Simon de Mont-

---

[1] *Records of Norwich* (1906), pp. 81, 85. They complained that the commonalty had elected mayors " nient faisantz les citizeins de dite citee a ceo en ascun manere pryuez," *i.e.*, not making the *gens d'estat* privy to the election. Mr. Hudson mistranslates this sentence.

[2] *Ibid*. I, lxxvii.   [3] *Ibid*. pp. 67 ff.   [4] *Ibid*. pp. 93 ff.
[5] *Ibid*., p. 36.   [6] *Ibid*., p. 113.   [7] P. 166.

fort's time, to be the community (*le commun*), to the exclusion of the échevins. On the other hand, a count of Nevers could address an order " au commun de la vile de Bruges et as maitres qui les gouvernent." [1] But this antagonism was not always in an acute stage, and in quieter times and in formal documents there is reason to believe that *communitas* in the style " mayor, échevins, and (whole) community " carried its original wider meaning,[2] as it appears to have done in the corresponding formula in England.

It seems possible that the local use of the term in its narrower sense in English boroughs was to some extent forwarded by parliamentary precedent. There was an even more sharply marked practical distinction between the magnates and the " commonalty " or " commons " (*i.e.* the representatives of the *communitates* of the shires and boroughs) in Parliament than there was between the council and the " commonalty " of a borough, although magnates and commons could together speak in the name of the *communitas Anglie*, the whole nation.[3] The borough council was, in origin at least, an emanation of the civic *communitas*, whereas the " commons " in Parliament were merely a royal addition to the baronial council of the king. It is difficult to account for the use of " commons " in towns as a synonym for " commonalty," " commoners," *communitas* in the narrow sense, except as a case of direct borrowing from parliamentary usage.

The narrower use of *communitas* received a great impetus when in many boroughs, at a comparatively late date, these " commoners " or " commons " obtained special representation in the governing body by the creation of a " common council" alongside the original town council, which if it had ever really represented their wishes, had long ceased to do this. This share in municipal administration, however, whether won by their own efforts or, as sometimes happened, forced upon them to end their tumultuous agitation in the borough assembly, did not long preserve its popular character.

---

[1] *Hist. de la Ville de Saint-Omer* (1877), p. 163.

[2] See for example a petition of the mayor and échevins of St. Omer " et pour tote la communalte de yceli " to the king of England on behalf of certain " bourgois marchans de la dite communalte " (*ibid.* p. 440).

[3] For a note by M. Petit-Dutaillis on the parliamentary meaning of " Commons," see *Studies Supplementary to Stubbs' Constitutional History*, iii. 447.

APPENDIX I

Merchant Gild, Fee Farm, Commune

IN his recent book,[1] to which we have so often had to refer, Dr. Stephenson claims that the light thrown in the preceding article upon the part played by the Norman merchant gild in municipal development during the twelfth century confirms his contention that the new commerce of that age was the vital force which converted the " military and agrarian " Anglo-Saxon " borough " into the self-governing " town " of the later Middle Ages. In a subsequent chapter he does, however, admit that the process of conversion had begun before 1066 and even had there been no Conquest would have led to the same result, though more slowly.[2]

So far as this process worked through merchant gilds, it was of course only partial, since even important towns, including the greatest of all, had not this institution. Perhaps Dr. Stephenson is a little too ready to presume that a group of well-to-do traders in the borough court of such a town would have much the same influence as the " caucus in the Gild Hall." [3] In London the aldermen owed their weight to their official position as judges of the Husting and heads of the wards rather than to their being traders, while in less prosperous boroughs the absence of an elected head and of the gild's power of raising money for communal purposes, must have severely restricted the burgesses' activities, though they were not precluded from voluntary assessments for the purchase of charters. It was only the gild town which before 1191 had, in some imperfect measure, that permanent officer of their own choice and that *unio communitatis* which were later the tests of a self-governing town.[4]

The gild itself was not, however, a final solution of the problem of town government. Created for purely commercial ends, it was external to the deeply-rooted borough organization, the royal provostry and the borough court. In strict legality the gild alderman had no authority to act, as he often did, on behalf of the community in non-commercial matters nor is there any evidence that he ever used any seal but his own in such business. It was not until towns received the

---

[1] *Borough and Town*, pp. 151, 171. [2] *Ibid.* p. 212.
[3] *Ibid.* p. 172. [4] Above, p. 230.

farm, usually in fee, of the provostry that the burgesses would normally provide themselves with a common seal, but whether the mere grant of the farm entitled them to do this is a point which will come up for discussion presently. However, this may be, in royal reeves chosen now by themselves from their own number and, in the case of the more ambitious towns, a new officer, the mayor, who was as much their own as the gild alderman, they had heads who represented the whole community and not primarily and in strict law its trading element.

It is not surprising that the gild phase should have left its traces in the continued domination of the gild in a few towns and in the wording of certain charters, especially those to Winchester and Gloucester.[1] Burgesses and gildsmen were probably already identical or nearly so in those cities, but they were not so at Southampton or it would not have been thought necessary to obtain a royal grant in 1249 that they should never have a mayor.[2] The gildsmen, who were the most influential section of the freemen, had no mind to exchange their alderman for an officer who would represent the whole community.

When, from the thirteenth century, other qualifications for the freedom of the town were substituted for burgage-holding in the larger boroughs, the single avenue was some-times, at Winchester for instance, membership of the gild. The distinction between burgess and gildsman, if it had existed, was effaced but, at Winchester at least, the gild meetings became little more than social functions.[3] At Exeter the gild organization disappeared early and left no trace save that its four stewards became municipal officials.[4] While fully recognizing the vital part that trade had played in the growth of the boroughs, especially from the reign of Henry I, it is still necessary to reiterate Gross's warning that the constitution of the corporate borough of the later Middle Ages was not borrowed from that of the gild, but was a re-organization and expansion of the structure of the

---

[1] Above, p. 229.
[2] *B.B.C.* ii. 363. For the " borgeis de la vile " who were not gildsmen see *The Oak Book of Southampton*, ed. Studer (Southampton Record Soc.), I, xxx.   [3] Furley, *City Government of Winchester*, pp. 71-6, 106.
[4] Above, p. 227. Admission to the freedom followed the London practice (B. Wilkinson, *The Mediæval Council of Exeter*, p. 26 *n.;* cf. *Calendar of Plea and Memoranda Rolls of the City of London, 1364-81,* ed. A. H. Thomas, pp. xxvii ff.).

pre-Conquest borough. Its basis lay in the community not in any section of it, however wide. Of the new institutions, the office of chamberlain, the chief financial official may have owed something to gild precedent and the mayor sometimes succeeded the gild alderman as first officer of the town, but both offices were essentially communal in origin and for that reason the mayoralty was liable to come into conflict with the aldermanry, as happened at Southampton. After all, too, the mayor was not an indispensable member of every urban corporation as were the ancient reeves or bailiffs, once their elective status was established. The new councils, like all these officers, were in theory elected by the whole community in its time-honoured court. The gild had no council, as distinguished from a small group of officers, except when, as at Leicester [1] and Andover, it had occupied the whole field of communal administration and the Leicester council coalesced with the communal jurats within half a century, though the *forewardmanni* [2] of smaller Andover did not become a normal body of *probi homines* until the gild, as a gild, practically ceased to exist in the sixteenth century.

What act or acts created an urban corporation, a *communa* or *communitas* in a new fuller sense ? The setting up of such a *communitas*, with elected officers and council and communal seal, at Ipswich in 1200 on receipt of a royal charter which, apart from the usual urban liberties and merchant gild, granted only the fee farm of the town and election of reeves and coroners, [3] may seem to supply the answer to this question. Yet in Richard's reign at least similar grants did not produce the same result. Northampton had a grant of fee farm and election of its reeves as early as 1189, confirmed by John, who added election of coroners, a few weeks before the Ipswich charter, but in sending this confirmation to Lancaster, which had just obtained the liberties of Northampton, the reeves did not use a communal seal, merely authenticating their

---

[1] See above, p. 233.

[2] The history of this unique body, originally twelve in number, later twenty-four, can be studied with some clearness in the very full extracts from the Andover records printed by Gross (*Gild Merchant*, ii. 3-8, 289-348). In the thirteenth and fourteenth centuries their main duty seems to have been to decide questions arising out of succession to or transfer of gild membership. Their Old English name, meaning " covenant-men " and their number suggest a possible connexion with Edgar's twelve witnesses of bargains in the hundred court (Liebermann, *Ges.* i. 210). Andover had a hundred court, but it met separately from the gild court in which the forewardmen appear.   [3] Below, pp. 270 f.

letter with the seal of the provostry.[1] London again obtained, or rather regained, the fee farm in 1190, yet a year later demanded and received recognition of a " commune " of the city.[2] That this was no mere confirmation by Count John and the barons of the concession made twelve months before by his opponent, the chancellor Longchamp, is clear from the horror which Richard of Devizes expressed at the later step.[3] Moreover, some boroughs had farmed themselves and elected their reeves even under Henry II who certainly recognized no commune. His grants were indeed only made " during pleasure," he allowed no fee farms, but there is no doubt that a perpetual farm was not an essential condition of early municipal incorporation of the type with which we are dealing.[4] Exeter had no fee farm until 1259,[5] Winchester none before 1327.[6] It is doubtful whether the citizens of Exeter had a continuous series of temporary grants. Yet these were among the earliest towns to have the specially communal office of mayor. Still more significantly, we have in Oxford a borough which begins to use a communal seal at a time when, as the Pipe Rolls clearly show, the burgesses had not yet even a temporary tenure of the farm.[7]

It has to be remembered, too, that the men of purely rural manors sometimes farmed them, though perhaps not in fee farm,[8] and that election of their reeves was common enough.

For the creation of the new type of urban commune, then, it seems necessary to postulate something beyond the farm, not put into charters, where charters were granted, but subject of unwritten concessions or acquiescence. It will be found, we believe, in the allowance of sworn association. The absence of any clear record of reorganization consequent on the recognition of a *communa* at London in 1191, save the institution of a mayor, has caused surprise, but may not the explanation be that the essential and perhaps the only other change is contained in the oath of the citizens to adhere to the commune and be obedient to the officers of the city, while similarly binding themselves to continued loyalty to the king?[9] It is possible that Miss Bateson was

[1] Above, p. 239.   [2] Above, p. 181.
[3] Stubbs, *Select Charters*, ed. Davis, p. 245.
[4] It was not of course incorporation in the full legal sense of the later Middle Ages. See above, p. 239.   [5] *B.B.C.* ii. 316.
[6] Furley, *op. cit.* p. 32.   [7] Above, p. 235.
[8] Pollock and Maitland, *Hist. of Eng. Law*, i. 628, 650.
[9] Round, *Commune of London*, pp. 235-6.

right and that the "skivins" of the oath were only the aldermen in the new communal setting,[1] though later attempts may have been made to substitute a body differently constituted. Oxford's contemporary assumption of a communal seal was perhaps an immediate repercussion of the movement in her mother city.

The circumstances in which the commune of London was granted were tumultuous and, though Richard of Devizes is not supported by other accounts in asserting that the magnates were forced to swear to preserve it,[2] it bore at least a superficial resemblance to the more violent kind of continental *communa jurata*, it was a *conjuratio* which, he says, neither Henry II nor Richard would have permitted for a million marks of silver. Neither Richard on his return nor John as king ever created a sworn commune by charter in England, though John at least founded them freely in his continental dominions. Nevertheless, the essential principle of the commune, the obligation on oath to preserve the town and its liberties and for that end to obey and assist its officers was silently recognized and incorporated in borough practice. There is an unmistakable likeness to the London oath in that which the burgesses of Ipswich swore on July, 1200, to be obedient, intendant, advisory and assistant to their officers and portmen to preserve and maintain the town and its honour and liberties everywhere against everyone, except against the lord king and the royal power.[3]

At Ipswich there was much reorganization, but that was because they had had so little up to then, not even a merchant gild.[4]

The Ipswich evidence that the new form of commune, though introducing local loyalties which might easily, in spite of protestations to the contrary, become a danger to the royal power, and which therefore were never formally authorized by charter, was recognized by the Crown finds

---

[1] Below, p. 266.

[2] According to the *Gesta Henrici et Ricardi* ("Benedictus Abbas"), ii. 214, they only swore to do so *quandiu regi placuerit*.

[3] Gross, *Gild Merchant*, ii. 118.

[4] From 1194 the men of Ipswich held the farm of the borough, doubtless "during pleasure," at an increment of £5, but it was three years before they paid anything (*P.R.* 6 Ric. I, p. 47 ; 9 Ric. I, p. 226). In 1197 and 1198 they paid off arrears (*ibid.* and 10 Ric. I, p. 95), but were again in debt for nearly a year's farm at Michaelmas 1199 (*ibid.* 1 John, p. 263). They had not yet paid the 60 marks they had offered "to have their liberties" as far back as 1191 (*ibid.* 3 Ric. I, p. 42).

confirmation in an unexpected quarter. The ordinance of 1205 for the defence of the realm against a feared French invasion and for the preservation of the peace, which Gervase of Canterbury embodied *verbatim* in his *Gesta Regum*,[1] has been noticed by historians as a reorganization of the fyrd,[2] but its importance for the enlarged meaning of *communa* and as the first general reference to the office of mayor, has escaped them.

In introducing his transcript of the ordinance Gervase says that it ordered the formation of a *communa* throughout the realm, and that all men over twelve years of age should swear to keep it faithfully. The ordinance does not actually speak of a national commune, but of local communes of shires, hundreds, cities, boroughs and groups of minor vills, though, as these covered the whole country, they might be regarded as constituting one national commune, a reorganization of the *communa liberorum hominum* of the Assize of Arms.[3] The chief novelty was that the command of the various units was to be entrusted to new officers called constables, with or without the co-operation of existing local officials. Several chief constables (*capitales constabularii*) replaced the sheriff in the county for this military and police duty, with subordinate constables, normally one for each of its hundreds, cities, boroughs and groups of townships, the *hundredi*, *burgi* and *visneta* of the Assize of Arms. These subordinates and the communes they commanded were to obey the orders of the chief constables. All men over twelve were to swear to observe this " ad honorem Dei et fidelitatem domini regis."

Interesting as it is as a link that has been overlooked between the Assize of Arms and the establishment of constables for the preservation of the peace in the next two reigns,[4] the

---

[1] *Works*, ed. Stubbs (Rolls Ser.), ii. 97.

[2] Stubbs, *Const. Hist.* i. 592, § 162 ; Davis, *England under the Normans and Angevins*, pp. 351-2 ; Norgate, *John Lackland*, p. 104.

[3] Stubbs, *Select Charters*, ed. Davis, pp. 183-4.

[4] The ordinance was an emergency measure to meet a danger which, so far as foreign invasion was feared, did not arrive and it may be doubted whether constables were generally appointed, though, for the preservation of the peace, they re-appear in the hundreds in 1242 (Morris, *The English Sheriff to 1300*, p. 228), and more widely in the writ of 1252 (*Select Charters*, p. 364), and in the Statute of Westminster of 1285. The mayor, or the reeves or bailiffs where there was no mayor, acted in cities and boroughs in 1252, while constables were appointed elsewhere. Though the scheme of 1205 was apparently abortive, it was embodied by London writers in additions to early Norman law books with especial emphasis on the part to be played by *fratres coniurati* and particularly in cities and boroughs (Liebermann, *Ges.* i. 490, 655, ii. 375, iii. 282).

S

ordinance would have told the municipal historian nothing, had not some cities and boroughs required special treatment. To meet their case the general rule that each subordinate commune should have one constable was qualified by the following clause:

"In civitatibus vero et burgis ubi major communa fuerit constituantur constabularii plures vel pauciores secundum quantitatem civitatis vel burgi una cum majore et constabulario castri quod ibi fuerit; eodem modo in burgis ubi prius communa non fuerat constituantur constabularii cum constabulario castri si ibi fuerit."

There are two points of importance for us here, first the precise meaning of a commune which some urban centres already possessed in 1205, while others did not, and, secondly, the evidence that despite the absence of any trace hitherto of royal authorization or approval of their institution, mayors were now fully recognized local officials. (1) The statement that cities and boroughs "ubi major communa fuerit" were to have several constables, according to their size, might seem to imply that *major communa* merely meant a large commune, but this interpretation seems to be precluded by the rest of the clause which prescribes the same treatment of boroughs "ubi prius communa non fuerat." They were *ex hypothesi* large nor could they be denied the name of *communa* or *communitas* in the sense in which it was applied in the twelfth century to any administrative or economic group. It would appear that *communa* in this clause means more than that, and the suggestion seems allowable that *major communa* should be translated: "greater (or more advanced) commune." (2) The suggestion gains support from the fact that every city and borough where there was a *major communa* is assumed to have had a mayor. We remember that there was a sense in which London itself had not a *communa* until 1191, and that Ipswich regarded itself as a *communitas* in a new and fuller sense after the charter and reorganization of 1200. It is true that if the mayoralty was an integral part of a "greater commune," Ipswich and more important boroughs than Ipswich did not possess it. In fact its possessors must have formed a very select class indeed. We do not know for certain of more than four towns that had mayors by 1205: London, Winchester, Exeter, and Lincoln.[1] All these, of course, had royal castles which the town with a

---

[1] See below, p. 291.

" greater commune " is also assumed to have. But it is hard to believe that John and his advisers were consciously drawing the line quite so high as that. It is perhaps more reasonable to suppose that they exaggerated the number of towns that had mayors. Medieval officials were often ill-informed on local conditions and chancery clerks sometimes addressed writs to the mayors of towns which had no such head officer. However, if Lynn was not the only borough which set up a mayor *proprio motu* [1] uncertainty rather than carelessness may have been the cause of such errors.

The ordinance of 1205 is not without its bearing upon the question whether the new communal movement in England with its sworn association, mayors and town councils owed anything to the influence of the contemporary continental commune. Dr. Stephenson maintains that the French commune had no more influence upon municipal development in England at this juncture than it had exercised at any time since the Norman Conquest.[2] The new form of commune was, he holds, a purely natural development from what had gone before. " Mayor " was a foreign title, indeed, but no more than a new name for an existing type of magistrate.[3] This is surely an untenable position. Before the creation of mayors there were only reeves whose first duty was to the king, and aldermen who were legally only heads of trade associations, though, as we have seen, they sometimes assumed the character of quasi-communal officers. The mayor as legal head of the community in all its aspects filled a place in the English town which had not been hitherto occupied, but which was normal in the foreign commune. It is true that the sworn association had a precedent in London under Stephen, and very likely in Gloucester and York where Henry II suppressed " communes," though Dr. Stephenson is inclined to conjecture other than municipal aims for these.[4] The idea was not new, but when it was at last allowed to be put in practice, some reference to those foreign models which had originally inspired it was inevitable. Even if the " skivins " of the communal oath of the citizens of London in 1193 were only the aldermen, the use of a foreign title of which there is no other instance in English borough

---

[1] *B.B.C.* ii. 362. [2] *Borough and Town*, p. 184.
[3] *Ibid.* p. 173.
[4] *Ibid.* p. 184, n. 2. The York case had clearly nothing to do with those of communication with the king's Flemish enemies.

organization, as distinguished from that of the gild, shows clearly to what quarter the eyes of the Londoners were turned. It was as the setting up of a continental commune in England that Richard of Devizes denounced the step then taken.

John's policy as king showed a realization that the sworn commune, under proper control, might be a bulwark instead of a danger to the Crown. He made use of it on both sides of the Channel for state purposes. There is little doubt that his, whole scheme of defence in 1205, with its exhaustive system of communes, in which every male over twelve was bound by an oath of obedience to his officers and loyalty to the king owed something to his earlier defensive policy in Normandy. He—and others—not only founded single-town communes bound by oath to render military service, but combined towns and even groups of ordinary vills, like the English *visneta*, in such communes for the same purpose of defence.[1] Of one of these, not set up by John himself, headed by Evreux in 1194, Adam the Englishman was mayor.[2]

APPENDIX II

The Barons of London and of the Cinque Ports

THE civic use of " baron " in England was peculiar to its chief city and to its unique naval confederation.[3] Much uncertainty has prevailed about the application of the term in London. It seems to vary in content at different times.

[1] Giry, *Établissements de Rouen*, i. 47 and *n*.

[2] Powicke, *The Loss of Normandy*, p. 147 ; Giry, *loc. cit.* ; Round, *Cal. of Docs. in France*, p. 138.

[3] Spelman's claim that Chester, York, and Warwick had barons seems unfounded. His barons of Warwick are probably the external barons the number of whose houses is given in the first paragraph of the Domesday description (i. 238). A charter of Henry I and two of Henry II addressed respectively to the barons of Hampshire and Winchester and to the barons of Lincoln and Lincolnshire (*E.H.R.* xxxv. (1920), 393 ; Gross, *Gild Merchant*, ii. 278) stand quite alone and are probably eccentricities of chancery scribes, who sometimes extended the title of barons to the burgesses of other ports than the Cinque Ports when the same writ was directed to them (*Foedera* (O), iii. 222, iv. 284). In the first case the common and correct " barons of London and Middlesex " may have been running in their minds. As a civic title baron is also found in French usage, but sporadically and in a narrow sense. Du Cange indeed says that it was applied in the twelfth century to the citizens of Bourges and Orleans. But at Bourges at any rate, where it seems first on record in 1145, the barons were four officers who administered the city under the royal prévôt (Luchaire, *Manuel*, p. 397).

King John grants the right of electing a mayor annually
(1215) to the barons of the city and the city's common seal
bears to this day the legend SIGILLVM BARONVM LONDONIARVM,
yet in the second half of the thirteenth century barons are sometimes distinguished from citizens in official documents, and in
the fourteenth they are identified with the twenty-five aldermen.   The late William Page took a middle line,[1] equating
them with the *burhthegns* of three of the five London writs of
Edward the Confessor and with the oligarchic party of the
twelfth century, the *probi homines* of the communal oath of
1193,[2] the " great council " of the Fitz Walter claim of 1303.[3]
Mr. A. H. Thomas, while prepared to accept the first identification, with the great sea-merchants who had become thegn-
worthy, adduces evidence to show that from the twelfth
century onwards " barons " had a wider meaning and was
in fact synonymous with " citizens." [4] Professor Stenton,
though not taking notice of the similarity of name, is in substantial agreement with this view, speaking of a transformation
of a patriciate of birth by an influx of a new wealthy element,
in part French and Italian, and by an equalization of London
wergilds at the 100 (Norman) shillings of the ordinary freeman.[5]
There certainly seems to have been a readjustment of wergilds
after the Conquest,[6] but it is hardly safe to say that the change
is clearly indicated in the writs of the Norman kings.   William I
preferred the *burhwaru* of two of the Confessor's writs [7] to
the *burhthegns* of the others in his English charter and writs,[8]
whether or not there was any real distinction involved, but
in one Latin writ addresses the barons of the city [9] and this
became the common form from the reign of Henry I, though
citizens is also occasionally used and exclusively in the Pipe
Rolls and in all charters but that of 1215 granting yearly
election of the mayor.   In the chancery rolls, from their
beginning in John's reign to the middle of the thirteenth
century, royal mandates on administrative matters are generally addressed to the barons and the occasional substitution
of citizens or prudhommes (*probi homines*) does not, as Mr.

[1] *London : its Origin and Early Development* (1923), pp. 219 ff.   Thegn
was of course usually Latinized as *baro*.   [2] See below, p. 266.
[3] *Liber Custumarum* in *Mun. Gildh. Lond.* (R.S.), II, i. 147 ff. ; Stow,
Survey, ed. Kingsford, i. 62 ; ii. 279.
[4] *Cal. of Plea and Memoranda Rolls of London, 1364–81*, pp. xxi. ff.
[5] *Norman London*, 2nd ed., 1934, p. 19.   [6] See above, p. 82.
[7] *B.B.C.* i. 126 (1042–44), *Mon. Angl.* i. 430, Kemble, 856 (1058–66).
[8] Davis, *Regesta*, nos. 15, 265.
[9] *Ibid.* no. 246.   In full in *Essays presented to T. F. Tout* (1925), p. 51.

Thomas remarks, seem to imply any distinction. This conclusion is strongly supported by the clear evidence given below that the barons of the Cinque Ports were the whole body of burgesses, not a governing council within it. If the analogy is complete, the barons of London were those who held land in the city and contributed to all the city's expenses, who were, in contemporary language, in scot and lot.

The connexion with " burhthegns," if it existed, may not be the sole source of their title. Their constant administrative association with the barons of Middlesex, their close relations with and service to the king—London was " the King's Chamber " [1]—and that inherent importance of the city which according to Henry of Blois made the Londoners to be regarded as *optimates* and *proceres*,[2] were sufficient in themselves to earn the distinctive appellation. It has been pointed out, in the case of the barons of the exchequer, that even lowborn men who enjoyed the king's confidence could be so entitled. " They were barons because it pleased the king to treat them as such." [3] It is not surprising that in course of time the barons of London should have claimed (1250) the privileges of their " peers," the earls and barons of the realm.[4]

When this proud claim was made, the process was already at work which in little more than half a century was to restrict the application of the title to the aldermen and ultimately leave it an archaic survival on the city seal.[5] The chief factor in this revolution was a change, which had begun early in the century, in the method of admission to the freedom of the city. Until then the qualification for citizenship, as in boroughs generally, was the possession of land and houses. When, towards the end of Henry II's reign, the maternal grandparents of Arnold Fitz Thedmar, alderman and chronicler, came from Cologne to visit the shrine of St. Thomas at Canterbury and, on hearing of the death of the wife's mother, decided to settle in England, they bought a *domicilium* in London and became (*facti sunt*) citizens.[6] In such cases descendants of the newly enfranchised inherited the freedom by patrimony. But by 1230 there were two other avenues to

---

[1] For the king's chamberlain in London, who was also his butler and coroner, see *Liber Albus, Mun. Gildh. Lond.* i. 15.
[2] Will. of Malmesbury, *Hist. Novella* (R.S.), ii. 576-7.
[3] Stenton, *English Feudalism 1066–1166* (1932), p. 85.
[4] *Liber de Antiquis Legibus*, Camden Soc., p. 17.
[5] See below, pp. 259.   [6] *Lib. de Ant. Legg.*, p. 238.

citizenship, apprenticeship and purchase (redemption), purchase not of land, but of the freedom. Less than a century
later, in the reign of Edward II, of nearly 1100 citizens enrolled in twenty-one months, only seventy-five were free by
patrimony.[1] It is true that the number of admissions was
abnormal and that the large proportion of redemptioners,
656, in particular, shows that the (temporary) victory of
the commonalty over the aldermen in 1319 was not unprepared
by the creation of votes. Nevertheless the decline of franchise
by patrimony was of long-standing and permanent. The
growth of the gild system, the democratic uprising during
the Barons' War and the development of the conception of
the civic *communitas* had shifted landmarks, and the day of
the old landed barons of the city was over. " Mayor and
barons " had yielded place to " Mayor, aldermen and community." To that extent its common seal became an
anachronism.

Even in the second half of the thirteenth century, royal
mandates were no longer addressed to the hereditary barons,
but to the smaller official aristocracy of elective aldermen,
whose position remained essentially unaffected by changes
in the constitution of the citizen body. The commonalty
asserted in 1312 that London, with its wards corresponding
to rural hundreds, had a shire constitution as well as a sheriff
and that the aldermen were its barons.[2] Their motive was
a practical one, to confine responsibility for a riot to the ward
in which it arose, but their statement shows how completely
the wider meaning of *barones* had passed out of use. The
aldermen themselves, whether on the strength of the parallelism in question or as survivors of the wider body, are
said to have regarded themselves as barons and even after
1350 to have been buried with baronial honours, until frequent changes in their body and recurrent pestilences caused
the rite to be discontinued. So, John Carpenter, town clerk,
writing in 1419, informs us,[3] and for a custom so recently
in use he is good authority. But his inference that barons
was the original name for the aldermen and for them only
cannot be accepted.

In the case of the barons of the Cinque Ports, there is the
initial difficulty that until 1206 there is no evidence that any
of the ports but Hastings had them. Henry II gave a charter

---

[1] A. H. Thomas, *op. cit.*, p. xxix.　　[2] *Ibid. 1323–64*, p. xxiv.
[3] *Liber Albus* in *Mun. Gildh. Lond.* i. 33.

to its barons early in his reign [1] and this was confirmed by John in 1205,[2] but both Henry and his son's charters to the other ports are granted vaguely to their men (*homines*). This might be regarded as merely chancery laxness, were it not that the early seal of Dover, which was in use in the first quarter of the thirteenth century, bore the legend: SIGILLVM BVRGENSIVM DE DOVRA [3] and was later replaced by one with the legend: SIGILLVM COMMVNE BARONVM DE DOVORIA.[4] Hastings even in its later decadence was held to be the chief of the ports [5] and service at court, the bearing of the canopy at coronations, is confirmed to it alone by Henry II and John. A coronation service, however, did not confer the title of barons upon the burgesses of Oxford and Hastings' early ship-service, though four times that of Romney, Hythe, and Sandwich, was no greater than that of Dover.[6] Was there some recognition of its proximity to the scene of the decisive battle of 1066 in the honours bestowed upon its burgesses?

The sudden extension of these honours to the other ports admits of more satisfying conjecture. Less than a year after John's simultaneous charters of 1205 in which barons are still confined to Hastings, mandates were issued to the barons of all five,[7] and two years later to those of Rye, Winchelsea, and Pevensey as well.[8] It is impossible not to associate this change with the greatly increased naval importance of the ports after the loss of Normandy in 1204, and with the consequent tightening of their hitherto somewhat loose bond of union into a close confederation. The more frequent demands upon their ships and the unusual liberties they enjoyed might well be recognized by this heightened status of their burgesses. Like the barons of London they were proud of their special relation to the Crown, and those of Pevensey and Winchelsea described themselves on their seals as " barones domini regis." [9]

That the barons at this date comprised the whole body of citizens is fortunately not in doubt. It is true that the Sandwich seal, which Birch attributes to a thirteenth-century date, has the legend: SIGILL' CONSILII BARONVM DE SANDWICO,[10]

---

[1] *B.B.C.* i. 99 ; for his charters to other ports, see *C. Chart. Roll*, iii. 219 ff.　　　　　　　　　　[2] *Rot. Chart.* (1837), p. 153.
[3] Round, *Cal. of Docs. in France*, p. 33.
[4] *Brit. Mus. Cat. of Seals*, ii. 68.　　　[5] *C.C.R. 1369–74*, p. 24.
[6] *B.B.C.* i. 90 ; *D.B.* i. 1.　　　[7] *Rot. Litt. Pat.* (1835), p. 64 *b*.
[8] *Ibid.*, p. 80.　　　[9] *B.M. Cat. of Seals*, ii. 160, 210.
[10] *Ibid.*, p. 180.

but, however this may be explained, it cannot controvert a precise definition of a baron in these ports which has accidentally been preserved, when local municipal records of its period have mostly perished. In May, 1336, one Arnald Camperyan of Dover complained to the king that the royal collectors exacted custom on the goods and merchandise he caused to be brought into the country, as if he were a foreign merchant, whereas, as he brought letters patent of the mayor and barons of the community of Dover to testify, he was a baron of that town, holding lands there both by hereditary right and by acquisition, and contributing to all things and expenses touching the town with the other barons.[1] Two years later the mayor, bailiffs and community of Sandwich laid a complaint against the exchequer for distraining them because they had admitted certain Gascons from Aquitaine to the liberty of the town as barons, to enjoy the same liberties and contribute to scot and lot with the others.[2] Their grievance was still under consideration in 1340.[3]

The scanty survival of early archives of the ports renders a reconstruction of their civic administration difficult, but from the earliest extant custumal we learn that about 1352 the council of the jurats (*jurés*) at Romney was chosen from the barons.[4] Refusal to serve was punished by sequestration of the offending baron's house. The chief ruler of the year was acquitted at its end in a regular form by his combarons.[5] They were the judges of the town court.[6] But just as at London the elected and sworn council of aldermen ultimately overshadowed the barons, from whom they were originally taken, so the jurats of the ports seem from the fourteenth century to have drawn administrative control into their own hands, while there was also perhaps some extension of citizenship. We hear less of the " mayor (or bailiffs) and the barons " and more of the " mayor (bailiffs), jurats and community." [7] As early as 1383 the Dover court was held by the mayor, bailiffs, and jurats.[8] It is under this title that

---

[1] *C.C.R. 1333–37*, pp. 675-6. [2] *Ibid. 1337–39*, p. 512.
[3] *Ibid. 1339–40*, pp. 216, 627.
[4] Bateson, *Borough Customs* (Selden Soc.), ii. 39.
[5] 4 Rep. *Hist. MSS. Comm.*, App., p. 424.
[6] Bateson, *op. cit.* i. 144, ii. 16, 116-17.
[7] *C.C.R. 1364–68*, p. 326; 5 Rep. *Hist. MSS. Comm.*, App., 493b *et alias*. Sandwich was incorporated in 1684 as the mayor, jurats, and community of the town.
[8] *S.P.H.*, Statham, *Dover Charters*, p. xxii. The Hythe seal in the fifteenth century had the legend : SIG' IVRATORVM VILLE HEDE (*B.M. Cat.* ii. 94).

the ports join in the Brodhulle assemblies, which dealt especially with their contributions to the expenses of the confederation.[1] If the designation baron survived here, while it vanished altogether in London, the main reason no doubt is that the ship-service and their membership of the ancient court of Shepway kept it alive.[2] A contributory cause may be that in these comparatively small and non-industrial communities the attainment of the freedom by patrimony possibly held its own more largely than it did in London against the newer qualifications of apprenticeship and purchase.

[1] Statham, *op. cit.* 120 ff.   [2] *Ibid.*, pp. 60 ff.

X

THE ORIGIN OF TOWN COUNCILS [1]

In the two preceding articles it has been seen that the ancient royal boroughs acquired a new status during the reigns of Richard I and John. At the death of Henry II they had enjoyed but a humble measure of self-government. By charter or custom they possessed a number of valuable privileges, especially separate jurisdiction in domestic cases short of the pleas of the Crown and freedom from toll elsewhere. There was no sharp line, however, between their judicial privileges and those allowed to the greater feudatories, to religious houses [2] and to the ancient demesne of the Crown. The ancient demesne also enjoyed general exemption from toll and shared with the boroughs the right to admit into their community villeins not reclaimed by their lords within a year and a day. In fact, though the Crown was not the sole landlord in the borough, its status approximated, *mutatis mutandis*, to that of ancient demesne. The privilege of farming the royal revenue and of electing the local reeve is found in both, but as yet it was always revocable. The one important privilege that was peculiar to boroughs, though not universal, was the merchant gild. Though granted only for the regulation and advancement of their trade, it was utilized in practice to give a kind of semi-corporateness to the borough community. In the gild alderman the burgesses found a head who was not a royal official but a quasi-municipal officer of their own, whose seal could be used to authenticate their communal actions.

Even where it existed, however, this was an obviously illogical solution of the problem of urban government. Its normal effect was a dual control of king's reeve (with the

---

[1] Reprinted, with revised introduction and incidental additions, from *E.H.R.* xliv. (1929), 177-202.
[2] *Cf.* Henry II's grant to the canons regular of St. Paul's church, Bedford (later Newenham Priory) of " all the liberties which the burgesses of Bedford have " (*Mon. Angl.* vi. 374).

sheriff behind him) and gild alderman.   Nor was the borough
community always co-extensive with that of the gild.   The
ultimate solution, reached at the end of the twelfth century,
was attained partly by chartered concession, partly by formal
or tacit recognition of communal self-assertion in the boroughs: [1]
(1) borough communities were enfeoffed by charter with the
permanent management of the royal farm of the town, the
royal reeves, who were still primarily responsible for it,
becoming their elected officers and taking the place of the
sheriff as their accountant at the exchequer ; (2) at London
with some show of authorization and elsewhere usually, it
would seem, without even this, the boroughs with grants of
fee farm celebrated the end of revocable autonomy and dual
control by re-organization and the introduction of official and
communal oaths.   The essential corporateness of the new
regime was marked not only by the oath to maintain the new
privileges and ancient liberties against all save the king, but
by the first appearance of borough seals and, in the more advanced towns, of a new single head of the community, the
mayor.   To assist the mayor in the name of the community
there were sooner or later set up small councils of *prudhommes*, generally twelve or twenty-four in number, sworn
to do the duties assigned to them faithfully, to uphold the
liberties and customs of the town, and to ordain and do everything that needed to be done for its status and honour.

As councils of *jurati*, as well as mayors, were already
familiar features of the continental communes, well known
to the Anglo-French on this side the Channel, it seems not
unreasonable to assume that in the one case as in the other
the influence of the foreign commune may be discerned.
Bishop Stubbs long ago suggested [2] this as one of the con-
current sources of town councils, the others being the gild
organization, the decadence of the old judiciary and the jury
system.   His suggestion, however, left the time and corre-
lation of these forces too vague to be very helpful.   A simpler
explanation was propounded by Maitland who expressed
his opinion that the borough council was a natural development from the borough court and ignored foreign influence. [3]
That seems also to have been the view of Miss Bateson [4]

---

[1] Above, p. 234.   [2] *Constitutional History*, 2nd ed. iii. 584 (§ 488).
[3] *E.H.R.* xi. (1896), 19.
[4] *Ibid.* xvii. (1902), 481 : " nowhere must town jurisdiction be neglected
as the source of town constitutions."

and of Charles Gross,[1] and obtained wide acceptance. At the other extreme, Round, without formulating any general theory, was evidently inclined to see the origin not only of the first city council of London, but of many others in southern England in close imitation of the institutions of foreign communes.[2] The assertion of such detailed copying of continental models did not stand the test of criticism and even their general influence has been denied, since my article first appeared in print, by Professor Stephenson who reverts to Maitland's theory of a purely native development, but with a different emphasis. The prototype of the council is not the doomsmen in the borough court, *qua* doomsmen, but the " caucus " of merchants in the Gild Hall or (where there was no gild) in the court.[3]

I

Although, or indeed perhaps because, some of these differences of opinion and uncertainties have been removed by the disclosure of new evidence, it will be well to begin our investigation by bringing together, as briefly as may be, the earliest records before 1300 [4] that we now have which describe the setting up of borough councils or contain an early mention of such a council with an indication of its functions. There are not many of these, about a dozen in all, and, with one very doubtful exception, none of them is earlier than the last year of the twelfth century. The dubious case in question is the supposed mention of a municipal council in London more than a century before that date, which could not be excluded, because Liebermann and Miss Bateson are responsible for the suggestion. Apart from this, however, London must be given priority in our list of first mentions of a council.

1. *London.* (a) In his defence against charges of disloyalty at the accession of William Rufus, William de St. Calais, bishop of Durham, claimed to have damped down revolt in London, particularly by bringing " (the ?) twelve better citizens of the said city " to speech with the king.[5]

---

[1] *Gild Merchant,* i. 90.
[2] *Commune of London,* pp. 219 ff. ; *Feudal England,* pp. 552 ff.
[3] *Borough and Town,* pp. 172 ff.
[4] The strong English influence at Dublin and Berwick will excuse their inclusion.
[5] " Meliores etiam xii eiusdem urbis cives ad eum mecum duxi ut per illos melius ceteros animarem " (Simeon of Durham, *Opera* (Rolls Series), i. 189 ; *E.H.R.* xvii. 730).

This body has been described by Liebermann as " a permanent city college of twelve," [1] but the absence of the definite article in Latin leaves it quite uncertain whether it was a fixed council or a selection of the more prominent citizens made *ad hoc*, like the twelve *de melioribus civitatis* who watched over the king's safety when he lay at Shrewsbury, before the Conquest. [2] It may be added that Miss Bateson did not attempt to reconcile the existence of such a body with the position she claimed for the aldermen, who, if they existed before 1087, [3] must almost certainly have been more than twelve in number [4] and for long were not fixed in number at all.

(*b*) The oath of the commune of London in 1193 bound its members " to be obedient to the mayor of the city of London and to the skivins (*skivini*) of the said commune . . . and to follow and maintain the decisions of the mayor and skivins and other good men (*probi homines*) who shall be (associated) with them." [5] Here we undoubtedly have to do with a governing body, whether, with Round, we see in the skivins an imitation of the twelve *scabini* (*échevins*) of the communal constitution of Rouen and in the " other good men " the twelve *consultores* associated with them, or, with Miss Bateson, regard skivins as merely a foreign name for the native aldermen and the good men as additional councillors whom the mayor might choose to summon to represent the opinion of the community, predecessors of the later common councillors. It must be said that the indefiniteness of the reference to these good men is a point in Miss Bateson's favour, [6] but both she and Round have so confused the issue by identifying the twenty-four who took an oath of office in 1206 with the council of 1193 (or the aldermen only, in Miss Bateson's case) that

---

[1] *Gesetze der Angelsachsen*, ii. 573, 662. The date is misprinted 1187–88. A Brihtmer *senator* of London before the Conquest is mentioned in a document of 1098–1108 (Cotton MS. Faustina B. vi, fo. 100 ; cf. *Mon. Angl.* i. 97), but this is too indefinite to serve as earlier evidence of such a college. It would be less rash to suggest that it points to the pre-Conquest existence of aldermen.

[2] *Domesday Book*, i. 252.

[3] The first mention of a ward alderman is in 1111 (Page, *London*, p. 180), and Mr. Page places their creation after 1100, but with so little evidence the argument *ex silentio* is dangerous. *Cf.* note 1 above.

[4] There at least were twenty *c.* 1128 (*op. cit.*, p. 176 ; *Essays presented to T. F. Tout*, p. 47).

[5] " Obedientes erunt maiori civitatis Lond[onie] et skivin[is] eiusdem commune . . . et quod sequentur et tenebunt considerationem maioris et skivinorum et aliorum proborum hominum qui cum illis erunt " (Round, *Commune of London*, p. 235).

[6] See also above, pp. 251-2.

it will be well to defer further discussion until the events of the former year are reached.

(c) In the *Chronica Maiorum et Vicecomitum Londoniarum*, ascribed with great probability to a leading citizen, Arnold fitz Thedmar (1201–74 ?), there is the following entry under 1200 [–1201] : " Hoc anno fuerunt xxv electi de discretioribus Civitatis, et iurati pro consulendo Civitatem una cum Maiore."[1] Miss Bateson in 1902 questioned this " story," partly because the early meagre section of the chronicle has more than one serious inaccuracy and partly because evidence that the sworn four-and-twenty of 1206 were elected was (it was thought) wanting.[2] We now know that it existed and had been in print for seventy years. The case against the " story " thereby loses weight, and the close parallelism of its wording with the description of the duties of the alderman's council at Leicester in 1225,[3] including the somewhat rare transitive use of *consulere*, is positive evidence in favour of its authenticity. Nor does the history of the manuscript lend support to any suggestion that the entry is a late concoction in the interests of popular government. If accepted as genuine, it is important as first emphasizing the function which gave the name of council to all such bodies, and as disclosing, taken in connexion with the episode of 1206 to which we shall come next, a state of things in the city which appears irreconcilable with Miss Bateson's hypothesis of unbroken government by twenty-four aldermen with the occasional assistance of other councillors.[4] The history of London in these vital years is provokingly obscure, but there does seem evidence of at least an occasional election by the citizens at large of a governing body of twenty-five or twenty-four who were not (necessarily) aldermen. William FitzOsbert's agitation a few years before (1195–96) reveals the existence of strong popular feeling against the city rulers, whom he accused of defrauding the king on the one hand and of shifting the burden of taxation to the shoulders of their poorer fellow citizens on the other,[5] and as these grievances can be recognized among the charges on which King John in 1206 ordered a new body of twenty-four to be elected, it is not improbable that they provoked the election of a somewhat similar body five years earlier.

[1] *Liber de Antiquis Legibus*, p. 2.
[2] *E.H.R.* xvii. 508.
[3] Below, p. 274.
[4] *E.H.R.* xvii. 508, 511.
[5] William of Newburgh (Rolls Series), p. 468.

(*d*) On 3rd February, 1206, John wrote to the barons of London, that he understood his city of London was much deteriorated by the faults of those who had hitherto been in power (" qui fuerunt superiores ") in administering justice in the city (" iure civitatis tractando "), in assessing and raising the king's tallages, a large sum collected from the common people not having been yet paid over, and in concealing pur-prestures. Wishing to safeguard his rights and honour and also the utility of the city lest . . . there grew up any dissension among them [1] he ordered them to have elected by their common counsel, in the presence of the archdeacon of Taunton and Reginald de Cornhill,[2] twenty-four of the more lawful, wise, and discreet of their fellow citizens, " who best know how and are willing to consult your (? our) rights and honour and the amendment of your city in administering its laws," etc.[3]

There can be no doubt that this body is the twenty-four whose oath " made in the seventh year of King John " was printed by Round from a totally different source before attention had been drawn to the writ of 3rd February in that year. The oath bound them briefly to enforce the king's rights according to the city custom (" ad consulendum, secundum suam consuetudinem, iuri domini regis "),[4] and much more fully, with special reference to possible evasions, not to accept gifts or promises of gifts in their administration of justice, on pain of disfranchisement of any offender and exclusion from the company (*societas*) of the twenty-four.[5]

As only the oath, and not the writ for election, was known when the interpretation of the communal oath of 1193 was discussed, Round found in it confirmation of his identification of the " scabini et alii probi homines " of that document with the twenty-four *jurés* of Rouen, while Miss Bateson regarded the twenty-four of 1206 as simply the aldermen. The writ does not seem to support either inference from the oath. Round was clearly wrong in assuming the existence of an elected council of twenty-four throughout the period 1193–

---

[1] Disturbances arising out of the assessment and collection of a tallage came before an eyre at the Tower in this year (Page, *London*, p. 120).

[2] The justices who held the eyre mentioned in the previous note.

[3] *Rotuli Litterarum Clausarum*, i. 64*a*.

[4] Mr. Page translates : " administration of the law of the king according to the custom of London." But this is inadmissible, if only that there was no such thing as *lex regis*.

[5] Round, *Commune of London*, p. 237.

1206, and the number of the body specially elected in the latter year cannot fairly be used to fill up the vaguer description of the former. There is no hint in 1206 of that distinction between *scabini* and *consultores* on which the affiliation to Rouen rests nor indeed of any distinction at all. On the other hand, the writ seems fatal to Miss Bateson's view. It is not certain that the aldermen in general were elected at this date—one of them, the alderman of Portsoken, assuredly was not—and if they were, it would not be " by the common counsel of the city." Indeed, Miss Bateson virtually admitted that evidence of election of the twenty-four would rebut her contention. Moreover, it was apparently the misgovernment of the aldermen which led to the appointment of this body.[1]

It has, in fact, been suggested that it was not a council at all, but merely a commission of inquiry and reform, purely temporary and *ad hoc*, and for such an interpretation of the writ and oath something may be said. Of inquiry we hear nothing, but much of reform. It was not a consultative council to act with the mayor like the twenty-five of 1200–01. The mayor is never mentioned and Round and Miss Bateson were mistaken in reading " counsel " [2] into the phrase " consulere iuri domini regis " of the oath, which must be interpreted in the light of the " iuri et honori nostro [3] providere " of the writ. Still the texts leave a distinct impression that the *superiores* were superseded in favour of the twenty-four, whose oath shows them sitting in judgement, not merely correcting unjust decisions. They were, we may believe, entrusted with the government of the city for the time being. They certainly were not permanent ; so that it is almost needless to point out that the method of their election would in any case have discountenanced Round's suggestion [4] that in them we have the germ of the later common council ; which, originating in selection by the mayor, was elected by wards.

[1] Of this Miss Bateson was of course unaware, but with this further information Mr. Page still adheres to her view. He assumes that aldermen (including deputies of the prior of Holy Trinity for Portsoken ward) were elected at this date and regards the writ of 3 February, 1206, as an order for the election of a new set of these officers, the wardmotes (by which the aldermen were afterwards elected) being perhaps called before the two justices or representatives of the justices meeting the wardmotes (*London*, pp. 227-8). This is very strained and does not explain why old-established officers should be described as the twenty-four.

[2] " Twenty-four councillors " (*Commune of London*, p. 238) ; " twenty-four councillors in judgement " (*E.H.R.* xvii. 508).

[3] Assuming this obvious emendation of the MS. vestro.

[4] *Commune of London*, p. 241.

T

They may be more correctly viewed as an anticipation by the Crown of the frequent interference in the government of the city by the appointment of *custodes* in the following reigns, though in this case the citizens are merely required to amend the defaults of their rulers by elected representatives.

Summing up the evidence for the whole period of the quarter of a century following the concession of the commune in 1191, it is hardly possible to say more than that it seems insufficient to justify a decision between the rival interpretations of the " scivini et alii probi homines " of 1193, except in so far as the government of the city immediately after appears to have been in the hands of the mayor and aldermen.[1] Their rule provoked a popular resentment, which led to the election of the twenty-four in 1206, and one would suppose, though here we know nothing of the circumstances, to the election of the twenty-five five years earlier. These, however, were only temporary set-backs, and by the beginning of the next reign the aldermen were firmly established as the council with whose aid the mayor administered the affairs of the city.

2. *Ipswich.* That a governing body whose number was fixed could be instituted without a mayor or any other formal borrowing from foreign communes appears from what happened at Ipswich in 1200. A singular chance has preserved for us in its case a unique description of the re-organization of a borough which had received a royal grant of fee farm with permission to elect its two bailiffs, hitherto Crown nominees, and also the newly created four coroners who were to watch over the rights of the Crown in the borough.[2]

Although not expressly authorized by King John's charter, the central feature of the new organization, which was very deliberately brought into being during the summer months of 1200, was the election of " twelve Chief Portmen sworn (*Capitales Portmenni iurati*) as there are in other free boroughs in England." [3] It was they who, for themselves and the town, were " to govern and maintain the borough, to render its judgements and to ordain and execute all things which behove to be done for its status and honour." They were no mere council of assistants to the chief officers of the community but a governing body, in which were included not only the

---

[1] As would appear from the story of FitzOsbert's rising. It would be rash to suggest that Richard's return in 1194 brought about a reactionary change in the government of the city. On the contrary. See above, p. 182.

[2] Gross, *Gild Merchant*, ii. 116 ff.

[3] Sicut in aliis liberis burgis Anglie sunt, *ibid.*, p. 117.

bailiffs but all the other principal officers of the town. Apart from their membership of this body the bailiffs had only one defined duty, that of keeping the provostship (*preposituram*) of the borough,[1] *i.e.*, of seeing that the farm of the town was duly paid, though it appears incidentally that they presided in the borough court and had administrative duties not directly relating to the payment of the farm.[2]

Despite the fact that the new constitution, in accordance with the charter, recognized the ultimate sovereignty of the community, all officers (portmen included) being elected and all ordinances drawn up by them submitted to the whole town for approval, it was actually a close form of government that was set up. As the eleven chief offices of town and gild were concentrated in the hands of eight of the twelve portmen, there does not seem to have been much freedom of election, and in the case of the portmen direct election was avoided, the bailiffs and coroners " with the assent of the town " choosing four good and lawful men from each parish as electors who were sworn to elect the twelve " from the better, more discreet, and more influential (*potencioribus*) of the town." Nothing is said of annual renewal, and as a matter of fact, though these elections took place in June and July, only the bailiffs, who by charter were removable, were re-elected in September for the new municipal year.[3]

---

[1] *Gild Merchant*, ii. 116.   [2] *Ibid.*, pp. 119, 121.

[3] This remarkable account, of which the briefest summary is here given, is only preserved in an early fourteenth-century transcript in the " Little Domesday " of Ipswich. There seems no reason to suspect serious tampering with the original, but anachronistic interpolations are always possible in medieval copies. Such in the opinion of the Rev. William Hudson is the assertion that councils of twelve were common in free boroughs in 1200 (*Records of Norwich*, I, xxiii.). That there were not twelve " portmen " in other boroughs, as the passage taken literally implies, needs no demonstration. The only other borough which ever had such portmen is Orford, in imitation, no doubt, of Ipswich. It is, assuredly, incredible that *all* free boroughs had a sworn council under any name at the end of the twelfth century, in view of the very special circumstances in which one was set up at Ipswich. If the statement is not a later interpolation, " alii " must be used in the sense of " some other." In the charter the liberties are those of " ceteri burgenses liberorum burgorum nostrorum Anglie," though not all shared by every borough (*cf.* p. 217). It is possible that the title *Capitales Portmenni* has been interpolated. It has a later ring (cf. *Capitales Burgenses* in many boroughs). In the borough custumal drawn up in 1291 we hear only of " twelve jurez " and in a document of 1309 they are spoken of as the " twelve jurates " (*Hist. MSS. Comm., Rept. IX*, pt. i., App., p. 242). The first occurrence of the title portmen in any document quoted by the Historical Manuscripts Commissioners is in 1325 (*ibid.*, p. 246). That the suggestion of these interpolations is not unjustifiable is shown by the description of Roger le Bigot in the copy of an accessory document (Gross, *op. cit.*, p. 124) as Marshal of England, a title which only came to his grandson fifty years later.

Four other towns, Shrewsbury, Lincoln, Gloucester, and Northampton, obtained charters essentially identical with that of Ipswich in this first year of John's reign,[1] a promise, not destined to be fulfilled, of a standard type of borough charter. Unluckily, none of the four has left a record of the steps taken on receipt of its charter to compare with the procedure at Ipswich. Before the end of the reign two of them, Lincoln and Northampton, made a further advance and took unto themselves mayors after the London fashion.[2] There is some reason to think that we have a definite record of the first institution of a mayor and a council to act with him in the second of these towns.

3. *Northampton.* On 17th February, 1215, the king informed his *probi homines* there that he had accepted (*recepimus*) William Thilly as mayor, and therefore ordered them to be intendent to him as their mayor and to elect twelve of the more discreet and better of their town to dispatch with him their affairs in their town (" ad expedienda simul cum eo negocia vestra in villa vestra ").[3]

The early date and unquestionable authenticity of this enrolment, unknown hitherto to the historians of Northampton,[4] make it, despite its brevity, perhaps the most valuable piece of information we have on the creation of town councils in this country. The king's acceptance of the mayor need not in itself imply that Thilly was the first mayor of Northampton, but the instruction to elect a council to assist him makes it almost certain that he was.[5]

Notifications of the acceptance of mayors and mandates of intendence can be paralleled from the next reign,[6] but the second part of the mandate is so very exceptional as to seem to need some special explanation. Perhaps this may be found in the fact that it was issued from Silverstone, fourteen miles south-west of Northampton, which John reached two days later. He was then seeking support everywhere against the barons who were demanding his confirmation of the charter of Henry I. His writ may be compared, from this point of

---

[1] *B.B.C.* i. 244-5, and for Northampton, *cf.* Markham, *Records of Northampton,* i. 30-1.

[2] *Infra,* p. 198.   [3] *Rotuli Litterarum Clausarum,* i. 188a.

[4] I must share the credit of calling attention to it with Miss Cam who independently noted it in preparing a history of the borough for the Victoria County Histories.

[5] Three days later a writ was addressed to " the mayor and reeves of Northampton " (*Rot. Litt. Pat.,* p. 129).

[6] *Patent Rolls,* Henry III, vols. i. and ii.

view, with his more formal recognition of the London mayoralty some eleven weeks later (9th May).

The duties of the twelve elected *discretiores* of Northampton are described in general terms, but with sufficient clearness to indicate a marked divergence from the Ipswich type of governing body. They are to transact the business of the town along with the mayor, and though the relation may have been one of equality at first, it is easy to understand how such a body of well-to-do burgesses developed later into a close " mayor's council." The Ipswich *jurés*, on the contrary, were elected to govern the town without any reference to the bailiffs, though these were members of their body. They would not, one would think, have developed naturally into the later " bailiffs' council " found in towns which had not mayors. Indeed, as described, they are not colleagues or assistants of any magistrate but a committee of the community, two-thirds of whom were officials, invested with wide powers of administration. We must suppose that this was a solution of the problem of urban government which was found unsatisfactory or at any rate not generally adopted. Which of these contrasting types of administration, if either, the burgesses of Northampton had set up when they received their charter in 1200, it would be idle to speculate. So far as the wording of the writ of 1215 goes, they might never have had a governing body at all until then, but we must not strain so concise a document. The Northampton council of twelve was afterwards doubled, perhaps within half a century. It is not until 1358 that there is definite mention of " the Mayor's 24 co-burgesses," [1] but two lists of twenty-four burgesses in the third quarter of the thirteenth century may represent the enlarged council. (1) The second custumal (*c.* 1260) is headed: " Consideraciones facte per xxiiii iuratos Norhampton' scilicet Robertum Speciarium maiorem, Robertum filium Ricardi [twenty-two other names]." [2] This suggests an official body rather than a jury of inquiry. (2) A writ of 2nd June, 1264, addressed in the name of the captive king to twenty-four named burgesses headed by Thomas Keynne, but not describing him as mayor.[3] If both lists represent the council it is strange

---

[1] Bridges, *Northants*, i. 364. I owe this reference and the suggestion of the early date of the doubling to Miss Cam.

[2] Bateson, *Borough Customs*, I, xlii. Contrast the heading of the first custumal (*c.* 1190) with its forty names, probably representing an assembly of the community.

[3] *Foedera* (Rec. ed.), i. 441.

that, with three exceptions, the whole membership should have been changed within four or five years.

The Northampton writ of 1215 serves as a warning not to assume that the twenty-four afterwards recorded in many boroughs was necessarily the original number of councillors.

4. *Leicester.* Leicester is the only mediatized borough in our list, and it has the further peculiarity that its council seems to have originated in the merchant gild which had grasped administrative control of the town. In its archives is a list, conjectured to belong to 1225, of those elected by the common counsel of the gild " to come at every summons of the alderman (of the gild) to give counsel to the town and to assist the alderman in the business of the town to the best of their power, . . . penalty (for neglect) 6*d*." [1] There are twenty-four names, in which the alderman's is included, but a new list incorporating just over half of these names contains twenty-five, the alderman making the twenty-fifth.[2] In 1264 a body described as the twenty-four *jurés* (*jurati, juratores*) of Leicester first appears in the records, sentencing a thief, *coram communitate*, to lose an ear.[3] Nine years later a list of these *jurés*, " elected by the community," is preserved in close association with one of a twenty-four chosen by the gild to maintain its laws and liberties.[4] The personnel of the two bodies was largely identical, completely according to Miss Bateson, but the evidence in her note only shows that they had two-thirds of their members in common. There is no mention of the gild body (which does not appear again) being bound by an oath. Though the primary duty of the *jurés* was to render judgements in the portmanmote, they are soon found transacting administrative business, constituting, with the mayor and bailiffs, the governing body of the town. The office of alderman of the gild and head of the community had been converted into a mayoralty in or shortly before 1250,[5] and the analogy of similar bodies elsewhere would suggest that as a sworn council, elected by the community, the twenty-four *jurés* came into existence at the same time. Even if the ancient doomsmen of the city court had been

---

[1] " Ad veniendum ad omnes summoniciones Aldermanni ad consulendam villam, et ad eum sequendum in negociis ville pro posse suo . . . sub pena de vid " (Bateson, *Records of Leicester*, i. 34).

[2] *Ibid.*, p. 35.   [3] *Ibid.*, p. 104.

[4] *Ibid.*, pp. 111-12 and note.

[5] *Ibid.*, p. 64. In my original article (p. 185) by an unfortunate mistake, I placed this change in 1257.

limited in number to twenty-four, they would not have been bound by oath or elected by the community.[1] The oath of the *juré*, while first of all binding him to render justice indifferently to rich and poor, required him also to maintain loyally the assize of bread and ale *with his mayor* and to keep the franchises and good customs of the town to the best of his power.[2]

5. *Dublin.* The citizens of Dublin seem to have instituted a council of twenty-four on receiving, in 1229, a grant of the right to elect a mayor from their own number. The charter was a copy *mutatis mutandis* of that granted to London in 1215,[3] and the number of councillors may have been imitated from that of the London aldermen. In the French custumal, which was apparently drawn up at this time, the amercement for striking one of the twenty-four was fixed at £10, one-fourth of the penalty for striking the mayor.[4] But in addition to the twenty-four, Dublin had two wider bodies of a sort unknown in England and only to be explained by the peculiar conditions of Ireland. At the end of the custumal there is a statement that :

" The citizens who have bought the franchises of the city . . . have established . . . that the above franchises shall be guarded . . . against all . . . that is to say that there shall be twenty-four *jurés* to guard the city, besides the mayor and bailiffs, and the twenty-four are to elect of young people (*ioesne gentz*) forty-eight and the forty-eight are to elect ninety-six. And these ninety-six shall guard the city from evil (*mal*) and damage." [5]

It was part of the duties of the twenty-four to look after the manners of the " young people." They took the forty-eight by relays to *festes* " pur eus sure et curtesie aprendre." When a tallage had to be raised, each of these bodies in turn assessed

---

[1] The story of the origin of gavelpence, given by a jury in 1253 (Bateson, *Records*, i. 40 ff.), carries back the twenty-four *jures* as doomsmen to the first quarter of the twelfth century, but is not a good authority.

[2] *Ibid*. ii. 33.

[3] Except that it was definitely a grant in perpetuity (*B.B.C.* ii. 361).

[4] Gilbert, *Historical and Municipal Documents of Ireland* (Rolls Series), p. 244.

[5] *Ibid.*, p. 266. The same triple arrangement was adopted at Waterford soon after 1300, but the numbers here were twelve, twelve, and six, and it was the thirty thus made up who were to guard the city against damage (Bateson, *Borough Customs*, I., liv). It may be mentioned here that the community of Kilkenny in 1230 regulated the election of sovereign, provosts, and *councillors* (*Hist. MSS. Comm., Rept. I*, Appendix, p. 130a).

its own members and then together assessed the community (*communalte*). The common seal was in the keeping of the mayor, bailiffs, and twenty-four, but they could not enfeoff any man or woman with land or tenement without the assent of the whole community of the city.[1]

It is just possible that the twelve citizens of Dublin who in 1222 or 1224 had, on behalf of the *universitas* of the city, lent over £300 to the justiciar of Ireland to be used against the rebellious Hugh de Lacy, and who in 1229 were to be reimbursed by the citizens, whose resulting claim upon the Crown was set off against the cost of the new charter,[2] represent an earlier council. Dublin had been granted in fee farm to its citizens by King John in 1215,[3] and its governing body may date, as at Ipswich, from that change in its status.

6. *Berwick*. The constitution of this border town was strongly affected by its proximity to England, long before its annexation to the southern kingdom. It already had a mayor, unlike other Scottish boroughs, when in 1249 an ordinance of the town prescribed that its common affairs should be administered by twenty-four good men of the better and more discreet and trustworthy of the borough elected for this purpose along with the mayor and four reeves.[4] Possibly, as in the case of other *statuta* passed at the same time, the ordinance merely confirmed unwritten practice.

7. *Oxford*. From a petition of the " lesser commune " of the town to the king against their treatment by the *maiores burgenses*, which is endorsed with the date 1257 in a hand of Edward II's time, we learn that Oxford was governed by a mayor and fifteen *iurati*. Together they passed ordinances and levied tallages. The jurats are spoken of, without the mayor, as judges of the town court, and are said to have chosen the two bailiffs, who were responsible for the royal farm, yearly from among themselves.[5] Allowing for *ex parte* colouring, all this, except for their number, is normal enough, but the presence of the university introduced a disturbing

---

[1] Gilbert, *Historical and Municipal Documents of Ireland* (Rolls Series), p. 267.   [2] *Ibid.*, pp. 92-3.   [3] *B.B.C.*, p. 231.
[4] " Statuimus insuper per commune consilium quod communia de Berwico gubernentur per xxiiii probos homines de melioribus et discretioribus ac fidedignioribus eiusdem Burgi ad hoc electos una cum maiori et quatuor prepositis " (Gross, *Gild Merchant*, i. 236). The mayor of this year had been mayor in 1238 (John Scott, *Hist. of Berwick* (1888), p. 478).
[5] *Cal. Inq. Misc.* i, no. 238. The endorsement is : " inquisitiones et extente de anno, etc.," and as the document is neither of these, the date may possibly be that of an inquest and not of the petition.

complication. At its instance and in its interest, a royal writ of 1255 ordered that there should be four aldermen (instead of two) and that eight of the more discreet and lawful burgesses should be associated with them, all of whom should swear fidelity to the king and give assistance and counsel (" sint assistentes et consulentes) to the mayor and bailiffs in preserving the king's peace, in keeping the assizes of the town (sale of bread and ale), and in detecting malefactors and disturbers of the peace and night-walkers and receivers of robbers and malefactors, and should take their corporal oath to observe all the premises faithfully.[1] Owing to a gap of nearly two centuries in our information as to the municipal constitution, it seems impossible to decide whether this body imposed from above, superseded the fifteen jurats or merely took over the delicate relations between town and gown, leaving the fifteen to deal with matters which concerned the burgesses alone. When the extant municipal records begin in the second half of the fifteenth century, there is no trace of either, the " mayor's council " consisting of thirty-five persons.[2]

8. *Cambridge.* In the case of the sister university there is the same difficulty. An order was sent in 1268 [3] identical with that to Oxford thirteen years before, except that the new body was to be only half as large, two aldermen and four burgesses. Here there is no record of a previous council, though there was a mayor as early as 1235. The history of the body set up in 1268 is, however, better known. In 1344 provision was made for their election with other officers,[4] and they still appear in the middle of the sixteenth century. The stringent oaths administered to them by the university [5] were resented, and in 1546 the two aldermen and four burgesses (called councillors in 1344) refused to take them ; this, on the complaint of the vice-chancellor of the university, brought down upon the townsmen a severe royal rebuke, whereupon, though " with some stomache " the required oath was taken.[6] Between 1344 and 1546, however, the town had added some seven aldermen to the original two, and the four councillors were perhaps included in the common council of twenty-four

---

[1] *B.B.C.* ii. 367-8.
[2] Salter, *Munimenta Civitatis Oxonie* (Oxf. Hist. Soc.), p. 232. The same number in 1519 (W. H. Turner, *Records of Oxford, 1509–83*, p. 22).
[3] *B.B.C.* loc. cit. ; Cooper, *Annals of Cambridge*, i. 50-1.
[4] *Ibid.*, p. 96.   [5] In what was known as the " Black Assembly."
[6] Cooper, *op. cit.* i. 441-2 ; ii. 65.

set up in 1376.[1] Thus a double council of the normal type was evolved and the assimilation was completed when in 1566 it was decided to have twelve aldermen at the least.[2]

9. *Yarmouth (Great)*. The first known council at Yarmouth, as at Cambridge, was called into existence mainly to cope with local disorder, but here it was the doing of the burgesses themselves. In 1272 the bailiffs and community obtained a royal *inspeximus* of certain ordinances which they had made with this object, for the execution of which and to support their bailiffs they had provided twenty-four good men (*prodes hommes*) of the town elected and sworn, who in case of negligence were to forfeit forty marks to the king.[3]

This might seem to be a temporary measure *ad hoc*, but, as a matter of fact, it was the institution of the council with which the bailiffs henceforth governed the borough. The town still possesses letters of appointment by the burgesses and community under their common seal in the tenth year of Richard II, appointing twenty-four persons to do all things in accordance with Henry III's charter.[4] It is surprising that Yarmouth, which had had a grant of its fee farm and the right to elect its bailiffs from King John eight years after Ipswich,[5] should have gone so long without a council. Were its burgesses so much more democratic than those of Ipswich, or was an earlier council replaced in 1272 by one bound by more stringent oaths and penalties ?

10. *Winchester*. The French custumal of Winchester, which its editor dates about 1275, records the existence in the city of twenty-four sworn persons elected from the most trustworthy and wise of the town loyally to aid and counsel the mayor in saving and sustaining the franchise.[6] They were to attend on proper summons from the mayor, and if absent without reasonable excuse forfeited a bezant (2s.).[7]

---

[1] See below, p. 335.

[2] Cooper, *Annals of Cambridge*, ii. 226. For earlier numbers see *ibid.*, pp. 59, 105, 108.

[3] *B.B.C.*, p. 368 : " Et pur aforcer nos bailifs et ces avaunt-dites choses susteiner et parfurmer, si avum nus purvou vint et quatre prodes hommes de la vile et a ceo eluz et juriz, etc."

[4] *Hist. MSS. Comm.*, *Rept. IX*, part i, Appendix, p. 305a.

[5] *B.B.C.* i. 230, 244.

[6] " En la cite deiuent estre vint e quatre iurez esluz des plus prudeshomes e des plus sages de la vile e (*sic*) leaument eider et conseiller le avandit mere a la franchise sauuer e sustener " (J. S. Furley, *The Ancient Usages of the City of Winchester*, pp. 26-7).

[7] *Ibid.* The same amercement at Berwick. None of the twenty-four was to maintain a party in court or appear as an advocate in prejudice of the liberty of the city.

As the city had had a mayor since 1200 at least, the council of twenty-four may go back to the beginning of the century, but unfortunately there is no record of it during the interval. Its participation with the community in the election of the mayor, and with the mayor in the selection of the four *prodes hommes* from whom the community elected the bailiffs, does not look a very early feature.

11. *Exeter.* The rolls of the Exeter city court, which are fragmentary until 1286, contain lists under 1264 and 1267 which may represent an elected council of twenty-four, divided in one case between *maiores* and *mediocres*,[1] but it is not until 1296 that there occurs notice of the election of twenty-four, by consent of the whole community of the city, to rule the city with the mayor for the year, to guard its franchises in every particular, to observe properly its ordinances (*statuta*), to advise the mayor wisely and loyally, to keep his good counsel, to come at his summonses, to maintain the king's peace, showing no favour to disturbers thereof, and to do common justice to all.[2] To all of which they were sworn. The enumeration of their duties, which is unusually full, marks them as full colleagues of the mayor in the general administration of the city and lays no particular stress on their judicial function.

12. *Southampton.* At Southampton about 1300 it was the custom for the community every year on the morrow of Michaelmas Day to elect twelve *prodes hommes* to ensure the execution of the king's commands along with the bailiffs—there was no mayor—to maintain the peace and protect the franchise, and to do and keep justice to all persons, rich and poor, denizens and strangers, all that year.[3] Their oath bound them *inter alia* to be aid and counsel (" eidaunt et consaillaunt ") to the bailiffs in executing the king's commands, etc., to be present at every court, and to attend on every summons of the bailiffs to hear the king's command or to render judgement in court.[4]

13. *Lincoln.* Certain provisions made by the mayor and community for the government of the city, probably about the same date, order that the community with the advice of the mayor shall choose twelve fit and discreet men to be judges

[1] B. Wilkinson, *The Mediæval Council of Exeter* (1931), xxvii. ff. ; 1 ff., 64 ff.   [2] *Ibid.*
[3] *Oak Book of Southampton* (Southampton Record Society), i. 44.
[4] *Ibid.*, 52.

of the city.[1] The mention of judicial functions only is a
difficulty in the way of taking this body as an early council
and identifying it with the twelve aldermen, who, owing to
the loss of most of the city's medieval archives, are not on
record until 1511. The object of this provision, however, as f
that relating to the mayor, which immediately precedes it,
was not apparently to define the duties of the office, but to
settle a question of financial privilege. The mayor was
allowed exemption from all public taxes and dues during his
year of office, but the twelve were denied this privilege. It
is not then perhaps necessary to assume that they were purely
judicial officers, though their title would imply a greater
prominence of that aspect than in the case of the other early
councils we have been considering.

2.

Making allowance for varied and mostly meagre sources,
a certain diversity is observable in these early councils, which
agrees well enough with their generally local origin. As to
numbers, six of the thirteen (I exclude the doubtful early phase
at London)[2] had twelve or (in one case) six members and the
rest twenty-four. This bare majority was increased, apparently before the end of the century, by the doubling of the
Northampton council ; on the other hand, some or all of the
other cases of a body of twenty-four, except that of London,
due to the accident of the number of wards, may represent
unrecorded doublings. And while the Berwick town council
numbered twenty-four, its merchant gild had twelve *feeringmen*,
a name of ancient sound. Excluding exceptional London,
our earliest cases are the Ipswich and Northampton twelves,
and the influence of the London precedent on some communities
which adopted the larger number must not be left altogether
out of account. At the same time it has to be allowed that
both numbers were used for temporary local purposes before
the era of town councils and that, in the greatest towns especially, there were some practical advantages in the larger one,
which may help to account for such doubling as took place

---

[1] The original Latin text of these " Provisions " has disappeared from
the archives since 1870, but an eighteenth-century translation is printed
in *Lincolnshire Notes and Queries*, xx. 25 ff. My attention was called to
it by Mr. F. W. Brooks.
[2] Also the unique early fifteen at Oxford.

at Northampton and later Shrewsbury. For one thing, the problem of non-attendance, which the penalties for absence show to have been serious, must have been much eased.

Other towns which appear after 1300 and before 1500 with councils of twelve are : Axbridge (13), Beverley, Canterbury, Carlisle, Exeter,[1] Gloucester, Godmanchester (town on ancient demesne), Nottingham, Pevensey, Plymouth, Portsmouth, Preston, Shrewsbury, Wycombe (?), and York, to which there must be added the Cinque Ports with their twelve jurats in each town. Other boroughs on record with councils of twenty-four are Barnstaple, Bridgenorth, Chester, Colchester, Lynn [Regis], Newcastle-under-Lyme, Newcastle-upon-Tyne, Norwich, Salisbury, Wells, and Worcester. As boroughs were mostly small, the greater prevalence of the council of twelve is not surprising.[2] Its persistence in some larger towns such as Lincoln and York (generally under the later name of aldermen) may be in part accounted for by the addition from the latter part of the fourteenth century onwards of larger common councils, double or even four times its number, nominally representing the community at large,[3] which the original twelves and twenty-fours had ceased to do, but belonging to the same class and readily coalescing with them in close corporations.

That the early municipal councils were elected by the communities of their towns, and were therefore supposed to represent them, is stated or implied in most of the cases we have discussed and is probable in the rest. It does not follow that election was always annual. Nothing definite is reported of the method of election, except at Ipswich where the direct participation of the citizens at large was confined to a public assent to the nomination of electors from each parish by the bailiffs and coroners, who were, however, themselves directly elected.[4] But Ipswich was exceptional in other respects,

---

[1] From 1345.

[2] Instances of the doubling of the twelve in some growing towns have been given above.

[3] At Newcastle-under-Lyme this object was attained in the fifteenth century without increasing the total number by adding twelve for the community to twelve representing the older twenty-four (T. Pape, *Medieval Newcastle-under-Lyme* (1928), pp. 135, 176).

[4] In 1309 the electors are said to have been appointed by the community (*Hist. MSS. Comm., Rept. IX*, part 1, App., p. 242a), but the officials may still have suggested names. This record shows that the power which the jurats had, according to the custumal of 1291 (*Black Book of Admiralty* (Rolls Ser.) ii. 167), to fill vacancies in their body caused by death or misconduct, does not justify my rash inference in 1929 that by that date they

and the practice of Southampton at the end of the thirteenth century, where the twelve were elected by the community at Michaelmas, at the same time as the town clerk,[1] is more likely to have been typical. It is not to be supposed that, in quiet times at any rate, this meant unfettered popular election. Serious responsibilities, as well as privileges, were incident to the government of a town, and these devolved inevitably upon the small body of more substantial burgesses, the *divites* or *maiores burgenses*.[2] With the increasing prosperity and political unrest of the second half of the thirteenth century, it is true, strong opposition was encountered in the more advanced towns from the *mediocres* and *minores*, but it was mainly directed against differential taxation and other abuses of their monopoly of power.[3] Attempts to use their electoral power to secure friendly officers were regarded as revolutionary.[4]

Except at Ipswich in 1200, at London in 1206 and at Lincoln *c.* 1300, the association of the *jurés* or *prodes hommes* with the mayor or other chief officer(s) of the borough is more or less strongly insisted upon, the phrase " aiding and counselling " several times occurs and, as is well known, such a body is often later referred to as a mayor's (or bailiffs') council. At Winchester the sole duty ascribed to the twenty-four in the clause of the custumal defining their function is this aid and counsel to the mayor.[5] " In this," says the latest historian of the city, " there is no idea of administrative or legislative powers . . . they are purely an advisory body . . . their relation to the mayor is a personal one—they are his advisers and supporters and the relation is expressed by calling them his ' peers '." [6] Winchester, however, at the end of the thirteenth century was comparatively advanced in municipal constitution, the twenty-four being less an emanation of the community than " an estate of equal importance in some matters) with the Commonalty." [7] The

held office for life. It was evidently only a provision to keep their number full during their term of office.

Systems of double election similar to that of Ipswich are found at Exeter, Lynn, Cambridge, and probably elsewhere.

[1] *Oak Book of Southampton* (Southampton Record Soc.), i. 44.

[2] A list of those of Oxford in 1257 contains only thirty-two names (*Cal. Inq. Misc.* i., no. 238).

[3] E. F. Jacob, *Studies in the Period of Baronial Reform and Rebellion, 1258–67*, pp. 134 ff.

[4] *Liber de Antiquis Legibus* (Camden Soc.), pp. 55, 58, 80.

[5] Above, p. 278.

[6] J. S. Furley, *City Government of Winchester*, p. 67.

[7] *Ibid.*, p. 68.

description of some of the earlier select bodies suggests co-operation with the chief officer on behalf of the community rather than a merely advisory function. At London in 1200–01 and at Leicester in 1225 it is the town and not the mayor or alderman that they are to advise. John instructs the burgesses of Northampton to elect twelve of the more discreet to transact their town's business along with the mayor, not merely to give him counsel. The twenty-four of Exeter in 1296 were to rule the city along with the mayor. At Berwick they were elected to conduct its common affairs (" communia . . . gubernentur ") " along with the mayor and reeves." These cases seem almost to bridge over the gap to Ipswich whose twelve *jurés* were to govern and maintain the borough in their own right,[1] though the bailiffs were members of their body. It may be added that the aldermen of London, though they became so closely associated with the mayor, were not created as his assistants.

The twenty-four at Great Yarmouth were a new creation, and it was part of their duty to support the bailiffs, but they were elected by the community, to whom the fines for non-attendance went,[2] and forfeited a large sum to the king, if they were negligent. Their functions were primarily concerned with the maintenance of the peace, and this reminds us that, whatever may be the case with administration and legislation, some of the bodies we have been considering had a judicial position which does not appear to have been derived from mayor or bailiffs. These officers presided over the borough courts, but the aldermen of London were the ancient judges of the Husting, and at Ipswich, Leicester, and Southampton, and more generally at Exeter, the councillor's duty of " rendering judgements " is laid down without any reference to the chief magistrates. The twelve of Lincoln, whose relation to the mayor is not indicated, were called judges. This, however, raises the question of origins, which will be dealt with later.

---

[1] Dr. Stephenson says that the jurats of those of the Cinque Ports which had not mayors formed similar " governing boards " (*Borough and Town*, p. 178). But where is the evidence that the bailiff was ever a jurat during his term of office ? *Cf.* Bateson, *B.C.*, i. 146, ii. 39 ; Statham, *Dover Charters*, p. 60.

[2] It is noteworthy that they were not necessarily summoned by the bailiffs. They might themselves appoint some one to summon them (*B.B.C.* ii. 368). The bailiffs are not always mentioned with them when the " justicing " of misdoers is in question (*ibid.*). They are called " le prodes hommes de la vile " or " le jurez " (*ibid.*, p. 234, 368).

Only very tentative conclusions can be drawn from the imperfect evidence which has survived. In the communal age an elected chief magistrate, whether new mayor or old bailiff, seems sooner or later to have been associated with an elected body of twelve or twenty-four. Both represented the community, and the earliest conception of their relation seems to have been rather one of co-operation than of subordination. Perhaps, even less consciously, they may have been regarded as checks upon each other. At Ipswich the influence of the *potentiores* would appear actually to have subordinated the chief magistrates to the portmen. This was, no doubt, possible with bailiffs who had long ruled as royal nominees and had still a divided duty to king and town. It could not have happened with a mayor, a new officer created by the town itself [1] to express its new unity and independence and free from all financial entanglement with the Crown. Typifying the new municipal régime before the world and made the mouthpiece of royal commands, the mayor naturally and inevitably acquired a dominance over the twelve or the twenty-four which was perhaps not originally intended. The strong class consciousness of his colleagues and the weak organization of the community fostered the growth of an oligarchical system of government in which the council's representation of the community was lost sight of and the narrower conception of a close body " aiding and counselling the mayor " came into existence. At Winchester as early as 1275 the twenty-four had become an estate in the civic constitution, sharing with the community the election of the mayor, dividing with it the nomination of certain minor officers and (with the mayor) naming the four from whom the community chose the two bailiffs. At Southampton, where the chief officer in the thirteenth century was the alderman of the gild merchant, the twelve elected the bailiffs, the clerk, and the serjeants.[2] They were themselves, however, elected by the community, whereas it is unlikely that the Winchester council was still elected by the borough moot.

[1] This is an inference from the absence of any charter by John, except his *ex post facto* one to London (1215), and the fact that the bishop of Norwich's burgesses at Lynn were afterwards accused of having set up a mayor without his consent (*B.B.C.* ii. 362-3). It is perhaps doubtful whether royal burgesses went so far without some permission less formal than a charter. By 1205 at any rate the existing mayors were officials recognized by the Crown. (Above, p. 254; *Rot. Litt. Claus.* i. 2a.)

[2] *Oak Book*, i. 44.

The development, indeed, proceeded at varying rates in the very diverse borough communities of these times. There is direct evidence from the *Red Register of Lynn*,[1] in the first quarter of the next century, of a council elected by the community " to consult with the mayor (' ad consulendum cum maiore ') when necessary," having been chosen *pro communitate*, and of the mayor refusing to give an important decision in the absence of his " consules." [2]   At Norwich, too, a mayorless city at that date, we have a record of the election in 1345 of twenty-four from the city " pro communitate et [? ad] negotia eiusdem ordinand' et custodiend' per idem tempus," without the concurrence of the whole of whom, it is said, the bailiffs, down to 1380, could not transact any important business.[3]

It is evident that, even in the fourteenth century, the mayor or bailiffs were not always at liberty to take just as much or as little advice from the council as they pleased. At Lynn and Norwich, however, the development of the original town council into a close body may have been slower than was generally the case, for the end of the second quarter of the fourteenth century saw the beginning of the movement which in so many boroughs added a second council to represent the community at large.[4]

Of the theories or suggestions that have been advanced to explain the origin of the first councils, that which regards them as for the most part a purely native growth is the only one that has been argued at any length. Its appearance in the *History of English Law* has given it wide publicity and up to the present time it may be said to hold the field. A critical examination of the problem as a whole may therefore properly begin by inquiring whether this view is tenable.

3

The suggestion that London had a municipal council of twelve members more than a century before the first-known creation of such a body may, I think, be dismissed as insufficiently supported and otherwise improbable, though it

---

[1] Ed. H. Ingleby, i. 64, 73 ; *cf.* ii. 169.

[2] They are said to have been " iurati ad villam hoc anno custodiendam." The date was February, 1324. The council of twelve at Beverley were known as *custodes*.

[3] W. Hudson, *Records of Norwich*, i. 64, 79, 262.

[4] See below, ch. xi. The germ of such a common council appeared, of course, much earlier in London.

U

comes from Liebermann and Miss Bateson. Still less can we accept the authority of the Ipswich Domesday for an apparent assertion that by 1200 all free boroughs possessed councils of this kind.[1] It occurs, indeed, in a copy of a contemporary document, and was therefore accepted by Liebermann,[2] but it is either an ambiguous statement or a later interpolation. We may, indeed, admit, with Miss Bateson, that in the complete absence of any other evidence " there has been a tendency to underrate somewhat unduly the amount of municipal unity in the twelfth-century ' shire ' of London before the days of the mayoralty," and perhaps to underestimate the extent of administrative work in other important towns. It is not known what re-organization, if any, took place in London during the short period when the citizens held the fee farm and elected their officers under Henry I's charter, but it is absurd to suppose that his grandson, who sternly repressed " communal " ambitions in the boroughs,[3] allowed the election of bodies so closely associated with the dreaded *commune* of the Continent. Much more probable is the view that the town government, so far as the burgesses had any share in it, and so far as that share had not passed into the hands of their merchant gilds,[4] was still transacted by the *probi homines* of the undifferentiated borough court, though that doubtless in practice meant the wealthy few, the *meliores, discretiores, potentiores,* or *probiores*,[5] as in the case of the aldermen at London, themselves perhaps not yet fixed in number. The close association of councils of defined number and functions, when they first appear in our sources, with the new office of mayor, seems to stamp them as a product of the communal spirit released by the abandonment of Henry II's restrictive policy in the reigns of his sons.

Such a conscious creation of a novel municipal organ as is here suggested is totally opposed to the evolutionary theory of the growth of town councils propounded by Maitland in

---

[1] Above, p. 270. Dr. Stephenson prefers to take *alii liberi burgi* in the restricted sense of " some other free boroughs " (*Borough and Town*, p. 177), and the references to the royal free boroughs in the Ipswich charter lend some support to this. See p. 217 and note 3, p. 271.

[2] *Gesetze der Angelsachsen*, ii. 662.

[3] Above, pp. 162, 176.   [4] See above, pp. 232-3.

[5] *Probi homines* itself came to have this narrower meaning and in the next century was used of the councillors of Southampton and Yarmouth, but in the address of royal writs it was a common equivalent of *barones, cives,* or *burgenses* (*Rotuli Litterarum Clausarum, passim,* and *cf. ibid.* i. 223b, 224 (Droitwich)). See also *C.P.R.* 1266-72, p. 522 (Colchester).

the *History of English Law* (1895, 2nd ed., 1898), and more shortly in an article on "The Origin of the Borough" which appeared in the *English Historical Review* in 1896. Admitting that the known facts did not justify any wide inferences, he formulated in 1895 a theory of conciliar development within the borough court :—

" In the town, as in the realm at large [he wrote], ' court ' and ' council ' are slowly differentiated, the borough court becomes a mere tribunal and by its side a distinctly conciliar organ is developed. This, however, except perhaps in exceptional London and a few other towns, seems to be rather the work of the fourteenth than of the thirteenth century." [1] Little attempt is made to fill in this general outline, and the details suggested do not seem altogether consistent. In the *History* he throws out a suggestion that councils may have been formed " by a practice of summoning to the court only the more discreet and more legal men," a practice, one may comment, which would leave unexplained the fixed numbers of the councils, but in a footnote he speaks of the development of an old body of doomsmen or lawmen into a council as the typical case, and this was the view he stated more prominently in his latest treatment of the problem : " When first we meet with a select group of twelve burgesses which is beginning to be a council, its primary duty still is that of declaring the judgements or ' deeming the dooms ' of the borough." [2] That the borough court was normally the urban equivalent of the rural hundred court, not infrequently retaining its name, and that there is some evidence of a select body of doomsmen in it in some parts of the country at all events,[3] is not disputed. But as Maitland himself emphasized the great variety in the number of doomsmen in rural hundreds and did not adduce more than one clear case where they were

[1] Pollock and Maitland, *History of English Law*, ed. 1898, i. 659.
[2] *E.H.R.* xi. 19.
[3] Judges (*iudices*) of the borough of Buckingham, whose number is not specified, are mentioned in 1130 (*Pipe Roll, 31 Hen. I*, p. 101). One or two citizens of London appear about the same date with the title of *iudex* or doomsman, presumably of the folksmoot (Round, *Ancient Charters* (Pipe Roll Soc., no. 10), p. 27 ; *Hist. MSS. Comm., Rept. IX*, Appendix i, p. 66a). There was an early tradition (*c.* 1250) that the twenty-four *iurati* or *iuratores* of the Leicester portmoot went back to the Norman period (Bateson, *Records of Leicester*, i. 41), which, if credible at all, can hardly be correct in regard to their name. At Chester doomsmen (*iudicatores*) of the portmoot are mentioned as late as 1293 (*Chester County Court Rolls* (Chetham Soc., N.S., 84), p. 181). *Cf.* below, pp. 300-1.

twelve,[1] it seems very unsafe to postulate the general existence of exactly that number in borough courts. Maitland seems to have had in his mind the twelve lawmen of certain midland boroughs and the twelve *iudices* of Chester who are recorded in Domesday Book. It should be remembered, however, that the former at any rate were a Scandinavian institution which apparently did not long survive the Norman Conquest, while Chester was within the area of Scandinavian influence.[2] Liebermann was inclined to reject any derivation of borough councils of twelve from the lawmen.[3]

If the new councils had developed from bodies of twelve or twenty-four doomsmen, we should have expected, but do not find, that, as in the case of the continental *scabini*, the old name would have remained attached to them, especially if their work was still primarily judicial. Apart from the Lincoln case, which has its difficulties, such a primacy is, indeed, very doubtful, as a glance through the earliest notices of councils collected in Section 1 above shows clearly enough. It is true only of those bodies at London (1206), Oxford, Cambridge, and Yarmouth, which were specially created to repress local injustice or disorder and which had obviously no continuity with the judiciary of the old borough. In all other cases " the rendering of judgements " either appears as one only, and not the first, of the councillor's duties or is not mentioned at all. Executing the king's commands, governing the town, advising the town or the mayor, saving and keeping the town liberty, these are functions prominently assigned to the councils.

There is, indeed, one clear case, and that the most important of all, of the slow development of an administrative council from the judiciary of a borough court. But, though the aldermen of London, the judges of its Husting court (but not a fixed number from the first), established themselves as the ruling council of the city, it was not, as we have seen, without opposition and some apparent attempts to set up a council chosen by the community as a whole. London, moreover, was an exceptional borough, and the Leicester tradition that the twenty-four *iurati* of their portmoot, who appear as a

---

[1] *E.H.R.* iii. 420 ; *History of English Law*, i. 557.

[2] But as the thirteenth century *judicatores* were at least nine in number (below, p. 300, *n.* 3) it is possible that the full number here was twelve as in 1066.

[3] *Gesetze der Angelsachsen*, ii. 566, 6 *d.* Cf. 622, 19 *b.* For the lawmen, see also Vinogradoff, *English Society in the Eleventh Century*, pp. 5-6.

council in the second half of the thirteenth century, were very ancient does not establish a case in point, since their administrative functions were taken over from a council of the merchant gild.[1] Leicester, indeed, affords a striking instance of a town council originating not in the gradual development of the borough judiciary but in the conscious action of its burgesses in their trading capacity.[2]

Neither the London nor the Leicester case can have contributed to the formation of Maitland's theory, for until 1902 it was not known that the aldermen of London were judges of the Husting court in the twelfth century and the Leicester evidence was first published in 1899. The evolutionary explanation of the growth of town councils must, indeed, have been based on general probabilities rather that on established facts. Most of the thirteenth-century evidence collected above was still in manuscript in 1896 or lurking unnoticed in the printed folio of the *Rotuli Litterarum Clausarum*. It was this apparent absence of evidence which led Maitland to place the general appearance of councils not earlier than the fourteenth century. With the fuller material now available and the probability that it is only a fragment of what once existed, we shall not be far wrong in expressing a belief that by the end of the thirteenth century most of the important towns had councils busily engaged in administrative work, though also in the generality of cases rendering judgements in the borough courts, not indeed, usually, because they were old bodies of doomsmen, but as one of a number of functions entrusted to a new municipal organ. It was actually, we may surmise, that decay of the old judiciary owing to judicial changes in the courts, assumed both by Stubbs and Maitland as an element in the development of town councils, which cleared the ground in many cases for a new arrangement.

[1] Above, p. 274.
[2] Sworn administrative councils believed to be old were not unknown in non-urban areas in the thirteenth century. In 1257 the supervision of the walls and ditches of Romney Marsh was in the hands of twenty-four *iuratores* who are then said to have existed from time immemorial. It was only five years before this, however, that the judicial enforcement of the duty of maintenance upon the tenants of the marsh had been transferred from the sheriff to them (N. Neilson, *Cartulary of Bilsington Priory* (Brit. Acad.), pp. 42-3). Besides the twenty-four each " watergang " had its twelve *iuratores* (*Black Book of St. Augustine's* (Brit. Acad.), i. 610). The bailiffs, jurats, and community of the marsh were incorporated in 1462 (*Cal. Charter Rolls*, vi. 181). The jurats of Portsmouth were also called *iuratores* (East, *Portsmouth Records*, p. 116).

Maitland was too cautious a scholar to maintain that his theory of uninterrupted development covered every case. In the light of what happened at Ipswich and of certain German analogies—no reference is made to the parallel evidence from the communes of France and Flanders—he could not, he said, exclude the type of council " newly and deliberately instituted," [1] but he evidently regarded it as quite exceptional. The thirteenth-century evidence, however, so far as it goes, points to special creation as the normal origin of a borough council, and the slow development at London seems exceptional.

It is surprising that in dealing with this problem Maitland, unlike Stubbs, should seem to have entirely ignored the influence of the foreign commune in England, though he elsewhere notes its effects in London [2] and suspects " the influence of the sworn *communa* of the French town " in the Ipswich burgess's oath to maintain the freedom and conceal the secrets of the town.[3]

No suspicion that the sworn council might show the same influence appears to have crossed his mind, nor did he draw any inference from the rapid diffusion of the office of mayor after its adoption in London. Of course Round had not yet discovered the London communal oath and that of the twenty-four there, while the close association of mayor and council in the thirteenth century was not yet fully revealed. Nevertheless, there was sufficient evidence for a repetition of Stubbs's suggestion of the continental *iurati* as one of the sources of our town councils. There may be a danger of pressing the suggestion too far and of underestimating the power of like circumstances to produce like institutions. Still it seems *prima facie* significant that foreign influence was admittedly at its zenith just when such councils make their first appearance in English records. It remains to inquire how far this influence shaped English municipal institutions.

4

The repercussions of the communal movement on the other side of the Channel had been felt in England from at least the middle of the twelfth century. Sworn communes had been formed or attempted at London, Gloucester, and

---

[1] *Hist. of Eng. Law*, i. 659.
[2] *Ibid.*, p. 657.
[3] *Ibid.*, p. 671.

York, but Henry II speedily stamped the latter two out and nothing is known of their organization.[1] The concession of a commune by count John to London in 1191 [2] was, however, accompanied or soon followed by the introduction of the foreign office of mayor,[3] and within the next quarter of a century at least a dozen towns copied London and provided themselves with mayors.[4]

By the side of the mayor (or officers with native names but like powers) appears for the first time, so far as evidence or indeed probability goes, a sworn administrative council of twelve or twenty-four burgesses. It is all part of a movement for a larger measure of urban self-government which had found its opportunity in the financial needs of Richard and John.

As sworn councils of just these numbers had long been a prominent feature of those city communes of France and Flanders which had clearly inspired municipal ambition on this side the Channel,[5] there can be practically no doubt that the general conception of such councils came from abroad, and the English bodies might therefore seem as foreign as the mayor. But here we must distinguish. The mayor filled a position which had not existed until then in English towns, while the new councils were merely the old *potentiores* more closely organized and with wider functions. In other words, there was the germ of a council already in existence, but none of a municipal magistrate who was not a royal

[1] Above, pp. 161, 176. The first may not have been municipal.

[2] Above, pp. 181, 182. See further J. H. Round, *Commune of London*, pp. 224-45.

[3] The mayor of London is first actually mentioned in April, 1193 (Hoveden, iii. 212), but must go back at least to the previous autumn and perhaps to the institution of the commune a year earlier. Round, however, regarded a final concord of 30th Nov., 1191, in which Henry Fitz Ailwin appears after Henry de Cornhill and his brothers and without the title of Mayor, as at least strongly opposed to the view that he was mayor then, three weeks after the grant of the commune. *Archæological Journal*, l. 263.

[4] Winchester by 1200 (*Rot. Chartarum*, p. 60b); Exeter by 1205 (*Rot. Litt. Claus.* i., p. 39b); Lincoln by 1206 (*Earliest Lincolnshire Assize Rolls*, ed. Stenton, no. 1448); Barnstaple and Oxford (probably) by 1210 (Round, *Cal. of Documents in France*, p. 462; *Cart. Oseney*, I, viii); Lynn by 1212, (*Rot. Litt. Claus.* i. 123a); York by 1213 (*ibid.*, p. 150a); Northampton by 1215 (*ibid.*, p. 188a); Beverley (*E.H.R.* xvi. 563), Bristol (*Rot. Litt. Claus.* i. 281b), Grimsby and Newcastle-upon-Tyne (*ibid.* i. 362b, 247a), by 1216. The view that " mayor " comes from *maior ballivus* is of course untenable, though the title of mayor may have been occasionally given to the senior bailiff in the thirteenth century (*Archæological Journal*, l. 254-5).

[5] Hegel, *Städte und Gilden*, and Luchaire, *Manuel des Institutions Françaises, passim*.

official as were the bailiffs. We must be on our guard against assuming any close copying of continental precedents. The sacred number twelve and its double had long been in use in England, as elsewhere, for local bodies affected to various purposes; and their comparatively recent application to the sworn inquests of presentment in the courts leet (to use their later and not very accurate name), which were to exercise no unimportant influence upon the administration of the medieval town,[1] might have suggested further developments of the idea. The names most usually applied to borough councillors, *jurés* (*iurati*), *prudes hommes* (*probi homines*), and *pairs* or *peers* (*pares*), were used in the foreign commune too, but they belonged to the common stock of French-speaking lands. Only once—in the London communal oath of 1193 —is the term most characteristic of the continental councils, *scabini*, *skivini*, *échevins*, given to the members of an English town council, and this has been thought by some to have been a merely casual use of a foreign name.[2] However this may be, London did not copy any foreign model in the end. There are some signs of hesitation under John, though no proof of any such direct imitation of Rouen as Round maintained,[3] but the city was ultimately content to adapt its native body of aldermen to the new purpose. This is noteworthy since it was the first English town to come under foreign influence and the sole recipient of formal permission to set up a commune.

Ward aldermen were not sufficiently general, or numerous enough where they existed, to supply councils on the London pattern in other boroughs,[4] but as London's constitutional influence was widespread, the use of the number twenty-four may have been imitation of the capital. Something approaching positive evidence of this is forthcoming in the case of Dublin, where the receipt in 1229 of licence to elect a mayor couched in the form granted to London in 1215 was apparently followed at once by the appointment of a council

---

[1] There is, indeed, reason to believe that such a jury developed into an administrative council in at least one small town on ancient demesne: Godmanchester.

[2] Above, p. 266. Eskevyns or skevins are otherwise only known in England as officers of the merchant gild (Gross, *Gild Merchant*, i. 26).

[3] See above, p. 266, and the criticism of Corbett, *E.H.R.* xvi. 766.

[4] Canterbury seems to have converted its six " borghs " into aldermanries with (hundred) courts in the twelfth century in direct imitation of London, but even here the aldermen cannot have furnished more than half the council of twelve.

of twenty-four.[1] Neither here nor elsewhere is there any hint of that duality which existed in the twenty-four of the Rouen group of communes, and which Round rather hastily thought he had traced to London.[2]

London influence need not necessarily be excluded even where so large a council was not considered to be advisable, for the only lesser number generally possible was the half of twenty-four. This is but one, however, of the possible sources of the very common municipal council of twelve members.

One well-known group of such councils, the twelve jurats of the Cinque Ports and their members, has been ascribed by Round to direct borrowing from abroad, but not from Rouen in this case.[3] Starting from the penalty of house demolition for offences against the community, which he thought peculiar to the Ports on this side of the Channel, but found both in northern and south-western France, he seemed inclined for a moment to suggest direct influence from Gascony, which had commercial relations with the Ports, and where, as he learnt from Thierry, " the form ' jurats ' more especially belongs." But on realizing that the punishment in question was probably derived in Gascony from the north, that Amiens afforded the only exact parallel to the Cinque Ports' infliction of it for refusal to serve as mayor or jurat, and that Picardy had communal confederations to explain the confederation of the Ports which he persisted in believing to have been formed as late as the thirteenth century, he put forward his hypothesis of the Picard origin of the Cinque Ports organization. The subsequent discovery that the penalty of house demolition, even for refusal to serve as mayor, was in use elsewhere in England, Scotland, and Ireland,[4] and that the confederacy was at least fifty years older than the joint communes of Picardy,[5] has long since demolished his hypothesis, but no one seems to have pointed out that, after explaining that the form " jurats " especially belonged to Gascony, he silently treated it as a possible Picard form. As a matter of fact " jurat " was confined to the south, the northern form being everywhere " juré." [6] Unless, therefore, we are prepared to affiliate the Cinque Ports to Bordeaux or Bayonne, " jurat "

---

[1] Above, p. 275.   [2] Above, p. 266.
[3] *Feudal England*, pp. 552 ff.
[4] Bateson, *Borough Customs* (Selden Soc.), i. 30, 264, 280 ; ii. 38-40.
[5] *E.H.R.* xxiv. 732 ; Petit-Dutaillis, *Studies Supplementary to Stubbs*, i. p. 87.   [6] See Littré, s.v.

or " jurate," as it is often spelt, in the former must be regarded
as an English word derived from *iuratus*, and for this there is
sufficient evidence. Whenever the councillors are referred
to in documents written in French it is translated " juré " ; [1]
it was used in towns remote from the Ports [2] and occasionally
alternated with " juror." [3] In 1379, in the assessment for
the poll-tax, it was employed as a class name for all municipal
councillors. [4] The oath of office was universal, they were
all *iurati*, but local usage determined whether they should
be colloquially described by the French form (*jurés, joures*)
or the English (*jurat(e)s*) or by some designation not referring
to their oath such as good men (*prudes hommes*) or portmen
or, most commonly, by their number, the twelve or the twenty-
four. Instead, therefore, of disclosing a specially French application, the Cinque Ports usage actually shows an unusual
local consistency in the use of an anglicized Latin word.

Any other conclusion would be difficult to reconcile with
the comparatively late and incomplete introduction of mayors
into the constitutions of the Ports. There is no evidence of a
mayor in any of them before 1290, and in the early part of
the fourteenth century Romney, Hythe, and Hastings had
still bailiffs as their chief magistrates. [5]

So far all attempts to establish a direct connexion between
the constitution of any English town and that of a particular
foreign commune or group of communes must be regarded
as having failed. Municipal growth in England owed a great
debt to the communal movement abroad, but its borrowing,
except in the case of the mayoralty, was general, not specific.
It derived thence the full conception of a self-governing urban
community, presided over by a chief magistrate and council
of its own choice, and with all its component parts cemented
together by binding oaths which inculcated a high ideal of
civic loyalty and service. [6] The general idea of a council
emanating from the community and sworn to serve and uphold
its interests seems to have been derived from foreign example,
but it is not necessary to look abroad for the details of its

---

[1] Cf. *Borough Customs* (Selden Soc.), i. 41, 85, 121-2 ; ii. 17, 22, 152,
154.

[2] *E.g.*, at Bridport (*ibid.* ii. 39), at Southampton (*Black Book*, ii. 60),
and at Portsmouth (R. East, *Portsmouth Records*, p. 1). Its use in the
Channel Islands seems to be due to English influence.

[3] *Borough Customs*, i. 212.

[4] *Rot. Parl.* iii. 58a ; *cf.* v. 515b ; vi. 338a.

[5] *Foedera* (Rec. ed.) I, ii. 730, 945. Yet Round assumed that all had
mayors (*Feudal England*, p. 552).   [6] Above, section I.

organization, its number, or the various names under which it went. There were features of English local life which had prepared the way for and were readily adaptable to the new conception. The spirit of the commune pervaded the proceedings at Ipswich in 1200, but the new constitution bears a thoroughly English impress. It lacks even a mayor, and Ipswich was one of many self-governing boroughs which were content with the right to elect their royal bailiffs.

It was only in this general way, indeed, that even the broader features of the communal system, itself far from uniform in detail, could be adopted in England, so different were the conditions of a fairly compact national kingdom from those of the throughly feudalized lands beyond the Channel. Urban government in England was a good deal less closely aristocratic than in the communes of France and the Low Countries, in which its organs developed out of the old local colleges of judges, usually twelve in number and known as *scabini*, who were appointed for life, originally by the Carolingians and afterwards by the feudal lords among whom their empire broke up. Annual election seems only to have been introduced, in Flanders at any rate, towards the end of the twelfth century, to prevent their making themselves hereditary, and it was always some form of self-election or at the most election by a select body of citizens, such as the hundred peers at Rouen and its daughter cities, who were themselves apparently hereditary.[1] Election by the whole body of citizens as prescribed by king John for the appointment of the bailiffs of Ipswich was a thing unknown in the foreign commune, an insular peculiarity explained by the necessity of making every citizen responsible for the due payment of the fee farm by those officers. Even in the election of a council, where they were left a free hand, the ruling class at Ipswich, while (through the bailiffs and coroners) appointing a limited body of electors, thought well to obtain the assent of the community at large to this procedure.[2] As late as 1300 the council of Southampton, we have seen, was elected by the whole community.[3] Little is known of the election of English mayors in the first century of their existence, but it points to an original selection, in form at least, by the general body of the burgesses, and at

---

[1] Giry, *Histoire de Saint-Omer*, p. 169 ; *Établissements de Rouen*, p. 14 ; Luchaire, *Manuel des Institutions Françaises*, p. 418. Thus the foreign communes conform better to Maitland's theory of the origin of town councils than the English boroughs for which it was devised.

[2] Above, p. 271.   [3] *Oak Book*, i. 44.

Winchester about 1275 the community still shared the choice with the council.[1] In England, too, the king merely reserved a veto on a single name, while in his foreign dominions he insisted on nominating from a list of three.[2]

In England the towns were indebted to the communal movement abroad for the mayoralty and in a more general way for their municipal councils, but both these institutions were developed by them from the outset on native lines consistent with their close dependence upon the Crown or, in the case of mesne towns, in imitation of the royal boroughs.

APPENDIX

Dr. Stephenson on the Origin of Town Councils

LIMITED as is the influence upon municipal developments in England attributed to the foreign commune in the foregoing article, it does not commend itself to Dr. Stephenson. He goes even further than Maitland in assuming a native evolution, though correcting his post-dating of the emergence of elected councils and finding their nucleus not in the borough judiciary, but in mercantile associations. The abortive communes at Gloucester and York need not, he suggests, have had any municipal significance nor can he see in the granting of the commune to London in 1191 and its sequel any trace of French influence beyond that which had naturally been in force since the Norman Conquest. The only change in the civic constitution as settled by Henry I and now revived was the institution of a mayor, and this officer was no more an essential feature of the foreign commune than he was of the boroughs which received self-government from Richard and John. " Henceforth the head of the administration (of London) bore the prouder title of mayor, but that was the extent of foreign borrowing." The mercantile aristocracies in the boroughs obtained a closer organization and wider powers, but there is no need to call in continental influence to explain what was a natural development.[3]

Such a view takes no account of the traces of that influence not merely in the title of the new officer, but in the

---

[1] Furley, *Ancient Usages of Winchester*, p. 27.
[2] But the Rouen type of commune was of course an imperfect one.
[3] *Borough and Town*, pp. 183-5.

clear implications of Richard of Devizes' denunciation of the
" Conjuratio " [1] and in a significant word in the Londoners'
oath of loyalty in 1193 to Richard and to their commune and
its officers. [2] Even if the *skivini* (*scabini*) of the oath were
only the aldermen, as Miss Bateson thought, the use of a
title so generally applied to civic councils abroad, [3] but in
England confined to a few officials of the merchant gild,
shows to what quarter the eyes of the Londoners were then
turned. In swearing to hold to the commune (*tenere c.*)
too, they were using a phrase found in French documents. [4]
Without tracing so much to imitation of Rouen as Round
did, would it be very rash to suggest that the " major commune Rothomagi " [5] may well have been in their minds in
instituting the office of mayor ?

If in financial and judicial autonomy the city won no more
than Henry I had given, it breathed in a new spirit, adopted
a new bond of union in the civic oath and found a spokesman.
Such a revolutionary cry as Robert Brand's " come what
may, the Londoners shall have no king but their mayor " [6]
became possible. Yet Professor Stephenson says that " neither
function nor origin distinguished mayors from magistrates
with other names. . . . They were no less seignorial or
royal than other magistrates." [7] What do we find in the
evidence ? The ancient reeves, now usually renamed bailiffs,
are first of all and above all financial officers. When the
licences for their election mention any function it is that of
accounting to the king for the revenue of the borough. [8]
The mayor of London in John's licence for his annual election (1215) is assigned no such specific function. He is to
be " idoneus ad regimen civitatis." [9] He will be drawn
into financial as into all other kinds of business, but at the
outset he is essentially the head of the community, without
special charge. It is true that when London's example is
copied, a senior bailiff will occasionally double the parts, [10]

---

[1] Stubbs, *Select Charters*, ed. Davis, p. 245.   [2] Above, p. 266.
[3] With the " quod sequentur et tenebunt considerationem (decision)
maioris, et skivinorum," etc., of the oath, *cf.* the passages quoted by Ducange
(*Gloss. Latinitatis*, s.v. considerare) which refer to " consideratio maioris "
and " consideratio scabinorum." For an oath of the burgesses of a French
commune to their *jurati*, see Giry, *Établ. de Rouen*, ii. 101.
[4] *E.g.*, Giry, *op. cit.* ii. 74.
[5] Round, *Cal. of Docs. in France*, p. 7 (1170-75) *et alibi*. The Londoners
must have been perfectly familiar with the civic institutions of Rouen.
[6] Palgrave, *Rotuli Curiæ Regis*, i. 69, (a. 1194).
[7] *Op. cit.*, p. 173.   [8] *B.B.C.* i. 245.
[9] *Ibid.*, p. 247.   [10] See above, p. 291, *n.* 4.

but this in itself implies a distinction. A long struggle between the episcopal lords of Lynn and its burgesses ended
in the recognition of a mayor instead of their reeve.[1] The
mayor allowed to Drogheda in Louth (1253) had in charge
to see that the reeves and other bailiffs justly treated both
poor and rich.[2] Nottingham obtained a mayor in 1284 to
improve the condition of its burgesses and other men by pre-
siding over the bailiffs and other officers of the town in all
matters relating to the government and advantage of its
two boroughs.[3] When the mayoralty of Northampton was
sanctioned in 1299, after more than eighty years of recorded
existence, the professed object was to associate the mayor
with the bailiffs in the trial of pleas, once their exclusive
province.[4] The suggestion conveyed by the excessive rarity
of these licences that the new communal spirit often took
the form of setting up a mayor without seeking permission
finds confirmation at Lynn. It had a mayor from 1212 at
least, but a final concord between the bishop of Norwich
and the burgesses in 1234 reveals that he had never had
the lord's recognition.[5] It is significant that the burgesses'
assumption of a mayor was accompanied by assertion of the
right to tallage themselves for municipal purposes. At
Lynn, as at London, the mayoralty is the creation of communal self-assertion and this no doubt marks its general
character at the outset. It accounts for the almost complete
absence of formal authorization. Only by insistence on the
presentation of the mayor elect to the king or other lord,
as John's London charter of 1215 shows, was control over
the new officer secured. The express permission which John
gave to London was extended to Dublin in 1229 and was
shortly afterwards sought by Bristol.[6] But its request did
not result in a grant, and after 1229 there was no other
chartered allowance of the privilege to an English royal
borough for half a century.

It might with some plausibility be argued, though Professor Stephenson does not do so, except perhaps by implication, that there is no need to look abroad for the prototype
of the English mayor when he often succeeded a civic head
who also was not in origin a financial or judicial officer or

---

[1] See below.   [2] B.B.C. ii. 363.   [3] Ibid., p. 364.
[4] Ibid., p. 364.   [5] Ibid., pp. 362-3.
[6] Close Rolls, 1234–37, p. 363. It is interesting to note that the burgesses also asked that they might have the London pondus.

invested with any burghal authority by the Crown. Were not the mayors of the thirteenth century modelled upon the gild aldermen who appear at Oxford and elsewhere in the twelfth as chief officers of their boroughs? At Leicester and Southampton the change from alderman to mayor seems to have been little more than change in name. But in these cases the conversion came comparatively late. That earlier in the century, in 1249, the burgesses of Southampton should have obtained from Henry III a grant that neither they nor their heirs should ever have a mayor in their town [1] shows that the transition had not always been so simple. Where the gild community and the burgess community were practically identical, as would seem to have been the case at Oxford, there would have been little or no difficulty. But the Southampton gild, strong as it was, did not include the whole of the burgesses.[2] The mayoralty was a burgess office, unconnected with trade; the mayor was the head of the whole community, gildsmen or no gildsmen. So the gild majority at Southampton would have none of him. Although Lynn resembled Southampton in having a powerful gild which did not include all burgesses, it was one of the first boroughs to set up a mayor. As its liberties were those of Oxford (and so those of London), example may have played its part, but the need of presenting a solid front to their episcopal lord perhaps weighed even more with the burgesses.

It is no mere coincidence that borough seals appear about the same time as mayors. They are both expressions of the new communal movement in the more ambitious boroughs.[3]

So far it was only the foreign commune that had an officer comparable with the new burghal head. The borrowing of his title shows that the Londoners of 1191 were fully alive to any features of continental municipalities which could be with advantage adopted in their own city.

As the mayor, despite his foreign title, is for Dr. Stephenson a purely native development, so *a fortiori* is the elected and sworn council of fixed number which assisted him (or elected bailiffs) in the rule of the town. Here he may seem to be on

---

[1] *B.B.C.* ii. 363.

[2] *Oak Book* (Southampton Rec. Soc.), i. Introd., p. xxx f.; see also above, p. 249.

[3] *Cf.* the decision of St. Louis in 1235 that the citizens of Rheims " non debebant habere sigillum cum non habeant communiam " (Ducange s. Commune, etc.), and the later surrender of their common seals by English boroughs whose charters were cancelled (above, p. 237).

firmer ground. That such part as the burgesses had been suffered to take in the government of the purely dominical borough had been exercised by a well-to-do minority is undeniable. Far back in the eleventh century we have record of *burhwitan* in the Devonshire boroughs, and similar traces are found in charters and other evidence of the twelfth century.[1] They have been usually identified with the doomsmen of the borough court, but Professor Stephenson, as we have seen, holds that after the Norman Conquest this power fell to the leading gildsmen, where there was a merchant gild, and to the chief merchants where there was none. In the former case the Gildhall was the earliest council house. Some obvious objections to this assumption have already been stated, and to these we may add that the aldermen of London owed their administrative status not to their connexion with trade, but to their being heads of the wards and judges of the husting. At Lincoln, too, it was perhaps the twelve judges who formed the thirteenth-century council. Of the three outstanding features of the borough council of the thirteenth century, election, the oath and the fixed number, there is no earlier evidence at all of the first two and no convincing proof of the third. There is evidence, indeed, which points to the absence of any restriction of numbers. While the first custumal of Northampton, the date of which is about 1190, was drawn up by forty persons, whose names are given in the preamble, the second, about 1260, was issued by " the twenty-four *jurati* of Northampton." [2]

It would be easier to make out a plausible case for Maitland's theory of the origin of town councils in the old borough judiciary than for that which traces them to " the caucus in the Gildhall." It fits London and possibly Lincoln. The constant insistence in the Cinque Ports custumals on the judicial functions of the jurats of the ports in their hundred courts, might seem to strengthen the argument. More impressive still, at first sight, is the case of Chester, where, despite its early merchant gild, the doomsmen (*judicatores*) of the portmoot apparently formed the administrative body in the thirteenth century, judging by their attestations of charters and known position in the community.[3] On the

---

[1] Above, pp. 273, *n.* 2, 286.

[2] Bateson, *Borough Customs*, i. Introd., p. xli f.

[3] *Journal of Chester Archæological Society*, N.S. x. 20, 29. They were not elective, the obligation to serve resting on particular houses, an obligation still in existence, formally at least, in the fifteenth century (*Chartul. of*

other hand, the earliest gild council, concerning itself with town business, of which there is record, that of Leicester, dated only from 1225, when councils were already no novelty. It is true that the evidence for Maitland's view is not so strong as it looks. The Cinque Port jurats at Romney and probably generally were chosen from the barons, the original doomsmen.[1] The Chester case, too, is apparently merely one of slower development, for it is quite unlikely that the ruling council of twenty-four *seniores* which appears by 1400 was the same body as the *judicatores* of the thirteenth century. But the really important question is not so much whether the " lawful men " of the old portmoots became councillors *qua* traders or *qua* doomsmen, but whether this was or was not the result of deliberate re-organization. The evidence for such reorganization at Ipswich, Northampton, Dublin and Yarmouth seems definite enough, but it does not satisfy Professor Stephenson. The council of twelve *discreciores* whom John in 1215 instructed the citizens of Northampton to elect to manage their affairs along with their new mayor, in his opinion, merely continued an existing practice under other chief officers.[2] But if so, why was it necessary to give any such instructions ? [3] Why should the burgesses of Ipswich in 1200 have recorded in such detail the election and functions of their new council ?

Chester Abbey, Cheth. Soc. N.S. 82, p. 341 ; M. Hemmeon, *Burgage Tenure in England*, p. 72, *n.* 3, from *Cal. Anc. Deeds*, iii. 350). The largest number of these judges witnessing an extant charter is nine (*c.* 1230, *J.C.A.S.* N.S. x. 20).

[1] See above, p. 261.   [2] *Borough and Town*, p. 178.

[3] The necessity would be even less apparent were he right in implying (p. 178) that the burgesses of Northampton had set up a similar council fifteen years before. This is an inference from the likenesses between five charters of 1200, of which the first in date was granted to Northampton and the latest to Ipswich. All five included fee farm and election of reeves. Professor Stephenson assumes that the Northampton charter served as a model for Ipswich and that " the action taken by the men of Ipswich followed the precedent set of Northampton." But as all five charters were issued within five weeks, that of Northampton was certainly in no real sense the model for those of Shrewsbury and Gloucester granted three and four days later respectively or even for that of Ipswich.

NOTE

The force of " free " in " free borough " may be compared with that in " free manor " (*liberum manerium*), a term applied to those manors for which were claimed franchises (*libertates*) which, the Crown insisted, must be justified by the evidence of royal charters (*Feudal Aids*, ii. 24). The term occurs as early as 1212 (*Book of Fees*, i. 87).

XI

THE COMMON COUNCIL OF THE BOROUGH [1]

THE character of the development in town government, which ended in the close corporations swept away by the Municipal Corporation Act of 1835, has been variously judged, because for a century and a half it was discussed with party bias and for even longer the true facts were largely buried in the disorderly muniment rooms of the boroughs. Brady in 1690 [2] and Merewether and Stephens in 1835 [3] propounded with equal confidence exactly opposite theories of the origin of borough oligarchy. Brady contended that the close corporations existed from the first, Merewether and Stephens that the boroughs were free and happy democracies until the introduction of municipal incorporation in the fifteenth century. Approaching the subject in a more scientific spirit, Gross [4] and Colby [5] in 1890 corrected many of the errors of their predecessors. Gross showed that even formal incorporation was a century older than Merewether and Stephens maintained, but so far agreed with them as to hold that " a popular and not an oligarchic form of government prevailed in English boroughs of the twelfth and thirteenth centuries." [6] From the fourteenth century, however, " the development in England was from government by a democratic burghal community to the exclusive sway of a narrow aristocratic ' select body '." [7] Neither Gross nor Colby, however, had gone very deeply into the early history of town councils, and it was reserved for Mrs. J. R. Green two years later to discover the essential unreality of this early democracy and the existence of " an oligarchical system of administration which was

---

[1] Reprinted from *E.H.R.* xlv (1930), 529-51.
[2] *An Historical Treatise of Cities and Boroughs.*
[3] *The History of the Boroughs and Corporations of the United Kingdom.*
[4] *The Gild Merchant.*
[5] " The Growth of Oligarchy in English Towns," *E.H.R.* v. 633 *seqq.*
[6] *Gild Merchant*, i. 108.   [7] *Ibid.*, p. 171.

in its full strength in the English boroughs as early as 1300 and can even be traced back at least fifty years earlier." [1] All the evidence which has since come to light tends to confirm and carry farther back the practical oligarchy of the thirteenth century *potentiores*, to whom, in the nature of the case, the actual administration inevitably fell. The complaints of the " lesser commune " at Oxford in 1257 [2] could hardly be paralleled in the next century, and the grievances of the London commonalty half a century before the Oxford petition are sufficiently attested by Fitz-Osbert's movement and John's supersession of the city *superiores* in 1206.[3] It is significant of the weakness of " democracy " in that age, and of the control over the boroughs exercised by the Crown, that in normal times popular recalcitrance was generally confined to petitions against unjust taxation and similar oppression. Attempts on the part of the borough commonalty to seize the direction of municipal administration were only possible when the Crown itself was temporarily under baronial control. It is the great merit of Mrs. Green's work to have shown that democratic self-assertion was far more general and for a time more successful towards the close of the middle ages than it had ever been before. The new " common councils " which were set up in the last quarter of the fourteenth century and in the fifteenth gave the commons a share in the actual work of administration.[4] Unfortunately, inadequate systems of election and more generally the use of nomination soon put the common councils out of touch with the mass of the commonalty, and in the end they did no more than broaden the basis of civic oligarchy.

I

The first common council of this type, and the only one still existing, was that of London, which dates from 1376. The name was, indeed, applied in the preceding quarter of a century to new councils at Bristol, Exeter, and Colchester, and in the same year as at London to one at Cambridge, but these were single councils, the result of movements initiated or headed by the *potentiores* in the name of the

---

[1] *Town Life in the Fifteenth Century*, ii. 243.
[2] Above, p. 276.   [3] *Ibid.*, pp. 267-8.
[4] For the establishment of similar popular bodies in some of the great foreign communes, as early as the beginning of the fourteenth century, under the name of *jures* or *prudhommes du commun*, see Luchaire, *Manuel des Institutions Françaises*, p. 424.

whole community against arbitrary proceedings of the borough officers. They therefore require separate treatment.[1]

The London common council differed from nearly all those which were created later in being an adaptation of a pre-existing selected assembly of the community. The only organ of burghal democracy, such as it was, in the thirteenth century, was an assembly which bore various names in different towns and was not always of the same origin. It might be the undifferentiated city court, as apparently it was at Exeter, or a *burwaremote* that had thrown off a separate judicial court as at Winchester or the assembly of a merchant gild as at Leicester. London had originally two assemblies, the open-air folk(es)moot at St. Paul's and the smaller husting which, by the thirteenth century, met in the Guildhall. Already in the twelfth, however, the folkmoot had ceased to have any part in ordinary legislation and administration, and the work of the husting had become predominantly judicial in the thirteenth century, though it was even yet not entirely free from administrative business.[2] The affairs of the city, so far as they could not be dealt with by the mayor and aldermen alone, were transacted in a new common assembly (*congregatio*), meeting in the Guildhall, which seems to have grown out of the husting. The most striking feature of this assembly is that it met by individual summons, and the judges in the London *iter* of 1221 were told, in reply to a question, that its business could not be held up by the absence of a certain number of aldermen " or others " and that there was no penalty for default.[3] It is not here called a *congregatio*, but the recurrence of the question of non-attendance in the assemblies of the fourteenth century, when it was at last found necessary to amerce absentees, shows that we are dealing with the same body. It may go back to at least the earliest days of the city

---

[1] See Appendix I, p. 330.

[2] As late as 1312 it was still regarded as a court in which the whole community could give its assent to admissions to the freedom of the city (*Cal. of Letter Book D*, p. 283) ; a clerk of the chamber was elected there in 1320 in the presence of the mayor, aldermen, and commoners (*ibid. E*, pp. 20-1) ; ordinances of the tapicers were approved in 1322 (*ibid.*, p. 252) ; auditors were assigned there by the mayor, aldermen, and community in 1337 (*ibid. F*, p. 4) ; and an ordinance about the conduit was made by the mayor and aldermen with the assent of the community in 1345 (*ibid.*, p. 128).

[3] *Munim. Gildhall. London.* i (Liber Albus), 69-70. For the suggested origin of the *congregatio* in the husting, see A. H. Thomas in the *Calendar of Plea and Memoranda Rolls of London, 1364–81*, Introd., p. xv.

" commune," if Miss Bateson was right in identifying the " skivini et alii probi homines " in the freemen's oath of 1193 with the aldermen and others specially summoned.[1] Whether others than those who received summonses had ever had a right to appear there is nothing definite to show.

The reluctance to attend administrative assemblies did not extend to those which met to elect the mayor and sheriffs. In the fourteenth century, although a larger number of citizens was summoned for this purpose, difficulty was found in excluding others, and a royal writ forbidding their intrusion had to be obtained. Mr. A. H. Thomas is, indeed, inclined to trace the *magna* or *immensa congregatio* for elections or other specially important business to a different origin as " a diminished survival of the old Folkmoots." [2] In the days of sheriffs appointed by the Crown the citizens had met in folkmoot every year at Michaelmas to know who was to be sheriff and to hear his charge.[3] The later election assemblies no doubt continued the tradition, but they were rather a substitution than a survival. When the right of election was secured for the community, it could not be left to a civic mass meeting without obvious risk of disorder and danger to the aldermanic monopoly of power. The same principle of selection was adopted as for the ordinary administrative assemblies of the community and, until the fifteenth century, the same method of selection. Like them the election assemblies met at the Guildhall, not at St. Paul's, the ancient meeting-place of the folkmoot. Folkmoots were occasionally summoned in the thirteenth century, at any rate in the civic crises of the Barons' War, but the name never clung to the election assemblies.

In these assemblies the commonalty had very little more real voice than they had had in the folkmoot of the twelfth century. The claim of the aldermen and magnates in the thirteenth century to rule the city and decide the choice of its chief officials is written large over the contemporary chronicle of alderman Arnold fitz Thedmar.[4] They might voluntarily obtain the assent of *universi cives* to an important ordinance, as was done in 1229–30,[5] but unluckily we are not

---

[1] Above, p. 266.
[2] A. H. Thomas, *Calendar of Plea and Memoranda Rolls of London, 1364-81*, Introd., p. lviii. This was Norton's view also. See *infra*, p. 312, *n*. 2.
[3] *Munim. Gildhall. Lond.* i. (Liber Albus), pp. 118-19; *E.H.R.* xvii. (1902), 502.
[4] *Liber de Antiquis Legibus*, pp. 91, 149 *et passim*.   [5] *Ibid.*, p. 6.

told whether this approval was given by the folkmoot or by an enlarged meeting of the Guildhall assembly.[1] At the end of the century, it is the latter through whom the opinion of the community is taken. But even in the next century it is their assent merely that is asked for in elections.[2]

Owing to the imperfection of the early records of the city, nothing is known before about 1285 of the method adopted in the selection of those who were summoned to the assembly. It is not clear whether there was a standing list of those liable to such summons or whether the mayor or sheriffs summoned them (through the bailiffs or serjeants) *ad hoc* for each occasion, as was apparently the custom later for special financial duties or similar functions. There is a strong probability in either case that they were already chosen from the wards and in proportion to their size. No innovation was needed, for in the twelfth century the city watch was selected on this basis, and it is significant that the proportionate numbers for which the wards were liable in the watch reappear as the ward quotas for the common assembly as arranged in 1346.[3] The same method was used for the collection of tallage in 1227,[4] and thirty years later in the trial of a mayor for oppression of the people.[5] More direct evidence comes from Norwich, to which Richard I had granted the customs of London. In the thirteenth century, we learn from its custumal, it had a common assembly (*communis convocacio*) for the transaction of the city's business, to which were summoned twelve, ten, or eight from each of its four leets.[6] Now these were the (old)

---

[1] Perhaps *universi cives* was only a high sounding name for the ordinary assembly. See below (p. 307) for the narrow use of *tota communitas*.

[2] The record of the election of mayor in October, 1328, is enlightening as to the actual share of the commoners in the choice. The mayor and aldermen retired to the chamber and " made the election for themselves and the commonalty according to custom." But when they descended to the hall and announced their election of Chigwell, there were somes cries for Fulsham, and the assembly broke up in confusion. Both candidates were persuaded to withdraw and John de Grantham was elected (*Cal. of Plea and Mem. Rolls, 1323–64*, ed. Thomas, p. 72). *Cf.* statements that the mayor and aldermen have elected sheriffs in the presence of men of each ward summoned to receive (*ad recipiendum*) their sheriffs (*Cal. of Letter Book C*, pp. 101, 114, 173, ann. 1301–03).

[3] Round, *Commune of London*, p. 255, and below, p. 308.

[4] *Pat. Rolls, 1225–32*, 132.

[5] *Liber de Antiquis Legibus*, p. 32.

[6] W. Hudson, *Records of Norwich* (1906), i. 191. For the date of the custumal, see the editor's introduction, p. xxxix. As in London, difficulty was found in securing the attendance of those summoned, and a penalty of 2s. was already inflicted on absentees, though London managed to avoid one until 1346.

watch quotas of the London wards and their quotas for election meetings of the common assembly in the fourteenth century. As in London, where in 1293 the *tota communitas* was defined as " for each ward the wealthier and wiser men," [1] so at Norwich the *meliores* and *discreciores eiusdem civitatis* alone were summoned. The mention of the serjeant of the leet's " panel " suggests a fuller list from which those " somoniti ad dictum ˌdiem " were taken.

There is no record of an actual selection of ward representatives for deliberative purposes in London until about 1285, when the well-known list of thirty-nine *probi homines*, one to four from each ward according to size, sworn to consult with the aldermen on the common affairs of the city, appears in the first of its letter books.[2] As the city had recently been taken into the king's hands and the mayor replaced by a warden, this body may have been an exceptional one in some respects. There does not, for instance, seem to be any other trace of an oath administered to members of the common assembly until it was radically reorganized in 1376.

Until the middle of the fourteenth century, there was no permanently fixed number for those summoned to deliberative assemblies ; one to four from each ward seem to have been the normal numbers, twelve from each could be called a " very great " assembly,[3] and the meeting on 30th August, 1340, to which no less than 528 representatives, six to twenty-eight from each ward, were summoned, was entirely exceptional. It was called to confirm the death sentence on two rioters under special powers exercised by the city in the absence of the king abroad.[4] If two entries in the city letter-book towards the end of Edward II's reign are to be taken at their face value, the attendance of those who were summoned to regular meetings of the administrative assembly was not more satisfactory than it had been a hundred years before. In October, 1321, the commoners disclaimed any desire to punish absentees,[5] and a year later they agreed to a restriction of the representatives of the commonalty to two from each ward, with full powers on its behalf, " in

---

[1] *Cal. of Letter Book C*, p. 11.   [2] *Ibid. A*, p. 209.
[3] " Maxima communitas " (*ibid. E*, pp. 169, 174).
[4] *Cal. of Plea and Mem. Rolls, 1323–64*, ed. Thomas, pp. 128-9. If the old Guildhall (Stow, *Survey of London*, ed. Kingsford, i. 271, 292 ; ii. 337) could accommodate so large an assembly, it must have been capacious.   [5] *Cal. of Letter Book E*, p. 147.

order to save the commonalty trouble." [1] Their attitude
may seem surprising in view of the fact that in 1319, despite
the resistance of the mayor (and doubtless of the aldermen),
they had won from the king letters patent which imposed
serious restrictions on the ruling body and gave the commoners a share with the aldermen in the custody of the
common seal.[2] It has to be remembered, however, that
Edward was then under baronial control, from which at the
later date he had got free. But, though the commoners
were probably overawed, regular attendance in quiet times
was never much to their taste. Perhaps, too, they were
reconciled to the limitation of the number of their representatives by the permission, now apparently first given, to
elect them themselves.[3] The ordinary place of meeting was
the outer chamber of the Guildhall ; it was only when there
was an *immensa* or *maxima congregatio* that they met in the
great hall itself.

While the numbers fixed in 1322 for administrative assemblies were soon altered, the ward quotas for the larger
election meetings, held in the hall, had now settled down to
a maximum of twelve and a minimum of eight or six.[4] The
irruption of unsummoned commoners, which drew down a
royal writ of prohibition on 4th July, 1315, would naturally
provoke insistence on a definitely fixed number. The annual
assemblies for elections were thus distinguished from the
more frequent ordinary assemblies in numbers, in normal
meeting-place, and in the interest taken in them by the
citizens. A further and very important difference first appears
in 1322 when, as we have seen, the representatives of the
commonalty in ordinary assemblies were allowed to be
elected by the men of the wards, for those at election meetings
were merely summoned by the mayor or sheriff as before.
This difference was still preserved when in 1346 an " immense "
commonalty, which filled the hall, ordained a nearer ap-
proximation in numbers, fixing ward quotas of twelve, eight,
or six for elections, and of eight, six, or four " to treat of
arduous affairs affecting the community of the city." [5] In
the latter case, however, two from each ward, and even one,

---

[1] *Cal. of Letter Book E*, p. 174.
[2] *Munim. Gildhall. London*, ii. (Liber Custumarum), pp. 267-73 ; i.
(Liber Albus), pp. 141-4. Mayors and aldermen were to serve for only one
year at a time.   [3] *Cal. of Letter Book E*, p. 174.
[4] *Ibid. D*, pp. 26-7.   [5] *Ibid. F*, p. 305.

if the other wards had a corresponding excess, were to form a quorum, and only such absentees were to be amerced in 2s., the first mention of a penalty for non-attendance. A list of those chosen for their wards on 14th February, 1347, to come to the Guildhall when warned, on matters affecting the city, contains 133 names.[1]

A final organization of the assembly was so far from being reached in 1346 that even the unit of representation was still in dispute and remained so for nearly forty years longer. The political importance of the trade misteries or gilds in London opened with their utilization in the stormy times of Henry III by two mayors, Thomas fitz Thomas and Walter Hervey, in the struggle of the commoners against the municipal monopoly of power of the aldermen and their policy of free trade.[2] It was not, however, until the civic contests of Edward II's reign that this new form of social organization began to affect the constitution of the city. In 1312 the assembly seems for a moment to have been reorganized on gild lines,[3] and in October, 1326, there is mention of a proposed meeting of the mayor and aldermen with representatives of the misteries to treat and ordain of the needs of the city,[4] though this was apparently an *ad hoc* body since its decisions were to be confirmed by the community. Midway between these experiments the commoners by the letters patent of 1319 had secured royal approval of a rule which made the mistery the only avenue to the freedom for most applicants.[5]

Just a quarter of a century after the latest of these dates, assemblies representative of misteries were tried for a year or two from November, 1351.[6] As in the first place only forty-two representatives from thirteen misteries were elected and these were the chief gilds, in which the aldermen, no longer the general traders of a century earlier, had a predominant influence, this particular experiment looks more like the work of the ruling oligarchy than of dissatisfied commoners. It is perhaps significant that from 1352, save

---

[1] Riley, *Memorials of London* (1868), pp. liii-lv. They are said to have been chosen (" in their wards ") at an assembly, so that the election was not, apparently, always done locally in the wards.

[2] G. Unwin, *The Gilds and Companies of London* (1908), pp. 64 ff.

[3] *Cal. of Letter Book D*, p. 276 ; *cf.* 283 and *ibid. E*, p. 12.

[4] *Cal. of Plea and Memoranda Rolls*, 1323–64, ed. Thomas, p. 15.

[5] *Munim. Gildhall. Lond.* i. (Liber Albus), 142.

[6] *Cal. of Letter Book F*, p. 237 ; *ibid. G*, pp. 3, 23.

once or twice for temporary purposes,[1] no more is heard of gild representation until 1376.

In the interval a contemporary Westminster chronicler, John of Reading, reports serious discord between the *populares* and *majores* of the city in 1364,[2] apparently arising out of the parliamentary statute of 1363 which in attempting to suppress cornering of commodities by confining merchants each to trade in one commodity defeated its own object by creating monopolies which raised prices by one-third and was repealed in 1365. In the next year the king's sudden supersession of the mayor, Adam Bury, caused a riot which led, according to Reading, to the election of two hundred *periti* from the wards to act as a council with the aldermen for *ardua agenda* and to elect the city officers, "accessu vulgi prohibito et secluso sub gravi poena."[3] The not very intelligent chronicler seems unaware that ward representation for these purposes was the existing system and is obviously wrong about the quota, but if he is otherwise correct, the settlement of 1376 was anticipated in the abolition of any distinction between the election assemblies and at any rate the more important administrative meetings either in numbers or in mode of choice. Election had been used hitherto only for deliberative assemblies.

The condemnation of leading citizens by the Good Parliament revived internal dissension in the city which resulted, in August, 1376, in a definite change of electoral unit from ward to mistery. In future every sufficient mistery was to elect certain persons, the greater not more than six, the lesser four or two according to their size, against the day (28th Oct.) when the new mayor was sworn in and these and no others were to be summoned for one year to elections and whenever it might be necessary to take counsel with the commonalty in the Guildhall. The misteries were to be ready to accept whatever was done by the mayor and aldermen along with their representatives.[4] That no very democratic change was intended is evident from the further provision which, while declaring ordinances passed by mayor and aldermen alone to be void, allowed the consent of a majority of the twelve principal misteries to be sufficient, if no wider one could be

---

[1] *Cal. of Plea and Memoranda Rolls, 1323-64,* p. 267 ; *Cal. of Letter Book G,* pp. 280-1.

[2] *Chronica Johannis de Reading, etc., 1346-47,* ed. Tait (1914), pp. 161, 317.   [3] Reading, *op. cit.,* p. 169 ; *cf.* pp. xi. 331.

[4] *Cal. of Letter Book H,* pp. 36, 39 f.

had, and from the power given to the mayor of fixing the number of misteries to be represented according to the gravity of
the matter in hand.[1] As the scheme was completed on receipt
of an urgent royal order to come to a settlement, it may well
contain some trace of compromise.

In addition to the change of unit of representation, the
makers of the revised constitution retained or revived the
amalgamation of the representative machinery for elections
and for administration into a single body which, as we have
just seen, had been tried ten years before, but perhaps not for
long. Instead of the two kinds of assembly of the older system
differing in several respects and both normally called into
existence *ad hoc* when required, there was now only one body
elected for a year and bound to hold at least two meetings
in each quarter to consult about the common needs of the city.
A standing council was thus substituted for an occasional
assembly and from the first it was regularly known as the
" common council," though " assembly " (*congregatio*) was
not entirely dropped. An oath was administered to every
member which is essentially the common councillor's oath as
it became stereotyped in the next century.[2] Councillors were
relieved of judicial and taxative duties.

The new constitution was intended to secure for the
commoners[3] a really effective share in the government of
the city, putting an end to that arbitrary action of the mayor
and aldermen of which they complained at the outset. Not
only was the change from ward to mistery expected to give
a body of representatives more independent of the aldermen,
but an attempt was made to break the aldermanic front
itself. One of the early steps of the new régime was to put
in force again[4] the long neglected rule of 1319 that prescribed
annual election of aldermen and forbade re-election until the

---

[1] *Cal. of Letter Book H*, pp. 36, 39 f. To the king, whose chief anxiety
was for the preservation of order, the object of the changes was naturally
explained as prevention of tumult arising from large gatherings (*ibid.*,
p. 36).

[2] *Ibid.*, p. 41 ; *Munim. Gildhall. Lond.* i. (Liber Albus), p. 41. For
the minimum number of meetings, *cf.* Worcester practice in 1467 (Smith,
English Gilds, E.E.T.S., p. 380). The distinction between a representative assembly and a representative council may seem rather a refined
one, especially as the former had always existed to give the " commune
consilium " of the city, but it was a real distinction. The oath of the
representatives *c.* 1285 (above, p. 307) may point to an early conciliar
experiment.

[3] See Additional Note, p. 338.

[4] *Cal. of Letter Book H*, pp. 59-60.

lapse of a year.[1] The work of the reformers of 1376 was not, however, destined to be wholly successful.

The name common council has indeed been supposed by some writers to have been applied to the assembly as early as the beginning of the fourteenth century,[2] and the ordinance of October, 1346, has been regarded as instituting that council in its later sense.[3] But the supposed antiquity of the name rests mainly on a misinterpretation of the phrase *per commune consilium*,[4] used with the meaning " by the common counsel " (of the citizens), and though the arrangement of 1346 anticipated the fixed panel for administrative sessions, it required neither regular meetings nor an oath, and it is doubtful whether it remained long in force.   Nor was it called a council. At most, it must be reckoned, with the introduction of election of representatives in 1322,[5] as one of the changes which paved the way for the legislation of 1376.

At the meetings of the new common council the commoners voted by groups, not as individuals.[6] The aldermen also had votes,[7] and the term common council sometimes includes them,[8] though it is more often applied to the representatives of the misteries,[9] who at other times are still distinguished from the aldermen as the commonalty or commoners.[10]

The most " democratic " feature of the new council, its representation of the gilds or misteries, was not destined to last long. With the decline of the influence of John of

---

[1] *Munim. Gildhall. Lond.* ii. (Liber Custumarum), p. 269.

[2] G. Norton, *Commentaries on the Constitution, etc., of London* (1869), pp. 62, 85, 87 ; R. Sharpe, *Cal. of Letter Book C*, p. 4.   Norton is very confused on this subject.   He speaks of " the mayor's common council " under Edward I and Edward II, a careless inference from " per commune consilium maioris, aldermannorum," etc. (*op. cit.*, p. 102), and distinguishes the body of *c.* 1285 as mere assistants of the aldermen in their wards.   He also regards the " immensa communitas " of this period as a folkmoot (*ibid.*, p. 74).

[3] Riley, *Memorials*, pp. liii-lv ; Sharpe, *Cal. of Letter Book F*, p. 162 ; Kingsford ap. Stow, *Survey of London*, ii. 279 ; Thomas, *Cal. of Plea and Mem. Rolls, 1323–64*, p. 15 *n.*

[4] It is possible that " commune consilium " was occasionally used concretely, but " congregatio " or " communitas " was the regular term in the city records. So, too, at Norwich which followed London practice (below, p. 317) it was always " common assembly," until early in the fifteenth century a " common council," modelled upon the London council of 1376 as modified in 1384, was adopted (W. Hudson, *Records of Norwich*, i. 98-101, 263 ff.).   [5] Above, p. 308.

[6] *Cal. of Letter Book H*, p. 110. On this occasion (1378) thirty-one misteries voted one way and ten the other.

[7] *Ibid.* Cf. *Munim. Gildhall. London*, i. (Liber Albus), p. 451.

[8] *Cal. of Letter Book H*, pp. 122, 162.

[9] *Ibid.*, pp. 54, 175.   [10] *Ibid.*, pp. 54, 122.

Northampton, the leader of the reforming party, who had been one of the sheriffs in 1376, reaction set in. From 1379 a practice grew up of afforcing the common council with " other the most sufficient men of the city " or " the more powerful and discreet citizens," who were, sometimes at least, chosen by the wards.[1] In November, 1380, a royal writ ordered the aldermen to take the opinion of the inhabitants of the wards as to whether it was best for the common council to be elected from the misteries, as before, or from the best men of the wards, or partly from each, and, if they approved the second alternative, to act upon it at once.[2] Apparently this was the result, and although Northampton's two years mayoralty (1381–83) stemmed reaction for a time, his rival and successor Brembre, with the support of the king, reversed much of the work of 1376. In January, 1384, " an immense commonalty of honest and discreet men " approved of an experimental return to election by wards. They were to send six, four, or two to the common council, according to their size, with an average of four or ninety-six in all. The mayor was to see that they did not include more than eight of any mistery. The restriction on the re-election of aldermen was removed.[3] A few months later, the minimum number of council meetings was reduced to one each quarter, and the old distinction between administrative and election meetings was partially restored by a provision that for the election of the mayor and the commoner sheriff [4] the council should be reinforced by others of the more efficient men of the city, so many and such as seemed to them necessary, with the advice and assent of sixteen aldermen at the least.[5] In October, 1385, the change from misteries to wards was approved for ever.[6]

The controlling influence of the aldermen was thus restored and actually increased by the power virtually given to them (with the mayor) to pack the election meetings of the council. Ten years later they were made irremovable, except for reasonable cause.[7] There was saved, however, from the wreck of the work of 1376 a permanent common council,

---

[1] *Cal. of Letter Book H*, pp. 137, 155 ; *cf.* 121.
[2] *Ibid.*, pp. 156, 164.   [3] *Ibid.*, pp. 227-8.
[4] Since 1340, at least, one sheriff was chosen by the mayor, who had nominated him for election as early as 1328 (*Cal. of Plea and Mem. Rolls, 1323–64*, ed. Thomas, p. 129 ; *cf.* p. 69).
[5] *Cal. of Letter Book H*, pp. 237 ff. A proclamation of 12th October shows that the " sufficient men " were to be summoned from the wards (*ibid.*, p. 251).
[6] *Ibid.*, p. 277.   [7] *Ibid.*, p. 409.

not too large and not too small, which was elected by the citizens in their wards, and which the mayor and aldermen were bound to consult at least four times a year.[1] The downfall and execution of Brembre caused no counter-revolution.[2] More fortunate than most English towns, London not only secured but retained a representative council chosen by the citizens at large.

The control of the composition of the election meetings by the mayor and aldermen widened the distinction between the comparatively small common council and this fuller representation of the freemen, and confirmed the position of the former as a council rather than an assembly. Even in the period 1376–84, though the council was supposed to serve both purposes, it was always described as a *congregatio* when it met for elections and was then doubtless increased in numbers, which the many misteries made easy. On sufficient occasion, even after 1384, the common council itself could be specially enlarged, as it was for the condemnation of the book called *Jubile* in 1387, when the more reputable and substantial men of the wards were summoned in such numbers that the council had to remove from the upper chamber to the hall below.[3] A special meeting for the election of representatives in Parliament in 1388 could be loosely described in the margin of the letter book as a common council.[4]

It has been asserted that though election by wards for the common council was restored in 1384, no change was made in the machinery for the election of the mayor and sheriffs which, therefore, continued to be made by the council and an unfixed number of commoners summoned from those nominated by the misteries, down to the reign of Edward IV.[5] This view is in plain contradiction with the ordinance and

---

[1] Its meeting-place was now called "the chamber of the common council," *Cal. of Letter Book H*, pp. 279, 290).

[2] Election by wards was again called in question in 1389, but it was reaffirmed (*ibid.*, p. 347). For these elections, see *ibid. I*, pp. 71, 89, 98, and cf. *ibid. H*, p. 347, and *Lib. Albus*, pp. 40-2. By 1419 the numbers were sixteen, twelve, eight, or four from the wards, according to their size (*ibid.*).

[3] *Ibid.*, p. 303.

[4] *Ibid.*, p. 332. The commons numbered about 210, from three to nineteen being summoned from twenty-four wards. It was the custom for the mayor and aldermen to elect two of the four representatives and the commons the other two.

[5] Norton, *Commentaries*, pp. 126-7. He was followed by Gross (*Gild Merchant*, i. 112).

proclamation on the subject quoted above,[1] and though the record of election meetings usually mentions only " an immense commonalty " or " very many commoners," there is occasionally a definite statement that these were drawn from the wards.[2] When, therefore, the common council ordained in 1467 that thenceforth the election of mayors and sheriffs should be made only by the council, the masters and wardens of each mistery of the city, coming in their livery, and *by other good men specially summoned for the purpose*,[3] there is no reason to suspect any other change than insistence that the heads of the city companies should always be summoned along with those called from the wards. By carelessly overlooking the words I have italicized, Norton thought that the electing body was so narrowed that further legislation became necessary, and accordingly, he says, in 1475 there were added to the common council and the wardens and masters of the misteries, as electors to the corporate offices and to parliament, the liverymen of the misteries, *i.e.* those freemen of the misteries (being freemen of the city) to whom a particular distinctive clothing was assigned by them, none others being allowed to be present.[4] What actually seems to have happened in that year was that for an ill-defined body of commoners summoned from the wards by the mayor and aldermen to election meetings there was substituted a definite class of recognized standing, the liverymen of the city misteries or, as they were called later, companies. Their liveries would have the further advantage of calling attention to any intruders at electoral meetings. This may look like a reversion to the ideas of 1376, but in the course of a century much had changed. There is no trace of any conflict on this occasion or of any proposal to alter the ward organization of the common council. So far from being democratic even in the limited sense of 1376, the change must doubtless be connected with the oligarchic tendency which was then becoming more and more intense in the English boroughs. After four centuries and a half the ordinance of 1475 is still in force for the election of the officers of the city corporation,[5] but the Municipal Corporation

---

[1] Pp. 313-14. [2] *Cal. of Letter Book H*, pp. 251 *n.*, 320.
[3] *Ibid. L*, p. 73. [4] Norton, *Commentaries*, pp. 126-7.
[5] It was generally affirmed by statute in 1725 (11 Geo. I, c. 18), which provided a legislative decision on some disputed points (*ibid.*, p. 242). " It was assumed that only liverymen of a year's standing were qualified to vote in the assembly now known as the Liverymen in Common Hall assembled " (*Cal. of Plea and Mem. Rolls, 1364-81*, ed. Thomas, p. lix).

Act and later legislation greatly widened the franchise for parliamentary elections.[1]

Thus by the close of the middle ages the assembly of nominees, which in the thirteenth century normally represented the mass of the citizens in the government of the city, had definitely split into two distinct bodies, both elected,[2] though on different electoral systems. London stood alone in the evolution of a separate electoral assembly. On the other hand, the common council, which was supplementary to the court (or congregation) of the aldermen, corresponded to the similar but proportionately smaller bodies of the same name which in many boroughs replaced the general assembly of the commonalty, whether primary or nominated, and formed second councils alongside the older bodies of twelve or twenty-four, membership of which, like that of the court of aldermen in London, was now enjoyed for life. In London, however, and nowhere else, except for a time in one or two boroughs whose constitution was modelled upon hers, the common council remained elective. Everywhere else, sooner or later, it became as close as the twelve or the twenty-four.

2.

In the development of its elected common council from a select assembly the capital was exceptional as in much else. The common councils which during the next two centuries were substituted in many boroughs, voluntarily or under royal compulsion, for the ancient communal assemblies were specially created and, unless London was copied, not elective. Imitation of London is best illustrated in the case of Norwich. Although, as we have seen, Norwich had received the liberties of London from Richard I, its earlier constitution differed in some important respects from that of its mother city. Until 1404, when it was made a shire, it had no mayor, and until 1417 no aldermen, by that name. Its chief executive officers were four bailiffs, assisted in administration, as early apparently as the beginning of the fourteenth century, by twenty-four

---

[1] An act of 1850 and the reform act of 1867 also extended the qualification for electors of aldermen, common councillors, and ward officers in the wards (Norton, op. cit., pp. 249 ff.). Until then it was confined to freemen householders.

[2] Indirectly, of course, in the case of the electoral body, the liverymen being appointed by the companies.

elected by the community. As at London, however, the normal
assembly of the community was not democratic, being mainly,
if not wholly, composed of some thirty to fifty of " the better
and more discreet " of the city, summoned by the officers from
the four leets into which it was divided, twelve, ten, or eight,
according to their size.[1] A penalty of 2s. for non-attendance
shows that, as at London again, even this limited number was
difficult to maintain. By the middle of the fourteenth century,
the burden of compulsory attendance seems to have been confined to twenty-four persons, elected by the community from
the leets, who were perhaps identical with the twenty-four
assistants of the bailiffs.[2] Somewhat later, in 1369, there is
evidence of an anti-oligarchic opposition operating here, as
in London, through the misteries or gilds.[3] A resolution of
the assembly ordered that the city officers and the twenty-
four " pur les assemblez " should be elected by " lavis des
bones gentz et les melliores des metiers de la cite." The
twenty-four [4] were not to make grants of tallages, mises, or
common lands without the concurrence of the better of the
crafts. The resolution was not entered on the assembly roll,
but the mention on the roll of 1372 of craftsmen bound to
attend assemblies, on pain of half the sum levied on absentee
members of the twenty-four, seems to prove that the gilds
won their point, if only for a season.[5] Six years later the rulers
of the city, on the ground that many of the commune of the
town had been of late " grauntement contrarious," petitioned
the king to empower the bailiffs and twenty-four to make such
ordinances and remedies for the good government of the
town as they should consider to be needed,[6] and this was
allowed by charter in 1380.[7] The deliberate omission of the
words " with the assent of the commonalty " from a clause
of the London charter of 1341, otherwise copied verbatim,
remained unknown to the commons, they asserted, until,
at the beginning of Henry V's reign, they came into conflict
with the twenty-four and other *gens destat* over the election
of mayors.[8] A compromise was arranged by arbitration

---

[1] W. Hudson, *Records of Norwich*, i. 191.   [2] *Ibid.*, p. 269.

[3] *Ibid.*, pp. xlviii-lii, 195, 268.

[4] It is not clear from the terms of the resolution that these were the
same persons as the twenty-four " pur les assemblez," but the recorded
attendances seem to leave no other conclusions open (*ibid.*, p. l.), unless,
indeed, the names of the latter who attended were not recorded on the
rolls.

[5] *Ibid.*, p. 269.   [6] *Ibid.* i. 64 f. ; *Rot. Parl.* iii. 41.

[7] *Ibid.* ; Hudson, *op. cit.*, p. 30.   [8] *Ibid.*, pp. 66 ff.

Y

(1415) [1] and embodied in a new charter (1417). [2] The omitted
words were restored, but the assent of the commonalty was
to be given by a common council of sixty chosen by the four
wards, as the leets were now renamed. The opportunity
was taken to revise the whole constitution on the London
model. The twenty-four were henceforth to be called aldermen, and, though elected by the wards, were to hold office for
life or until removal for reasonable cause. The procedure
arranged for the election of mayor and sheriffs also closely
follows their model, except that, in addition to the aldermen
and the common council, all resident citizens were allowed
to be present, not merely those summoned by the mayor
from the wards as in London—down to 1475. Acute civic
troubles in the period of the Wars of the Roses were not primarily due to defects in this constitution, and although changes
were proposed and even temporarily adopted, the only permanent alteration of vital moment was the exclusion after
1447 of the general body of freemen from the elections of
mayor and sheriffs, [3] which therefore became less popular than
those of London. With this exception and a more fatal change
in the eighteenth century, which restricted the freemen's
election of the sixty common councillors to twelve, who co-
opted the remainder, [4] the city's constitution, as settled in
1415–17, survived down to 1835.

Superficially, the constitutions of London and Norwich,
as they stood at the close of the middle ages with their popu-
larly elected common councils, might seem to differ little
from that of modern boroughs. There was this vital difference, however, that the aldermen, though elected, were
chosen for life and formed a separate estate of the governing
body, with magisterial powers in which the common council
had no share.

It is a striking illustration of the influence of London on
other municipalities that, somewhere about the time of the
Norwich compromise of 1415, constitutional changes on the
London model were effected at the bishop of Norwich's borough
of Lynn in Norfolk, then one of the most prosperous English
seaports. The chief organ for legislation and administration
at Lynn was a common assembly (*congregacio communitatis*), [5]

---

[1] W. Hudson, *Records of Norwich*, pp. 93 ff. [2] *Ibid.*, p. 36.
[3] *Ibid.*, p. cv. [4] *Ibid.*, p. cxv.
[5] At Lynn the community seems to have included the semi-privileged
class of episcopal tenants, who in the accounts of civic strife are called
inferiores.

which for very important business might number from seventy
to a hundred and ten persons or more, though the mention of
individual summons and of a fine of 2s. for default suggests
that the same difficulty of securing a quorum at ordinary
meetings was experienced as at London and Norwich.[1] Tumultuous interference with elections was obviated here, not as
at London by forbidding all but those specially summoned
to take part in them, but by the more effective device, which
is found also at Exeter and Cambridge, of an electoral committee. The election of the mayor and other officers and
—down to 1395 at least—of the twenty-four counsellors of
the mayor was entrusted to twelve persons, the first four of
whom were named by the alderman of the gild merchant and
then co-opted eight others.[2] About the beginning of the
fifteenth century, annual election of the twenty-four was
abandoned in favour of co-option for life or until resignation
or removal, and it was perhaps now that they came to be
commonly called jurats.[3] The mayor and other officers
continued to be elected by the twelve eligors. It was very
likely this closing of the council by the *potentiores* and its
results which provoked an agitation for a more liberal constitution among the mass of the burgesses (*mediocres*). In
1411–13 they had joined with the *inferiores*, as they had done
a hundred years before,[4] in resisting the financial burdens
laid upon them by the ruling class on unfair assessment or
as in this case, without their assent. The king was appealed
to and the *potentiores* were obliged to make concessions. These
financial disputes were closed by a solemn agreement, which
inter alia bound the mayor not to deal with the rents, etc., of
the community without the co-operation of a committee including both *mediocres* and *inferiores*.[5] But fresh contests
arose over the election of officers and councillors. The
committee of twelve eligors was abolished and the election of
the mayor and four chamberlains was conformed, so far as
possible, to the London practice. The burgesses named two

---

[1] A fairly continuous record of its more important meetings during the
second half of the fourteenth century is contained in the *Red Register of
King's Lynn*, ed. H. Ingleby, vol. ii.

[2] *Ibid.* ii. *passim ; Hist. MSS. Comm., Rept. XI*, App., pt. iii., pp.
195-6. Burgesses for parliament and coroners were appointed by committees of twelve who were similarly selected (*ibid.*, pp. 146 ff.).

[3] *Ibid.*, pp. 105-6. They were still elected yearly in 1395 (*Red Register*,
ii. 15).

[4] *Hist. MSS. Comm., Rept. XI, u.s.*, pp. 187, 240.

[5] *Ibid.*, pp. 191-4.

sufficient jurats or ex-jurats from whom the sitting mayor and the twenty-four jurats chose one for the next mayor; the burgesses elected two non-jurats as chamberlains, the other two being appointed, with the same restriction, by the mayor and twenty-four. The life tenure of the jurats was left untouched, but vacancies by death, etc., were to be filled by the burgesses nominating two sufficient persons from whom the surviving jurats should choose one or demand a fresh, nomination, if both were considered unsuitable.[1] The dissensions, however, continued, and probably owing to the unordered constitution of the borough assembly, the *potentiores* succeeded in 1416 in getting the new system revoked and obtained royal approval of the step.[2] Elections were again conducted by committees appointed in the old way, the burgesses at large having no voice in this matter and no organized or regular voice in any other. Naturally dissatisfaction broke out once more, until at last in 1420–21 the episcopal lord of the town negotiated an agreement which gave the town a common council on the same representative basis as those of London and Norwich, but proportionally smaller. Each of the nine constabularies of Lynn was to elect yearly three of the more competent and peaceful of its burgesses to take part " in the causes and affairs touching the town " which, as carefully defined in the document, are purely financial. Whatever the mayor, the twenty-four, and the twenty-seven (or the majority of these in each case) ordained in these matters was to hold good.[3] Lynn therefore withheld from its common councillors that share in the election of municipal officers and burgesses for parliament which was enjoyed by the corresponding bodies at London and Norwich. The name common council was from the first applied, as in many other boroughs, to the whole body of which they formed a part, as well as more particularly to themselves as representing the commonalty. Owing to the existence of a privileged non-burgess element at Lynn, however, the common councillors did not here entirely replace the commonalty. Down to 1524 the assembly remained the *congregatio communitatis*. Few but councillors normally

---

[1] *Hist. MSS. Comm., Rept. XI, u.s.*, pp. 196 ff. The date is uncertain but it was Henry V whose intervention brought about the settlement (*ibid.*, p. 197 : " our present dread lord.")

[2] *Ibid.*, pp. 202–3 ; *cf.* 160, 169. Mrs. Green's narrative of the events of 1411–16 has several erroneous dates and some confusions (*Town Life*, ii. 411 ff.). For example, she places Henry V's intervention after, instead of before, the new election ordinances (*ibid.*, p. 414).

[3] *Hist. MSS. Comm., Rept. XI, u.s.*, pp. 245-6.

attended it, but an instance is recorded—in 1463—when six
from the commonalty were appointed in addition to six from
each of the two councils to assess a tax,[1] and the election of
burgesses for parliament took place in the presence of the
commonalty.[2] It must be added that the popular basis of
the common council was not very broad, even for the burgesses.
Under Henry VI the constabulary actually electing seldom
numbered more than twenty voters, and sometimes as few as
twelve.[3] Such as it was, this popular element in the Lynn
council, together with the assembly, was swept away by the
charter of 1524, which made Lynn one of the closest of close
boroughs. The government of the town and the admission
of burgesses were placed in the hands of a mayor, twelve
aldermen, and eighteen common councillors. The councillors
were to be chosen by the mayor and aldermen from the burgesses at large whenever they pleased, with power to remove
any and to fill vacancies. The aldermen, who were to hold
office for life, were chosen by the Crown in the first instance ;
vacancies to be filled by the common councillors, who were
also to elect an alderman as mayor annually.[4] Thus every
vestige of popular participation in the town administration
disappeared. The aldermen and the common councillors
were so interlocked in this close oligarchy that they came to
be described as one " house " or " company," and down to
1835 the only breach that was effected in their monopoly of
power was during the Commonwealth, when the commons
demanded and obtained the right to elect their representatives
in parliament, which was more than they had possessed in the
middle ages.[5] For the complete failure of " democracy " at
Lynn, the early loss of all share in the choice of the borough
officers and council of twenty-four may have been largely
accountable, and the decline of her medieval prosperity no
doubt riveted the chains upon her.

3.

The addition of a " common council " to an older council,
which we have traced at London, Norwich, and Lynn, became

---

[1] *Hist. MSS. Comm., Rept. XI, u.s.*, p. 168.
[2] *Ibid.*, p. 169.   [3] *Ibid.*, p. 162.   [4] *Ibid.*, p. 206.
[5] *Ibid.*, pp. 149 ff. Since 1524 the representatives had been elected by
the town council directly, not through a committee (*ibid.*, p. 148).

frequent during the fifteenth and sixteenth centuries,[1] but unfortunately in other cases we have no such precise accounts of the events which led to their institution. It was usual to make the second council double the number of the old twelve or twenty-four and to rename these aldermen. The new twenty-four or forty-eight are but rarely stated to have represented the wards as in the three boroughs we have examined.[2] These additional bodies were created by local agreement, by royal charter, or by act of parliament. The first procedure is well illustrated by what happened at Winchester in 1456. The ruling body there was the ancient twenty-four, which formed a separate estate, though the commonalty was not without influence in the communal assembly—an offshoot of the primitive *burghmote*—and elected one of the two bailiffs. In the year mentioned, it was decided to reduce the number of the twenty-four to sixteen,[3] and to associate with them in the government of the city eighteen citizens " de parte communitatis coelectis." [4] If the reason given for the change, the reduction of the burden upon the time of the twenty-four, be the real one, it is perhaps not surprising that nothing more is heard of the scheme. Yet a similar arrangement at Newcastle-under-Lyme proved workable. At some date between 1411 and 1491 a body of twelve *pro communitate* was associated with another twelve representing the twenty-four *seniores* who had hitherto constituted the town council.[5] This was part of a kind of division of power, for there were also bailiffs and serjeants for the twenty-four and the commonalty respectively. The twelve *pro communitate* (doubled by 1547) came to be known as " the council of the town " and later as the common council (*consilium communitatis*).[6] An early example of a second council created by charter is found at Colchester. By Edward IV's charter of 1462 it was to consist of sixteen of the better and more discreet burgesses chosen from the four wards by the bailiffs,

[1] The second council of twenty-four recorded at York before 1411 seems to have been of a less popular kind. (*York Memorandum Book*, ed. Sellers (Surtees Soc.), i. 30, 119 ; ii. 256).
[2] An exception was Colchester, where the second council, here only sixteen in number, were drawn equally from the four wards (*Cal. of Chart. Rolls*, vi. 150).
[3] Of whom seven were ex-mayors.
[4] *Black Book of Winchester*, ed. W. H. B. Bird (1925), p. 86.
[5] T. Pape, *Medieval Newcastle-under-Lyme* (1928), pp. 176 ff.
[6] MS. Book of the Corporation of Newcastle-under-Lyme, s. 1547 and 1588. Mr. Pape kindly lent me his transcript of this book.

aldermen, and (old) council of sixteen, itself to be chosen by the bailiffs and aldermen. The whole body, including the second sixteen, was, in words which were to become common form in royal charters, to be and to be called the common council of the borough, and it was given full powers of legislation and taxation.[1] Thus, though the town was in the same charter incorporated as " the bailiffs and community of the borough of Colchester," the powers of the community were transferred to a small self-electing body of forty-two persons, and the government of Colchester became as closely oligarchical as that of Lynn sixty years later.

The moving cause of such changes is clearly stated in the acts of parliament which in 1489 vested popular rights of participation in elections of officers and assessment of taxation at Leicester and Northampton in close bodies consisting of the mayor, his twenty-four brethren, and a new element, consisting of forty-eight of the wiser inhabitants, chosen by them and changed by them as often as seemed necessary. Great discords, it is premised, had arisen in the two towns and in other boroughs corporate at the election of mayors and officers by reason of the multitude of the inhabitants being of little substance and of no discretion, who exceed in the assemblies the other approved, discreet, and well-disposed persons, and by their confederacies, exclamations, and headiness have caused great troubles in the elections and in the assessing of lawful charges.[2] At Leicester, the limited assembly which henceforth transacted the town business in " common halls " was careful for a century to describe itself as acting " for the whole body of the town," [3] but a charter of 1589 formally incorporated the mayor, twenty-four (now all called aldermen), and forty-eight as the " mayor and burgesses of the town of Leicester," reducing the rest of the population to the status of mere " inhabitants." [4]

[1] *Cal. Chart. Rolls*, vi. 150. The first sixteen had been evolved from an original twenty-four by the separation of eight auditors who became aldermen by 1443. See below, p. 335. Although the charter calls the whole body the common council, the town records usually distinguish the common council from the aldermen, and sometimes limit the name to the second body or even the first (*Red Paper Book*, ed. W. G. Benham (1902), pp. 26, 28, 31).

[2] Miss Bateson's summary of the act in *Records of Leicester*, ii. 319.

[3] *Ibid*. III, xviii. The two councils were sometimes distinguished as the " masters and the commynte " (*ibid*., p. 29).

[4] *Ibid*., p. 248. A further charter in 1599 gave to the forty-eight the formal title of common council (*ibid*., p. 361).

Until the fifteenth century the Crown had regarded the conciliar arrangements of the boroughs as a matter of purely local concern. The new policy of fixing councils by charter or act of parliament, reflects the increasing difficulties experienced by the ruling class in dealing with democratic agitation and its desire to secure a decision which would leave everything in its hands and could not be challenged. Welcome light is thrown upon the matters in dispute, election of officers,· etc., by two compositions between the bailiffs and commonalty of Shrewsbury, which were approved by parliament in 1433 and 1444. They illustrate the variety as well as the general likeness of the expedients adopted to end such dissensions. The earlier agreement created (or reorganized) a body of twelve assistants to the two bailiffs, to sit for life, with the usual reservations. They were to be appointed in the first place by the bailiffs and commonalty, who were to fill vacancies as they arose.[1] Much less favourable to the commonalty was the composition of 1444. The twelve were renamed aldermen and (with the bailiffs) were to fill their own vacancies. A second council of twenty-four " sufficient and discreet " commoners was added, who were also appointed for life, in the first instance by the bailiffs and commons, but afterwards by co-option.[2] Thus the Shrewsbury corporation was slightly less close than those of Colchester, Leicester, and Northampton, where the first council filled the vacancies in the second. Nor were meetings of the whole commonalty entirely given up, though provision was made against disorder by requiring them to express their views through a speaker taken from the twenty-four.[3] The common speaker (*praelocutor*) is found also at Norwich [4] and Lynn.[5] It is a feature which was perhaps originally derived from parliamentary procedure. The Shrewsbury commons elected the chamberlain and auditors, but the more important officers, bailiffs, coroners, etc., were chosen by one of those nominated committees of which we have noticed examples at Lynn and elsewhere.

The well-known Worcester ordinances of 1467 [6] furnish

---

[1] *Rot. Parl.* iv. 476 ff.   [2] *Ibid.* v. 121 ff.   [3] *Ibid.* v. 122.
[4] Where he was chosen by the common council of sixty (Hudson, *Records of Norwich*, i. 104 ; *cf.* pp. 95 f.).
[5] Here the speaker was a feature of the short-lived constitution which was suppressed in 1416 (above, p. 319). He was elected by all burgesses, excluding the jurats, there being as yet no common council at Lynn (*Hist. MSS. Comm., Rept. XI*, App., pt. iii., p. 200).
[6] *English Gilds*, ed. Toulmin Smith, pp. 370 ff.

another detailed description of the working of a two-council
system, but, so erratic is the preservation of municipal documents, no account of its institution has come down to us.
The chief differences from the Shrewsbury arrangements
were that both councils contained double the Shrewsbury
number of members, and that those of the first council were
not called aldermen, but the twenty-four of the great clothing
(*i.e.* livery), a term used also at Nottingham, but differently.
They were forbidden to grant the common good without the
advice of the forty-eight. The commoners elected one of
the chamberlains, as at Shrewsbury, and were equally represented on assessment committees and among the " judges "
who sat with the auditors. Later, at all events, they might
in certain cases be elected bailiffs. Here again the officers
were elected by committees. The enactment of these
ordinances by the citizens in their gild merchant reveals a
feature of the city constitution which must have been very
rare, if not unique, by this date.

Exceptions have already been noted, at London and elsewhere, to this normal type of two-council borough, in which
the number of the common councillors was just double that
of the aldermen or men of the great clothing, or otherwise
described members of the first council. In these exceptions
the numbers were at least fixed, but cases occur in which the
number of either one or the other council was left or became
undefined. In the first councils of twenty-four, the growth
of a sort of inner council of ex-mayors, the mayor's brethren,
and of a class of ex-bailiffs, occasionally tended to strain
both the unity and the fixed number of the body. This
was what happened at Northampton, at any rate, where the
original twenty-four began to split into two on these lines
in the fifteenth century, and by the end of the next was
represented by a body of ex-mayors (the bench), tending to
be about twelve on the average, and a body of ex-bailiffs,
tending to number about twenty-four.[1] There was nothing,
however, so far as we know, in the composition of common
councils to lead to a similar vagueness, though there were,

[1] Markham and Cox, *Records of Northampton*, ii. 17 ff., where, however,
it is misleading to say that the old twenty-four " disappeared in favour of
the forty-eight common council men." They survived as the undefined
body of ex-bailiffs with certain powers, and if they lost control of town
policy, it was to the aldermen, not to the forty-eight. The same process
may account for the large and not quite fixed mayor's council at Oxford.
See Appendix II, p. 337.

of course, differences of standing within them, and it is not obvious why that of Gloucester was not even limited to a maximum of forty until 1627, and not fixed absolutely at that number until 1672.[1] Sometimes, as at Coventry, though the number was fixed, it was not very strictly adhered to.[2]

Even where numbers were fixed, variations from the standard type were caused by special local developments, such as the part in municipal government won by the crafts in northern boroughs. A somewhat complicated council was evolved at Beverley by 1536, which consisted of three benches of twelve, the first being the twelve governors (formerly keepers), the original council and future aldermen, who were elected by the crafts from the other two benches, who together formed the twenty-four councillors or assistants. When vacancies occurred in the twenty-four, the whole thirty-six named two persons, of whom the community chose one. As the whole council was thus in some sort an emanation from the burgesses at large, there was more propriety than usual in its being described as the common council of the town.[3] The power of the crafts and popular election of common councillors (in the strict sense) is seen also at York, the mother city of Beverley. A charter of Henry VIII created a new common council, to which the thirteen principal crafts contributed two each, and fifteen inferior ones one each, forty-one in all.[4]

4

Even in the south we have seen that the common councillors at the end of the fifteenth century were not always

---

[1] G. S. Blakeway, *The City of Gloucester* (1924), pp. 55 ff.

[2] The constitution of Coventry, a corporation of comparatively late origin (1345), was in general exceptionally fluid and wanting in clearly defined bodies. Its common council, as fixed by a charter of James I, contained thirty-one superiors, who were apparently ex-officials, and twenty-five inferiors. Coventry was also exceptional in the prominence of its court leet in the government of the town (see the *Coventry Leet Book or Mayor's Register* (1907–13), ed. Dormer Harris). A somewhat similar part was played by the three Inquests at Hereford (*Hist. MSS. Comm., Rept. XIII*, iv. 316-17, 326), and by the two Inquests at Newcastle-under-Lyme (Pape, *Medieval Newcastle-under-Lyme*, p. 136).

[3] *Rept. Hist. MSS. Comm. on Beverley Corporation MSS.*, pp. 53-5.

[4] Gross, *Gild Merchant*, i. 111 ; *E.H.R.* ix. 279. For the share in the election of mayors given to the workers by Edward IV, see *Foedera*, xi. 530, quoted in *York Memorandum Book* (Surtees Soc.), introd., p. viii. There is evidence of the representation of artificers in assemblies between 1380 and 1392 (*ibid.* i. 39, 173).

the nominees of the mayor, as seems to have been the custom at Coventry, or of the mayor and aldermen, or of the common council itself, or of both councils. To these cases in which the common council was not yet closed there must be added that of Canterbury, where, in 1473, it was still elected *per communitatem*.[1] The permission to the " citizens and community " of Chester in a charter of 1506 to elect *annually* twenty-four aldermen, and forty other citizens as a common council, suggests an even more liberal constitution,[2] but was perhaps open to more than one interpretation. At any rate, the mayor incurred a rebuke in 1533 for filling vacancies in the common council himself, and the mayor, aldermen, and residue of the common council were directed to appoint from wise, discreet, and substantial commons.[3] This was in accordance with the general development which was embodied in numerous royal charters during the sixteenth and seventeenth centuries, though the selection of common councillors was more usually left to the mayor and aldermen alone.

As the two councils acted together for all business in which the common councillors participated,[4] and acted for the community at large, it is not surprising that they were, from this point of view, regarded as a single body, and that the term common council came to be used either for the whole or for the element which was supposed specially to represent the commons. At London, we have seen, " common council " sometimes included the aldermen and sometimes excluded them.[5] The Crown itself had no fixed usage. In the Colchester charter of 1462, the term is used in the wider sense,[6] in that of 1506 to Chester in the narrower.[7] By the middle of the sixteenth century, it could be employed officially where there was no special representation of the commonalty. The charters of Warwick (1554)[8] and Barnstaple

---

[1] *Hist. MSS. Comm., Rept. IX*, pt. i., App., p. 170.

[2] Morris, *Chester in Plantagenet and Tudor Times* (1893), p. 525.

[3] *Ibid.*, pp. 218-19.

[4] The common councilmen were often described as assistants of the superior body. At Shrewsbury, for instance, " thei . . . shall be continuell assistentz and of counsell to the seid bailiffs and aldremen " (*Rot. Parl.* v. 121).

[5] The present traditional title of the whole body is : " the Lord Mayor, Aldermen and Commons of the City of London, in Common Council assembled."

[6] Above, p. 323 n. 1.   But the narrower usage prevailed locally.

[7] See above.

[8] *The Black Book of Warwick*, ed. T. Kemp (1898), p. 110 ; *cf.* p. 341 *n*.

(1556),[1] for instance, set up in each a single council of principal or capital burgesses, filling up its own vacancies, to be " the common council of the borough."

The Warwick charter is particularly interesting, because it gave the bailiff and twelve principal burgesses discretion to make, constitute, and admit from time to time " tantos alios burgenses de inhabitantibus probioribus burgi illius in burgenses eiusdem burgi." This rather ambiguous clause [2] was interpreted by the council as giving it the right to appoint a certain number of assistants, not to be members of the common council, but " as it were the mouth of all the commons." [3] As the twenty-four so appointed contested this reading, they were first suspended and then (1576) reduced to twelve, " to do those things that the comon multytude should ells doo," i.e. choose the bailiff out of two named by the principal burgesses, which the charter directed to be done by the inhabitants at large, and to assist in the election of burgesses to parliament in order to satisfy the conditions prescribed by a statute of Henry VI.[4] In 1663, however, the constitution was assimilated to what had then become the normal type by the conversion of the principal burgesses into aldermen and the assistants into a common council, in the original restricted sense.[5]

As the addition of a common council (in this sense) in many boroughs had more or less vested the powers of the community in the joint council, the frequent application of the title assembly to its meetings may perhaps be considered as a survival, though assembly could be used for the meetings of even smaller bodies, e.g. those of the mayor and aldermen of London in the fourteenth century.[6] Northampton affords a clear case of this survival, for after the forty-eight had displaced the mass of the burgesses in 1489, the meetings of the enlarged council were called common assemblies and its ordinances were described as made by " the mayor and his brethren the twenty-four comburgesses and all the hole comynaltye (or hole body) of the towne." [7]

---

[1] Gribble, Memorials of Barnstaple (1830), pp. 379 f.
[2] A closely similar one in some charters merely empowered the council to admit new burgesses in the ordinary sense : e.g. see Mayo and Gould, Municipal Documents of Dorchester, p. 62 (Charter of 1629).
[3] Black Book, p. 16.
[4] Ibid., pp. 106, 393 ; Statutes of the Realm, ii. 340. The assistants were sometimes called " commoners " (Black Book, p. 379).
[5] Ibid., p. 434 ; Carlisle, Topogr. Dict. (1808), s.v.
[6] Thomas, Cal. of Plea and Mem. Rolls, 1364–81, p. 215 et passim.
[7] Markham and Cox, Records of Northampton, i. 340 ; cf. 329, etc.

The usual meeting-place of borough councils was a chamber in the gildhall, town hall, or otherwise named civic hall; and at Exeter, York, and elsewhere the council came later to be known as the council of the chamber, or simply as the chamber, but with the increase of their numbers and of civic business in the fifteenth and sixteenth centuries separate council houses were provided in some towns.

Other names for their meetings besides common assemblies or assemblies were common halls and councils simply. With few exceptions, councils which comprised two or three sections or companies, as they came to be called, seem to have sat in the same room and to have had equal votes, though the aldermen or other superior company occupied a bench at the upper end of the chamber, sometimes raised above the general level. At Plymouth, in 1683, it was said to be a rule that constitutions could only be altered by a majority of the whole body, which ought to consist of thirty-seven persons.[1] It is only at Lincoln that we distinctly hear before the seventeenth century of a twelve and a twenty-four forming an inner and an outer house and voting separately.[2] Laws were made in the inner house, and the outer, it was complained, was not always allowed sufficient time for their consideration. Something of the kind, however, seems to have obtained at York from the sixteenth century onwards, for the common council is said to have proceeded largely by petition to the mayor and his brethren.[3] At Norwich the sixty common councillors, though they sat with the mayor and aldermen, could ask leave—like the commons in parliament—to go apart in a house by themselves.[4]

Much administrative business was, however, everywhere disposed of by the mayor (or bailiffs) and their brethren, the aldermen or other primary council, who could no doubt in most cases practically decide what should come before the whole body. At Canterbury, we are definitely informed, the share of the common council, even in legislation, depended

---

[1] *Hist. MSS. Comm., Rept. IX*, pt. i., App., p. 277.

[2] *Ibid., Rept. XIV*, App., pt. viii., pp. 78, 90. The twenty-four were added to the twelve aldermen (mayor's brethren) in 1511, " to keep and order all acts to be made in the common council " (*ibid.*, p. 24). The mayor and aldermen sometimes sat as a " secret council."

[3] *E.H.R.* ix. 279 ; Raine, *York* (Historic Towns), p. 195. In the seventeenth century there was an upper and a lower house (*ibid.*). At Coventry by 1617 the mayor and aldermen had possession of the council-house, though the common council could be summoned to it for certain business (*Leet Book*, pp. 335-7).   [4] Hudson, *Records of Norwich*, i. 100.

upon the mayor and aldermen.[1] On the other hand, municipal legislation and taxation were sometimes expressly
reserved by charter for the full council.[2]

The variety of law and usage which makes a general
description of English municipal institutions in the Middle
Ages, and even later, so difficult, was characteristic of them
from the first and was only gradually mitigated by natural
assimilation and royal policy. There was nothing in England
corresponding to the Scottish *Leges Quatuor Burgorum* and
convention of royal boroughs. Until the fifteenth century,
English kings were content to exercise a firm control over
their boroughs through the municipal officials, over whose
choice they reserved an ultimate veto, and left them free
to hammer out local organization for themselves. Even in
the charters of Henry VI and Edward IV the clauses which
fix the number and powers of municipal councils perhaps
reflect local desires rather than any definite policy of the
king or his advisers. It is only from the sixteenth century
that royal charters seem to be aiming deliberately at greater
uniformity in municipal institutions.

APPENDIX I

Some Single Common Councils of Early Date

THE widespread common council of the fifteenth century
and onwards, added to an oligarchical council to represent
the commonalty, has obscured the earlier existence in a few
boroughs of a single common council of well-to-do burgesses,
established primarily to curb the arbitrary action of mayor
or bailiffs. The first recorded institutions of such a council
occur almost simultaneously at Bristol and Exeter in the
middle of the fourteenth century.

Before that date the municipal history of Bristol is far
from clear, but there is some evidence, arising out of a severe
conflict between the *potentiores* and the commons in 1312–13,
which may perhaps point to a small council of twelve.[3] If
such a council existed and survived that crisis, it was superseded in 1344 by a larger one on a different basis. Reforms

---

[1] *Hist. MSS. Comm., Rept. IX*, pt. i., App., p. 170.
[2] As at Colchester (above, p. 323).
[3] Hunt, *Bristol* (Historic Towns), pp. 63 ff.

were called for, " many good customs having been abused and some almost forgotten." And so, runs the official account, though the mayor is appointed to see to their conservation, at the instance of Stephen le Spicer, who was elected mayor this year for the better rule of his office (*status*) and the town,[1] there were chosen forty-eight of the *potentiores et discretiores* of the said town to be his counsellors (*consultores*) and assessors and to assist and expedite the town's affairs.[2] Five years later the forty-eight are described as " electi ad tractandum in communi consilio," [3] and common council was the name by which their body was afterwards known.[4] The charter of 1373, which erected Bristol into a shire, generally confirmed the new constitution, but reduced the number of the councillors to forty, probably to bring them into relation with the five aldermen, at that time elected by the wards. The council was to be chosen by the mayor and sheriff with the assent of the community, and this assent was still required by the charter of 1499, which, however, put an end to the popular election of the aldermen, now increased to six by the inclusion of the recorder. He was appointed by the council, but the others were chosen for life and were only removable by the mayor and their fellow aldermen. As the mayor was taken from the aldermen, and the aldermen from the ex-mayors and common council men, the government of the town became wholly oligarchical, except for the shadowy consent of the community required for the appointment of the forty councillors. Later charters allowed the council to fill its own vacancies, and the corporation became close in form as well as in fact. The increase of the aldermen to twelve in 1581 assimilated it to the normal double council type.

In 1345, the year after the establishment of the Bristol common council, a similar change was carried through at Exeter. Owing to the preservation in great part of the city court rolls from 1264, a good deal more is known of the early constitution of the city than in the case of Bristol.[5] The election of a council of twenty-four of the usual thirteenth-century

---

[1] This seems to be the only authority for Mrs. Green's statement that " the popular party insisted on the appointment of the forty-eight " (*Town Life*, ii. 268).

[2] *Little Red Book of Bristol*, ed. Bickley, i. 25-7.

[3] *Ibid.*, p. 20.   [4] *Ibid.*, p. 86.

[5] For the substance of the brief summary of the evidence in the archives of the Exeter Corporation which follows I am mainly indebted to Dr. B. Wilkinson's monograph on *The Mediæval Council of Exeter* (M.U.P. 1931).

type is recorded in 1296–97, and entries on the rolls of 1264 and 1267 have been claimed as showing the existence of a similar body at those dates. The general silence of the rolls, however, hardly supports the assumption of a permanent council of twenty-four, though under 1333 there is a list of twenty-six persons who are described as elected by common counsel to be with the mayor and four stewards in all the great affairs of the community whenever summoned beforehand by the bailiffs. This certainly looks more like a council than such a selected assembly as we have found at London and Norwich in the thirteenth century. The suggestion of continuity from 1296–97 is, however, confronted by the appearance in 1324 of an elected body of twelve with the same function, but whose consent is expressly stated to be necessary for the validity of the mayor's acts. This experiment was recurred to with more success in 1345, when the misdoings of mayors and stewards " contra voluntatem meliorum civitatis " and tending to its impoverishment and disinherison provoked the creation of a body of twelve citizens " of the better and more discreet," excluding all the higher officers, without whose consent and counsel, or that of the greater part of them, no amercements, fines, or arrears beyond a small fixed amount should be pardoned, none admitted to the freedom of the city, no letters or obligations touching the city sealed, and no important civic business determined. This council of twelve was annually elected along with the mayor and stewards, and in the same way for more than a century, and the record of its appointment always insists on the necessity of its consent in the " ardua negotia " of the city.

It is clear that, like the change at Bristol the year before, this was no triumph of a popular party over the *potentiores*,[1] but the successful assertion of the control of the well-to-do over the officers of the city. A few years before, in 1339, it had, indeed, been necessary to forbid tumultuous assemblies of freemen at the election of these officers, but the ruling class had clipped the wings of the commonalty very effectively. The appointment of officers was in the hands of one of those elaborately nominated election committees of which we

---

[1] A possible case of popular agitation for representation, but at a much earlier date, may be contained in a too brief entry on the Exeter Court Rolls (now called Mayor's Court Rolls) to which my attention was kindly called by Miss R. C. Easterling. " On the first roll (1264)," she writes, " very inconspicuously placed, is a list containing 24 (or 25) names headed ' Isti electi sunt per mediocres.' "

have seen a typical example at Lynn.[1]   At Exeter a first four
chose thirty-six who made the elections.   These were always
meliores.   In fact, though everything was done in the court of
Exeter in the name of the community, and the new council of
twelve discreets was described from 1365 at least as the common council of the city, the municipal government was in
practice oligarchic.   Here, as in so many other boroughs,
the fifteenth century saw a democratic uprising against the
domination of the *meliores*, which was at first successful, but
produced no lasting effects.   Nothing is known, unfortunately,
of the circumstances in which there appeared in the council
in 1450 a second body of twelve, " elected by the community
for the community," and not by the thirty-six who chose
the first twelve, now distinguished as *de magnatis*.   But
assimilation must have gone on rapidly, for from 1455 we hear
only of a single common council of twenty-four, elected
apparently by the thirty-six.   In the last years of the century
fresh dissensions seem to have arisen, apparently over the
election of the mayor, and a royal ordinance is said to have
abolished the thirty-six and to have given the selection of
the two ex-mayors or receivers from whom the commons
were to choose the mayor as well as the direct choice of the
other officers to the council of twenty-four.   By Henry VIII's
charter of 1509, which professed to follow his father's ordinance, the councillors sat for life, and were not removable
save for serious cause, and then only by their own body, which
moreover filled all its vacancies.   As the two from whom
the mayor was selected were councillors, the government of
Exeter at the beginning of the sixteenth century could hardly
have been more oligarchic.

Nearly thirty years later than the setting up of common
councils at Bristol and Exeter, a somewhat similar step was
taken at Colchester.   Here again it was the arbitrary proceedings of the town officers, not the privileged position of
a ruling class, that it was sought to curtail.   Until 1372 the
whole income of the town had passed through the hands of
the two bailiffs, who were its chief officials, as there was no
mayor.   They were alleged to have spent it at their will in
defiance of constitutions made by the whole community and
the more worthy of the sworn men of the town, from which
it would appear that there was already a council, but that it
was not unanimous in opposition to the action of the bailiffs.

[1] Above, p. 319.

z

It was partly composed no doubt of ex-bailiffs. This being so, " certain lovers of the borough " carried through the assembly a series of ordinances designed to limit the power of the bailiffs and their brethren, which are fortunately set down in great detail in the extant Oath Book of the corporation. The town finances were transferred from the bailiffs to two new officers, called at first receivers and later chamberlains, who with the bailiffs and eight auditors were to administer the revenue they received and to present accounts annually in the presence of their colleagues and such of the community as desired to attend. To exclude the influence of the ex-bailiff class upon the election of these and the other officers, a committee of eligors was established after the fashion of Lynn and Exeter, but in this case not a mere body of nominees. Four sufficient persons, one from each ward, chosen by the advice of the whole community, were sworn to add to themselves twenty others, and the twenty-four, none of whom might be an ex-bailiff, took an oath to choose fit and proper persons as bailiffs, receivers, and auditors. No ex-bailiff could be appointed as receiver.[1]

A new council was a necessary part of the re-organized constitution. The bailiffs and auditors were annually to co-opt sixteen of the wisest and best of the wealthier burgesses (*ceaux que plus ount*). The bailiffs and the twenty-four councillors were to manage all the affairs of the borough, and to make necessary ordinances for its common profit. They were bound to meet at least four times a year.[2] That these changes were in no real sense democratic is plain from the provision that any representations by the commonalty touching the common profit or damage must be made by bill to the bailiffs at one council assembly, considered there, and answered at the next. Clamorous interposition was forbidden on pain of imprisonment.[3] And so we hear of ordinances made in 1425–26 " by the bailiffs and the general counseill of the town at the request of the commune people." [4] With this restriction, the general or common council replaced any wider assembly that may have existed before 1372, except that in a constitutional crisis it was still open to the bailiffs

---

[1] *The Oath Book of Colchester*, ed. W. Gurney Benham (1907), pp. 31 ff.
[2] *Ibid.*, p. 33. For quarterly meetings of council as a minimum number at London from 1384 and at Worcester, see above, pp. 311, *n.* 2, 314.
[3] *Oath Book, loc. cit.*
[4] *Red Paper Book of Colchester*, ed. W. G. Benham (1902), p. 49.

to summon the whole community to a meeting with the council.[1] At elections all burgesses were entitled to appear, but men's children, apprentices, and others who were not full freemen must not intrude.[2]

The distinction of status between the eight auditors and the other sixteen councillors, ended in the separation of the auditors as aldermen before 1443,[3] and was seemingly increased four years later by the acquisition of the right to have four justices of the peace in the borough, in addition to the bailiffs.[4] The offices of bailiff, justice, and coroner were now confined to aldermen, who in turn were only to be drawn from the councillors.[5] The effect, of course, was to restrict election within very narrow limits and to pave the way for co-option. The charter of 1462 enlarged the council by the addition of a second sixteen, but gave the choice of these to the bailiffs, aldermen and first sixteen.[6] In 1524 ordinances were made which, though enacted only " for a year and further if profitable," show a continued tendency to close up the corporation. The twenty-four eligors who elected the aldermen (with other officers) were forbidden to remove them without the consent of the bailliffs and remaining aldermen.[7] Also the aldermen and common council asserted the right to appoint one of the chamberlains for life, leaving the selection of the second chamberlain only to the eligors, who five years later were limited in their choice of the four serjeants of the town to eight persons named by the bailiffs and aldermen.[8]

It is possible that a council which was instituted at Cambridge in 1376 should be classed with the type of common council we have been examining. Unluckily in this case there is no more to go upon than a brief entry in one of the borough books. Until the third quarter of the fourteenth century, the mayor's only assessors seem to have been the two aldermen and four burgesses or councillors imposed upon the town by Henry III in 1268, at the instance of the university, for a special purpose, the preservation of the peace.[9] These were elected along with the town officers by eighteen eligors chosen in an even more complicated way than those we have already met with. The mayor and his assessors

[1] *Oath Book*, pp. 34-5.
[2] *Ibid.*, p. 35.
[3] *Red Paper Book*, p. 159.
[4] *Cal. of Chart. Rolls*, vi. 84.
[5] *Oath Book*, p. 186.
[6] Above, p. 322.
[7] *Red Paper Book*, p. 30 ; *cf.* 29.
[8] *Ibid.*, p. 31.
[9] Above, p. 277.

named one of two first eligors, and the commonalty the other, and these two chose twelve approved persons, who co-opted six others.[1] In 1376, however, a body of twenty-four councillors appears, described as " lately elected in the name of the whole community," [2] and this remained the common council of the borough down to 1835. If the six assessors of the mayor were regarded as a first council and the twenty-four as a popular addition, Cambridge would share with London the distinction of being the first to set up a common council of this more usual type. But the assessors were rather few to be considered as a council in the strict sense, and the institution was always disliked as a mark of university dictation to the town.[3] If there was actually no superior municipal body until the number of the aldermen was raised,[4] it is conceivable that the establishment of the council of twenty-four in 1376 was not the result of democratic pressure but of a more general movement against the mayor and his unpopular associates. Fifty years later, in 1426, the whole government of the town is said to be in the hands of the mayor and the twenty-four burgesses of the more discreet sort; no mention is made of the aldermen or other assessors. There is nothing specially " democratic " about the election of the twenty-four, when it comes into view at this date. They were chosen by an even more complicated arrangement than that for the election of officers, and here, too, the commonalty's part was confined to the selection of one of the original two eligors.[5] Still it was a freer system than that which obtained later at Colchester and elsewhere, and it was not until 1599 that the election of the twenty-four, now all ex-bailiffs, was transferred to the mayor and aldermen with power to displace and replace the unfit.[6]

The most important inference to be drawn from these municipal developments at Bristol, Exeter, Colchester, possibly at Cambridge, and perhaps in other boroughs where information is lacking, is that, so far as they go, and leaving London out of account, they confirm the view that the fourteenth century was not a period of much " democratic " activity and advance in the English borough.

[1] Cooper, *Annals of Cambridge*, i. 96, s. 1344.   [2] *Ibid.* i. 114.
[3] Above, p. 277.   [4] Above, *ibid.*
[5] Cooper, i. 174-5.   [6] *Ibid.* ii. 597.

APPENDIX II

List of Old Councils and Common Councils before 1550

ONLY those common councils are included which were added to an older body, usually by the end of this period called aldermen, as a representation of the commonalty. The list is doubtless incomplete, as information is lacking for some boroughs and for others it is confused and uncertain :—

Borough.				Aldermen, etc.	Common Council.
Beverley	.	.	.	12	24 (before 1536)
Canterbury	.	.	.	12	36 (before 1456)
Chester	.	.	.	24	48 [1] (before 1459)
Colchester	.	.	.	8+16 [2]	16 (1462)
Exeter	.	.	.	12	12 (1450–55 [3])
Gloucester	.	.	.	12	number undefined
Ipswich	.	.	.	12	24 (before 1520)
Leicester	.	.	.	24	48 (1489)
Lincoln	.	.	.	12	24 (before 1520)
London	.	.	.	24	number variable [4] (1376)
Lynn (Regis)	.	.	.	24	27 [5] (1420–21)
Newcastle-under-Lyme	.			12	12 [6] (before 1491)
Northampton	.	.	.	24	48 (1489)
Norwich	.	.	.	24	60 (1415)
Oxford	.	.	.	35 ?	24 [7] (before 1519)
Plymouth	.	.	.	12	24 (before 1521)
Salisbury	.	.	.	24	48 (before 1463)
Shrewsbury	.	.	.	12	24 (1444)
Winchester	.	.	.	16	18 [8] (1456)
Worcester	.	.	.	24	48 (before 1467)
Yarmouth	.	.	.	24	48 (before 1538)

[1] Reduced to 40 by the charter of 1506.

[2] The original 24 had split into a body of 8 aldermen and 16 councillors. In one sense, therefore, Colchester had 3 councils from 1462.

[3] After five years the two councils coalesced. See above, p. 333.

[4] When their election was transferred to the wards in 1384, their number was fixed at 96, but this was afterwards increased. See above, p. 313.

[5] Reduced to 18 by the charter of 1524.

[6] See above, p. 322.

[7] Both numbers seem to have varied slightly. In 1518 a list of the *Consilium Maioris* contains 37 names and that of the *consilium commune* 28 (Turner, *Oxford City Records, 1509–83* (1880), pp. 20-1). But the numbers in 1523 were the same as in 1519 (*ibid.*, p. 32).

[8] Perhaps only a scheme, never put in force. See above, p. 322.

APPENDIX III

A Criticism Considered

WHEN the preceding article was first published in the *English Historical Review*, the author was criticized for describing as " democratic " or " popular " the opposition to municipal governing bodies and in particular that in London in 1376 the outstanding feature of the success of which was the substitution of gild for ward as election unit.[1] It is true that, taken in their strict sense, these terms would be used more correctly if confined to those disorderly intrusions into election assemblies which led to royal intervention at the instance of the ruling class. But, if properly guarded, they are convenient short expressions not wholly inapplicable to the widespread movement against such narrow oligarchies as that of the London aldermen. As " democratic " is the more ambiguous of the two, I have put it within inverted commas or substituted " anti-oligarchic." Though there were many cross currents in the London of 1376 and the popular character of the change from ward to gild may easily be exaggerated, the enforcement of the long neglected regulations of 1319 for annual election of the aldermen and prohibition of immediate re-election directly connects the movement of that year with the violently anti-oligarchic episodes of the reigns of Edward II and Henry III. To have entered into the much debated problems raised by the cross currents just referred to in a brief summary of the institution of common councils would have unduly swollen the already disproportionate space allotted to that of the capital. The reader will find the problems in question fully treated in the late Professor George Unwin's *The Gilds and Companies of London* (1908), especially c. x. and in Dr. Erwin Meyer's article on " English Craft Gilds and Borough Governments of the Later Middle Ages " in *University of Colorado Studies*, xvii. (1929-30), 384-401. In an unprinted London thesis on " Civic Factions in London—their relation to Political Parties, 1376-99," Miss Ruth Bird adduces evidence for the view that the conflict between the victualling and non-victualling gilds had less to do with the municipal crisis of 1376 than antagonism to the aldermanic capitalists of the type of Richard Lyons and Adam Bury, just then condemned by the Good Parliament.

[1] E. F. Meyer in *Speculum*, vii. 249 f.

XII

THE STUDY OF EARLY MUNICIPAL HISTORY IN ENGLAND [1]

THE twentieth century opened with the brightest prospects for the study of early municipal history in this country, prospects which have since become lamentably overclouded. A group of distinguished scholars had made a remarkable and unprecedented advance in the solution of the most obscure problems presented by the initial growth of urban life in England. In the past the subject had been chiefly in the hands of lawyers and local antiquaries, and neither class was well equipped to grapple with its real difficulties. One outstanding work there was, the *Firma Burgi* (1726) of that admirable eighteenth-century scholar, Thomas Madox, but, great and permanent as is its value, it deals with an aspect of municipal growth which was comparatively simple to one of his immense knowledge of the national archives. Much more complicated problems were attacked, and to a large extent solved, in the last decade of the nineteenth century and the first lustrum of this. Charles Gross dispersed the cloud of error which had exaggerated the part played by the merchant gild in the evolution of our municipal constitutions. Mary Bateson found a French key to some of the most striking peculiarities of the post-Conquest borough, revealed the great mass of archaic law which the boroughs preserved throughout the middle ages, and edited the most complete collection of the records of a single borough which has yet appeared. Maitland showed that the oldest English boroughs were rooted in the soil, that the medieval burgher was still interested in agriculture, had one foot on mother earth outside his walls. His gifts of subtle insight and bold suggestion were never more evident respectively than in the analysis of the transition

[1] A paper read at the British Academy on 10th May, 1922, and now reprinted, with some revision, from vol. x. of its *Proceedings*.

from " commonness " to " corporateness " in the English borough which rounds off a famous chapter of the *History of English Law* and in the more debatable treatment of the Domesday boroughs in *Domesday Book and Beyond*. We may think that the boldness has gone too far in the latter case, without withholding from him and his zealous disciple, Adolphus Ballard,[1] the credit of having made what is really the first of our documentary materials for the history of English boroughs more intelligible and more significant.

A later stream of French influence than that detected by Miss Bateson was explored by Dr. Horace Round in articles on the Cinque Ports [2] and the Commune of London,[3] though the direct affiliation to foreign communes which he thought he had shown has not found acceptance.

All these workers were in the prime of life, and in the ordinary course many years of fruitful investigation might have been expected from them. But a sort of fatality seems to have attended on the group. Dr. Round is still happily with us, though he has not pursued the municipal studies of earlier years, but all the others had died before the end of 1915, Maitland, the longest-lived of them, at the early age of fifty-six. The loss to this particular branch of historical research was irreparable. The barrenness of the last decade in this field, with the notable exception of an excellent study of *Burgage Tenure in England*,[4] by an American scholar, Dr. Hemmeon, a pupil of Gross, who himself died early, cannot be attributed wholly to the war and its sequel.

Maitland's chief contributions to the story of the evolution of our oldest towns emphasized two somewhat opposite features of their origin—continuity with the nucleus of an agricultural township and the stimulation produced by a period of foreign invasion, the latter perhaps over-emphasized.[5]

In impressing upon us that " those who would study the early history of our towns have fields and pastures on their hands," Maitland did not claim originality. The very word " town " is an unmistakable finger-post. Beginning as an Old English word for a village, or even a single homestead, it has been narrowed down in this country, though not in

[1] *The Domesday Boroughs*, 1904.
[2] *Feudal England* (1895), 552 ff. *Cf.* above, p. 293.
[3] *The Commune of London and other Studies* (1899), 229 ff. *Cf.* below, p. 347.
[4] Harvard Historical Studies, xx. (1914).
[5] Still more subsequently by Dr. Stephenson. See above, *passim.*

New England, to mean an urban as distinguished from a rural community. The transition thus indicated had been noted by Stubbs, but the vivid picture of the agricultural aspects of medieval Cambridge in *Township and Borough* placed it in a new and stronger light.

More novel was Maitland's attempt to account for the possession by our chief towns, when they first come well into view after the Norman Conquest, of a court which was not that of a rural township, if indeed the township had a court, which he did not believe,[1] but parallel with the court of the hundred which was an aggregation of townships. He traced this borough court with some other features of later town life to the age of the Danish invasions. The necessity of defence brought about the fortification of many old and new centres, and he suggested that courts were established in them to settle the quarrels of the ruffling warriors placed in them by the landowners of the county, upon whom the burden of their upkeep was thrown. The general application of the term " borough," which means a place of defence, to such towns was regarded by him as supporting this " garrison theory " of the origin of our oldest towns. Though whole-heartedly adopted by Ballard, it has not secured universal acceptance. Maitland himself explained, in answer to criticism, that he did not mean to offer it as a solution of the problem in all towns, or even as completely covering the ground in those where it is most plausible. It does not profess, therefore, to account for the urban organization of towns which, like London, Lincoln, or Canterbury, had existed, if not from Roman times, at any rate from a date not much later, or even of a distinctly later town like Norwich. There were other influences making for urban aggregation and organization, especially the growth of trade. It is significant that the general spread of the term " borough " in its urban sense was accompanied by the use of a word which expressed the trading aspect of the same community. This was " port," the derivation of which from *portus*, " harbour," seems, like the parallel word " poort " in the Netherlands, to point to the first seats of trade having been on the coast or navigable rivers.

The existence of a military element, fleeting or more durable, in many boroughs need not be denied, but it was not the only element, and its identification with the burgesses who in Domesday Book are recorded in most of the greater boroughs

[1] Professor Vinogradoff is less sceptical (*Growth of the Manor*, 194, 274).

as belonging to some rural manor and paying rent to it, or occupying houses which paid such rents, is more than dubious. Domesday itself shows that the lordship of burgesses and houses was being transferred pretty freely before the Conquest, and the burgesses' right of sale may account for a good many of these manorial ownerships. The tendency of the rural landowner to acquire property in the local town, and even to reside there occasionally, is early evidenced and continued down to modern times. " Tenurial heterogeneity," the awkward phrase which Maitland coined to express the fact that such boroughs were on no single lord's land, whether king's or subject's, may have grown up quite independently of military arrangements.

The borough which was the property of one lord was not, however, unknown in Anglo-Saxon times, witness Dunwich in Suffolk with its lay lord and Sandwich in Kent, which belonged to the monks of Christ Church, Canterbury.[1] Not the least striking of the effects of the Norman Conquest in the field of municipal history was the wide extension of this class of dependent or seignorial boroughs, of which more will be said later.

Another result of the Conquest is the real beginning of our evidence for municipal history. We have no genuine pre-Norman town charter, much less any civic record, judicial or administrative, of that date. For these latter, indeed, we have to wait until the later years of the twelfth century, but there is a growing stream of charters from the first establishment of the new dynasty. More than three hundred had been issued by the Crown and private lords before the end of John's reign, and these have been brought together in a form convenient for students of borough formation and organization by Ballard in the first volume of *British Borough Charters*.[2] Materials for a further volume, extending to the death of Edward I, had been largely collected by him before his death, in 1915, and will shortly be published.[3]

It is noteworthy that the most liberal grantor of charters to royal boroughs was John, whose appreciation of the sums they were ready to pay for privileges was probably not checked by much consideration whether the permanent interests of the Crown would be served by the greater independence he allowed to the towns. However, the leases of Crown revenue which he gave were such hard bargains that there is no

---

[1] *D.B.* i. 3a, 1.   [2] Cambridge, 1913.   [3] *Ibid.*, 1923.

reason to suppose that those interests suffered materially. His son was less lavish, except when in dire financial straits, as in the year or two before the Barons' War, and his grandson even less so, save where the foundation and enhancement of towns served his general policy.

The policy of enlightened self-interest on the whole pursued by our Norman and Angevin sovereigns can be well studied in their treatment of those older towns which may now be called royal cities and boroughs in a fuller sense than before. Hitherto the king, though in possession of the borough administration and receiving the danegeld and the revenue of its court and market, had been but one, if the greatest, of its landlords. It was, however, in these centres of growing wealth that the replacement of the antiquated danegeld by more remunerative forms of (non-feudal) taxation was begun and its extension by Henry II, ultimately under the name of tallage, to the ancient (rural) demesne of the Crown [1] brought the boroughs under the general head of *dominia* and, aided by the gradual extinction of manorial lordships (sokes) paved the way for the theory that all land in the borough was held of the Crown by socage or burgage. The tallage and subsequent revenue developments were fruitful in results for the towns. They yielded a revenue which, even when ultimately made dependent on parliamentary consent, retained traces of its origin in the higher rate at which the towns and the ancient demesne were charged, and it disposed the king to grant to them such privileges as would enable them better to meet this and their other financial obligations to the Crown. Indeed, we need not limit royal graciousness quite so narrowly, for, where nothing was lost by so doing, the claim of the Crown dependents to special favour was fully recognized. From this point of view the curious parallelism of some of the privileges of royal boroughs and those of ancient demesne is instructive. Both were quit of suit to shire and hundred courts and in general exempt from taking their cases to outside courts, other than the highest. They both ultimately almost excluded the sheriff. The privilege of freedom from toll throughout England, or even the whole of the king's dominions, was generally enjoyed by both. Both gave freedom to the serf unclaimed by his lord for a year and a day. Moreover, some communities on ancient

[1] Stephenson, *Borough and Town* (1933), pp. 160 ff., has cleared up the order of these events.

demesne are found in enjoyment of such special features of borough tenure as the right of sale and bequest of their tenements, and larger urban communities thereon, *e.g.* Basingstoke and Kingston-on-Thames, though not formally called boroughs, attained a status which was practically indistinguishable from that of recognized boroughs. This burghal aspect of ancient demesne [1] becomes troublesome when we attempt to define a borough, just as it created difficulties when the demesne was taxed at the borough rate by parliament. There was some uncertainty at first as to who should give the consent of the men on ancient demesne, and, in default of a more logical solution, it was finally settled in favour of the knights of the shire,[2] whose normal constituents paid at a lower rate and to whose expenses the demesne men successfully refused to contribute.[3]

A familiar feature of royal charter-giving to towns is the grant of the liberties of highly privileged communities, like London, Winchester, or Hereford, to other boroughs, new or old. Although these liberties were usually set out in full, the standardization of formula must have greatly lightened the labour of the clerks of the royal chancery. So mechanically, in fact, were the models followed that many towns which received the liberties of London had in their charters references to that peculiarly London institution the Portsoken, as if it were a local area.

Privileges of such imposing lineage were highly valuable to a growing community, but could not arrest the decline of a weak one. Not all the liberties of Winchester availed to save Henry III's new borough of Warenmouth (1247), in Northumberland, from early extinction, and by 1585 the site of the *Nova Villa*, founded by Edward I in Dorset, with the liberties of London, was marked only, as it still is, by a single farm called Newton, near the port of Ower Passage in the Isle of Purbeck.[4]

---

[1] See Pollock and Maitland, *Hist. of Eng. Law*, i. 384, and Hemmeon, *Burgage Tenure in England, passim.*

[2] *Rot. Parl.* i. 457 (16 Edw. II, 1322).

[3] *Ibid.* iii. 44, 64 ; Benham, *Red Paper Book of Colchester*, p. 58.

[4] Hutchins, *Hist. of Dorset* (1861), i. 462, *cf.* 652 ; *Calendar of Patent Rolls*, 1281–92, p. 217, gives the appointment on 7th January, 1286, of commissioners to lay out a new town at Gotowre super Mare in the parish of Studland. Merchants and others taking plots and beginning to build were to enjoy the liberties of Lyme and Melcombe (which were those of London), and a charter to that effect was promised. The well-known charter to *Nova Villa*, granted on 10th May following (*Cal. Chart. Rolls*, ii. 337), fulfilled this promise.

As the word " liberties " implies, these chartered privileges were usually, and especially at first, of a negative rather than a positive kind. The simpler sort exempted the recipients from some onerous service or payment. The most valuable privilege of the latter kind was a general exemption from local tolls, which was sometimes extended to the foreign dominions of the Crown. An exception was often made for the tolls of London. A good example of release from burdensome services was the exemption from finding lodging for the king's retinue, whether demanded by force or by the billet of the marshal, which spread from London through Bristol to the larger Irish boroughs. Canterbury and Rochester, being on the Dover Road, had to be content with the requirement of an order from the marshal.

Even such a liberty as that of electing a justice to try Crown pleas, *i.e.* homicide and other serious offences arising in the borough, which looks positive enough, was really negative, for it was chiefly prized as excluding the sheriff or other royal officer from entering the town to try such cases. This rare privilege, so far as I know, was only granted twice, to London by Henry I and to Colchester by Richard I. The Colchester case was belated, for Henry II's institution of regular circuits of the royal justices, who superseded the sheriffs for this purpose, proved fatal to the extension of the privilege. From this time, however, many towns were empowered to elect a coroner or coroners to take the preliminary steps for the trial of Crown pleas, which had been one of the duties of the town justice, and the sheriff was thus excluded even from this humbler interference in the town. A few boroughs which were not shire-towns were favoured by special visits of the royal justices to try Crown pleas, but only in one exceptional case was there any reversion to the old expedient of municipal justices. It is significant of the abnormal position of Chester that in it alone of all the towns within the four seas Edward I allowed Crown pleas to be tried by the mayor and bailiffs.[1]

It was the position of the sheriff as the local financial agent of the Crown which made the towns eager to take perpetual leases of the royal revenue derived from them, even at rents so oppressive that their chief citizens were frequently mulcted for arrears or, as a last resort, the liberties of the town were temporarily taken into the hands of the

---

[1] Charter of 1300 (R. H. Morris, *Chester in Plantagenet and Tudor Reigns*, p. 492 ; *B.B.C.* ii. 146).

Crown and the elective officers superseded by royal nominees. For the right of dealing directly with the exchequer they were willing to pay large sums down and to incur burdens which many of them found almost too heavy to be borne. It is striking evidence of their dislike of the sheriff. The nearer tyrant was the more to be feared.

The rapacious John was the great distributor of such leases, fee farm grants they were called, and so, more than any other king, made himself responsible for the develop-ment of the greater boroughs as areas locally within but administratively outside the counties. The process was not even approximately complete, however, so long as the sheriff had the right of entry to serve writs of the exchequer for non-payment of the farm, or general judicial writs in cases arising in the town courts or those of the justices on circuit. It was not until Henry III had involved himself in a morass of debt and exhausted the patience of his barons that this further step was conceded, in order to raise the wind. In 1255–57 nearly a score of towns bought the privilege of return of writs, the right, that is, of receiving writs of the Crown and reporting their execution. The Crown still sent the writs to the sheriff, and so far the administrative unity of the shire was preserved, a point of some importance when parliamentary writs came later into question, but his officers were not allowed to do more than deliver the writs into the hands of the town bailiffs. The Crown, of course, retained the right of authorizing the sheriff to enter the town by special mandate, if its wishes could not be otherwise enforced. This expedient was resorted to when the citizens of Oxford and Cambridge showed themselves impotent to deal with the many doubtful characters who resorted to the Univer-sities, we are told, " for mischief and not for study." [1]

Emancipation from the sheriff, though it had gone far, was not absolutely complete until a borough was constituted a county of itself with its own sheriffs receiving all writs direct from the Crown and its mayor acting as royal escheator. The only towns in this position before 1373, when Bristol got it, were Chester (in part) and London.

The virtual emancipation of the greater royal boroughs from the shires in which they lay was accompanied by the growth of a special town spirit and organization which seems to have been greatly stimulated by the communal movement

---

[1] *B.B.C.* ii. 161-3 ; *Rot. Parl.* v. 425.

on the Continent. Here again king John is in the front of the stage. It was he who in his factious days during Richard's absence authorized the setting up of a sworn commune in London, and as king he issued the first charter, also to London, which arranged for the annual election of a civic head with the new French title of mayor, whose first appearance had closely followed, if it was not coincident with the swearing of the commune. Scholars have differed as to the length of life of the London commune. Dr. Round, in 1899, held that the oath of the twenty-four in 1206 to do justice and take no bribe, which he found in a manuscript collection of London documents of this period,[1] implied a body derived from the " vingt-quatre " of Rouen, and probably the parent of the later Common Council, as well as the practical existence of the commune so late as the middle of John's reign.

These conclusions were vigorously disputed by Miss Bateson [2] and M. Petit-Dutaillis,[3] who convinced themselves that the twenty-four in question were none other than the aldermen. If disproof of this identification would suffice to prove Dr. Round's view, it might seem to be established, for my friend Professor Unwin has called attention to the existence, in the printed Close Roll of the year in question, of a royal order, unknown to all the disputants, which is clearly a mandate to the barons of London to elect this very body of twenty-four.[4]

Some doubt may, however, be felt whether this body, which was to be elected to remedy the misgovernment of the existing civic administration, was intended to be permanent, and it is not easy to meet Miss Bateson's point that their oath says nothing of consultative functions, while the oath of the later common councillor says nothing of anything else, for he had no judicial function. On the other hand, the order for the election of the twenty-four does mention financial as well as judicial duties.[5] Moreover, this was

[1] *Commune of London*, 237. *Cf.* above, p. 256.
[2] *Eng. Hist. Rev.* xvii. 507-8.
[3] *Studies Supplementary to Stubbs*, i. 99.
[4] *Finance and Trade under Edward III*, p. 13. Professor Unwin was mistaken in supposing that they were merely to report on the maladministration of the city.
[5] Round, in ignorance of the writ for their election, identified them with the *skivini* of the citizens' oath to the commune in 1193, in whom Miss Bateson saw only the aldermen under a foreign name (see above, p. 266). The aldermen in any case succeeded in maintaining their position as city executive. Nevertheless the commune in the sense of a sworn association of the citizens was a permanent result of the crisis (*cf.* above, p. 252).

just the period at which similar bodies were coming into existence in less prominent English boroughs.

When Ipswich, in 1200, received a charter granting to the burgesses the fee farm of the borough with the right to elect bailiffs and coroners, they decided to elect twelve sworn chief portmen " to govern and maintain the said borough and its liberties, to render its judgements and to ordain and do what should be done for the state and honour of the town," and they took an oath to that effect. As soon as the port-men were elected and sworn, they exacted from the assembled burgesses an oath upon the book to be loyal and assistant to their bailiffs, coroners, and twelve portmen. The unique record from which this is taken [1] may only seem to assert the existence in 1200 of such bodies in all the other free boroughs of England, but the Ipswich case was clearly not an isolated one, and it is a new institution which is in question. The whole proceedings at Ipswich, of which the election of the portmen was only part, are strongly reminiscent of sworn communal organization abroad. In the case before us the councillors bore a neutral name, but similar bodies appear not long after with the significant title of *jurés* or *jurats*. The oath of the twenty-four *jurés* of Leicester, for instance, was almost identical with that of the twelve portmen of Ipswich. Add to this that before the end of John's reign a dozen of the most important English towns had instituted civic magistrates with the French name of mayor, a number largely increased under Henry III, and we come to the con-clusion that the influence of foreign civic progress on England at the end of the twelfth century has probably not yet been fully appreciated.[2]

Until comparatively recently little was known of these sworn bodies of twelve or twenty-four during the thirteenth century, and there has consequently been a disposition to post-date the rise of town councils, but the publication of municipal records has revealed the existence of at least thirteen.[3] The Ipswich example shows that, except in such a special case as arose in London in 1206, the creation of such select bodies was left to the voluntary action of the burgesses, and so, save for an occasional appearance in preambles, their existence would hardly be suspected from royal charters.

[1] Gross, *Gild Merchant*, ii. 116 ff. See above, p. 271.
[2] See further above Chapter IX and App. I.
[3] See above, pp. 265-80.

In the personality of the mayor and bailiffs, who represented the communities in their relations with the central power, the Crown took a closer interest. Yet, if we may judge from the silence of many charters, express licences to appoint mayors and bailiffs were not always required. They had, however, commonly to be presented to the king or his representative for approval.

In days not yet remote the gild merchant was very generally held to have been the germ and vital principle of the constitution of the medieval borough. This error was dispelled once and for all by the late Charles Gross, whose epoch-making monograph appeared no longer ago than 1890. It was an error which illustrated the worst features of English historical amateurishness, unjustifiable generalizations from partial and misunderstood evidence, and incapacity to grasp a complicated problem as a whole. Those who held it managed to ignore the fact that towns of the first importance, London itself and Norwich, never had the institution which they regarded as the source of municipal structure. Cases like that of Leicester, where the personnel of the borough court and of the gild was apparently the same, and the town's business done in the latter was on the whole more important than that which came before the portmanmoot, seem to have hypnotized even so good a local antiquary as James Thompson. It is not strange that in a community predominantly commercial the newer and more flexible organization of the gild should sometimes have been preferred to a court which was primarily judicial and greatly tied by ancient precedent. In the words of Gross " this fraternity was not the germ of the English municipality, but only a potent factor in its evolution." How potent in the twelfth century before election of officers and councils was secured he did not realize.[1]

The thoroughness with which Gross executed his task is well illustrated by the fact that, though Ballard and others have ransacked all available sources for fresh charters during the last thirty years, only three towns possessing merchant gilds have been added to his list : Brecon, Exeter, and Pembroke.[2] We may add that Gross was misled by Summers, the historian of Sunderland, into the attribution to that town of a gild to which it was not entitled. Henry III's " new

---

[1] See above, pp. 222 ff.
[2] Rawlinson MS. 465 (Bodl. Lib.), f. 230 ; B. Wilkinson, *Medieval Council of Exeter* (1931), p. xviii. ; *Cal. of Pat. R. 1377–81*, p. 107.

borough of Warnemouth " or Warenmouth in Northumberland disappeared so completely that by the end of the seventeenth century its unclaimed charter was calmly appropriated by the burgesses of Sunderland, an offshoot of Bishop Wearmouth in Durham. That their pretension should have been admitted by the royal courts, as it was, is evidence that the early history of the palatinate of Durham was as little understood by the judges of Charles II's time as the etymology of place-names. For, of course, a medieval charter to Sunderland would have been granted by the bishop and no eccentricity of sound-change could have converted Wearmouth into Warnemouth.

Leaving the royal towns, we pass to that great class of boroughs which stood on the lands of feudal lords, lay or ecclesiastical, and were mostly of their creation, for the Crown seldom granted a royal borough to a subject, however great. Outside the palatinates, the mediatized town was exceedingly rare.

Unlike the towns which had no lord but the king and in the great majority of cases boasted immemorial origin, the mesne or seignorial borough was, with rare exceptions, a post-Conquest creation which we owe to the Norman lord's recognition of the value of urban centres in the peaceful penetration of newly conquered districts, and as sources of larger income than could be raised from purely agricultural communities.

The second motive continued to operate long after the first had ceased to exist, except in Wales and Ireland, where it was largely responsible for the creation of many boroughs, both by the Crown and by private lords. In Wales and Ireland the medieval boroughs were English outposts in an unfriendly country, as the first Norman boroughs in England had often been.

As they were more artificial than the older boroughs, these new creations show a much greater uniformity in the size and rent of tenements or burgages, as the Normans called them, and of their appurtenances in the town fields and meadows. There was probably also more uniformity of legal custom. It is not surprising that their founders should have been apt to take as models for these new towns the little *bourgs* of their native Normandy. Yet until the beginning of this century their predominantly foreign origin had not been grasped. We owe its recognition and the discovery of

the widespread influence of one small Norman *bourg* to the
now famous articles of Miss Bateson on the " Laws of
Breteuil." [1] An unfortunate confusion of *Britolium*, the
Latinized form of Breteuil, with Bristol had misled even the
very elect, and of the list of nearly fifty boroughs which Gross
had entered in his table of affiliations as directly or indirectly
drawing their institutions from Bristol, nearly half were at
once struck out. This would have been a notable achieve-
ment, even if it had not been accompanied by a patient and
elaborate attempt to recover the lost customs of Breteuil from
the charters and custumals of her daughter towns on this side
the Channel. This part of Miss Bateson's work has more
recently been subjected to severe criticism by Dr. Hemmeon [2]
with greater acumen than good taste, and more fully and
courteously by Ballard.[3] It must be admitted that, as was
natural enough in the first flush of so striking a reversal of
preconceived ideas, Miss Bateson showed somewhat less than
her usual caution in the work of reconstruction. She did not
allow sufficiently for the intermixture of English with Norman
customs in documents, few of which belong to the first age of
Anglo-Norman borough-making. The strength of this influence of the native English borough upon the new foundations is attested by the prevalence in some of them of that
power of free or restricted bequest of land which was so
striking a feature in the normal English borough, but did not
exist in those of Normandy. The possibility of the inclusion
of some custom which, though Norman was not Bretollian,
does not seem to have been quite excluded by Miss Bateson,
and there was a distinct element of danger in assuming the
general identity of the customs of Verneuil, which have been
preserved, with those of its neighbour Breteuil which mostly
have not. The mere fact that king John granted the liberties of Verneuil to Breteuil in 1199 suggests that there must
have been important differences. In drawing exactly the
opposite conclusion from this grant, Miss Bateson seems
unconsciously to have let the wish be father to the thought.
It is not very safe to ascribe Verneuil customs to Breteuil
unless there is strong support from other quarters. There is
some reason to believe, therefore, that her reconstruction of
the laws of Breteuil errs by excess, but Ballard himself inserted

---

[1] *E.H.R.* vols. xv, xvi.
[2] *Burgage Tenure in England*, pp. 166 ff.
[3] *E.H.R.* xxx. 646 ff.

in his alternative draft exemption from the assize of *mort
d'ancestor*, which was only devised in the reign of Henry II, on
the strength of an obviously absurd legal argument of the
thirteenth century. Nor did either of Miss Bateson's critics
do adequate justice to the general merits of articles which
revolutionized the study of medieval urban institutions in
England.

In considering some features of this class of seignorial
boroughs in which French influence played a very important,
though not exclusive part, we may put aside the small number
of boroughs, Bath, Chester, Leicester, Newcastle-under-Lyme,
Stamford, Warwick, and for a short time Colchester, Northampton and Exeter, which were mediatized by the Crown
in favour of a member of the royal house or other great
magnate. His interest was mainly financial and did not very
seriously retard their growth. Leicester, it is true, had no fee
farm grant from her earls until long after most royal boroughs
possessed it, but, as we have seen, the farm was a doubtful
blessing except in so far as it prevented the financial inter-
meddling of the sheriff, and from that Leicester was already
exempt. Chester had its own purely urban sheriffs, before
any other English city,[1] for the sheriff, later sheriffs, of
London had jurisdiction over Middlesex as well as the city.[2]

The boroughs which were founded by Anglo-Norman
lords, with or without a written charter, were very numerous
and varied greatly in size and importance. Local magnates
anxious to increase the revenue from their estates were not
always good judges of the economic possibilities of the sites
at their disposal. Many such foundations were still-born
or failed to reach maturity. Of the twenty-three boroughs
created in the poor and backward district of which Lancaster
was the capital between 1066 and 1372, with burgesses ranging
in number from six up to one hundred and fifty or so, only
four retained an established borough status at the end of the
middle ages. Many had become extinct, though vestiges of
burgage tenure in some cases kept their memory alive, the
rest, such as Manchester and Warrington, had lost any
germs of independence they had once possessed and lapsed
into a sort of urban manors. As early as 1300 a lord of
Warrington, alarmed at the growing aspirations of its borough

---

[1] Before 1150, *Chart. of St. Werburgh's Abbey, Chester,* ed. Tait (Chetham
Soc. N.S. 79 (1920)), p. 53.

[2] Round, *Geoffrey de Mandeville*, pp. 347 ff.

court (*curia burgensium*), had forced the townsmen to renounce it and take their cases to his manorial court.[1] Some of these extinct and dormant boroughs were revived by the industrial revolution, but at the present day seven have no higher rank than that of urban districts (or part thereof) and five are governed by parish councils.

Lancashire laboured under some special disadvantages, but economic difficulties and the dead hand of manorialism were operative everywhere, and arrested the progress of many a promising borough. The extent to which they were at the mercy of their lords is well illustrated by the story of Burford in Oxfordshire, to which Mr. R. H. Gretton has recently devoted an admirable monograph.[2] Under the lordship of great absentee earls, and afterwards of the Crown by escheat, the little borough attained a status which superficially seemed as well established as that of many a small royal borough, but the sale of the Crown rights early in the seventeenth century and the settlement of the purchaser in the town proved fatal to its liberties, already undermined by the loss of substantial trade.

A point which has been much discussed is the exact basis of the application of the term borough on the one hand to such large and ancient towns as Leicester or Northampton, not to speak of those which enjoyed the higher title of city, and on the other to petty manorial communities with a mere handful of burgesses. In other words, what was the lowest qualification for borough rank, or, as Maitland put it, " the inferior limit of burgality " ?

Some common features all boroughs had, which were essential but not distinctive. Every borough, large or small, possessed by prescription or by royal licence a market[3] if not also a fair or fairs, but in England licences were freely granted to feudal lords for manors which they had no intention of converting into boroughs.[4] I say "in England" because in Scotland such licences seem to have been confined to boroughs. In an article published posthumously on " The Theory of the Scottish Borough," Ballard showed that the Scottish kings

---

[1] *V.C.H., Lancs.*, iii. 319, where " burgesses " is a slip for " community " (*communitas*) ; *B.B.C.* ii. 182.

[2] *The Burford Records*, Oxford, 1920.

[3] For possible abnormal exceptions, see above, pp. 67, 207, *n.* 1.

[4] Before this practice began in the later Anglo-Saxon period, the market was a more distinctive feature of the borough, for other buying and selling merely required official witnesses. See above, p. 28.

went on the principle of giving each borough, royal or baronial, the latter comparatively few, a complete monopoly of trade in a definite area, which was in some cases a whole shire.[1]

The court of the borough has been confidently claimed as a distinctive feature, and if all boroughs had possessed the full hundredal court which the greater towns enjoyed perhaps the claim might be allowed. But the usual court of a seignorial borough, even when called a portmoot, was the ordinary feudal court of the normal rural manor, and like it might or might not possess some criminal jurisdiction. At Manchester this criminal jurisdiction (in cases of theft) was deliberately withheld and reserved for the lord's higher court. Any growth of independence was repressed by the presidency of the lord's steward or bailiff, and in the significant case of Warrington, where a long minority had enabled the burgesses to assert some freedom, the court was suppressed altogether. This seems to have been a court of burgesses only, but the courts in all boroughs were not so limited. At Bakewell, for instance, the freeholders of the manor were joined with the burgesses both in the court and in the privileges granted by the charter. Clifton-on-Teme, chartered in 1270, had only a seignorial court and owed suit to the sheriff's tourn.[2]

We are not justified, therefore, in regarding a court of burgesses as a universal criterion of a borough, and, even if it were, it would be rather a reflection of the essence of the institution than the essence itself. For it seems obvious that where there were burgages and burgesses there was in some sense a borough.[3] It is the great merit of Dr. Hemmeon's book on *Burgage Tenure in England* that it emphasizes this tenure as the vital principle of the borough everywhere. It is true that he has to admit the presence of some features of burgage tenure on ancient demesne in places where there

---

[1] *Scott. Hist. Rev.* xiii. 16 ff.

[2] R. G. Griffiths, *Hist. of Clifton-on-Teme* (Worcester, 1932), ch. V, pp. 42-3.

[3] This is clear in the case of Higham Ferrers. In 1251 William de Ferrers, earl of Derby, emancipated eighty-eight serfs there, converting their lands held at his will into free burgages " sicut continetur in carta nostra quam eisdem fieri fecimus de libero burgo in Hecham habendo (*E.H.R.* xvii. (1902), 290). *Cf.* p. 206 above.

Professor Clapham holds that the forty-nine burgages of Linton, Cambs., in 1279, did not make it a borough (*Cambr. Hist. Journal*, iv. (1933), 198), but, for all we know, it may have been called so for a time.

was no borough,[1] but there are exceptions to all rules, and the middle ages were full of them. Complication, cross-divisions, and blurred outlines, rather than logical categories and clear-cut definitions, were the characteristic features of their slow and painful process of evolution.

In the widest sense of the word, then, the medieval borough may be defined as an urban area in which the tenements were held by low quitrents in lieu of all or nearly all service,[2] and were more or less freely transferable by sale, gift, and bequest, subject in many cases, in varying degrees, to the rights of the family and of the lord, where there was one. The latter sometimes exacted a transfer fee, more rarely reserved a right of pre-emption, and very generally prohibited alienation of burgages to certain categories of persons, chiefly religious houses and Jews.

Charters tended to stereotype custom in boroughs just at the time when the royal judges were developing the common law outside them. Among the peculiarities of borough law which resulted, the most striking was the not uncommon, though often restricted, right of bequest of land by will, which had been suppressed in the common law. Hence in some borough records we find a double system of probate, for after the will had been proved before the ecclesiastical authority, bequests of tenements and rents were approved before the mayor or bailiffs.[3] This right of devise of land was less usual in the Anglo-Norman boroughs than in the old English ones because their Norman models did not know it.

The wide use of the term " borough," which has just been explained, could not efface the practical distinction between the larger towns and the host of petty boroughs which had been called into existence since 1066. With the expansion of the national administration and the growth of

---

[1] The prevalent tenure was not burgage but privileged villeinage (or villein socage). Such likenesses to burgage tenure as the allowance of sale and devise of tenements were due to the common favour of the Crown. Leases of the farms of some manors of ancient demesne created quasi-burghal constitutions and those which, like Basingstoke and Kingston-on-Thames, had really urban possibilities became ultimately incorporated boroughs. Of the two places quoted by Maitland (*H.E.L.* i. 640) as having burgage tenements but not called boroughs, one had been a borough and the other may well have been (*B.B.C.* II. l.)

[2] As late as *c.* 1202 the founder of the seignorial borough of Egremont reserved an annual day's ploughing and a day's reaping (*B.B.C.* i. 95).

[3] See, for instance, H. Ingleby, *The Red Register of King's Lynn*, i. *passim.*

Government demands upon the purses and services of the nation, this distinction was emphasized and a new and narrower use of " borough " began to appear in official documents.   It was only the larger boroughs as a rule which already in the late twelfth century sent a full delegation of twelve to meet the justices on circuit, and when, in 1252, boroughs were ordered to set a night watch of twelve men from Ascension Day to Michaelmas for the arrest of suspicious characters, and other vills one of four or six according to their size,[1] it is probable that the mass of small boroughs fell into the latter class.

This suggested interpretation of the order of 1252 is borne out by the regulation of the same date that the musters of the local force afterwards known as the militia should be held in boroughs by the mayor or the bailiffs, if there was no mayor, and in other vills by new officers called constables.[2] Constables are henceforth a feature common to the rural township and the manorial borough.[3]   It seems significant that the carrying out of these measures was entrusted to commissioners who met the reeve and four men from each vill and twelve burgesses from each borough.[4]

Thus, for practical reasons, official nomenclature drew a line between boroughs and non-boroughs on a basis of population and administrative equipment.   This narrower sense of " borough " was evidently in the mind of Edward I when in his early experiments in parliamentary representation he twice ordered the sheriffs to send up representatives of boroughs and *villae mercatoriae*.[5]   The accepted translation of *villa mercatoria* by " market town," which might mean the ordinary manor with a market but without burgage tenure, has concealed the fact that, though some of these were apparently included under this head, undoubted boroughs in the wider sense were also comprised.   Indeed the sheriffs in 1275 drew the borough line so high as to exclude even Shaftesbury, which had appeared in Domesday Book as a borough.   This is only comprehensible when it is realized that *villa mercatoria* really meant " merchant town," [6] as *lex mercatoria* meant " merchant law " and *gilda mercatoria* " merchant gild."   It

---

[1] Stubbs, *Select Charters*, ed. Davis, p. 363.
[2] *Ibid.*   *Cf.* an earlier arrangement in 1205 (above, p. 253).
[3] In the larger towns they appear only as ward officers.
[4] Stubbs, *op. cit.*, 4th ed., p. 374.   [5] In 1275 and 1283.
[6] It was sometimes written *villa mercatorum*.

implied a town with the larger trade transacted in fairs of general resort rather than in the weekly market frequented chiefly by local buyers and sellers. " Fair law " was almost a synonym for the " law merchant." [1]

Unfortunately for clearness, Edward dropped this distinction between borough and merchant-town after 1283. From that date the parliamentary writs to the sheriffs mentioned boroughs only. This did not, however, bring about a reduction in the number of representatives. On the contrary, there was a large increase in the parliament of 1295 which continued on the whole for some time. In view of the new principle of taxing boroughs at a higher rate than the counties, it was not the interest of the Crown to limit their numbers, and this at least was well understood by the sheriffs, upon whom it fell to decide which towns in their counties were boroughs. But they were sadly confused by the king's wide use of " borough " in the writs, and the Pipe Rolls show that they described certain parliamentary boroughs as *villae mercatorum*. Indeed, the sheriff of Cornwall, in 1295, had so lost his bearings as to enter four undoubted boroughs as merchant-towns.[2] There was some excuse, therefore, for those contradictory accounts in their returns of the number of boroughs in their shires which have rather shocked modern historians. In the evident hope of clearing up the confusion, the Government in 1316 called on the sheriffs to make a special return of all boroughs and vills in their bailliwicks, but the result can have given little satisfaction, for uniformity is certainly not the strong point of the reports which are known to us as the *Nomina Villarum*.[3] There was a tendency, it is true, in a number of counties, to revert to the stricter interpretation of

---

[1] Fleta explained *lex mercatoria* as *ius nundinarum*.

[2] *Parl. Writs*, i. 35. In his valuable article on " Taxation Boroughs and Parliamentary Boroughs, 1294–1336 " (*Hist. Essays in honour of James Tait* (1933), pp. 417 ff.), Professor J. F. Willard has shown from the Enrolled Accounts of Taxes that the lack of uniformity went even further. The lists of boroughs chosen by the sheriffs for representation were far from exactly coinciding with those selected by the chief taxers for taxation at the higher, borough, rate. In their zeal for the royal revenue the taxers were considerably more liberal in their estimate of what was a borough. It is more surprising to find that they omitted at least 12 per cent. of the parliamentary boroughs, including Beverley and Maldon. Professor Willard considers that the taxers were guided in making their selection by the economic activities, population and local reputation of towns. A town so selected became, for the time being at least, a borough, even though it had not hitherto been accounted as such.

[3] Printed, so far as they survive, in *Feudal Aids* (P.R.O.).

BB

borough which was official under Henry III, but there were conspicuous exceptions, the most glaring being that of Devonshire, where the sheriff returned twenty boroughs, most of which were seignorial. In the long run, the canon of parliamentary boroughs was settled from below by the inability or unwillingness of the weaker towns to bear the burden of sending representatives, and not by any neat scheme imposed from above.

In what has been said, I have attempted, very imperfectly, I fear, to indicate in the first place the main results of the remarkable outburst of investigation of our early municipal history which began with Gross's work on the gild merchant and was unhappily so soon cut short, and secondly to sketch some of the conclusions to which I have been led in the course of the pious task of completing and editing Ballard's collections for a volume of thirteenth-century charters. The whole of the charters of the formative period will soon be accessible to students. The silence of charters, however, on many important aspects of urban development is profound. Much spade-work remains to be done in the unpublished records of some of our oldest towns before the ground is clear for the future historian of municipal growth in England. To trace that growth from the advent of the town-hating Angles and Saxons down to these latter days, when five-sixths of the population of Great Britain are massed upon pavements, is a task worthy of the best powers of an historian of institutions.

INDEX

Liber burgus is applied only to boroughs dealt with in Chapter VIII

A

Agardsley. *See* Newborough.

Agriculture. *See* Fields and Pastures.

Aids, of the boroughs, 166 and *n*. 3, 343. *See* Tallage.

feudal, 105 *n*. 6.

Ailwin, mercer, of Gloucester, 174, 177.

Alderman (1) of gild merchant, 227-8, 231-4, 248-50 ; council of, 274 ; and mayor, 299.

(2) of borough wards, 248, 266 *n*.3, 292.

(3) doomsmen, 288.

(4) councillors, 243-4, 251-2, 258-9, 266-70, 276-7, 280, 292, 304 *n*. 2, 318, 329-30, 335. *See* London.

Alfred, king, system of defence, 15-18 ; tolls from Worcester *burh*, 20 ; trade in his reign, 19 ; restoration of London, 23. *See* Mints.

Alodia, alodiarius, 104.

Altrincham [co. Chester], granted *in libero burgagio*, 216.

Amercement, low, 206.

Ancient demesne and the borough, 263, 343-4, 354-5.

Andover [Hants], 25, 52 ; gild merchant, 233 ; *forewardmanni*, 250 and *n*.

Arable, borough, leases of, 115-16. *See* Fields and Pastures.

Arundel [Sussex], 18 *n*. 7, 57, 83.

Assembly, borough, 304-10, 316-17, 318-25, 328.

Asser, bp., on Alfred's fortifications, 15, 17, 18.

Assistants, 327 *n*. 4, 328.

Assize of Arms, 221, 253.

Assize of bread and ale, 147 *n*. 4, 207-8.

Athelney [Som.], Alfred's fortifications at, 15.

Athelstan, king, 2 *n*. 3, 25, 27-9, 35.

Auditors, borough, 324-5, 334-5.

Avera, avra, carrying duty, 97 ; *cf.* 148.

Axbridge [Somerset], 19, 53, 65.

B

Bailiffs, 192-3, 234, 239-40, 270-1, 291 *n*. 4, 297, 330, 333-5, 349. *See* Reeves and Provostry.

Baker's custom, 94, 109 *n*. 4.

Bakewell [co. Derby], 24, 354.

Baldock [Herts], borough, 105 *n*. 6.

Ballard, A., develops " garrison theory," 4, 26 ; on borough and hundred courts, 32-3, 47, 60 ; on criteria of the borough, 64 ; on *firma burgi* and election of reeves, 185 ; on *liber burgus*, 195-6, 198, 208, 213, 217 ; criticism of Miss Bateson's " laws of Breteuil," 351-2 ; on the Scottish borough, 353-4.

Barnstaple, 18 *n*. 7 ; Athelstan's alleged charter, 2 ; *burhwitan* of, 42, 82, 124 ; mediatized, 57, 68, 128 ; seal, 236, 239 ; mayor, 291 *n*. 4; " common council," 327-8.

Barons, civic : (1) of London, 256-9 ; of Cinque Ports, 259-62 ; of Bourges [France, Cher], 256 *n*. 3 ; of Orleans [France, Loiret], 256 *n*. 3.

Basingstoke [Hants], 52, 218, 355.

Bateson, Mary, 26 *n*. 1 ; on borough and hundred courts, 32, 35, 38, 60 ; on influence of French *bourgage* tenure, 106-7, 339 ; on commune of London, 266-70, 305, 347 ; on laws of Breteuil, 351-2.

Bath [Somerset], 33, 51-2, 53, 55, 65, 91 ; hundred, 45 *n*. 1 ; *see* Edith, Queen ; farm, 150 *n*. 5 ; third penny, 151 ; mediatized, 154.

71, 73-4, 114-15; king's burgesses, list of, 73-4; custom of burgesses, 87; poor burgesses, 64, 88; commendation ?, 92; the burgage, 215 *n*. 1; borough account, 124-5; communal (?) property, 129; mediatized, 155; farm, 152, 154, 156, 178-9, 188; councils, 322-3, 333-5; auditors (later aldermen), 334; justices of the peace, 335. *See* Lexden.
Colombières, Phil. de, 61 *n*. 5.
Commendation by A.-S. burgesses, 89-90, 92.
Committees, electoral. *See* Election, double.
Communa, communia, commune, communitas, (1) Community, any established group of men, 221, 240, 242-3 (of vill).
(2) the poorer majority of such a group, 241 *n*. 3.
Commune, the sworn: on the Continent, 159-61; the London *communio* of 1141, 161; Henry II and the Commune, 162, 176-7 (Gloucester, York); c. of London, 1191, 181-3, 251-2; general, 234, 237, 251-2, 264.
Sworn military communes (1205), 253-5; in Normandy, 256; *major communa,* 254.
Influence of foreign commune in England, 264-5, 290-301, 347.
Communitas, commune (1) borough community, body of burgesses, corporation, 234, 237-8, 240-6. *See* Assembly, Council, Election; in France, 246-7.
(2) body of unofficial burgesses, *communarii, minor communa,* commonalty, 243-7, 305-9, 311, 313, 324, 331-6, 338. In France, 246-7.
(3) majority contrasted with a small oligarchical class of burgesses, 243.
Compotus civitatis, 124.
Congleton [co. Chester], *liber burgus,* 216.
Congregatio, convocatio. *See* Assembly.
Consilium, commune, 312.
Constables, military (1205), 253-4. of the peace (1242, 1252, 1285), 253 *n*. 4, 356.
Constabularies, wards at Lynn, 325.
Conway [co. Caernarvon], liberties of, 203; seal, 239 *n*. 4.

Corbett, W. J., on the Burghal Hidage, 16. *See also* 292 *n*. 3
Cornhill, Henry of, 182.
Coroners, borough, 48 *n*. 2, 204, 250, 258 *n*. 1, 270-1.
Cotes [by Warwick], 142.
Cottars (*coscez*), 86. *See also* Bordars.
Councils (1) early town, 234-5, 240, 264-301; nature of, 280-5; origin of: Maitland's theory, 286-90; Round's view, 292-4; limits of foreign influence, 291-2, 294-6, 348; Dr. Stephenson on, 299-301; lists of, 281, 337.
(2) Supplementary common, 247, 281, 310-30, list of, 337; meeting-places, 329; procedure, 329-30.
(3) Single common, 330-6.
Courts, borough, 38-66, 200, 204, 206-7, 249-50, 286-90, 341, 353-4; meeting-places, 63 *n*. 2. *See also* District, Five boroughs, Folkmoot (London), Husting, Leet, Portmoot, and Borough.
Coutances, Walter of, chancellor, 182.
Coventry [co. Warwick], 25; incorporation, 238, 240; common council, 326, 329 *n*. 3; court leet, 326 *n*. 2.
Cricklade [Wilts], 18 *n*. 6, 50 *n*. 3, 51, 55.
Culcitra, coverlet, 109.
Custom from borough fields, 114-16, 129. *See Landmol.*
Customs, tenure by, in boroughs, 86-99; 100, 104, 109, 127. and burgage tenure, 96-108. in French *bourgs,* 109-10. "servile," late survival of, 84, 98, 105 *n*. 6, 135.
Custos, keeper, 151-2. Cf. 326.
Custumarii, liberi. *See* Chester.

D

Danegeld, in boroughs, 47, 76, 77 *n*. 1, 123, 343.
Danelaw, 36, 44, 65; boroughs, 118, 131-2, 137.
Danes, invasions of, 15; reconquests from, 24; later invasions, 31, 39.
Democracy, burghal, 302-3, 338. *See* Common councils.
Derby, 25, 69, 71 *n*. 2, 75 *n*. 5; minor burgesses, 87.

S

Sagus[m], cloak (?), 10 *n.* 4.
St. Albans, surrenders charter and seal, 237.
St. George, hundred of [Dorset], 52-3, 56.
Saint-Omer [France, Pas de Calais], 110, 247 *n.* 2.
Sake and Soke, 125-6, 128.
Sale of burgages, 101, 355.
Salford [Lancs.], heriot, 99.
Salisbury, episcopal man. and bor., 57. New, seal, 236-7.
Saltash [Cornwall], 105 *n.* 6.
Sandwich, hundred, 45 *n.* 1, 49 *n.* 2 ; reliefs for ship-service, 125-6 ; mediatized, 140 ; farm, 152 ; barons, 260 ; seal, 260 ; incorporation, 261 *n.* 7.
Sarre [Kent], 10.
Scabini (*schöffen*), 61 *n.* 3, 266, 269, 295. See *Skivini.*
Scandinavia, early trade with, 118 ; mercantile settlements in Danelaw, 131-2.
Scarborough [Yorks], farm, 172 ; liberties, 204, 211; non-burgesses, 215 *n.* 1.
Sceaftesege [Bucks], 18 *n.* 4.
Seals, municipal, 230, 235-7, 250-1, 257-8, 260-1.
in France, 299 *n.* 3.
Seasalter [Kent], "little borough" of, 67, 141.
Sea-service. See Cinque Ports and Maldon.
Seniores, senatores, 301. See Borough.
Senlis, Simon de, lord of Northampton, 155-6.
Shaftesbury [Dorset], east gate of, 15 *n.* 5, 18 ; 51, 55, 356.
Sherborne [Dorset], burgages at, 207.
Sheriff, the Anglo-Norman, 149-51, 225. See *Firma burgi.*
the A.-S., 147-8. See *Firma burgi.*
exclusion of, 217, 345-7 ; borough, 44, 331, 352.
Shrewsbury, 44; hundred, 45; liberty, 48 *n.* 3 ; heriot, 81 ; merchet, 82 ; French borough, 105 ; mediatized, 149, 155 ; lease of farm, 174-5, 178 ; fee farm, 187 ; councils, 324.
Skivini, ? aldermen, 252, 266, 292, 297.
Skynburgh [co. Cumb.], *liber burgus*, 201, 209.

Socage, tenure by, in boroughs, 82, 107 and *n.* 2, 134, 218, 343.
Socager, heriot of, 80.
Soke of king and earl, 146.
Sokemen in boroughs, 78, 80, 87.
Sokes, 23, 43, 97.
Southampton [Hants], 28, 57, landgable, 90, 100, 109 *n.* 2 ; farm, 170, 178 ; fee farm, 185 *n.* 11 ; gild merchant and non-gildsmen, 230-1, 249 *n.* 2 ; alderman and mayor, 232-3 ; council, 279.
Southwark, 58.
Sovereign, of Irish borough. See Kilkenny.
Speaker, common (*praelocutor*), 324.
Stafford, 24 ; comital houses, 145 ; third penny, 149 *n.* 2 ; farm, 153-4 ; *liber burgus*, 197, 199, 217 *n.* 1.
Stamford, lawmen, 43, 80 ; wards, 60 *n.* 3 ; arable, 71 *n.* 1 ; sokemen, 78, 80 ; abbot of Peterborough's ward, 94 ; baker's custom, 94; mediatized, 162 *n.* 1.
Stenton, Prof., on meaning of *burgensis* in A.-S. times, 78, 95 ; on sokemen of Stamford, 78, 87.
Stephenson, Dr. Carl, conception of the A.-S. borough, 4-5, 27, 130-8, 248 ; on borough and hundred courts, 33, 61 ; on *burhgemot*, 38 ; on the agricultural character of the ordinary A.-S. borough, 68-77 ; on effect of Norman settlements, 103-8, 131-2 ; on the meaning of *burgensis* in A.-S. times, 78-9, 86, 95-6 ; on " villein " and " serf " burgesses, 83-5 ; on origins of Cambridge, 131-2 ; on Scandinavian trading settlements in Danelaw, 131-2 ; on borough aids, 166 *n.* 3 ; on *firma burgi* and election of reeves, 185-93 ; on *liber burgus*, 217-20 ; on municipal development in twelfth century, 248 ; on the origin of mayors and town councils, 296-301.
Sterkeley hundred [Wilts], 53.
Steyning [Sussex], borough and hundred, 56, 83.
Stockport [co. Chester], *liber burgus*, 201.
Sudbury [Suffolk], transferred to Thingoe Hd. for danegeld, 59.
Sunderland [co. Durham], 349-50.